# MISTER SATAN'S APPRENTICE

*For my father, Alan Gussow (1931–1997)*
*Earth-friend*

# CONTENTS

gh when I reread my book now, a decade later: James
d Ralph Ellison.

, the author of *Another Country,* gave me the courage
out interracial desire as though it were, in fact, at the
American experience, and not to confine my gaze solely
of the opposite sex. The youthful white blues apprentice
these pages takes notice of the bodies of his two older
ers at various points in ways that deserve to be called
not expect that dynamic to surface when I sat down to
I allowed it and I'm okay with it. Desire refuses to be
a yearning for musical communion sometimes expresses
ghtened attention to the embodiment of musical wisdom.
women I write of here, the blues they inspired me to feel,
lay would have made far less sense had I tried to silence
s or mute the various registers in which they thrilled, dis-
wrecked, challenged, and educated me.

stands squarely in the path of any author who would do
he blues paradoxes of American experience. As I meditated
rlem sojourn and thought about the challenge of repre-
daily musical odyssey with Mister Satan, I found myself
eatedly to the Prologue of *Invisible Man.* Ellison's protag-
kes a joint while listening to Louis Armstrong's trumpet;
lic question "What did I do to be so black and blue?" pre-
spatio-historical reverie, a Dantean descent in which the
consciousness gives way and the protagonist sinks down
he generations, back through black history, until he finds
dialogue with a maternal ancestral figure, a slave who
hated her white master. This tableau resonated profoundly
ral transformative musical experiences I'd had, and its in-
overs over my narrative: that first night in La Famille,
rab hold of the groove and find myself dragged downward
more challenging confrontation with black music than I
cipated; the first afternoon I play with Mister Satan and
out on Randall's Island and suddenly sense the possibility
er musical communion; and the day that Nat Riddles sup-
e at Mister Satan's side on 125th Street, signifying power-

# PREFACE TO
# THE NEW EDITION

WHEN I SAT DOWN in the fall of 1995 to write the
memoir that would become *Mister Satan's Apprentice,* I
felt the pressures of what journalists were fond of calling
"America's racial divisions" weighing on me like a clear and present
danger. O. J. Simpson had just been acquitted in the killing of his
ex-wife Nicole and her friend Ron Goldman. Many African Americans responded with glee, viewing O.J. as a latter-day Staggolee
who beat the (white) system at its own game thanks to the brilliant
forensics of his black lead attorney, Johnnie Cochran, and the overt
racism of Los Angeles cop Mark Fuhrman. Most white Americans
viewed the same acquittal with incredulity and rage. *Not guilty?* Were
blacks crazy? Or were whites simply beginning to taste the crest-
fallen disillusionment in a "justice system" that black folk had known
for far too long? *Newsweek* proclaimed, "Whites v. Blacks: Were We
Watching the Same Trial? After the Verdict, the Two Communities
Talked Past Each Other, with Passionate Misunderstanding."

I was a second-year English graduate student at Princeton University when the verdict came in. Less than an hour after it arrived,

I was sitting in Nell Painter's seminar on African American intellectual history, one of two white students in an otherwise all-black class, and I was filled with the same anxieties that always filled me in such settings. Those anxieties certainly weren't Professor Painter's fault: a brilliant, probing, and contrarian scholar, interracially married, a fan (she once confessed to me) of country music, she repeatedly challenged us to ask unsettling questions, counterintuitive questions, the questions nobody else was brave enough to ask. If I'd had the nerve, I would have asked the question that preoccupied me in those days, the same question a black man named Rodney King asked despairingly when another jury verdict three years earlier led to what were referred to as either the L.A. Riots or (if you were a hip leftist) the L.A. Uprising: "Can we all get along?" But I didn't have the nerve. Demoralized by an academic culture that seemed determined to see me as white, to reify whiteness as what Aaron David Gresson has termed a "spoiled racial identity," and to transform those who shared my race, class, and gender—straight white middle-class males—into emblems of racial bad faith, I'd lost my public voice, or whatever voice I possessed in the racially mixed classroom.

But I had a book contract in hand and a story to tell. It was here, I swore to myself, that I would do what Nell Painter had insisted we do—go for broke. I'd write a book about the black men and women I had known and loved, the *people* I had known and loved and hated and learned from and gotten my heart broken by and made music with—white, black, whatever. I'd strive to represent both Uptown and Downtown as I had experienced them, the full catastrophe of a race-maddened New York that was also, and simultaneously, bubbling with transracial alliances that couldn't wholly be accounted for by the rhetorics of suspicion then fashionable in the academy. And I'd start exactly where I had started my own blues journey, with the smart, naïve, lonely, and wild-hearted suburban kid I'd been back in my hometown of Congers, New York. To imagine that such a white boy—a prep-school townie, off to the Ivy League—would ultimately transform himself into a blues performer with any legitimate claim on the music was counterintuitive, to put it mildly. But here I was, Mister Satan's sideman, a touring pro with

a Harlem pedigree and the respect o[...] pened? Did I, in fact, have a legitima[...] one more cultural thief, a ravenous a[...] the sort eviscerated by bell hooks in [...] the Other" in *Black Looks: Race an[...] do was tell my story and trust the an[...]

I wrote *Mister Satan's Apprentice* in[...] two, three, and four hour blocks sand[...] inars. The writing process was facilita[...] kept from 1984 onward—more than[...] though many pages were taken up wit[...] European busking scene that I had b[...] decade, I had also managed to docume[...] York City blues musician. My unlikely [...] La Famille was there to be harvested, [...] downtown episodes. Mister Satan, on[...] naire and streetside Harlem's prophetic [...] presence. I had accumulated a bag of ca[...] recordings of our performances on 125t[...] made in Sterling's apartment on 116th St[...] ica lessons that my soon-to-be mentor, [...] Nat Riddles, gave me in Morningside F[...] two stints on the road with the bus-and-tru[...] musical called *Big River* (each day a new[...] were made for journaling and ripe for tra[...] more substantial.

In stylistic terms, what guided my w[...] middle ground between the onrushing [...] Kerouac and the signifying terseness [...] spilling it all out and holding some of it [...] been a conscious goal for years. One way [...] *Apprentice* is as the protagonist's gradual e[...] ian innocence—alternately buoyant and sh[...] like a bluesman's ability to reconcile euph[...] cept life's paradoxes with good humor. Two[...]

fully on my still-shallow soundings and thrusting me into a series of fresh insights about what the blues are and where they come from.

Chapter 9, "Sweet Harlem Summer," which follows Nat's blow-down, is one of the book's pivots. It represents not just a turning away from the melodrama of romantic despair (the principal source of my "white boy's blues" to that point) and toward a deeper commitment to my craft, but an acknowledgment that death haunts the blues and must be confronted and transcended with the help of the community. I listen for the first time, as that chapter begins, to the silence behind my notes. I hear a dance with death in the stylings of a half-dozen sax players. I encounter Death himself in the form of a comically terrifying Harlem specter named Mr. Sims, who threatens repeatedly to slit my throat until I confront him one day, find my voice, and make peace.

Death is everywhere in *Mister Satan's Apprentice*. Death shadows Nat Riddles. Every "bastard" who has ever worked with Mister Satan or taken his handouts eventually gets himself killed, it would seem. Sterling's wives prior to Miss Macie all have died. Our street-partnership is shadowed by New York's sensationalized racial violence: the beating and death of Michael Griffith in Howard Beach, the murder of Yusuf Hawkins in Bensonhurst. The lesson I begin to absorb in "Sweet Harlem Summer" comes home to roost—a blues line repeated, with emphasis—on the day that I am threatened by two men who view my presence in the neighborhood as a political affront. Death waits for me, too. It's no longer just a black thing, a regrettable but containable threat that has profoundly shaped the Harlem blues people with whom I have cast my fate while leaving me exempt. My ass is also on the line, if I choose to continue my journey. That I have a choice at all is a mark of my racial privilege, but the choice I make is not trivial.

Death haunts *Mister Satan's Apprentice* for a more personal reason. As I raced to complete the manuscript in the spring of 1997, my father, Alan Gussow, was diagnosed with pancreatic cancer and died within five months. That wrenching experience of loss, and the open-heartedness with which my father and I said our goodbyes, weaves its way into the final pages of this memoir.

An alert reader will notice moments where I am signifying with subversive intent on the African American literary and intellectual tradition. At the beginning of chapter 8, I speak about the "vague cringing empathic defensive stab—a kind of quadruple consciousness" I feel as I walk through the Village with my black lover Robyn. I was trying to up the ante on W. E. B. Du Bois and his celebrated claim about the "double consciousness" that marked African American life, much as I strove musically to go beyond Little Walter, James Cotton, Magic Dick, and my other musical precursors. There's an edge to my writing in such passages, a defiance of political correctness bred by frustration. An admirer of Du Bois, a child of the Civil Rights movement, I found myself painfully and unwillingly at odds with the black cultural nationalism that had emerged in the late 1960s with Larry Neal's call for "the destruction of the white thing" and that had persisted in various forms through my college years and beyond. I was happy to see the white thing destroyed, god knows, but not if it included my harmonica and me! The most deliberate affront I could offer to ideologies of blackness and whiteness, particularly when they sought to render my experience invalid or invisible, was to write of the creole blues culture I knew. The white-boy-lost-in-the-blues story was familiar, but certain complications had been left out. Both Nat Riddles and Sterling Magee are African American bluesmen animated, in part, by white musical exemplars—Kim Wilson in Nat's case, Elvis Presley in Sterling's. I give blues harmonica lessons to an older black man who pays me for my services. "Thunky Fing," an original composition dating from my Harlem years, begins as another flipped script: an unconscious inversion of the *Sanford and Son* theme song that I recast on the harp in an innovative way and then bring down to 125th Street to try out. Sterling matches me with backing chords, then flips the script again by renaming my—now our—song. Where, precisely, is "black music" in all this? Or "white blues"? *Mister Satan's Apprentice* rises to a climax in which a representative musical text, *Harlem Blues*, is produced against all odds—black-and-white music, I call it. That choice of words, and hyphens, is deliberate. As author, I felt as though I were committing an act of gentle vengeance against black cultural nationalism and white racism alike. We *can* get along, I thought, as I finished my manuscript. Modern blues life is exhausting, exhilarating, unlikely. But this is what it looks like. This is what it sounds like. Power to the people!

In retrospect, the racial discord that frames both the events narrated in *Mister Satan's Apprentice* and the writing of the text itself have come to seem like dispatches from a peculiarly dark and distressing time. Our own moment seems charmed by comparison, although only a fool who knew nothing about the blues would presume a definitive pronouncement. As I write these words, Barack Obama has just been sworn in: America's first black President—and first black-and-white President. The underlying commitment to transracialism that drove me to write my memoir seems uncannily aligned, ten years down the line, with the American national purpose. I make no claim to prophetic intent, but I'm delighted at where we have arrived.

Oxford, Mississippi
January 2009

# MISTER SATAN'S APPRENTICE

# PROLOGUE:

# 1969

I DIDN'T BELIEVE IN GOD, I'd have said, if anybody had asked me. I took the question personally because of my name. A bearded old man in the sky, watching over an eleven-year-old kid? The best thing about being half-Jewish was not having to waste time going to church or synagogue. My mom and dad never took us, or made us say prayers.

Katydids were the closest I came. The *ch-ch-ch* sound they made, floating through the window of my third-floor bedroom late at night, the last two weeks of August. Like a huge starry bath that cradled and held you. And made you want to cry, for no reason except summer was over and school—where bullies lurked—was about to start. My invisible musical friends. They'd chatter at each other through the heavy dark oak leaves, play off each other. I'd tap my toes under the sheets, grind my teeth, match their beat. Filled to the brim for two weeks. Then school would come along, a breezy cold snap, and wipe us out.

We lived in an old green Victorian house at the top of a hill. A handyman's special, bought for cheap; twice as big as anybody's around. It had huge drafty windows, no air conditioners, not enough heat in the winter. Each of us had his own room. My brother Seth—the electronics genius—spent most of his time soldering down in the basement, trying to invent new circuits that sounded cool. Fuzz boxes, phase shifters. Congers was a random little town, twenty-five miles north of New York City. There were three lakes—Rockland, Swartwout, and Congers—within a mile, and dozens of vacant lots filled with butterflies. My mom gave me her old collection, which included cicadas and dragonflies. She made me a net out of mosquito netting sewn around a bent coat hanger jammed into an old broom handle. She showed me how to make a killing jar: an old Skippy jar with a screw top, a crumpled paper towel in the bottom soaked with carbon tet death fumes. All summer long I'd hunt. Fritillaries, Mourning Cloaks, huge Polyphemus moths with eyespots. She showed me how to pin the wings to a balsa-wood mounting board with strips of paper, after they'd stopped shivering.

My mom knew about katydids and other outdoor things. She'd grown up in California when Orange County was orange groves. *Stalking the Wild Asparagus* was her favorite book. She'd hang pineapple juice cans around our necks and lead us down into Dead Man's Gulch, where the best wild strawberry spots were. She'd show us how to identify sassafras bushes—three different kinds of glove-fingered leaves—and harvest the roots. Chop them up, boil in water, add sugar to make syrup, add seltzer to make root beer. Like the Indians, she'd say. Think of how much money we're saving!

My dad had no job, those days. He'd had one at the Parsons School of Design when we were little kids and then quit. He spent most of his time hiding out in his third-floor studio—painting landscapes on huge canvases, puffing on a cigar, listening to records. Sgt. Pepper's Lonely Hearts Club Band, Ravi Shankar, Doc Watson, Bessie Smith. He was writing a book called *A Sense of Place: The Artist and the American Land*. In 1965 Robert Kennedy came to our house—we had a photograph—and Alan Gussow showed him the Hudson River, pointing out how polluted it was. He worked for Kennedy in '68, out in Oregon. The morning after the California primary he called upstairs to my brother Seth and me and told us something very bad had happened.

"Kennedy lost?" I said, worried.

It was the second assassination in two months. Martin Luther King's was April 4th, the day after my tenth birthday. My dad flattened the side of our Dodge Polara station wagon a week later, accidentally. He was distracted and just missed a telephone pole, he told us. Swerved at the last minute.

PART ONE

# NEW LIFE

CHAPTER ONE

# IF THAT DON'T BRING HER BACK

*I sent my baby a brand-new twenty-dollar bill*
*If that don't bring her back, I'm darn sure my shotgun will.*

—John Lee "Sonny Boy" Williamson

NOBODY ACTUALLY KNEW what had happened to Nat. One moment he was the crown prince of New York's downtown blues scene, double-parking his cab in front of Dan Lynch's Blues Bar on Sunday afternoons, striding indoors with a harmonica in hand to blow chorus after squalling chorus at the weekly jam sessions; the next moment he was gone, fled South to his father's or sister's in Norfolk or Newport News. He'd been shot in the chest on the corner of Thirteenth Street and Second Avenue, just down the block from Lynch's. That was the only fact everybody seemed to agree on. The guy who shot him was either a drug dealer or a jealous lover or pimp connected to Doreen, Nat's brilliant white girlfriend, a prostitute and junkie. Nat had either been yelling at Doreen or slapping her around or both. The shooting wasn't supposed to have happened—Nat was too smart, too generous, too self-disciplined—and yet it seemed fated. Everybody who knew him was shocked; nobody was surprised. Nat Riddles *would* go get himself shot, and disappear.

He'd be back. He always came back, after the stories people told

9

had had a chance to swell and ripen. Some Sunday afternoon when the jam session was flying high he'd shoulder back through the swinging doors of Dan Lynch, flash his dazzling smile, bear-hug ten or twelve dear old friends, yell out to Chuck Hancock on the bandstand, kiss Karola and Diana at the bar—"I love it!" he'd say as a cold Heineken found its way into his hand, "I *love* it!"—and stand there beaming as Chuck's alto sax screamed, honked, and snarled. Nat was back! He'd been president of the student government at Long Island University, a Tae Kwon Do adept, a trophy-winning disco dancer, a graphic artist at Pratt. He'd freebased cocaine in the days before crack. He was perpetually on the verge of becoming the blues world's Next Big Thing. A young black harp-player with the Sound. White guys who loved blues couldn't get enough of him. "Nat!" they'd yell. "Hey, Nat!" He called all waitresses "darling" and made the older ones melt where they stood. He was my master. One of two.

WE MET ON a cold April night in 1985. The lovelorn neighborhood harmonica player—recent dropout from the graduate English program at Columbia—had just made his big-stage debut on the steps of Hamilton Hall, where three hundred sitters-in protesting the university's investment policies in South Africa were being entertained by various campus bands. A Marine Band harp blown through a large outdoor P.A. system ruled the world. I was bopping home down Amsterdam Avenue, lost in the sound of my own notes decaying as they spiraled up and collected under the walkway between the Law School and Philosophy Hall. Bird was my model: sweet, angular, endlessly unfolding lines.

A yellow cab heading uptown passed me, slowed, then hung a U-turn and pulled up to the curb. The driver leaned over and rolled down the passenger-side window. He was older than me but not much, and black. He smiled as if we knew each other.

"Was that you?" he asked.

"You mean playing just now?"

"Yeah."

I shrugged. "I was noodling."

"It sounded nice. I thought I oughta see who the hell you were."

Still leaning on his elbow, he flipped open a tool kit sitting next to him on the front seat. The trays were cluttered with harmonicas, cables, a ball microphone.

"You play?" I said.

"I've been accused of that more than once." His smile was a promise, an effortless seduction. He selected a harp, cupped it beautifully with enfolding hands, and stared at me as he played, eyes narrowing slightly as he bore down. I stood at the open window, struck dumb. The gods had blessed me with another visitation. I blinked in the glare outside Plato's cave. The records I'd been listening to—Little Walter, James Cotton, Junior Wells, my old high school collection—were mere shadows of the true and beautiful.

"Shit," I said.

"You like that?"

He shut off the engine, got out of the cab, came around front, set his open toolbox on the hood.

"You've got the music in you," he said, selecting another harp. "All you need are a few of the subtleties."

We stood on the corner of 118th Street and Amsterdam in the cold wind for forty minutes while he recapitulated the stylistic evolution of American blues harmonica. John Lee Williamson—the first Sonny Boy, not to be confused with Rice Miller—was our honored forefather. You wanna build a mansion, you gotta pour some concrete. Little Walter and Junior Wells were blowing straight John Lee stuff before amplifiers came along and shook everything up. Kim Wilson of the Fabulous Thunderbirds is an awesome motherfucker and blows some shit that would spin your head. Not to mention Sugar Blue, the baddest street blues harmonica player ever to come out of New York.

"Man," he said, "Sugar used to walk the streets with his head down, practicing, and he was *always* high. I mean *always*. And he was the only player I've ever seen who could stop a street full of people *dead* with his playing, just like that. Set his little amplifier on the sidewalk, plug in, and go. Diddleyotten rebop, wabba dabba doo-bop! They wouldn't throw no change, either. I'm talking bills—ones, fives, tens, fluttering through the air. A whole *blockful* of people, man. Taxicabs would pull over, women—beautiful women, gorgeous women, *luscious* women—would stop dead in their tracks. That was Sugar. I ain't tellin' you no lies. He was *always* practicing, too. Every time you'd see him he'd be walking down the street with his finger in his ear, figuring things out."

The cold finally chilled us. He gave me his card before he went. Nat Riddles, Harmonica for All Occasions.

HE SHOWED UP at my apartment for our first lesson in one of those ten-dollar Panama hats the tourists buy down on Bleecker Street in Greenwich Village. He knew how to wear it. Without apparent effort he'd nailed the precise angle where Superfly meets Bogey.

"I like it," he said, glancing around the large livingroom. I had lots of space now that Helen was gone.

He tossed his hat on the bed, set down his tool kit. He inspected my record collection. No Big Walter Horton?

The windows were open—a warm May afternoon—and occasional yells and honking horns floated up from the street as I slipped a tape into my boom box and we took out our harps and went at it, face to face. His sound was a groaning joyous stridency swelling between his hands, explosive but contained. Mine was Little Cricket fidgeting before the Dancing Master. When he tapped his foot, Time shuddered. I leaned forward—hungering, imitating, holding back. He could have flipped me off my chair with one shoulder-feint.

"Open your hands," he admonished.

My vibrato was spirited but lightweight, ungrounded. His was rich, slow, dark, controlled, powerful, effortless.

"Are you really doing it just with your throat?" I asked.

He gazed at me and played a soft quivering low note.

" 'Cause I can get it, you know." I played my staccato, chattering version.

He said nothing. His note grew softer, more liquid. He continued to gaze at me. He lifted his chin slightly so I could see. His

Adam's Apple quivered softly, effortlessly. His throat was very dark and smooth and beautiful.

I stared. He kept the note going—soft, humming, deadly. My eyes fell.

"I'll work on it."

The note burned into me, silencing me. Somebody yelled in the street down below.

"I can't do it, Nat," I murmured, pleading.

We moved onto tongue-blocking. Chicago-style blues harmonica—Big Walter, James Cotton—depended on a forceful tongue-slap against the wooden comb to produce octaves alternating with chords. Maximum control, big sound. Nat was somehow able to articulate in multiple dimensions at once, vibrato behind double-tonguing punctuated with throat-pops.

"Naw, man." I laughed when he described his technique. "You can't be doing that."

He waved his hand. "There's *nothing* I do that DeFord Bailey wasn't doing fifty years ago."

"You got this stuff off records?"

"Off records, whatever. From guys like Bob Shatkin and Lenny Rabenovets. We've got some *awesome* harp-blowers in this city, man, guys who were doing it and doing it *properly* long before I came along."

"I've never heard anybody play like you."

He smiled. He had a corroded wire retainer around one of his front teeth. "They're out there, believe me. Chicago ain't shit next to Brooklyn and the Bronx."

He made a fluttering, feathery sound in the middle register. I tried and couldn't get it.

"Flutter your tongue," he said.

I fluttered my tongue. A pale imitation.

"It's like eating pussy," he said.

I laughed. "Do you ever meet women—you must meet women who'll say, like, that guy must . . ."

"Oh, they know. They'll come up smiling and say, 'I know you. You're a harmonica player. I know about you guys.' "

. . .

*1974.* I'D SEEN MY first naked woman's breast in the spring of junior year at the Rockland Country Day School, a couple of months after turning sixteen. Eric Balch and I had gone skinny-dipping with Laurie Stillman during ninth period in the lake down below the back woods. The Day School was in Congers, two miles from our house. Seth and I were the townies. The rich kids from Upper Nyack and Sneden's Landing drove Mercedes's and BMWs, skied on Rossignols and Nordicas, took Christmas vacations in Aspen and Sun Valley; we rode our bikes. Congers had nothing going on except the same old shit: vacant lots, lakes, and Dr. Davies' Apple Farm up on Route 9W. And now, amazingly, sex.

I'd gotten a good enough look—two gumdrop-sized nipples, brownish aureoles, a heartstopping twin jiggle—to last me all summer. I'd gotten buzzed on the quart bottle of Schaefer we'd passed around, too. Drinking beer at school! This flirtation with evil was unprecedented; it stunned everybody and thrilled me. *Adam* was doing this shit? The Day School was 120 kids grades six through twelve, most of whom were tripping or smoking pot or both. I was a holdout—for no good reason—and about to crack. My reputation was so spotless that the druggies often brought me along as insurance during reefer-jaunts into the back fields, in case Mr. Goldstein, the bearded stuttering art teacher, came snooping.

"Oh," Mr. Goldstein would say, noticing me dawdling just outside the circle of red-eyed kids, "it's you, Adam. I . . . I . . . well, never mind." And he'd turn and go.

I was *that good.* It was humiliating. Plus my nickname: Lips. Glenn Alynn, a pudgy, spit-spraying ski bum in the grade below me, had started it. My lips weren't any bigger than his, but he'd managed to convince everybody through sheer repetition. Lips! Hey *Lips!* I already knew I was ugly, with my squinty eyes and big butt; I'd never had a girlfriend and obviously never would. The nickname just made it worse. One day, despairing, I went to the headmaster, Mr. Downs, and asked him to make Glenn stop. Mr. Downs gazed at me.

"Lips?" he said.

"That's right. I could take it at first, but it's gotten ridiculous."

"I can't *make* people stop calling you names, Adam," he explained, trying hard not to smile.

School had always been this kind of nightmare. Public school was worse, one reason I'd transferred to the Day School back in ninth grade. You get skipped into first grade early because you can read, you're smaller and weaker than everybody else from then on, you get hairy balls a year later in junior high. If it wasn't bullies slapping me around and getting girls to laugh, it was the fact of being hopelessly uncool. Doing my homework, not doing drugs, knowing nothing about rock music, not getting invited to the big weekend parties at Ellen Kurz's where everybody got wasted to the sounds of "Sympathy for the Devil" and had orgies they'd whisper about Monday morning. Sex was the problem. Everybody else at the Day School was getting some. I wanted some. A girlfriend, at least. A kiss or two.

The fall of senior year I decided to act. Skinny-dipping and beer drinking had broken the ice; it was time to kill off the hopeless brainiac reject I'd been. One gray October afternoon I drove over to the Nanuet Mall, walked into Allegro Music, and asked the sales guy if I could take a look at one of the Hohner Marine Band harmonicas. He unlocked the display case and handed me a small cardboard box. The only other musical instrument I'd ever owned was the white plastic flutophone I'd screeched "Claire de Lune" on back in fifth grade. Harmonica had been calling to me, recently. My dad would cycle through the same two or three records while daubing away in his attic studio; I'd overhear Bob Dylan wheezing on his and whooping "Honey jes allow me one more chancccce. . . ." The big hit on WABC during the summer of '74 was the Ozark Mountain Daredevils' "If You Wanna Get to Heaven," driven by a pesky little harmonica: "If ya wanna get to heavennnn . . . you got to raise a little helllll. . . ." Not to mention *The J. Geils Band Live Full House* album played at deafening volumes in senior class homeroom every morning, with Magic Dick blowing his face out on "Whammer Jammer" after Peter Wolf egged him on. Eric Balch and I knew all the words and acted them out:

We gotta get it crazy tonight. You gonna get it crazy tonight?

I'll get down to it.

Ah said you are gonna get it craaaaaazy?

I'll get down to it.

Ah said you gonna moogoomoogoomoogoogonna get it all down get it all night get it all right get it out of sight and get it *down,* baby?

Yeaaah!

Whammer Jammer, lemme hear ya, Dickie!

All that was waiting for me, down the line. I pried the chrome-plated grail out of the small cardboard box as the sales guy watched, cradled it lovingly, cupped it the way I imagined the pros did. You weren't allowed to play the thing until you'd paid for it. The sales guy fanned the bellows on a harmonica-tester to show me it worked. I shivered, thrilled. Eric would flip when he found out.

I picked up an instructional book, too, the only one that looked halfway cool: *Blues Harp* by Tony "Little Sun" Glover, with a picture of a wild-eyed black guy in a headband on the cover, wah-wahing through his cupped hands.

NAT HAD PLANS FOR ME. First thing we had to do was baptize my Mouse. I'd bought it right after Helen moved out and hadn't worked up the nerve to wail through it outdoors. I drove him downtown after my first lesson to pick up Charlie Hilbert, his guitar man. Charlie lived in a dingy fifth-floor walkup with a huge German shepherd named Snapper. Snapper went berserk on the landing—barking, roaring, howling—as we trudged up. Charlie was a smallish white guy with a goatee and a nasal New Yawk accent. He yelled at and whapped Snapper to shut him up. Snapper whimpered lovingly as Nat pulled his ears. Charlie had two beat-to-shit Mouses, which we grabbed and tossed into the back of my car along with his guitar case. Somehow I'd managed to fall in with real blues guys!

We drove down to the Village and set up against the north wall of Cooper Union's Great Hall: Charlie in the middle, our three little Mouses in a row. Nat had on the Panama hat and a pair of mirrored sunglasses. Blind Lemon Riddles, he joked. I gazed at the people strolling by. You were impossibly exposed out here—vulnerable,

alive, naked to the world. The groove floated between Nat and Charlie like a taut, durable rope. Where should I grab hold? I was a third
dancer with two left feet. Didn't I tell you he could blow? Nat said
later as we packed up.

A week later I was wandering through the Village with my new
girlfriend, a Bahamian woman named Andria, when we came across
Nat and Charlie. They were working the corner of Sixth Street and
Avenue of the Americas, squatting on their upended Mouses—
Charlie hunched over, Nat sitting tall with legs spread. Nat's lizardskin loafers were new and looked sharp with his white Panama. He
was preaching to a small crowd, telling them how the blues was
American music, Southern music, and how he and Charlie were
from the South—Charlie from southern Staten Island and he, of
course, from the South Bronx.

"If *we* don't have the blues," he laughed, "don't *nobody* have the
blues. Ain't that right, Charlie?"

I leaned against a trashcan with Andria in my arms, swooning at
the evening's luck. Nat supported his cupped harp and bullet microphone with a near-vertical arm, pivoting fluidly from his waist,
working the groove like a slow-motion boxer. Each phrase he blew
came from deep and led with flawless logic to the next.

"Another mule kickin' in my stall," he sang, winking at me.
"Adam knows all about that."

Andria and I got drunk around the corner in the BeBop Cafe and
floated back an hour later bearing a pair of ice cold Heinekens from
the deli next door. Nat saw the brown paper bag with protruding
green bottleneck coming at him and stopped blowing.

"For me?" he said, touching his chest. "Awww, you guys are just
too much."

He handed me the mike while he drank. It was round and light
and bigger than I expected, harder to cup.

"Don't be playing like no *white boy*, now," he admonished,
putting on a black Southern accent as he waved his beer. "Noooo.
Show the peoples how well Uncle Nat done taught you, son."

My hands got cold, my mouth went dry. Somehow you push
through. Then the notes start to come and you're playing, it's a

Friday evening in the Village and you're bathed in blinding light, struggling to hold the groove even as it sags away from you, your new master and new lover looking on. Old hurts flame through your heart, vaporize in a hot rush. People toss money. Where else would you rather be?

1974. I LAY ON MY BED with my new toy, angling the chrome coverplates in the light, trying to see down into the holes. "O, Susanna!" I'd figured out right away. Christmas carols were easy, once you got the hang of squeezing your lips to make single notes. Blues was harder. You had to wrestle with the airstream inside your mouth, lasso and choke it, feel the sadness in your throat, make the thing cry and wail. It had something to do with being a black guy. Tony "Little Sun" Glover was white—the back-cover photo had him squinting at the camera, a cigarette dangling from his lips—but every other picture in *Blues Harp* was of a black guy, either smiling or sucking on a harmonica: James Cotton, Jimmy Reed, Little Walter, Sonny Boy Williamson. Sonny Boy was standing outdoors between a guitar player and a drummer, glaring at the camera like an old buzzard, blowing harp into a big chrome mike.

Harp was a cooler word for harmonica. I'd figured this out a couple of weeks before taking the plunge. I'd borrowed Eric Balch's *J. Geils Band: Lookin' for a Love* album and was amazed to find Magic Dick listed on the back as "harp." Where's the harp? I thought, straining to hear plucked strings as I listened to the thing on headphones. Then it hit me.

1985 WAS THE SUMMER OF NAT. I tailed him everywhere—Central Park, the Astor Place Cube, jam sessions at Dan Lynch and Nightingale. Sometimes he worked just with Charlie; sometimes he rounded up the Dan Lynch Irregulars and threw whole bands onto the street. His nickname for his act, whatever the configuration, remained constant: El Cafe Street. A moveable blue feast. He'd raise his finger in the air between songs like Malcolm X, lift his chin, and preach in a voice that could swing from street to upscale and back:

"El Cafe Street, where there *is* no cover and no minimum. We will not be hawking drinks out here. Waitresses will not be coming up to you and saying 'Pony up or get out.' No bouncer will flex his biceps and prevent you from entering our exclusive establishment. El Cafe Street is open to all. Unlimited *free* entertainment, as long as the local authorities see fit. We come to give yah whatcha come tuh get. Where else in New York City can you get a deal like that? Hell if I know. Charlie, do you know? Charlie's shaking his head. Charlie don't know. All we ask is that you dig deep and give whatever you feel our music—our *American* music, the best in the world—is worth. Thank you, darling. What's that? Yes, we do accept credit cards, food stamps, chitlins, and collard greens."

The money poured in. His musicians loved him. He was an equal opportunity employer: if you could follow his stop-time signal— that finger in the air—and go with whatever craziness came down, you were in. He actually put instruments in guys' hands and got them started. Jerry Dugger was a plump black bass player from Brooklyn, shy and sweet, who wore dark lizardy Wayfarers indoors and out; Nat gave him a snare and said, "You're my drummer. Learn." Bill Durkin was a big, sleepy, cynical kid who twanged his white Gretch and duckwalked like Chuck Berry; he'd been there, done that—worked the Beaubourg in Paris, bedded Swedish au pairs he'd picked up at the Central Park Zoo. Nat collared him. Ted Horowitz, a huge furry-shouldered half-Italian guitarist who wore sweatpants with minimal underwear and later made it big on the national blues circuit as Popa Chubby, bought himself a Mouse and followed in Nat's footsteps, working Wall Street on Friday afternoons. Homeboy Steve Antonakis, Ron Sunshine, Canarsie Kenny: everybody had a Mouse hanging off his shoulder that summer. Guys would blow through the swinging front doors of Dan Lynch and plug their rechargers into the outlet by the pool table. Half the regular jammers seemed to be on Nat's El Cafe Street payroll, flashing thick wads of one-dollar bills.

My Mouse had been baptized; I wanted in. I was always subwaying down to Christopher Street and prowling eastward, looking for action. I'd been woodshedding furiously with the Nat tape and a Big Walter Horton record I'd picked up. Many late nights I walked home through Riverside Park, working shit out. "Wailing" was a cliché: what if you were *actually crying* while you played? I thought about Helen and Jack, her new boyfriend, and tried that. Every tunnel had its own decay rate, its sweetness of echo. Fourth of July morning found me in Central Park, haunting the men's bathroom behind the Sheep's Meadow snack bar, going for Big Reverb while homeless guys yawned and pissed.

Fourth of July night was Nat's epic throwdown at Dan Lynch, the gig they still talk about. All afternoon and early evening tens of thousands of people had been streaming through the East Village toward the Macy's fireworks extravaganza on the East River. Dan Lynch was just off the corner of Fourteenth Street and Second Avenue; at ten o'clock the place was empty except for two bored bartendresses, a worried band, and Nat in his cocked Panama. You could hear huge low thuds in the distance, like bundles of newspapers being dropped. Nat pulled me out through the front doors to sniff the gunpowdered air. After a final packed flurry at twenty past ten, he raised his finger and said, "Listen." Nothing except the vague taxicab roar of New York at night. Then the roar began to swell, a tidal wave foaming with whistling bottle-rockets and endless popcorn strings of firecrackers.

He laughed. "Do I know my business or what?"

"Damn."

"We serve no wine before its time," he said, tucking in his plain white t-shirt as he pushed back inside, notching his snakeskin belt tight.

I sat in the front window under the neon Bud sign, getting trashed, watching him go. He blew for forty-five minutes on the first song. He called his children home—jazzed-up masses yearning to breathe blues. It was Apocalypse Now. Wave after wave crashed against the front doors and poured through. The way he bopped, swayed, floated, stung. He was beautiful. A blonde in a clinging red dress got up on the narrow bar that separated the band from everybody else and did the bump-and-grind. Nat brought the band way down and flared the fingers of his free hand over his Panama like a coxcomb. "I got a little red rooster," he sang, eyeing her lovingly, "too lazy to crow for day. . . . Keeps everything in the barnyard . . . upset in every way." She shimmied down to his level, turned dreamily, pulled him close for a kiss which his hat partly hid. The place came apart. Then he eased her offstage with a "Thank you, darling" and kicked into an uptempo boogie. "I sent my baby a brand-new twenty-dollar bill," he cried. "If that don't bring her back, I'm darn sure my Uzi will." He cocked his free hand like a pistol and machine-gunned the place, all of us, with tongued chords.

People were screaming through the smoke. He could do no wrong. The first set lasted two and a half hours. The tip bucket—a dented tin champagne cooler—made two or three rounds, floating through the drunken waving arms like a holy chalice. The blonde, who he introduced me to between sets, turned out to be his girlfriend Doreen.

*1974.* I CARRIED IT EVERYWHERE I WENT, usually in the pocket of a fringed suede jacket I'd started wearing. I played it every free moment—in the Day School's various boys bathrooms, in stairwells and other echo-zones, in the five or ten minutes before morning assembly. I'd spend lunch and ninth period jamming in the upper school lounge with a couple of guys who played Led Zeppelin and James Taylor stuff on guitars they'd brought in. Glenn Alynn had given up; Lips had vanished without a trace. Who even *saw* my lips, these days? I walked around campus with a harp cupped, wailing and warbling. My new nickname was Wazoo. Waz, for short.

The girlfriend question was still open. I had zero nerve—I'd never actually asked a girl out—so I put off the moment of truth and went harp-crazy. I went back to the Nanuet Mall, bought a couple more Marine Bands in different keys, plus some records. You couldn't learn blues, according to Glover, unless you listened to the real shit. Older black guys. It was like learning French: you had to get over to France, surround yourself with garrulous French people.

So where was Blues Land? I'd never met an actual blues musician. The only older black guy I knew was Mr. Foreman, the Day School's caretaker. He lived with his wife and foster kids in a small house next to the basketball court. He smiled a lot, talked in a slow lazy way, limped around the school, kept things clean and fixed. His skull was brown and shiny when he took off his porkpie hat. One of his thumbs had been half cut off; he'd use it to nub through the hundred keys in his quadruple key-ring until he found the right one. I liked Mr. Foreman. I'd been his janitorial assistant during the fall of junior year. I'd bicycle up to the school on Saturday mornings and help him mop dirty floors and fix sticking locks. His favorite word was "mash." We'd be crouched next to a door, squirting 3-in-1 oil into the keyhole.

"Mash on it," he'd say, nodding at the frozen handle, smiling a little. "She'll open."

Same thing if I was mopping. "Mash it into the corner," he'd tell me. "We gonna *get* that dirt."

He was the gentlest person I'd ever met. He was a minister on Sundays, people said, at a church down in Nyack. I always wondered if my biblical name made him treat me extra nice. His house, when his wife opened the door, always smelled like warm delicious food: pork chops, buttered sweet potatoes, juicy long-cooked things. His foster kids would hang back, eyeing me.

Mr. Foreman, as far as I could tell, knew nothing about blues. He didn't sing while he was working or play an instrument. So he was a dead end.

But I did manage to find an amazing record. I'd been jamming with it every day, before and after school. *The Great Bluesmen* was a double LP with a cover you could lay on your bed and stare at for hours: scratched, faded, jumbled up black-and-white photos of older black guys—a couple of them in Mr. Foreman's same hat—picking guitars, grimacing, showing their teeth; one large photo of a guy with grainy pitted black skin and bloodshot eyes gazing right at you and smiling like Mona Lisa; two crumpled dollar bills; a Johnnie Walker Scotch bottle; nickels and dimes scattered across an ace of spades playing card; a brown-skinned woman with naked breasts and her head hidden by a gin bottle; tarnished looped guitar strings resting on the La Bella package they came in; and a harp. Exactly the same harp I had, in the flipped-open cardboard box lined with red paper. But this harp had been to hell and back: coverplates rusted and squeezed in, varnish worn off the splayed wooden comb. A real bluesman's instrument, obviously.

Every guy on the two-record set—Homesick James, Muddy Waters, Mississippi John Hurt, Jimmy Rushing—had his own way of yelling "Hey, baby!" at the woman he wanted, or couldn't get, or was being mistreated by. I couldn't understand some of the words, when Son House started beating his guitar and raving. But his crying feeling was my feeling. That sob in your throat when the cute girl you were silently crazy about started laughing at some other guy's stupid jokes and you *knew* he wasn't right for her. You knew you could make her happy, if she gave you the chance. But she was ignoring you. How could she be so cruel? How could you be such a fucking wimp and not talk to her? But you were. Zero nerve. If you could just break through and *yell at the top of your lungs* everything she made you feel—love, craziness, horniness, despair—you might have a chance of turning her head.

The Great Bluesmen and I had a steady date. Every morning before school, every afternoon when I got home. Keeping up with different tracks was tricky; you had to make small adjustments to your foot-tap so you didn't fall behind or race ahead of the beat. "Key to the Highway" by Sonny Terry and Brownie McGhee was the bounciest jam track. Sonny *squalled*. Brownie was my man, too:

> I got the key . . . to the highway
> Billed out . . . I'm bound to go
> I'm gonna leave here runnin'
> Walkin's most too slow. . . .

RIDDLES WAS GOD in the summer of '85. Then Labor Day came, El Cafe Street lost out to Homeboy Steve and the Mudcats in the Second Annual Village Voice Street Entertainers Festival—Nat's harps sounded worn and flat—and summer was over. The next time I saw him was the last for a while, in mid-September. He and the guys were slouched in the Kentucky Fried Chicken next door to Lynch's. Everybody looked beat. Jerry Dugger had been dating a young white blues singer named Joan Osborne and things were going sour. Canarsie Kenny—a barrel-chested white harmonica player and former junkie who rasped like Howling Wolf—was singing the praises of Tuinals gulped a handful at a time. Nat was bitter and spent. He'd been driving his cab for days. His eyes were red; there was a rageful edge in his voice.

"I will work for you," he said. "I got no problem working hard. Ask any musician that *ever* worked for me how hard I work. But do *not* tell me I gotta slave fifteen hours, twenty hours in a row *and* pay gas *and* take whatever insolent bullshit whoever gets in my cab wants to throw on me, and then come home with only seventy-five dollars to my name."

Kenny scowled. "The hack scene's fucked up, always has been."

"Look at me. Look at me. I literally cannot *see* straight. That's how dog-tired I am. My hands are shaking." He held out his hands so we could see. "See that? Trembling like a kicked dog. And I'm supposed to go back out there behind this kind of bullshit and *work* for you? Fuck that. Fuck that. I don't do that, I *will not* do that. Find somebody else to be your slave." He looked away, lips tight.

I was scared. I tried to cheer him up later, jamming for him on the sidewalk in front of Lynch's. He was working on a paper-bagged quart of Ballantine Ale and eyeing the cool September afternoon. Something I played caught his ear and he bent down to listen, eyes closed. I've never worked so hard for a smile. I had the crying feeling in my throat. I threw every lick I'd stolen off the Big Walter record at him with his own stuff mixed in, every tongue-blocked yelp and bark and woof and snarl, all in clappable, foot-tappable time. He opened his eyes and scatted along with me. He was starting to glow again. He buttonholed a couple of guys coming out the front door of Lynch's and made them listen.

"Now *who* taught you all that stuff?" he said, beaming.

I stopped playing and deadpanned in a breathless earnest white-boy voice. "Why, *you* did, Nat."

He poured a plastic cup of Ballantine's and handed it to me. "You're playing like a harmonica player now."

"Barely."

"Stop. Don't do that. What did I just say?"

"I'm a harmonica player."

His smile was gone. "I said *you can play.*"

"Thanks."

"The music was *always* in you. All I did"—he poked my chest with his finger—"all I did was say, 'Hello in there, I see you in there, come on out.' "

*1975.* I FINALLY HAD MY FIRST GIRLFRIEND. Sandra was half-Jewish, like me, and exactly my age. Long dark hair, tight bluejeans with flared bellbottoms. She played violin. She was smart, impatient, elbowy. She loved Broadway show-tunes. Her favorite makeout record was *Godspell.* We wore each other's lips out, lying tangled on her bed with her mom cooking chili downstairs. She let me touch her breast under her sweatshirt on our third date. It was this perfect thing.

I'd been hoping all fall. Finally, at Jodi Wax's New Year's Eve sleepover, I'd made my move. Twenty of us were crashed out at 4 AM on the floor of Jodi's basement rec room. Somehow I ended up next to the Girl I Wanted. People were dozing, murmuring, sagging. By five I was stroking her hair: gently, with love pushing through my fingertips. My heart was breathless. I'd never gone this far before. By six I was nuzzling her hair, smelling her shampoo. Just before people woke up, she sighed and turned. "Good morning," she said. And pecked me on the lips.

We were going out. My first girlfriend. It was like nothing I'd ever had. I said I love you two months in, after moving through the various stages of Like. The night I said it, she murmured it back. My heart tickled, feathery. Her breath smelled like chili with onions.

I was jumping around my bedroom at home between dates, blowing harp. Blues was unbelievably happy music. I'd picked up a copy of *The J. Geils Band Live Full House* and figured out Magic Dick's solo on "Whammer Jammer." The screaming bent high note was impossible. Finally I dunked my harp in a glass of water and shook it out. *Wheee-oooooh!*

A junior named Jordan showed me the blues scale. Jordan was

the Day School's best rock guitarist. He had stringy brown hair—as long as Sandra's—and wore cowboy boots and a major attitude. Clapton sucked; Jimmy Page ruled; Jethro Tull was the best. Blues was simplistic shit—nothing but three chords, over and over—but he was willing to back me up on acoustic guitar. And show me the blues scale. He'd play one note at a time, I'd find it on my harp. The blue third was a revelation. He'd smear a minor third slightly sharp, make it sad-happy and raw. I finally got it.

Sandra and I had been going out for three months, things were great. Suddenly they weren't. She'd act impatient at unexpected moments. I'd say something; she'd look bored. I got weird desperate feelings that wouldn't go away. I'd search for her during ninth period in the various buildings. I'd find her dawdling with Jordan on a sofa in the student lounge, laughing and snorting.

He was cooler than me, better-looking. This couldn't be happening. The world became one incredible sick hopless feeling. I had to do something.

I took her to a blues concert. I'd just turned seventeen and could drive at night. The James Cotton Band was opening for the J. Geils Band at a local community college gym. We were sitting in the bleachers. Cotton was stalking the stage, harp cupped as his band swung and grooved under the rainbow lights. He tore through "Creeper Creeps Again"—bellowing, snarling, taking no shit. I'd been blowing for six months; this was the first time I'd heard a pro, live. Cotton was God.

"Things aren't working out, Adam," she said testily.

"What are you talking about?"

She looked away, furious.

I put my head in my hands. "Please, Sandra," I said.

Cotton was finishing up. The gym was huge, shadowy, throbbing, with lots of room to dance. We sat side by side, frozen. The J. Geils Band strutted out in studded leather jackets and pants. This was 1975. They were bigger than God. Magic Dick had a huge Jewish Afro, dark sunglasses, a goatee. Magic Dick was the Devil's own spawn.

"Don't do it," I whined, trying not cry. "Jordan isn't right for you."

"How do you know?"

Magic Dick was strutting around the stage blowing "Whammer Jammer." His sound through the massive P.A. system was a shuddering blow. This was the greatest night of my life. I glanced at Sandra. A sob blossomed in my throat. The worst. How could it be both?

I drove her home after the show—no last kiss—and collapsed on my bed three towns over. The world had ended. She was Jordan's now. I clapped my headphones on and cranked up the stereo, letting B. B. King flood through me with "Sweet Little Angel":

I've got a sweet little angel. . . . I love the way she spreads her wings
I've got a sweet little angel. . . . I love the way she spreads her wings
When she puts her arms around me . . . she brings me joy in everything.

All I'd ever wanted, gone. The dams broke. It poured and poured, a river inside me.

IT WAS CHARLIE HILBERT who gave me the news. I bumped into him just before Christmas '85 down at Dan Lynch. The summer of Nat seemed like a distant golden age. I'd been through a couple of busking lifetimes since then—blowing harp behind an old black tap dancer named Gator, working the Astor Place Cube and Grand Central Station with a wild, drawling, thrashabilly guitarist who called himself Lonesome Harry but was really Bill Taft III of Cleveland, Ohio, a great-grandsomething of the U.S. president. Charlie had an indoor gig with the Jersey Slim Blues Band. His hipster goatee was gone; he had the same nasal Bensonhurst-meets-Piscataway accent and was cheerfully gloomy, the only way I'd ever seen him. He rolled his eyes when I asked about Nat.

"That guy. Did you hear about him getting shot?"

"Shot?" I said.

He grimaced. "Four times in the chest. Fucking Nat."

"Nat's *dead*?"

"He's fine. He was back in here a week later, bragging. Him and Sonny Boy both get shot, and the Riddles lives." He laughed. "One of 'em got him right here." He jabbed his sternum with his index finger. "It was only a .22 so it didn't do shit."

He'd been having a shouting match with Doreen in Dan Lynch, according to Charlie, and they'd taken it outside. Some Puerto Rican guy had come along and popped Nat. Maybe drugs were involved, maybe he'd gotten physical with Doreen. With Nat telling the story, who knew?

# CHAPTER TWO

# EVERYBODY IN HARLEM KNOWS SATAN

*If Bessie Smith had killed some white people she wouldn't have needed that music.*

—LeRoi Jones, *Dutchman*

STAY OUT OF HARLEM! was the first thing Helen and I had been warned when we moved into neighboring Morningside Heights back in 1980. Her fellow English grad students at Columbia—white folks, all—were adamant. *Never* make the mistake of taking the No. 2 or No. 3 express subway north past Ninety-sixth Street, or the A train north past Columbus Circle. *Always* transfer to the No. 1 local. Forget to do that and you'd end up in the middle of . . . *Harlem!* Mortal danger.

This was said with a nervous laugh, repeated like a mantra, taken as self-evident common sense.

A male grad student—a white guy—had been killed the year before, we were told. He and his girlfriend, walking home late at night, had been followed into the lobby of their apartment building on Morningside Drive by a black guy with a gun. They'd behaved like dutiful white people, handed over their money and watches. As the black gunman spun away, the white guy's wallet slipped out of his pocket.

"You dropped something," the white guy reportedly called out. With a trace, it was whispered, of inappropriate jauntiness.

The black guy turned and shot him in the face.

Helen's new colleagues shuddered as they warned us: Morningside Park is full of junkies. Harlem is only a couple of blocks away. The Heart of Darkness is at your doorstep. *Be careful.*

HARLEM WAS THE LAST PLACE on my mind during the summer of '86, half a decade later. Nat's vision of El Cafe Street as a moveable blue feast had become my own; I'd flown over to Paris in June with my Mouse and gotten loud. I'd taken trains down through Avignon to the Riviera and back up to Amsterdam, jammed with dozens of guitarists, drummers, singers. I'd sweated in the Metro tunnels and strolled seaside cafés, been teargassed by the *flics,* drunk too much *vin rouge* and draft Heineken. I'd had several memorable affairs and a regrettable one-night stand with a Milanese heiress who'd offered me two weeks at St. Moritz. Two years after losing Helen, my wounded heart had finally begun to heal, or at least scar over.

I put away my Mouse when I got back to New York in late August, spent. Found a part-time job tutoring writing at Hostos Community College in the South Bronx, picked up a few harp students to make rent. In my spare time I was struggling with a road novel that couldn't quite capture the unlikely romance my busker's life had been. I was blowing a little harp, jamming occasionally at Dan Lynch in the vacuum left by Nat. I hadn't seen or talked to him in more than a year. I missed him.

I'd recently moved to Inwood, at the forgotten northern tip of Manhattan Island. My usual commute to Hostos was down the East River Drive and across the 145th Street Bridge. One day in October, a hazy Indian summer noon, I suddenly got inspired. Why not take a shortcut through Harlem and stop off at Sylvia's Soul Food? Helen and I had been there once and enjoyed a delicious, if anxious, Sunday brunch: creamy scrambled eggs, sage-fragrant patty sausage, grits topped with half-melted hunks of butter. Biscuits, black coffee. The real American deal.

I jumped in my Honda and took off. Harlem from Inwood was

due south on the open road. I blew down the Henry Hudson Parkway, swooped under the George Washington Bridge, rolling down the window and punching up Jazz 88 as I went. A tenor sax—had to be Stanley Turrentine with those whooping-cough lines—was singing to me. River air whipped through. America was raw, fragrant, sprawling, jagged, electrical. I held seventy in fifth for three minutes and slid off the ramp at 125th Street.

I started to get nervous, rolling across Broadway past Kentucky Fried Chicken under the subway's webbed cathedral arc. This past spring I'd ventured alone to jam sessions at several Harlem jazz clubs; the only hands laid on me had been warmhearted and welcoming, but still. White anxiety dies hard. I locked both doors at Amsterdam Avenue and rolled up the window, cursed my sick soul, lowered the window a crack, turned up the radio. Stanley's sax shrieked, an aural mandala identifying me, protecting me, warding off bad vibes.

I'd made it to Adam Clayton Powell Jr. Boulevard, just past the Apollo Theater, when I heard a faint bluesy roar. The rawness and aliveness were uncanny. I turned down the car radio as I paused at the light. Nothing on the left except the State Office Building—tallest in Harlem—with the wide empty plaza fronting the street, a few old guys in Kangol caps and fedoras warming their bones on sunny benches. On the right were Senegalese street vendors in gold and purple dashikis, a hot dog cart, a crowded bus shelter plastered with posters for Regina Belle's next concert sponsored by WBLS.

I pulled through the intersection, came around the shelter, and saw the music source: an older man backed against the smoked glass face of a New York Telephone office. He had a fluffy gray beard, an electric guitar in his lap, was kicking one hi-hat cymbal in furious clattering time. I pulled to the curb, rolled down the passenger-side window. The heat radiating from him was not to be believed. He was Robert Johnson reborn as Parliament Funkadelic, a Mississippi flood roaring down Broadway. He rocked tautly on his hi-chair, tossed off withering flurries of bittersweet chords. His gold tooth flashed. His smile was fierce, beatified, sexual, self-contained, infectious.

It's *that guy*, I thought, shivering. I'd seen him once before, twenty blocks and a world away. He'd changed my life.

*1984.* HELEN AND I were walking home from Butler Library on an unexpectedly mild February night, arguing. What else was new? We'd been going through hell ever since Christmas, when she'd told me about Jack, her current love interest. A fellow English grad student, he, like the last guy, was somebody we both knew. I'd kicked a chair across a room, she'd slammed her pillow against the bed, inches from my head. We weren't violent people. We'd never laid a hand on each other. We just argued, endlessly and bitterly. Then reached out in desperation, fell sobbing into each other's arms, and kept going. I was beginning to wonder how long we could. I'd started to get serious about harp again, after years of occasional noodling. I'd wail mournfully in the service tunnel below the gym on my way to graduate seminars, hoping the security guard—whoever was on duty—would lift his head and notice me, hear the pain in my heart.

We heard the racket up the block before we could tell what it was. A crowd had gathered. I eased Helen to a stop. Three black guys were set up with their backs to the front of the Chemical Bank on the corner of 113th and Broadway. The trim-hipped guy on the left, with the scraggly black beard and trucker's cap, was contributing random licks on a cherry red Gibson ES 335. The light-skinned guy on the snare and cymbal had a big gut and chipmunk cheeks. The second guitarist—fluffy graying beard, flashing teeth—was laying down a greasy, driving groove that he interrupted several times to salute the heavens with a large paper-bagged bottle he'd just drained. He rocked on his heels, shimmied a little, eyes closed. His singing voice was a harsh rasp, pain blown wide with delight. Oh baby . . . you don't have to go. I'm gonna pack my bags and it's . . . down the road I goooooo.

Helen and I stood there, watching. I was transfixed. The groove was deathless. Three angels had descended like messengers from another galaxy. Grits and greens and smoking-hot barbecue. Rock me baby, all night long. Heart fluttering, I fingered the battered harp in my hip pocket. Who had the nerve to pull it out? I suddenly felt very young and very white. Several songs later—an endless flowing moment—the trio broke to light cigarettes and catch its breath while the open guitar case out front filled up. I reached into my back pocket for my wallet and pulled out a dollar. I was afraid to talk to the guitarist with the flashing teeth—awed, really—so I went up to Trucker's Cap and asked about the small trapezoidal amps both men were playing through.

"This here's my Mouse," the guy said, eyes narrowing at the flurry of bills and change. "Battery-powered."

"Where can I buy one?" I blurted out, surprised at myself.

"You know Manny's Music, downtown?"

"Sure."

He cocked his finger at me and pulled the trigger. "There you go."

"Mister Marvin!" the gray-bearded guitarist rasped, crouching in front of the guitar case. "Mister Pancho! Get on over here!"

I SHUT MY CAR OFF and got out, came around front, and stood on the Harlem sidewalk, stripped naked by awe. He was playing through a pair of Mouses and singing through a second set. His microphone stand was planted in a blue plastic bucket between his legs. Passing strollers paused to toss in dollar bills and change. A few older guys clutching paper-bagged bottles were cheering him on. He was wearing corduroy pants and Wallabees and had bone-thin legs. His forehead and cheeks were drenched above his beard. Tendons leaped and slithered in his smooth brown arms. His white t-shirt read "Kool: Alive with Pleasure."

A woman in a print dress was dancing a slow shuffle off to the side—hand touching her chest, elbow out. A scar creased her sunken cheek. She smiled to herself, eyes lowered. Teeth were missing. She had dark leathery skin. She was old and moved elegantly, swaying to an inner pulse. The music washed over me, bathing me. Long reckless harmonica lines spun through my head.

Somebody brushed by and I remembered where I was. A couple of older guys were leaning against my car, arms folded, watching me, not watching me. One was rail-thin and had a cane. I back-pedaled toward him; he eased sideways to make room. He had high Indian cheekbones. We stood propped against the car for a moment, side by side, grooving. Finally I blurted something about the guitarist being better than anybody I'd seen this past summer over in Europe.

"You right about that," he said, smiling as he shifted his weight. He had an artificial leg.

His name was Duke. He called me Adams. After a couple of minutes I felt he'd stick up for me if anybody tried to make trouble. We basked in the mild October afternoon. The men with paper-bagged bottles turned and stared whenever a woman with a particularly spectacular butt swished by. I risked a few looks. Duke caught me and grinned. "Yessir," he chuckled.

The music roared on, background and foreground, a crashing, driving flux, almost breathable, drilling into my bones. After a while I asked Duke who the one-man band was.

"Who, him?" he laughed with friendly disbelief. "I thought you knew about him. That's Satan. Uh huh."

"Satan," I said.

"That's right. Everybody in Harlem knows Satan. He's been playing right at this same spot since like—since maybe about four or five years. Oh yeah. This is Satan's spot, right here."

I stared at Satan, wondering. You couldn't make up a story like this. Watching him writhe, letting my hips and shoulders be tugged, remembering my own years as a funk-blues guitar-player back in college, I was starting to hear harp riffs that would work. I asked Duke if he thought Satan would let me sit in, a couple of tunes. It was hard saying the name out loud.

"What do you play?" he asked.

"Harmonica," I mumbled. "Blues."

He flashed a crooked smile. "Heyyyy, Stevie Wonder, my man." Then he said, "Sure, he'll let you play. *Can* you play?"

"I can play," I said, surprised at my own fierceness.

"Because people out here have seen *everything*, man, from flying elephants on down. They'll let you know how they feel."

We slapped hands before I left. I told him I'd be back the next day with my stuff.

1975. THE SUMMER AFTER high school graduation, with Sandra gone, I buried myself in the blues. Not just harp—amplified now, through an old suitcase-sized Epiphone amp—but electric guitar. My heros were Clapton and the three Kings: B. B., Albert, and Freddie. Once you'd figured out how blues scales worked, fingers could do the trick as well as lips and tongue. I couldn't be myself until my parents were out of the house. Then I'd heave open my bedroom windows, crank up the Kay until my guitar strings creaked, put Derek and the Dominos' live version of "Why Does Love Got to Be So Sad" on the stereo, and send shattering news out across the neighborhood. Electricity is instant mad power. I wanted to slash and knife. The connection between my aching throat, shredded fingertips, and throbbing eardrums was as perfect as anything I'd felt for Sandra. I didn't need *anybody* now.

I'd never hear my mom come home. She'd stand in the doorway of my room, hands over her ears, eyes clenched, screaming my name until I heard her and stopped playing.

"What?" I'd say sullenly, after I'd spun the stereo volume down to zero. Guilty, quivering, alive as shit.

"*What??*" she'd echo, incredulous. "I could hear you halfway down the block!"

"I was practicing."

"Turn it *down.*"

"It's *off,* Mom! What the hell else can I do?"

"Alan!" she'd shriek over her shoulder. "Talk to your son."

I was off to Princeton that fall. I wore tie-dyed t-shirts and had a bad attitude. I cleaned dorm bathrooms and sold hoagies at night to pay my bills. I'd heave my cooler of Italians, turkeys, and roast beefs from entryway to entryway, stick my head in, shout "Hooooagie Maaaan!" then wail on the harp holder around my neck. Sometimes I'd bring along a Tijuana taxi-horn and ah-ooh-gah until blond preppies in pink Lacoste shirts and Bean's hunting boots cursed me from upstairs. I hated them and their gorgeous blond girlfriends. I hated their eating clubs up on Prospect Street, where they drank too much on Saturday night, danced to live bands like the Good Rats and Valentine, and kept freshman slime like me out. I was ugly, lonely, out of the loop. An exile in my own mind, wolfing down all the sour grapes I could find.

I was a bluesman without a band. My first audition, freshman week, was from hell. Two local rock-blues legends, the Bordash Brothers, had put an ad in *The Daily Princetonian*. The legends part I found out about later. They needed a second guitarist; I'd jammed with lots of records in the past nine months. Nervous but nervy, I showed up at a garden apartment somewhere down behind the cemetery on Witherspoon Street and was let into a carpeted basement room lined with Marshall stacks and Les Paul Sunbursts. The Bordash Brothers had fluffy black manes, five o'clock shadows, lots of chest hair, huge invisible jism-dripping balls. They took one look at me and eyed each other.

"Whaddya wanna start with?" the brother on guitar asked.

"I was hoping maybe a shuffle blues in E."

"Can you handle that, Joe?" he snorted as Joe, sitting on a stool, dialed up the volume on his electric bass.

"Fuck if I know. I'm only a townie."

My hands shook. I'd played thirty seconds of a rhythm pattern I'd stolen off a Climax Blues Band album when Guitar Brother glanced at Joe, made a disgusted face, and unplugged.

"Thanks, man," he said.

"I blow harp, too."

"I'm sure you do."


I RAN UP INTO INWOOD HILL PARK after I got home from my tutoring gig—pockets bulging, Satan on my mind. I blew endless spiraling lines. My notes ricocheted off the girdered underbelly of the Henry Hudson Bridge, scattering pigeons. It was a question of reaching down into your guts and ripping. James Cotton used to suck so hard he'd tear loose brass reeds. Nat taught you that. I bounced back along the park road with my lips rubbed raw, drenched and panting. Cool currents eddied down off the wooded slope of Inwood Hill, like breath out of the Indian caves; lonely summer crickets whirred under fallen leaves.

I threw my Mouse and daypack in the back of my Honda at noon the next day and took off, Dyckman Street to 125th Street in two minutes flat. Bob Porter was playing Albert Collins on his Jazz 88 blues hour, icy knifing guitar lines that made my throat throb. I pushed across 125th, veering left at the firehouse past Sing's Lounge and the fried fish place, crossing Frederick Douglass Boulevard. I cruised past the Apollo Theater—amateur hour tomorrow—and strained to hear Satan's sound over the general roar. Street vendors hawking Coltrane tapes, Luther Vandross aching for my love from a helplessly overdriven loudspeaker on the sidewalk in front of Black Hair Now. I floated across Seventh Avenue in the diesel wash of a city bus, swung into the clear. There he was! Thrashing his guitar and hi-hat cymbal in front of the telephone office, with the same handful of wine drinkers egging him on. Everybody except the dancing woman. Duke leaning on his cane. I floored it and shot by.

I swung left onto Lenox Avenue, heading uptown. Lingering so long the day before, I'd left no time for breakfast before my tutoring gig. Sylvia's was a block and a half up on the right. I parked, slammed, heaved my Mouse out of the trunk. Older and younger men were loitering in doorways, laughing loudly, arguing, slapping hands, spinning away from each other, yelling over their shoulders. Nobody paid me much notice. I floated toward the front door and pushed through.

I stood awkwardly on the threshold, Mouse dangling. The room billowed with clatter and warmth: stocky powerful women in lemon yellow and birdshell blue uniforms slamming dishes into the sink below the counter, chatting with customers, swinging toward the steam tables and shouting, heaping heavy white plates with ham and eggs and grits and gobs of butter melting into fluffy homemade biscuits, clouds of steam rising off the dented steel coffeemaker, patty sausage sizzling on the grill. The gray-haired woman behind the register gazed at me through large glasses—lips pursed, skeptical. I floated toward the counter, slid onto a stool. An unshaven older man in a trucker's cap was hunched over a plate of ribs two stools away. He gave me a quick flat look and went back to work. One of the uniformed women behind the counter wiped her way to where I was sitting and smiled.

"You need a menu, baby?"

Scrambled eggs so creamy you'd swear they were laid to order, patty sausage bursting with peppery sage-juice, a mound of white grits with melting butter, strong black coffee to wash it all down. I ate silently, rhapsodizing over my homecoming meal. Parisians with their croissants and café crème couldn't touch this shit. Forget about McDonalds, Disneyland, Coca-Cola. America was built on breakfasts like this. Flapjacks, bacon. Keep you in the saddle all day. What did Satan eat? I suddenly wondered. My stomach tightened. I forked up the last of my grits with a browned biscuit bottom and signaled for the check, humming. I pulled out a five and, still sitting, stretched it and the check out toward the cashier lady.

My arm was a couple of inches too short. She glared through her glasses. "I'm not going to come over there and get it from you."

"Sorry," I murmured, sliding off my stool.

She took the check and bill and punched the register without looking at me. *Bam! Bam! Bam!* The change dripped from her hand like ice water; I slid back around the counter and grabbed my Mouse.

A moment later I was back on the street. Voices raged through my head. I was an asshole, self-centered, a fool out of my depth. Why the fuck are you here?

I looked up at the sky. Soft, hazy, October-sweet. Duke was probably wondering where I was. Yeah those white boys talk a good game but when push comes to shove.

I threw my Mouse in the back of my car and leaped in, throat tight. Slammed and gunned.

I blew back across 126th Street and around the State Office Building. Duke was leaning on his cane when I pulled up next to the fire hydrant. The music was high surf crashing against the shore, frothing. He grinned as we grabbed hands. "Heeeey, Adams, how's it goin' there?"

"He's on his game today."

"Oh yeah. That's Satan for you. Once he gets the spirit, you know—he might play that one song all night if he feels like it."

We let go and leaned back against my car. Satan was shouting something about Billy Joe jumping off the Tallahatchie Bridge. I could feel his groove so strongly it was like being connected with jumper cables. He brought the song to a close, a great thrashing crescendo of cymbals and phase-shifted guitar as the wine drinkers hollered Yeah! He fell back with his gold tooth flashing, bent forward to fiddle with the wires that kept his cymbal stand anchored to his battered, rusted chair.

Time shivered. Now or never. I floated toward him, weightless. Murmured something about enjoying his music. He glanced up and smiled distractedly, shook my hand, went back to tinkering.

"Um," I mumbled. "Any chance of me sitting in on a couple of tunes? I'm a harmonica player."

He looked up. Our eyes met. His gaze was level, thoughtful, impossible to read.

"I won't embarrass you," I added.

He leaned back in his chair and considered this. Combed his fingers through his gray beard. His fingertips had thick whitish calluses, grooved and peeling.

"Did you bring your instruments?" he asked.

I nodded at my car. "My Mouse is in the trunk."

Another pause. Then he raised his arm, burst into a gold-toothed grin, and roared, "Come on up!"

In a flash I was at my car, diving in and out, dodging pedestrian traffic as I veered toward the telephone office, crouching on the sidewalk, unzipping my daypack and slapping stuff together. I could sense appraising eyes already. Duke was explaining me to the wine drinkers. I upended my Mouse and faced it rearward, like Satan's. His amps were old and birdshit-stained. I plugged in my mike, switched on, blew a couple of test notes. Sidewalk traffic had frozen.

Thirty Harlemites—young, old, curious, dubious—were staring at me. I sat on my amp. Normally I would have stood, but standing taller than Satan on his own turf seemed politically unwise.

He was leaning back with his legs crossed, smoking a cigarette. "How you coming along there, Mister?"

He tuned up to the note I gave him, slam-dunk precise. He hit an open chord, I wailed.

"Yes sir," he chuckled. He leaned toward his mike. "Five!" he barked. He strummed random chords, brooding, then sat back. "I got a little thing called 'Mother Mojo' I want to groove on a while."

"Cool." If his version was anything like Muddy's, I was home free.

"Whooooooo!" he squalled into the mike, raking his pick across the strings, a phase-shifted thunderclap. "We're damn sure gettin' ready to do some kickin' and stompin' up here today." Then he hit.

The difference between watching him play and playing with him was the difference between sitting through a screening of *Twister* and being sucked skyward by a category five. I'd grooved with more than a few guitarists, live and recorded; I'd learned something about the small adjustments one makes to create flow. This was new. This was hanging onto the lion's tail. "Blow on, Mister! Blow *on!*" he roared, romping. Harlem loomed down on me as I careened wildly. A thin shouldery woman with tears in her eyes shook her head and yelled, "You got it baby! You got it!" A couple of young guys in baggy orange pants grabbed hands, laughing, "This shit is fucked up!" An older man with processed hair and a mustache staggered up openmouthed, paper-bagged pint dangling. "Blow, white boy!" he hollered, leaning in. *"Blow!* Lord have mercy! Lord have— Yeah! You got it now! Make it talk!" I heaved raw, bleeding notes up out of the lowest place I knew. He reached out, crooked his bottle arm around my shoulder, danced a little jig.

Satan writhed to a halt. "Hold it, Mister!" he roared, leaping up from his hi-chair as the crowd eased back. He grabbed the guy's shoulders. "You're drunk, man!" he cried. "You're filthy, stinking drunk and I won't have you up here making all kind of mess when we're trying to play our music!" The guy let me go, confused. Satan spun him around. "Get your snaggle-toothed black behind down the block and do *not* come messing with my harmonica man again," he shouted, giving him a push, "or you *damn* sure won't live to see Judgment Day!" People doubled over, slapped hands. The guy staggered backward, jerking to a wobbly stop. "All right white boy!" he yelled, toasting me with his pint. "You got it now! Play the blues!"

Satan slipped back into place and resumed. "Give me a dozen of your mojo hands!" he cried as I doubled him with frantic yelps. "Blow on, Mister!" he roared, flogging me with the beat until I almost passed out. My diaphragm was aching, my stock of licks was exhausted, a hundred people were shouting; I was the center of a delirious crapshoot with last-minute wagers pouring in. They weren't going to let go until I'd rolled sevens for everybody and rung in the jubilee.

Lifetimes came and went. Satan finished up with a clattering flurry; I hit a Magic Dick Special—the quivering bent high note from the beginning of "Whammer Jammer." We cut things off and Satan fell back as the sidewalk erupted, beaming like we'd just shared a very rich joke.

"Hell yeah!" somebody shouted. "Go 'head on, Devil!"

"That was some pretty playing, Mister," he chuckled as we slapped five. "Yes sir." He leaned toward his mike. "I want everybody to give Mister . . ." He trailed off, glanced at me.

"Adam," I said.

". . . Mister *Adam* a big hand," he chuckled as everybody roared. He licked his lips. "I guess they told you who I am."

"Yes sir."

"I am *Sa-tan*," he rasped, making two distinct syllables. "Mister Adam and I gonna take a very short break right now while I housekeep the money bucket, so don't anybody be running anywhere except right up here with your tips." He unplugged and stood up.

Paris was nothing next to this. Money was raining into the bucket—bills, change, subway tokens. One moment Duke was helping me to my feet and bragging about how I'd just come home from my European tour; the next moment a sweating, overmuscled little powerlifter with a scar knifing across his forehead who smelled of booze was elbowing in and grabbing me. He wanted to shake hands; he kept sticking his out, waiting for me to touch it, then grabbing mine and roaring "Yeaaaaaah! Yeaaaaaah!" before he yanked his away and mugged outrage at my trying to steal it. After four or five yanks he threw his arms around me and told me how he'd grown up down in Mississippi with this family, this white family down there and they had a white boy like me, the motherfucker looked *exactly* like me, motherfuckit, his name was Ricky and he and Ricky they used to . . . they used to—I mean Ricky and him were *close,* motherfuckit, he and Ricky used to go hunting and fishing and swimming together and lie around with the same girls—white girls, black girls, it didn't make no damn difference to *nobody,* motherfuckit, they always shared and . . . and—even Ricky's little sister, she was a white girl too but she treated him just like he was family even though he was black—they all did, every damn one of them, he could go into their house any time he felt like it, eat any food he felt like out of their refrigerator or anything, motherfuckit. Shit. I looked just like Ricky, too. Same red hair and everything. Motherfuckin' shit.

Satan burst through the crowd. "Mr. Murphy!" he roared, "I will *not* have you shooting off your filthy mouth and using all kind of disrespectful language in my presence!" Mr. Murphy let go and stood at attention with his hands behind his back, smirking. Satan gave him a disgusted look and then his scowl melted and he and Mr. Murphy were cracking up, people were howling, and Satan was waving me over, pushing a handful of crumpled bills into my hand and hissing, "No no no" when I started to protest, then bending down and scooping another four or five out of the bucket. "Shut up!" he whispered in my ear, not unkindly. I gave a dollar to Mr. Murphy and a dollar to Duke, shoved the rest into my hip pocket and stood there panting while the impossible Harlem afternoon—jangly, loose, simmering, cool—swirled around me, the tang of broiling shish kebab and heavy sweet Ethiopian incense wafting down from somebody's folding table just up the block.

We plugged back in and played a few more—"Stagga Lee," "Shake, Rattle and Roll," "Sweet Home Chicago"—and then I glanced at my watch, dropped to the sidewalk and began stuffing harps and cables into my daypack like a robber in mid-heist. Satan clanked to a stop and asked where I was off to. His face was drenched; he looked happy and transfigured, eyes pouring into mine. I told him about tutoring.

"I hate work!" he roared. "Ain't no job never gave me nothing worthwhile I couldn't get for myself some other way."

"You gonna be out here tomorrow?"

"Just as sure as you are handsome."

"Hey," I said, slinging my daypack over my shoulder, "I have to tell you about the street music scene over in Europe next time I come down. We would *destroy* them in Paris."

He smiled and stroked his beard. "We'll get us a little taste and you'll tell me all about it."

I stuck out my hand as I grabbed my Mouse. "Mister Satan, it's been a pleasure."

"Likewise, Mister Adam."

I let go, eased through the crowd, threw my Mouse in the car, and took off. I dipped my head for a last look as I pulled away. He was leaning back in his hi-chair with his guitar across his lap, smoking a cigarette and looking very, very relaxed.

# CHAPTER THREE

# YOUNG MAN
# WITH A HORN

*I didn't know where I was going; I guess I just had the feeling that a man who plays horn ought to go where people really understand about horns.*

—MEZZ MEZZROW

I WAS SO FOCUSED on getting to the New York Telephone office the next afternoon that I almost sped right by him. He was working a new spot—across the street from the Apollo Theater, in front of a shopping mall called the Mart 125. He had company: a bony old guy slapping at a washtub bass, yelling fiercely.

I flew around the block and parked on 126th Street, behind the State Office Building. Copeland's Soul-Food Kitchen, the Seville Lounge. I bounced around the corner—harp lines zinging through my head, tugging me—and past several women with dreadlocks sitting at a folding table heaped with bean and sweet potato pies and books. *The Blackman's Guide to the Blackwoman, The Autobiography of Malcolm X, Muhammed Speaks!* The Apollo marquee loomed like a candy cane dream. Amateur hour every Wednesday.

"All right now!" somebody shouted as I came up.

"Heeeeey, Adams!" Duke called out, waving me over. He was wearing a powder blue polyester suit and old sneakers, standing with a heavy quiet white woman who turned out to be his wife. He shook my hand and held it for a few seconds, leaning on his cane. His wife was a social worker at an office down the block. Satan's fingers crabwalked across the fretboard; his music crashed and swirled, buoying us up. Another hazy, lazy October afternoon. The washtub bass player yelled "Hey! Hey! Hey!"—one Hey! per beat—as he yanked on his broomstick, plucked the tautly bowed clothesline.

Somebody leaned toward Satan and yelled, pointing at me. His eyes opened. I felt strangely shy as he caught sight of me and smiled. He was wearing a blue knit watchcap over his cornrows.

"Get on up here, young man!" he rasped through his microphone.

The washtub bass player was named Professor SixMillion. His reddish brown skin was stretched tight across his skull and jaw. He smiled a taut, hard smile and nodded as I unpacked. "You better blow that harmonica, now! We might have to kill you if you don't. Ain't that right, Satan?"

I stared at the guy. He stared at me, smile fading.

"Shut up," Satan huffed playfully.

Professor cocked his finger at me, smile spreading again. "Gotcha," he said. "Aaaaaaaugh." He grabbed for me across Satan's hi-hat cymbal and hugged me to him, roughly. "I love you, baby," he said. "We gonna do that. We gonna fuck with you."

"Professor!" Satan barked. "I do not like your profanilizing."

". . . dick with you. Shut up, Satan. Shut up, shut up, shut up! We gonna dick with you." He gave a high jittery laugh.

Once again a crowd flowed to a stop, surrounding us. I did what I always did: try to make my harmonica sound as though an older black man—Nat, Little Walter, James Cotton—were playing it. My throat ached. I worked my flatted thirds hard, yanking them into the bittersweet spot between major and minor. Every note out here had to cut deep.

"What's your name again?" Satan asked when the song was over, wiping the sweat off his face as tips clanked and fluttered into the bucket.

"Adam," I said.

He laughed. "The reason I asked is because this other young man what was blowing the saxophone before you showed up is named Adam too."

I swiveled on my upended Mouse and saw a bearded white guy with small round John Lennon glasses holding a sax, waiting patiently behind me.

"You're Adam?" I said.

"I guess we're having a jam," he said.

Satan chuckled. "Too many Adams to keep track of."

Professor SixMillion blew me a kiss. "You bad, baby. We'll be talking."

Two or three songs later a guy in a suit came out of the mall doorway next to Professor and summoned Satan and me to follow. I got the other Adam to watch my stuff and followed, floating through aisles heaped with dishwashing liquid and discount sandals. The guy glanced over his shoulder as we reached his manager's office.

"You blow hell out of that harp. Stevie Wonder in some *serious* trouble, you know what I'm saying?"

He leaned back at his desk, loosened his tie. Satan was his main man—Monday Wednesday Friday, everybody around here knew Satan—but what I was doing sounded real nice along with his thing. Did I have some kind of a group I played with?

We exchanged cards. Satan came in. He was wearing maroon corduroy pants held up by a tight belt. We slapped; his eyes were liquid with heightened readiness.

"Here he come," the guy said. "Sit on down, Satan. Ease your feet."

He outlined grand but obscure plans. Everybody loves a salt-and-pepper act. Y'all sound too good. The Apollo is waiting. "Well," he finally said, rustling a few papers. "Satan and I have some business to discuss. I'll be calling you soon."

We shook hands and I jogged back out past the bins of discount blouses, neon plastic toys in bubble wrap, off-brand flip-flops. A woman in her mid-thirties with a flared nose and beautiful almond-shaped eyes that reminded me in a stabbing way of Helen's stopped me, hand on my arm, as I was coming through the door. "Baby," she said, "you can *play*." Her smile was luscious, enfolding a delicious secret.

THE OTHER ADAM was part of a Great Peace March—had joined the coast-to-coast trek in Pittsburgh—and invited us back to the group's encampment on Randall's Island. A sort of sixties be-in. We packed up and pushed Satan's shopping cart around the corner and down Seventh Avenue toward his apartment building. "That whole damn march came by the other day, right after you left!" he roared happily, elbowing me.

"Aaaah, I hadda work."

"Thousands of money-throwing bastards. I was mentally putting my foot on your behind. We could have cleaned *up*, Mister."

I asked Professor SixMillion how long he'd been playing the washtub bass. He glared. "Ain't no *washtub* about it," he spat hoarsely. "This a damn bass, a Harlem bass. Don't fuck with me, Adams." His taut smile curled upward. "Shit."

A moment later, as we rounded the corner onto 122nd Street, I ventured something to Satan about how we'd kicked some ass the day before. Professor smiled for real. "You talk like us. That's what we always say about kicking ass."

"Kicking ass and stomping dick," Satan added, puffing on a cigarette.

"Now you got it. Kicking ass and stomping dick. That's what we always say."

"Stomping dick," I said. "I've never heard that."

Satan yanked his shopping cart to a stop in front of a beat-to-shit Ford van, dirty white. "Stomping dick is a new addition. Kicking ass been around so damn many years we got tired of it like it was."

"Kick some goddamn ass," Professor chuckled fiercely, grinning at me. "You all right." A euphoria suddenly seized him. He waved his hand at the gutted buildings across the street, the broken glass glinting on the sidewalk, the four little kids and a dog splashing around an open fire hydrant, the fat guy in a smock selling freshly boiled crabs off a little handtruck. "You in Harlem now!" he shouted. "You in *Harlem* now! Anybody lay a finger on you, we'll kill 'em. They know that."

PROFESSOR AND I drove over in my car, tailing Satan and the others. I flipped on the radio as we cruised across 125th Street toward the Triborough Bridge. A sax was blowing—Willis Jackson or Arnett Cobb, a big tenor—and Professor scatted along. Wabba dabba do bop!

"Things's lightened up a whole lot since the last six or seven years," he rasped as we paused at a red light. "Six or seven years ago they'd kill me if they saw me in this car with you."

He turned from the shoulders like a man with a stiff neck and rolled his eyes at me. "I killed three men. Three. Satan killed two."

This time I waited for his smile to break through. It didn't.

"Can't let nobody mess with your shit." He rubbed his eyes hard with the heels of his hands. "Somebody fuck with your shit, ain't but one thing you can do."

I WAS STANDING in a gravel-strewn parking lot on Randalls Island next to Satan's white Ford van, drinking beers with Marshall. Marshall had cinnamon skin, a barrel chest, a snapping turtle's jaw, broken teeth, a jagged smile. One of Satan's assorted hangers-on. Satan and Professor were hiking the last load of Mouses up to the yellow nylon tent where the Great Peace Marchers had decided we were to play. I'd just asked about Satan's real name.

"Sterling Magee. Only he won't answer if you call him that."

"How long has he been playing the streets?" I asked.

"Satan? Hell if I know. We gave him that name. Clubs, streets, he don't care. He played on that—what's that called? 'Yakety-Yak, Don't Talk Back.' "

"The Coasters?"

"That's him. Only he likes the streets. Hundred, two hundred a *day.* Can't nobody tell him shit." He laughed. "His daddy was a preacher down in Mississippi."

THE AIR WAS COOL and meadow-fresh around the tents; people were frolicking on the big grassy lawn. An earnest young proctor politely asked Marshall and me to stop drinking and throw our beer cans in the recyclable trash. Satan, sitting on a picnic table, was surrounded by a fascinated group of white kids in tie-dyed shirts. His eyes were fiery.

"I am Satan," he declaimed. "God's people told you a lie. I am the most mannerable person you will ever meet. And guess what? Every single war that ever was—all the killing, all the disrespecting, all the mother effing this and that—every *bit* of that damned mess has been fought in the name of God. Ain't no wars been fought in the name of Satan."

Professor laughed harshly from the stage area. "Dammit Satan, let's play. Shut up." He kicked his washtub into place with a muffled clank.

Several kids tittered.

"Listen to me well," Satan hissed, ignoring him. "Let the words that come out your mouth be as beautiful as the smiles on your faces and you *damn* sure gonna live to be old and good-looking."

We set up under the tent—Professor in the middle, Satan and I on either side—and grooved into the ripening October dusk as dancers swayed, spun, leaped. "I create the music," Satan cried. "On a Hundred Twenty-fifth Street." Professor slapped and thumped a melodyless melody. I felt myself descending, pulled below the surface into a warm swirling flux of focused multidimensional attentions, calls provoking responses provoking hoohahs yelps and chuckles. Hey! yelled Professor. Hey! Hey! Hey! Time suddenly fell away and we were floating in space, working hard and smoothly for nobody but ourselves. Why hurry? A song was a neighborhood to be lingered in, tasted, known. The tangerine evening blew through me. Take your time, young man. Take your time.

IN THOSE DAYS I GAVE a lot of harmonica lessons, almost all of them to lonely white guys with time to spare and an aching desire to make a certain kind of sound on the instrument. Everybody I knew referred to this as the Sound. Nat had the Sound; he'd done his best to pass it along to me. The Sound was Southern-born, it was cocky, playful, manic, chuckling, resentful, edgy, comforting, relentless. It took incredible lip strength and finesse to produce. It was sexual. It was the haunted, restless feeling of a guy's apartment late at night after the woman who used to live there had moved out. It was whatever nasty things she was doing with the other guy—a virile sensitive soulmate—this very minute. It was the best way of beating those visions back into the ghoulish cave they had crawled out of. Working hard at the Sound was a socially acceptable way of sobbing, raging, and primal-screaming from a hot heart while pretending merely to be practicing.

When the weather was warm I used to give lessons outdoors down in the Village. Helen had left two years earlier and I still couldn't stand to spend much time indoors. I'd tell people to bring a tape recorder and meet me at the half-sized Arc de Triomphe in Washington Square Park. We'd wander past the Jamaican drug dealers, looking for a secluded bench. One of my occasional students was a balding guy with bad teeth from Brooklyn named Maury Weisberg. He was fifty-five or sixty, worked at Brooklyn Borough Hall. I don't know how he got my name. They find their way to you, Nat used to say.

On this day, for our first lesson, Maury showed up wearing blue polyester slacks and a dark blue raincoat. We found a bench off by ourselves. He punched RECORD on his Radio Shack cassette recorder and I started showing him stuff. I ran through a bunch of different rhythmic patterns in E. His eyes glittered. I messed with his head, the way Nat used to mess with mine. He had beautiful tone—like a choked sobbing child—but kept his hands cupped tightly around the harp so none of it got out. His hands trembled with effort.

"Open your hands!" I groaned. "Let it out."

"I've been working a lot on my tone. It's lines—I can't think of new stuff to play."

We went at it for a while, working through scales and patterns. His retention was almost nil. Indian summer rustled the few remaining leaves in the trees overhead. We looked at each other when enough was enough. He glanced at his watch, scratched behind his ear. "That's about an hour."

As he was pulling on his raincoat he said something about the last time he played the streets and getting stoned in order to do it.

"All right, Maury!" I said. "Where do you play?"

He hesitated. "I don't want anybody stealing my spots."

"Nah, man."

"Upper East Side. Eighty-sixth and Third."

"I'm amazed the cops leave you alone up there."

He shrugged, flashed his razor-tooth. "I play with this guitarist friend. We're up at Yale this weekend. You know Beinecke Street?"

"Yale!" I hooted.

"I get stoned, it's not so bad."

"I always play best on one cup of coffee and a couple of beers," I said. "Or a lot of beers."

"You look like a clean kid. Stay away from the strong stuff."

"Nah, I just drink my—"

"I did all that stuff. It'll mess you up."

He gazed at his hands. A car raced by on Bleecker Street. "Nineteen years I was on tranquilizers. Tomorrow it's three weeks I'm off. Not to mention whatever else including junk."

"Shit."

"Look at these." He unbuttoned his cuff, rolled up his sleeve. I could see a couple of whitish indentations, like tiny burn scars. He rotated his arm slowly in the glow from the streetlight overhead, smiling. "I started back in '46."

"After the war."

He unrolled and rebuttoned. "Second Armored Division—the first guys into that Buchenwald camp. Anyway, I just get stoned now. Even that not too often."

"I'm cool with a couple of Heinekens."

"I can't even do that. I can't do cocaine even, none of that crap."

"Coke did nothing for me the one time I tried it."

He made a raw face. "Those kids," he croaked furiously. "They think they're so smart. They don't know a damned thing. They look at me, they don't know."

We stared at each other.

He pulled on his raincoat, shoved his cassette recorder under his arm. "Here's fifteen dollars," he said. "Fifteen, right?"

"You've got great tone, Maury."

He smiled shyly. "It's a good deal," he said, easing away. "I'll call you."

THE THIRD OR FOURTH TIME I played with Satan on 125th Street, a trim-hipped guy in a trucker's cap with thin lips and a scraggly black beard stopped to talk. He clicked his heels and bowed, saluting. Satan introduced him as Mister Marvin. Except for the brown skin he could have been a cracker moonshiner from the hills of Kentucky. Hard-bitten, taciturn, not without antic wit. He looked vaguely familiar, then uncannily familiar.

"Mister Marvin and Mister Pancho Morales used to play with me when I had myself a little street group," Satan said. "Then I went down to St. Petersburg, Florida, and fired myself from the band when I got back."

"You enjoying yourself?" Mister Marvin asked, arm cradling my shoulders.

"Hell yeah."

"There you go. The master treating you okay?"

"He's damn sure enjoying the money!" Satan laughed as all three of us slapped.

"Good, good. Speaking of which—" He whispered in my ear about You blow harp like a motherfucker and by the way could I hold a dollar until next week?

This had already happened a couple of times, but not with guys I'd been introduced to.

"Aw, go ahead and *work*, Mister Marvin!" Satan rasped happily, bending to scoop some change out of the bucket and deposit it in Mister Marvin's waiting hand.

"I know you," I said, giving him two dollars.

"That's what my ex-wife told the judge last week."

"You were playing guitar with Mister Satan the first time I saw him, two or three years ago."

"Guilty as charged, Your Honor."

"This bastard can *play* some guitar, too," Satan said. "Don't be telling no stories."

He bowed. "All praise due the master."

"Thank you sir."

MY TUTORING JOB at Hostos Community College was beginning to wear on me, now that I knew Satan was expecting me down in Harlem. Who wouldn't rather be playing outdoors than working indoors, especially if the money was comparable? Tutoring paid seven dollars an hour; the tip bucket almost always did better than that. We were, of course, heading toward the winter months. I kept the job, adjusted my schedule to leave afternoons free. Bided my time.

One sunny Friday in mid-November, after I'd finished explaining the niceties of the past participle to Arelis Santana—whose café au lait complexion and gentle fluttery confusions destroyed me—I jumped in my car and blew back across the 145th Street Bridge and down through Harlem to 125th. Satan was kicking and stomping as I came up, a clattering inferno dwarfed by the five-story smoked glass facade of the telephone office. I double-parked on the uptown side, ran across, caught his attention, told him I'd be back in an hour, jumped in my car, drove over to Columbia, parked, hopped a subway down to 50th Street, walked over to Manny's Music, bought a C harp and an E-flat harp, subwayed back uptown, jumped in my car, drove back across 125th Street and circled onto 126th, packed my stuff around the block to where Satan was still roaring away— coulda been the same song—and unpacked, plugged in, sat down on my upended Mouse and started blowing. I hadn't yet played standing up, leery of towering over him.

"You know what I like about you?" he said later, as we were packing up, our pockets bulging. "It may surprise you."

"I can't guess."

"I like the way you tap your feet when you're playing. Don't ever lose that. The most pitiful thing a musician can do is oppress the enjoyment of his own music."

I was in the kind of crazy, jumping mood that had ravished me all summer over in Europe. It was Friday evening; I wanted to conquer new territory. Why not drive over and play that Chemical Bank where I'd first seen him?

He was surprisingly game, even eager. We loaded his four Mouses and my one onto his Waldbaum's shopping cart along with the hi-hat cymbal and folding hi-chair and pushed the cart around onto Seventh Avenue, past Black Hair Now. We were talking about women. I'd mentioned Helen.

"All my wives have died on me," he barked cheerfully, lighting up a cigarette. "My last one died back in February."

"I'm sorry."

"Sorry, hell. Ain't no wife good for more than worration and botheration and effin up. Every time you turn your back she's making eyes at some other no-good bastard."

I shook my head. "Tell me about it."

"Hello Miss Lady," he suddenly called out, bowing slightly and smiling as we passed a young woman in stonewashed jeans with Circean plaits bound up in a bun. She ignored him, her ass twitching dismissively as she strolled away.

He made a face. "More musicians been brought low chasing after women and their smelly little behinds than ever got messed up by drugs, crack, liquor, and all that mess put together, Mister." His dangling cigarette bounced between his lips. "I remember one time I was on the gig with Curtis—King Curtis, this is, man could blow a beautiful saxophone but however. Give him two drinks and the bastard acted the fool with women. Come on over to whatever table I'm sitting at, maybe I'm rapping with a pretty young lady or whatever, and here come Curtis, tongue hanging down to the ground, talking some mess about why don't *my* young lady come on back to the hotel we're all staying at and let a real horn man make her happy.

Wiggling his tongue and all that ugliness. No no. I ain't never had no crude ways like that with women."

He yanked his shopping cart around the corner onto 122nd Street, past the crab man. We rolled to a stop in front of his apartment building. For the first time I noticed the words "Shakespeare Flats" engraved in reddish brown marble over the doorway.

"Bastard got himself killed, too. Stabbed on the stoop of his own apartment building, telling some junkie in a disrespectful way to get a move on."

We worked side by side, loading the Mouses and hi-hat cymbal and chair and his several other bags of stuff into the back of my Honda. I flipped down the split rear seats. He was particular about the order in which we loaded: amps and bags first, then cymbal, then collapsible chair. He rearranged vigorously when the hatchback wouldn't close. He offered me a cigarette on the short crosstown drive—122nd Street and Seventh Avenue to 113th Street and Broadway—but I didn't yet smoke. He lit up and rolled down the window. I asked him about playing with the Coasters.

"They told you a story," he said, whipping the match out. "Ain't no way in the world. Fellow what played for the Coasters *looked* like me, but it wasn't me on guitar no kind of way."

"A woman last week told me you played for James Brown."

"I backed him up one time at the Apollo with my little group I had back in the seventies."

"You must have worked with a lot of people over the years."

"I hate interviews!" he yelled out the window, with comic book exaggeration.

"Sorry," I said, "I'm not trying to—"

Then he ticked them off. "King Curtis, Marvin Gaye—all them dead bastards played with me. Etta James, Little Anthony and the Imperials, Jordy and the Starlighters, Noble 'Thin Man' Watts. Not one of 'em worth a so-and-so."

As we cruised the Columbia neighborhood looking for parking, I mentioned I'd been in school there a couple of years earlier. He suddenly grew animated. He looped the homemade mandala from around his neck—a glittering assemblage of shellacked jigsawed shapes crusted with sequins and beads—and tapped it with his cocked finger.

"I got me more mathematics in my squared circle than a thousand mathematicians with a thousand monkeys banging away on ten thousand typewriters, Mister. I joke not. Check it out. How much is two and one?"

"Three."

"Wrong. Twenty-one is three sevens. The seven stars of Revelation, seven days in a week, and my throne is out there on Seventh Avenue. Likewise three sixes—they might of taught you in college that one and eight make nine, but they lied. Eighteen is three sixes, which is a *very* good number for me, namely 666. God's people got it bass-ackwards, talking all that mess about the Devil's corruption. Ain't no D-e-v-i-l in S-a-t-a-n. Right or wrong?"

I had to smile as we slapped hands. "Right."

He chuckled. "Seven and six is thirteen, three sixes makes eighteen, and get this: Revelation 13:18: 'Here is wisdom.' Mathematical understanding is but the gateway to wisdom. The Bible is my book—God's people may *believe* otherwise, but their belief ain't worth a damn. You ain't never took a belief test, did you?"

"No."

"Couldn't do it. God's people got a racket going, but it ain't my thing. I speak for myself and spread respect wherever I go. Somebody in Harlem say 'Good morning, Mister Satan,' I'm gonna bow to whoever is helloing me and say 'Thank you for that beautiful smile, Sir or Miss.' Two thousand years God's people been hullaballooing about Jesus told me this and that. Damn Jesus! Ain't been one damn time in two thousand years Jesus thanked anybody for anything. Same thing with God. You ever heard God say Thank you Mister Adam for blowing that pretty solo? Hell no. Big old ugly bastard won't show his no-good face. Throwing tornadoes and hurricanes down on people, flattening churches in Arkansas, killing people right and left. And all for what?"

He was staring hard at me—furious, mirthful—while I maneuvered into a parking spot.

"What?" I said.

"Trophy yards. God's people call them graveyards but they lied."

WE WERE ON my old stomping grounds now. These were streets I'd walked many a night after Helen had moved out, wailing into my cupped hands, honing my sound. A harmonica is the only musical instrument you can play while strolling up Broadway and be considered at least marginally sane. A trombone will get you committed. Marginal is a good word for what I was. My road novel—a self-reformulating project, like a series of shed skins—had until recently featured a young protagonist named Wild Bill Rasputin, a half-Russian cowboy who was trying to save the world from nuclear war through a series of strategic interventions involving spirited blues harmonica playing and womanizing. I'd started that draft in the summer of '84, when Reagan was president, the Evil Empire was our nemesis, and Armageddon was being floated as a workable concept. Next to Ronald Reagan, Mister Satan struck me as the voice of common sense.

We set up in front of the Chemical Bank, as we'd been setting up in Harlem, with our backs to the wall and me on his right. He'd taught me the trick of facing my Mouse rearward so the sound expanded and diffused without on-axis harshness.

It was a cool, beautiful evening. Five Mouses and one hi-hat cymbal make a lot of racket. Busking with amplification is illegal in New York City without a permit. Several police cruisers slowed, then moved on. The beauty of working the streets is the flicker of surprise that passes across the faces of people who suddenly lift their heads and catch sight of you, the two of you. What are you doing here? I am singing "Sweet Home Chicago" and Mister Satan is hurling lightning bolts; on this song he is backing me up, shadowing me so subtly that our two voices have become one. We are entrancing you, disturbing you, rephrasing an old question. You are looking at us and thinking: Huck and Jim. This is not how we see ourselves. We don't see ourselves. We *play* ourselves. Close your eyes. Stand in my sneakers. His sound is filling your ears, pressing against your left side and washing over you—a sharp blue flame, thousands of little cat's claws tugging at your feet, hips, shoulders, head, a swinging turquoise flux strewn with sweet gravel. You can live here. Genius builds the house and flings open the doors. The design is Mister Satan's but your help is essential. There's a hammer in your hand, nails clasped between your lips. Swing cleanly and well and you're in on one stroke. He's holding the board and his hands are very, very strong.

We made thirty each in an hour and a half, plus piles of loose change. It was the first time I'd stood up while playing with him. A tall dark-haired girl I'd gone to the Day School with ten years earlier had wandered by, watched for a while, come up and kissed me, given me her phone number. She'd had a rough time senior year after watching her best friend get torn in half by a drunk driver. She was a pothead back then, reigning bitch-goddess in the class ahead of me, and thought I was an immature little twerp. She couldn't get over my singing. This wasn't something she associated with me. "Call me," she said, pressing the slip of paper into my hand.

"What days you working?" Satan asked as we cruised back home to Harlem.

"It varies."

"Vary on, Jones," he laughed. "I got your phone number memorized."

His was 749-9297. SIX WAYS, he cheerfully pointed out. The phone company knew what he was about.

When I got home, there was a message on my answering machine from Nat. I hadn't heard from him in more than a year, since he'd dropped out of sight after getting shot. He was lonely down in Virginia and wondered how the hell I was.

# CHAPTER FOUR

# NO BAD FELLA

*Seems like everybody . . . in this world is down on me*
*You know I ain't no bad fella . . . I don't intend to be*

—BROWNIE McGHEE

NAT WAS LIVING IN HAMPTON, it turned out, with an older woman named Esther. He was ecstatic when I returned his call, as though my voice were a priceless gift. I was flattered and slightly unnerved. He was my master. He was summoning me. I grabbed my Panama hat and Mouse and harps, jumped in my car, and burned South for a long weekend.

The drive down to Virginia takes eight hours and always starts with the same endless flat stretch of Jersey Turnpike. I propped my boom box on the front seat and replayed the tape I'd made that first May afternoon, matching licks with him. My sound these days was closer to his than to Old Me, although a difference remained. Xeno's Paradox: an arrow travels half the distance from bow to target, then half the remaining distance, then half the remaining distance. When does it hit? You couldn't ever arrive at Nat's Sound. You could get usefully closer. My sound was darker and more Riddles-like than it had been. Slower, stronger vibrato; more kick. That's what you got for a year on the streets. Bill Taft, Gator, the summer in Europe. I was Satan's sideman now.

THE ADDRESS HE'D GIVEN ME was a two-story townhouse in the Foxhill Gardens complex. Virginia was still lukewarm in late November, air velvety with the smell of wild grapes and rotting leaves. Esther was an ivory-skinned woman in her late fifties with the South on her tongue—stocky, grandmotherly, kind. The house smelled heavily, deliciously, of cooking. Nat wasn't there, although he'd told her I was coming. I called the number she gave me. A gruff voice, not Nat's, answered over the clinks of glasses and bar chatter.

"Nat!" I yelled when he came on. "I'm at Esther's!"

"Adam!" He laughed violently, hysterically, turning away from the phone. "It's my buddy from New York!" he shouted. "I gotta get on home!"

I was out by my car with the hatchback raised when a dented blue wreck of a Toyota Corolla vroomed into the parking lot, heaved sideways, and screeched to a stop in the empty space next to me. He yelled, I yelled, he jumped out—door hanging open, no slam—and bearhugged me, almost taking my breath away. He'd grown a small mustache and looked trim and fit and smelled good.

"I am so happy to see you I can't *tell* you," he said. "Oh man. Ask Esther how I've been. I am just so *awesomely* happy I can't tell you."

"Well it's nice to know you're not dead."

"They ain't got me yet, which don't mean they ain't tryin'."

"Nat, man." I shook my head and couldn't stop smiling.

"So how the hell are you?" he said, hand rubbing my back.

"Look what I brought."

"A Mouse!" he shouted as I lifted mine out. It was plastered with stickers from Nice, Antibes, Amsterdam. "You brought a Mouse!" He hugged it to his chest, voice filled with wonder, eyes brimming.

WE SAT AT ESTHER'S KITCHEN TABLE and drank Colt .45 and ate the dinner Esther had quietly prepared, and talked. Dinner was salty Virginia ham, greens in pot liquor, honeyed yams, yellow squash. Esther said very little the whole night, gazing tenderly at Nat from time to time across the room.

He was working on a garbage truck now, getting his strength back. He outlined the various tasks he performed in sequence—riding shotgun, jumping to the ground, two-handed heaves, cycling the compactor, leaping back on board. He made it sound like noble work, a Zen discipline of enacted mindfulness. He'd gotten the job after he'd moved down here back in February. His father and stepmother lived across town. He'd lived with them for the first couple of months before moving out.

"She treats me like a stepchild," he said furiously. "I came down here, I got a job, I was sick as a *dog* but I went out and found myself a job—there was one point after I got shot, right after I got out of Bellevue, when I would crawl out of bed and try to put together enough bottles to trade in for subway fare down to the city, and I was *grateful* just to have that much. I mean actually *grateful*. And then I came down here and got a job, and I gave my father the first hundred dollars of every paycheck I got. Pow! In his hand every second Friday. Her two sons weren't working, they just sat around watching TV—twenty-eight and thirty, lives going nowhere—and *I* was working, I was breaking my back, and she treats *me* like a stepchild? Why? My own mother's dead, I got nobody I can call my own except my father, and my stepmother's gonna turn him against me? My own flesh and blood? I don't *need* that, man."

After dinner we pulled out our harps, I set my boom box on the kitchen table, and we got down to business. Esther sat quietly in the living room, sewing. I showed Nat a couple of the Sonny Terry tunes I'd worked up over in Paris, punctuated with hoots and whoops. This time he followed my lead; his harps had flat notes and sour octaves but all you finally heard was the voice behind the instrument—hollering across an open field, taunting and rope-a-doping, wheezing, sighing. My own sound wasn't as consistent or identifiable, although it was getting eerily close to his at certain moments. He had to smile when I played the El Cafe Street theme song, most of which I'd figured out from a recording I'd made down on Astor Place.

"Yeah," I admitted, sheepish but proud, "there's a little bit of family resemblance."

"Son," he laughed, "ya got my eyes. You can't *play* like you used to play."

"I can't even remember how I used to play." I sipped my beer. "I mean the first song I ever learned was 'Whammer Jammer,' Magic Dick was like—"

"Dick Salwitz is a *bad,* bad dude on harmonica."

"I mean he was It for me back in high school."

"Magic Dick was the guy *I* heard when I was twenty-three or twenty-four back at Pratt who first made me say, 'Whoa, what is *that?*' "

"I thought you were more of a Big Walter kind of guy."

He flashed his corroded wire retainer. "I'm a *All*-Those-Guys kinda guy."

1975. I WASN'T JUST a Bordash Brothers reject and bathroom-cleaning hoagieman. The Princeton English Department had put me in Lit 151—Remedial Writing for Jocks, Foreigners, and Retards—the second day of freshman week. My instructor, Mr. Heilbut, gave us idiotic worksheets I could have done in junior high. I told him as much. He gave me D's on the first four essays I handed in. The hockey recruits and Chem-E nerds were making B-pluses. I was the loneliest, ugliest, dumbest bluesman in the Class of '79.

All I had was my music, pitiful as it was. Saturday nights, while other freshmen at the Princeton Inn—my residential college—were mingling to disco bands in the darkened dining room, I'd hide out upstairs, blowing and jumping around, working up my nerve. My favorite inspirational text was Muddy Waters's *Woodstock Album* with Paul Butterfield on harp. Faster than James Cotton, more fluid than Magic Dick, Butter would hammer out endless triplets, buzzing around Muddy like a chuckling angry wasp. "I'm gonna take you downtown, put *cloooothes* on your back. . . ." Muddy would bellow, and Paul would diddly-diddly-diddly-*waaaaaah*. I'd dance around and between them until my lips ached, trying to soak up Muddy's swagger, Paul's wasp-chuckle.

The might-get-laid feeling I'd had around eight-thirty always turned to despair around one, after the fifth plastic cup of vodka-

and-Kool Aid punch downstairs. How could I *possibly* ask a cute girl to dance? Muddy's swagger had ebbed. I'd ache, brood, squeeze through the dancers to watch the bands up close, lose myself in the grooves. At least I had my woodshed to crawl back to.

The woodshed concept I'd just learned about in a course called Intro to Jazz. Charlie Parker had gotten his butt kicked at a jam session in Kansas City, crawled home, and locked himself in a small shed out behind the family house. Kicked aside the split logs and axe handles, blew sax for days, worked shit *out*. Made all his mistakes in private, with nobody around to say You suck! Next time he went to a jam session: *Boom!* Bird Lives. Clapton had done the same thing. Quit the Yardbirds, locked himself in his room at art school for six months. When he came out, *Boom!* The Bluesbreakers, Cream. Clapton is God.

The only problem with my current woodshed was the Roommate Question. Lou was away most weekends—fencing tournaments—but around during the week, doing homework. Then I made a discovery.

The stereo room was down in the basement, below everybody—right under the kitchen—and available. You could get a key. It was lined with orange shag carpet, had a good turntable and powerful speakers, and smelled like stale bong water. Yellow Naugahyde beanbag chairs cluttered the floor. Rows of sunken lights controlled by dimmers lit the place up like Times Square. Nobody used it except for an occasional pot party. The door was thick and could be bolted from inside.

I kicked the beanbags aside and took over. I'd bought a new amp at Sam Ash in New York—an Earth Revival, with tubes that glowed blue—and I'd haul it down there every night after dinner, a stack of records under my arm. There were no quiet rules, no distractions. No shrieking Mom or Bordash Assholes. Just me and B.B. King with Bobby "Blue" Bland, live at the Coconut Grove:

> Every day . . . every day I have the blues
> Every day . . . every day I have the blues
> When you see me worryin' . . . you know it's you I hate to lose.

I'd turn everything waaaaaaay up and go for hours. You could almost pretend the roaring crowds were real, and wanted you.

NAT AND I SPENT SATURDAY AFTERNOON tooling around Norfolk in his Corolla—windows down, passing beers back and forth, talking trash. We were loud. I couldn't tell whether we were getting looks from other drivers because of that or because this was the South. Down here, he said, he was the fast-talking guy from New York.

We lusted out loud after the women we passed, black and white and several shades of freckled brown I hadn't seen outside Virginia. This seemed deliciously liberating. I told him my sex life was lousy now but I'd had a wonderful affair with an American girl in Paris. Somehow the conversation turned toward the question of how long you could go, given the chance. I said I'd managed forty-five minutes with Jessie.

"Forty-five minutes?" he laughed. "Man, I went for fourteen *hours*. That's my record. Nine hours was the next closest."

I stared at him, he stared at me.

"Ask my girlfriend, Kathy, she'll tell you. My ex-girlfriend."

"The parole officer."

"The parole officer. That's the one thing we *always* had. All our friends knew about that."

It was a lambent fall day, warm in the sun and cool in the shade. We'd brought my Mouse and Panama hat along, in case a busking opportunity presented itself. The Hampton Mall seemed like a good bet. Neither of us wanted to blow solo and no guitar men were waiting outside Sears, so the plan collapsed. We bounced through the galleria like a couple of goofs—Mouse cradled under my arm, Nat instructing me in the finer points of Panama deportment. Mine was a real Stetson, cream white.

"I don't believe this," he said as he rotated it in his hands, tickled.

"It's been halfway around the world."

He folded down the brim, settled it on his head. He was wearing a black polo shirt, cranberry slacks, snakeskin belt, Gucci loafers, sweet Egyptian Musk. Back at Esther's he'd dabbed me with a sample from a small glass vial. He tilted the brim to the precise angle where his shaded eyes suddenly got cool, dark, vaguely menacing. His voice thickened.

"Mah man. Whatcha need?"

"No!" I laughed.

He tilted the brim way back, stuck his thumbs into his shirt like he was grabbing suspenders, splayed the tips of his loafers outward.

"I jes got inna town fum the country," he drawled. "Damn ef I ain't got me a taste for some fried chicken. Ah'm on steal me one ef I gotta, sho-nuff."

We slapped hands and howled. People really were staring now.

"You gotta watch out for these," he said, flipping the hat off and handing it to me. "They will mess with you."

His car was a wreck inside—torn vinyl, glove compartment wouldn't close—but he knew how to flog the gearbox for maximum torque. Cruising back from Norfolk along the ocean highway, he told me about Tae Kwon Do.

"I don't get scared," he said. "I *never* get scared. When I get excited, it just makes my sight get clearer—focused and clear."

I handed him another Heineken from the cooler in the back seat and we clinked. I pulled out my harp and wailed like a novice, warbling crazily. "One of these days," I said, "I'm gonna learn how to play this thing."

"I love it," he said. "What more do I want? I got the sunny day, I got the beer. . . ."

"Pussy," I suggested, guzzling.

"Don't get me started."

Later, back in Hampton, he pulled into a pizzeria parking lot and went inside to make a few calls. I sat in the car and practiced. He was gone for a long time. When he came out he looked stricken. He slipped into the driver's seat and slumped back, head lolling, eyes closed. I said nothing for a few seconds.

"What's up?" I said.

"I am so mad." His voice was a hoarse whisper. "I am trembling. I am *trembling*. Look at my hands." He held them out.

"Shit."

"I am so . . ." His jaw clenched. He was almost shrieking. "People talk about me, they tell lies about me."

I slipped my harmonica into my pocket and slouched in my seat. We sat quietly for a moment and then he pulled out of the parking lot, stopped off at Shorty's Liquors for three forty-ounce bottles of Colt .45, and drove us back to Foxhill Gardens.

WE SAT AT ESTHER'S KITCHEN TABLE until two o'clock Sunday morning, drinking. Esther had gone to sleep. Nat raged. He'd stripped his shirt off to show me where he'd been shot. There were several shiny black welts. The largest was just below his breastbone, about an inch long and a quarter-inch wide. He never made clear why the guy—a Puerto Rican—had shot him; I didn't push the point. Doreen was a prostitute and a junkie. He was worried about AIDS. Last he'd heard she was healthy.

The South was fucked up, filled with some two-faced Southern motherfuckers. The blacks were worse than the whites, although the rednecks got stupid when they drank. The blacks down here resented him, they distrusted him, they'd smile in his face and stab him in the back. He'd started a Monday night blues jam at a black club called the Metro. All the white blues players were coming down, it was a *scene*—the club was doing more business in one night than these backwoods Southern motherfuckers had managed to bring through the front door in ten years. Ask *anybody* in town, they'd tell you. Things were moving for him down here.

A month ago he'd been propositioned by Lanie, the wife of the guy who owned the place. Lanie was a sweetheart; the owner, Drake, was known to be the meanest guy in town. Drake knew about the proposition. He'd heard it through the grapevine. He'd killed men for less. This wasn't the problem. Nat hadn't gotten together with Drake's wife and wasn't going to, not once he found out. What kind of a suicidal motherfucker did they think he was? The problem was the awesomely beautiful nineteen-year-old he'd been dating for the last couple of weeks. We're talking about drop-deap *luscious,* built from the ground up. Eyesight to the blind. The fourteen-hour girl. That's who he'd been talking about with a buddy of his on the pizzeria phone: Denise. Denise was now telling folks down at the club that Nat had promised to marry her. Marry her! Which was a stone lie, regardless of whatever else he might have said.

The problem was—he didn't know this at first, he only found out last week: Denise was Drake's *daughter.*

Nat poured more malt liquor and raged. He couldn't sleep these days; it took two forty-ounce bottles to knock him out. Things were fucked up down here. People you thought you could trust would go and pull some devious, behind-the-back bullshit. His own father was being cold to him. Ask anybody what kind of a son he'd been. He was at his mother's *bedside* when she died of cancer, holding her hand. Twenty-three years old, looking out for his two sisters. Where the hell was his father?

It was getting late. I was drunk and a little overwhelmed. He was in the middle of a story about driving his cab up in New York.

"I pulled up in front of the Pierre," he said, "and this big tall white motherfucker in a suit got out *without paying*—some kind of businessman, I don't know who or what he was—and I said, 'Excuse me,' and he smiled in my face and said, 'You have a good night.' The bellhop took his bag. The motherfucker *hadn't paid me.* My blood went cold, man. I was out of the car, I slammed the door and came around front, I was *incredulous.* I couldn't even be angry. I came up to him—he was standing where you are, I was standing about two feet away—and I was calm outside and *trembling* inside. 'You forgot to pay me,' I said. 'I don't know what you're talking about,' he said. He started to go around me. 'Don't do this to me,' I said. 'Please don't do this to me.' I was almost laughing I was so mad. He said nothing. *Nothing.* The bellhop looked at me like I was trash."

His eyes glistened, burning into me. Suddenly he leapt up from Esther's kitchen table.

"I went *Pow!*" he screamed, making a wrenching, twisting turn in the middle of the floor. "I threw him down and then I went *Pow,* motherfucker, I said *Pow!*"

He paused, hands raised for a final blow, quivering. He was crying. Nat was crying.

"I had no *choice,*" he whispered. "You know me, Adam. The motherfucker left me *no choice.*"

# CHAPTER FIVE

# WHITE BOYS

*Fucking up white boys like that made us feel good inside.*

—NATHAN MCCALL, *MAKES ME WANNA HOLLER*

A FEW DAYS AFTER I got back from Virginia, New York suddenly turned sour. My Mouse and Panama hat were stolen, I got hassled on 125th Street. Then, just before Christmas '86, a gang of young Italian guys with baseball bats chased three black guys out of a pizzeria in a place called Howard Beach. One of the black guys ran across a highway and was whacked by a car, dead as a stray dog. The New York tabloids love nothing more than a nice juicy race-hatred story with bruised black bodies and fists raised in outrage. My Harlem honeymoon was over.

The equipment ripoff was my fault. I was working mornings at the Writing Center over at Hostos; trying to be discreet about my second career, I'd gotten into the habit of leaving my Mouse and hat in my car, parked just off the Grand Concourse. This was the infamous South Bronx, where cat-sized rats scurried across vacant lots. One noon I came back to find the rear window punched in, empty back seat glittering. Stupid! Raging inwardly, I tore the shit out of my harps on the drive home. Later I raided the cookie jar in which

I'd been husbanding my busking money, subwayed down to Manny's Music, and picked up a new Mouse—a pristine black trapezoidal cube, comfortingly heavy against my thigh as I swung back up chilly Broadway.

Mister Satan called the next morning, raring to kick and stomp. "You got my people asking after you, Mister," he laughed. "Fools be running me ragged with all *kind* of mess, talking about Hey Satan, where's that white boy at?"

I called my supervisor at Hostos, weaseled out of afternoon hours, drove down. He'd already worked up a small crowd, mostly men, several of whom leaned back against my car the moment I slid up next to the fire hydrant. Older cars were appropriated this way in Harlem, I'd noticed. Flashy new Benzes and Volvos driven by young guys with gold-capped teeth were not. Satan had undone his corn-rows and combed his gray-flecked hair out; he looked regal, leonine. My new Mouse delighted him: a material addition to our collective stock.

"Lift up on him," he rasped after clanking to a stop, leaning over to slide a strip of cardboard box between amp and sidewalk. "We *got* to keep this baby looking new."

"I coulda done without the upgrade."

"Feels like they snatched a rib clean out your chest, don't it?"

"You can see where they nailed me," I said, jerking my head at the garbage-bag-and-duct-tape rear window.

He lit up a cigarette and dug the three or four bills he'd made out of the tip bucket. "Ain't nobody broke into my step-van one damn time in Harlem, going on six years."

"You're lucky."

His smile vanished. "You said that. Hell, the best way you got to cover your back is show respect in front of your face and give away free liquor. Everybody out here know me. People see my van, ain't nobody gonna break in and mess with my altar. Half those bastards out on Seventh Avenue done got drunk in the back seat."

His preaching had drawn a couple of guys close; they roared as we slapped hands. One, in a dark blue security guard's uniform, I suddenly recognized: the stocky powerlifter with the scarred forehead who'd collared me that first afternoon with a story about a white boy he'd grown up with down in Mississippi. He looked sober now, if not quite legit.

"Hey Satan," he laughed, working his massive shoulders. "Hey Satan, listen, I gotta—"

"*Mister* Satan."

"Mister Satan. . . ." He hesitated, chastized, then leaned in conspiratorially, backhanding his mouth. "Aw shit, man, gimme a goddamn dollar."

"*Mister Murphy!*" Satan roared.

"Aaaaaaaaah!" Murphy howled, doubling over. His laugh seemed to have a life of its own, writhing and whoo-hooing as it swung him away from us. Satan tried to keep a straight face and couldn't.

"Get on back here you ugly bastard!"

He was back, mirthful but humble, clasping Satan's hand with both of his. "I'm sorry, I'm sorry, I can't help it, Sata—*Mister* Satan. Mister Satan. I'm sorry, you know I don't mean no—"

"Shut up," Satan huffed, chuckling, pulling a bill out of the side-of-the-knee pocket of his army surplus pants and crumpling it into Murphy's curled hand. Murphy's eyes sparkled.

"Thank you, Mister Satan. Thank you." He lumbered quickly away, disappearing into the crowds past the bus shelter.

I plugged in and we tuned up. Satan's guitar was an Ampeg Superstud—solid oak body, a couple of tuning keys missing—and he'd strung it with heavy jazz strings that made my fingertips ache the one time I'd strummed it. Unlike most blues harp players I was a pitch perfectionist, tweaking my reeds every night with a jeweler's file. Satan had the best ears I'd ever worked with, quickly aligning himself with the note I provided. It was a subtle, trusting, microtonal dance we did in the moment before our plunge, one of the few places where he allowed me to set the standard. Once he began thrashing, all bets were off. Mississippi tuning was an ever-present threat: six one-stringed diddly-bows masquerading as guitar strings, each cackling its own distinctive commentary on European Standard Pitch, all swirling together and swamping me like Big Muddy.

This afternoon we were in good shape until a wasted, hollow-eyed guy with ashy skin and laceless sneakers shuffled up, paused to eye the tip bucket, then snatched a couple of dollars and shambled away. Satan strangled the groove and leaped up, heaved the rusted steel mike stand out of the bucket and went after him. I sat on my Mouse, chilled. A couple of girls screamed. Sidewalk traffic stopped. Satan threw down the mike stand; the two men were grappling, Satan was roaring and shaking the thief without actually hitting him, the thief was cursing and crying, swinging his cane.

"The white boy!" he blubbered. "The white boy said I could take it!"

People who'd just come onto the scene glanced at me.

"I was *playing,*" I muttered.

Satan heaved the guy to his feet, shook him like a puppy, yanked the two dollars out of his hand. "You are *wrong,* Mister!" he shouted, voice high and taut. "Now you get on away from here and do *not* try that mess again!"

"White boy said I could!" the guy whimpered, staggering, pointing at me.

Satan retrieved his mike stand and stood in the middle of the sidewalk, hair dented from the tussle. "Listen up if you love your life!" he bellowed as the guy drifted away, lost in his own fog. "Jig with me again and I'll put my foot so far into your filthy black behind your nose will be pointing at next Thursday!"

Murphy and a couple of other hangers-on had rushed up, bristling and woofing, spoiling for the fight they'd just missed. Murphy backpedaled toward me, furious with concern.

"You okay, man? Ain't nobody laid a hand on you?"

"I don't know what that guy's problem was."

"That no-good coon-ass nigger lay a *hand* on you," he swore, "I'm on fuck him up *bad.* Can't nobody say I won't."

"I'm fine, I'm fine."

He flexed his massive shoulders, worked his jaw furiously. "Hey Larry," he called out to one of the others. "We gonna fuck him up?"

"The Master says no." Larry had cinnamon skin, tinted glasses, handsome full features.

"Hell no," Satan said, shoving the mike stand back in the tip bucket. "Miserable bastard gonna find enough worration wherever he goes."

" 'Cause I'm ready, I swear I am. Motherfucker *touch* Satan, we gonna fuck up his junkie ass till he can't crawl sideways."

I'D NEVER HEARD of Howard Beach until the racial lynching happened out there, five days before Christmas. "Racial lynching" were Mayor Koch's words. Three black men from Bed-Stuy, disoriented by the Queens highway system, had pulled into the parking lot of a random pizzeria and gone inside for a snack. Howard Beach was an Italian neighborhood. A group of white teenagers—early accounts claimed nine to twelve—confronted the blacks with baseball bats and sticks and the memorable words, "Niggers, you don't belong here." Then they chased them outside and beat them. One of the black men, a twenty-three-year-old named Michael Griffith, fled across Cross Bay Boulevard and was struck by a car and killed.

Three whites were arrested almost immediately: John Lester, seventeen; Jason Ladone, sixteen; Scott Kern, seventeen. I studied their pictures in the papers. I wasn't inclined to be objective. I'd had my share of run-ins with this sort of punk. Growing up twenty-five miles north of New York City, I'd spent much of my childhood and adolescence in public schools given their prevailing tone by what we used to call "the tough kids." Some of these kids were Italian, many had recently moved from the Outer Boroughs. They smoked in the boys' room and the back of the bus, slouched in class, had girlfriends, carved their initials into cinderblocks. Their fathers were often New York City cops or firefighters. They picked fights. Sometimes these were epic slap-fights between alpha males, strung out across several weeks, pursued from classroom to lunchroom to gym. Sometimes, for fun, they picked on smaller, weaker kids. White kids, since there were no black kids to abuse. I was a prime target, often hit. They'd make a fist with their middle knuckle protruding, hammer me in the shoulder-bone or thigh-muscle, give me dead arms and dead legs. Sneak up from behind and sucker-punch my notebooks out of my bent arm so my homework splattered across the hall and got trampled. Slap me around in front of the girls. I never went to the pizzeria in Congers, my own hometown. I was afraid to. That was where Danny Vivino and the other hoods hung out.

Black people were not my problem, growing up. So far as I could tell from the books I'd read, they'd suffered a particularly harsh version of my own fate: being beaten up by tough white guys who ruled the roost. Jews—as my German-hating Jewish grandmother was fond of reminding me—had suffered this fate. My boyhood reading leaned strongly toward the Holocaust and the Civil Rights era. I was transfixed by pictures of cowering Jews being herded into cattle cars by Nazis, black men and women knocked sprawling by water cannons as Bull Connor's deputies unleashed snarling German shepherds. Pictures like that had put the crying feeling in my throat. Black people weren't my problem, or hadn't been. My problem was with punks like John Lester, Jason Ladone, and Scott Kern. And, I suddenly realized, whoever in Harlem was inclined to lump me indiscriminately with guys like them. White boys, all of us. Ripe for payback.

SOMETIMES THE HONEYMOON has to end so the marriage can flower. January is not usually thought of as high busking season in New York. Mister Satan had bragged about previous winters he and Professor had brought along a broom to sweep space clear. This year the snows stayed away. It was cloudy and mild on 125th Street my first afternoon back after the dawn of 1987; Mister Satan and Professor had just packed up and were bickering loudly. I came around them and, for the first time, put my hand on Mister Satan's shoulder.

"You guys heading out?"

He smiled weakly. "Hey, Mister Gus."

"Merry Christmas," Professor sneered. "Happy New Year, goddammit." He kicked his washtub: *Blam!*

"You have your amplifier?" Mister Satan asked.

I nodded at my car. "I was thinking we ought to try over by Columbia."

The idea took a moment to sink in. He broke into a devilish grin. "Hell yes!"

"Fuck yes," Professor barked. "Shit yes, motherfuck—"

"*Professor!*" Mister Satan thundered, "I do *not* appreciate—"

"Shut up, shut up, shut *up!* Ain't no problem."

"Correct."

"We all goin'. Ain't nobody left out." He put on a huge tight grin and extended his hand toward me. "How you doing, baby?"

"Merry Christmas," I said.

"Satan don't believe in Christmas."

"Ain't no belief about it," Mister Satan harrumphed, heaving his loaded shopping cart toward my car. "God's people telling a story. Every damn one of us come from a drop of *something.*"

On the way over to Columbia, at Professor's instigation, we stopped at Shorty's Jamaican Kitchen and picked up a takeout cup of stewed pig's feet. This was new but I was game. I had one hand on the wheel and five fingers cradling a delicious greasy suckable cartilagenous lump. Sauce dripped, cymbals clanked. Mister Satan was next to me, working on a knuckle; Professor leaned forward, staring at me, incredulous.

"Look, Satan! A damn pigfoot. You eat the same food as us!"

I smiled over my shoulder. "I'm crazier than you think."

"Hah! What you know about crazy?"

"Nothing you don't," I parried.

"Shit. Me and Satan *forgot* more about crazy than . . . than . . ."

Mister Satan chuckled. "A Chinese chicken with American eyes."

"There you go. Whoo!" He slapped Mister Satan's shoulder. "Ain't we bad?"

"A Chinese *what?*" I said.

"Mister Adam," Mister Satan growled, glancing up, "please don't be tailgatin' no trucks."

Professor cackled. "I ain't had frog's legs in *years!*"

We set up across the street from the Columbia University bookstore, in front of a church. A wounded city paused to watch us flail and thrash under chill January skies. A hundred private smiles flowered. Mister Satan's open guitar case seemed to exert the magnetic force of a religious shrine. Dollar bills were confetti and coins were a tinkling silver shower, blessings and gifts intermingled.

"We are a threesome!" Mister Satan proclaimed when he finally broke for a smoke, bending down to scoop his fingers through our take.

Later, back in Harlem, we sat in my car in front of Shakespeare Flats and finished off the pint of Romanoff vodka we'd poured into three clear plastic cups. We looked like the victims of genital elephantiasis, front pockets bulging with bankrolls and change. Giddy is putting it mildly.

"We are the Creators!" Mister Satan roared. "You can blow that harmonica, too, young man. Don't be telling no lies."

"Thanks."

Professor blew me a kiss from the back seat. "I love you, baby. Merry New Year."

"Happy Christmas."

"Don't go there," he warned delightedly. "Satan might snap."

"I shouldn't say this," Mister Satan chuckled, slapping my thigh, "because it goes against verbal correctness, but you the best damn nigger I ever heard."

"Shit," Professor sneered, glancing out the window.

1976. I COULDN'T SPEND my whole freshman year playing blues in the stereo room. You had to emerge from the woodshed occasionally—hit classes and the library, eat, peddle hoagies, sleep. Eating was tricky. The Princeton Inn dining room was divided into cliques: preppies, jocks, blacks, and smart weirdos. Mealtimes forced me to figure out who I was.

I wasn't really a preppie. Preppies were the Andover/Exeter/Miss Porter's crowd, larval versions of the Ivy/Cottage/Cap-and-Gown eating club crowd. Preppies were blond, had perfect white teeth and midwinter tans. Preppies wore Topsiders and Lacoste polo shirts. I wore sneakers and tie-dyed t-shirts. Preppies sucked.

Jocks spent all their time talking about last weekend's Yale game and playing beer-prong until they booted. I wasn't a jock.

I wasn't black. So I'd pretty much fallen in with the smart weirdos. Many of them were upperclassmen who'd been assigned to the Princeton Inn as freshmen and never escaped. By senior year they were barnacled into weirdly shaped fifth-floor garrets—majoring in astrophysics and Sanskrit, translating *The Tale of Genji* from medieval Japanese, bonging it up. Some of them were re-admits who'd taken time off during the Vietnam War to wander, trip, join communes. Lawrence Watt Evans—hip-length brown hair, puckering red lips, World Expert on Everything—had renamed himself "Malachi" and was writing a sci-fi trilogy on the seven-year plan. One bearded, emaciated guy with a wispy Fu Manchu beard trudged barefoot around campus all winter. Saigon had just fallen, Gerald Ford was our stumbling president; here we all were, denizens of The Far Side of Paradise.

The smart weirdos overheard my practice sessions, a nightly frenzy from below, and decided I was one of them. I'd taken over their party room; the least they could do was wave me over at dinnertime. A relationship evolved. They were gentle, quirky, ingrown, self-dramatizing, endlessly fond of bad puns. Their dress code was a cross between Dungeons & Dragons and Early Druid, with seasonal inflections. They pulled all-nighters in the student lounge, smoking clove cigarettes and playing obscure forms of whist. They patted me on the head, happy to have a new mascot.

I got restless after a while. I always did.

One night in the spring of freshman year, just for the hell of it, I took my tray of cafeteria ravioli and salad and headed toward the Black Table. The Black Table had no sign on it reading Black Table. Nothing had been written down anywhere, as far as I knew, prohibiting me from sitting at it. It was a long table at the back of the dining room where only black students sat, eating and talking—laughing, sometimes, louder than the rest of us. I'd been watching it for a while, curious. I knew nobody at it personally, although I recognized a few faces, people I'd passed a hundred times in the hall. The two black people I actually *knew* on campus were roommates of smart weirdos and ate at outposts of the Smart Weirdo Table, not the Black Table.

I was an open-minded guy. I was willing to take the first step. Maybe I'd get into a conversation about blues, or civil rights. My dad had been a delegate for McGovern in '72. I was liberal.

I floated toward the Black Table, smiling weakly, and suddenly felt a very weird vibe. Were the three or four people who glanced up—and whose faces gave nothing away—hoping that I wouldn't sit down? Maybe I was hallucinating.

Awkwardly, panicking a little, I slid into the end of a row, leaving one chair free between me and the next person, a woman with large owlish glasses and Brillo-textured brown hair combed into a swooping curve. I murmured hello, or tried to. The guy across from her stared at me for a moment and went back to work on his Salisbury steak and mashed potatoes. Two guys farther down were arguing heatedly about Steven Biko, the struggle, the people. The air around my head was suddenly humming. One of the arguers paused and eyed me, his voice dropping, then getting louder, more cutting.

I forked up a couple of ravioli and chewed silently, heart pounding. Nobody said a word to me. I eased to my feet after a few minutes, pushed back my chair with the backs of my knees, and walked out of the dining room with my green fiberglass tray of ravioli, salad, and dirty silverware.

JANUARY '87 streamed by like an air-conditioned dream, huge gulps swallowed whole. Harlem slapped my hand, grabbed and pumped it, tossed me a quarter, refused to color me bad. Sometimes we were a trio, sometimes a duo; I'd taken to wearing a navy beret like Professor's—saucered sideways, shading my eyes. We swooped uptown, planting ourselves on the corner of 145th Street and Broadway against the wall of a Banco Popular. Winds whistled off the Hudson River, airfoiled up the steep hill, clawed at our faces. "We're damn sure a bunch of playing fools!" Mister Satan yelled, not unhappily. We rushed to set up and played furiously, picking, fretting, and plucking fingers and lips all thawing simultaneously as paper-bagged drinkers huddled and bickered in the winter twilight.

One sunny afternoon we lashed the shopping cart to the roof of my car and headed downtown to the New York Public Library, just the two of us.

"Hell," Mister Satan remembered fondly, puffing on a cigarette, "it was Professor who broke me out *onto* the streets back in the early eighties. I was scared to death, too."

"You?"

"It ain't no easy thing to get out there if the clubs been your main gig for a while. It's more like a freedom-release thing you got to *feel* before you can enjoy it. Up till then you naturally gonna be wondering where the stage is, where's my pay gonna be coming from, suppose nobody like what I'm playing, whatever. So that introduces a holdback element into the music. Professor's whole thing was about *damn* the holdback, just go and have a good time. So the old bastard loosened me up considerably."

I smiled. "As long as the cops leave me alone I'm happy."

"I got my police up in Harlem *very* friendly to our music, Mister."

The Midtown police no-noed him before I'd gotten back from parking the car—he sat glumly below a crouching stone lion, our gear clumped around his cart—but nobody raised a hand around back, on the sidewalk next to Bryant Park. An unleashed Mouse is a marvelous thing. Our bittersweet wash seemed to pour up the curved glass front of the W. R. Grace building across the street, rolling and frothing like a surging breaker. We were huge, puissant, indomitable. Fuck Howard Beach! A vacationing Parisian restaurateur who remembered me from the Beaubourg tossed a twenty in the bucket when we broke; a black record exec in tasseled loafers who remembered Mister Satan as Sterling tossed us two tens.

We could do no wrong, seemingly. A few days later, on 125th Street, we were tossing back Romanoff with orange-drink chasers. The State Office Building across the street softened slightly in the thin late sun. We were beginning to make summer plans—huge, staggering, unheard-of plans. Hit the road, head South, lay waste to America.

"We wouldn't need any hotels," Mister Satan insisted. "Just push aside my altar and sleep in the back of my van."

"Let New York stew in its own juices for a while."

"They definitely gonna do that whether we around or not. By the way," he added, "you free on Valentine's Day?"

"Unfortunately."

"I got us a little job that night, if you want. A social club thing down on Seventh Avenue."

"A juke joint."

"A joint what ain't *got* a juke and need one."

"Hell yeah, we can do that." I tossed back the last of my vodka. "I used to play a couple of jazz clubs around here."

"Not one of 'em worth a damn," he scowled. "Charge five dollars a drink and give the bandleader one. I gave up that whole mess back in the seventies."

MY BRIEF, SURREAL CAREER in Harlem's cabarets had come about through sheer chance, or fate. In February of '86—ten months before connecting with Mister Satan—I was wailing down Avenue of the Americas just past Herald Square when a young black guy pulled in next to me. He grooved as I blew, nodding his head. Naturally I gave him my best Nat-stuff.

"You play good," he said after a moment.

"I just got this baby up at Manny's," I said, holding out the shiny new F harp. "Some of the new ones sound great and some suck." I put it to my lips and yelped. I had a new gig these days, working the subways with a young Irish-American guitarist named Billy Collins. I'd play for anybody, anywhere, at any time.

"You ever been up to Harlem?" he asked.

"Ate at Sylvia's once."

He smiled. "You and Mayor Koch."

We walked and talked in the cold dusk, dodging garment workers heaving loaded dollies. His name was Kevin Rollins—Sonny's nephew, he said. He dishwashed in a restaurant called La Famille. One Hundred Twenty-fifth Street and Fifth Avenue. They had jazz in the front room, jam sessions on Wednesday and Sunday nights with a free buffet. You wanna talk about fried chicken? Peach cobbler? Couldn't nobody touch Miss Bea's peach cobbler. Bring my harmonica, they'd let me sit in.

"You won't be the only white person there," he said. "Plenty of Japanese come up. We're in the guidebooks."

We made a date. We grabbed hands again and he veered away, disappearing into the night.

What did I know about Harlem, except that I was supposed to steer clear of it? I'd been a grad student at Columbia, ten blocks and a world away. I'd once eaten brunch there with Helen. I'd read *Invisible Man*. I'd grown up during the sixties watching furious rioting blacks on the evening news. Heroin, junkies. These days all you heard about was crack cocaine.

The following Wednesday evening I drove down from my new home up in Inwood. M & G Soul Food with the garish orange and green sign, Lagree Baptist Church filling up a storefront. You knew you were in Harlem the moment 125th Street doglegged left past the firehouse. I pulled up to the curb just before Fifth Avenue, next to a shadowed series of gated storefronts. Got out, locked, tried not to look as though I was locking *against* anybody. Asked a couple of young loiterers in baggy jeans where the place was. "La Fam-ill?" they said. They jerked their heads. I floated around the corner into never-never land.

The front window was well lit and slightly fogged. It required an amazing act of will to push through the front door. Heads swiveled, none of them Japanese. I was a minority of one. I clutched at my harps in the pockets of my bomber jacket. A jukebox was crooning in back; there were drums and an electric organ on the small stage to my left. A light-skinned guy in a blue blazer was running through scales on a muted trumpet.

I smiled awkwardly and forced myself forward, easing through shoulders that magically parted. The men wore suits and sport jackets, the women were dressed up. Everybody smelled good. The narrow room had a warm, close, rippling, brandied feeling, as though low flames were gently massaging the floor and ceiling. Nobody knew who Kevin Rollins was. I found Miss Bea in back, overseeing the kitchen. Kevin had told me she was high yellow and warned me not to be put off. She gazed at me austerely through flat, withholding eyes. Kevin wasn't working tonight. She didn't know about the music. That was Tippy's thing, not hers.

I eased back the way I'd come and found a seat at the bar, next to the bandstand. A dark-skinned older guy in a smudged straw hat struck up a conversation. He had a Caribbean accent. His name was John Spruill, rhymed with "school." He spelled it out. He was from Panama and played organ, although he wasn't on the gig.

I did as he suggested, scrawling my name on a cocktail napkin and handing it to Tippy Larkin, the trumpet player. I was working on my second Heineken. My hands had stopped trembling. The trio swung to life. Tippy swayed hard as he spattered a fluid stream of high notes. The drums rocketed, riding on a gaudy swirling surge of chords from the Hammond B-3. Ten conversations around me suddenly kicked up thirty decibels apiece, shouted hilarities over a musical explosion-in-progress.

Two sax players crowded the mike after Tippy. I barely recognized "Things Ain't the Way They Used to Be" through a haze of organ flourishes. The be-bop drumming was a wilderness of sizzling off-beats. Where was the one? I'd never claimed I was a jazz cat. I ordered a third Heineken and dove mentally for the deep groove, humming and tapping my foot, a barely suppressed cry pirouetting in my throat.

The dueling saxes swung back into the head, triumphant; the rhythm section crashed home. People applauded with sudden attention as though it had just occurred to them that musicians were at work. Tippy had the paper napkin in his hand. He read off my name. The young man is going to play some harmonica.

I took a last sip of beer to scattered applause and walked the five impossible feet from my barstool up onto the stage. "Don't touch the mike," Tippy warned as he stepped down. I felt in my jacket pocket for harps, pulled out an E-flat: the high lonesome sound. I leaned toward the organist—dark red sunglasses, gray grizzle—and asked for a shuffle blues in B-flat. He grunted, "Count it off." The drummer wiped the sweat off his face with a white towel.

There was a brief, almost imperceptible hush after the rhythm section swung into gear and I leaned toward the mike. I was hovering, searching for a handhold, then grabbing and plunging in, knife-edging my blue thirds like Nat and Big Walter, yelping with panic and anxious yearning. Somebody was clapping in time. I yelped again, kicked from behind by the drums. A sudden electrical storm seemed to surge around me, hunger and rippling expectancy reaching out from all sides, supercharging the atmosphere. "Don't stop!" shouted somebody at the bar. I shivered and bore down hard, cut through the swirling surf, found the taut cable and held it, refused to let go, was dragged along the glass-strewn bottom, cut and bleeding, screaming—it was *hot* down here, burning the skin off my shoulders, scraping the skin off my knees, elbows, and chest, bursting through my heart as I streamed back to the surface, gasping, on fire. "*Do* it, goddammit!" somebody yelled. Flames licked at me, then spread wildly; the room was an open mouth—hot, demanding, loving, ferocious, dizzying. The drums hurled me forward, the organ boiled me alive. I held on. All I could do was hold on. I held and held, streaming.

We swung the shuffle home and the place exploded. It was scary. I started to step down. "Where you going?" yelled the organist. "You ain't going nowhere." I called out another B-flat blues—uptempo this time—and blew Sonny Boy Williamson's "Pontiac," swinging so hard I nearly threw myself off the stage. Another explosion, looser and more knowing, as though the crowd and I had already become old friends.

John Spruill collared me when I came off, dragging me onto my barstool, cackling. "You stole the show!" he hissed in my ear. "They *love* you, man. Ain't nobody come in and play like that for a long time. You own this house now."

The dream element was very strong for the next half-hour. Guys holding saxes and trumpets thumped me on the back. A woman sitting in one of the booths took my hand as I went for the men's room, giving me a luscious wistful look. If anybody was laughing at me, or resentful, I didn't notice. Miss Bea, allowing herself a small smile, wondered if I had a manager. A white-haired man in a dark gray suit, ahead of me on line for the lone urinal, grabbed my shoulder. "I ain't heard nothing like that up north since Jimmy Reed," he croaked. When I got back to the bar, John Spruill was guarding the two Heinekens I'd been sent. He pulled me close.

"There's two women in this place you could get right now.

*Nobody* comes in and plays like that. Sometimes we get white boys who come in—blow a little trumpet or something. Sometimes they start blowing and they are hor-ri-*bull*, man. And somebody gotta go up and say '*Do not play anymore.*' But you? No, man. People want something new and you is *it.*"

John was a visionary. His vision consisted of laying waste to Harlem in one night with me as his secret weapon. Why stop with La Famille? He spirited me out the door—Miss Bea, of all people, made me swear I'd come back Sunday for another jam session—and away, back to my car.

"Do you smoke?" he asked, holding out a joint as we cruised up Lenox Avenue into the Heart of Darkness.

I shook my head. "Nah, tonight I just drink."

"Well, mahn, we gotta get us a taste. You like vodka?"

"Sure."

"Gimme a buck. I'll match it."

He hopped out after I double-parked, then back in, handing me the small paper-bagged bottle. I baptized it. He killed it.

"Now we talking," he said.

We passed Sylvia's, the Lickety Split, Harlem Hospital.

"You like coke?" he asked.

"Never tried it."

"Gimme five, I'll put in five, we gonna have a *good* damn time."

This time he returned with a small foil package. I followed his lead, using a rolled-up dollar bill. A numbing whiff, like rubbing alcohol. Everything was suddenly glittering, careening with possibility.

Sutton's was our goal; Professor Spruill was in control. Panama Johnny and the Inwood Kid parked on 145th Street, swivel-hipping downhill and through the front doors. A wilderness of mirrors under soft lights, a keening jukebox in back, a grand piano on a darkened stage. A couple of guys in Borsalinos glanced up from the five or six occupied card tables. Soon Panama Johnny was holding a heated discussion with the dubious bartender.

"This is Adam, my man is a harmonica player, he just took the house *apart* down at La Famille. Come *on,* mahn, him and me gonna play a few tunes and entertain your customers."

Not on card night. A quick beer and we were trudging up Sugar Hill to the car, flying down St. Nicholas Avenue through the cold February night, double-parking outside a bar with no name. I followed Spruill down the front steps, ducking under the battered air conditioner. The place was empty except for a huge jukebox in back—lit up like a flying saucer with landing pods locked into place, thumping and wailing for my love. *Thursday* night was jam night. Spruill waved his arm at the slip-covered Hammond organ and sparred desperately with the bartender, a bored young guy forking Chinese food out of a foil tray.

"Come on mahn, give us a chance. Whaddya got to lose? My man Adam will *kill* you with his harmonica. He just tore up the house at La Famille—you couldn't hear for the screaming, mahn, women were throwing undies. I ain't telling you no lies. Come *onnnnnn,* mahn."

We heaved ourselves back up the cold, cold steps.

"I'm ashamed of my people," Spruill muttered. "Don't know a good thing when it's sitting on their own damn shoulder."

We pushed back through the front doors of La Famille after midnight, willing to settle. The band was gone, the crowd had thinned. A couple of people recognized me but Miss Bea would have none of it. John cajoled until she relented, then skipped toward the Hammond B-3. The power cord was gone—taken, presumably, by the guy on the gig. "God almighty!" John groaned.

Another couple of beers and we ended up at a small disco around the corner. I was standing alone in the middle of a checkerboard dance floor, harp cupped to my face. The jukebox had just been turned off; fifteen sharply dressed young black men and women were staring at me. I was drunk. Somebody tittered.

"Go and serenade her!" John kept hissing, jerking his head at a girl standing alone. "She'll love it."

I felt like somebody's stupid pet trick, suddenly. I was angry. I played hard and fast and the tittering stopped. I walked up to John

and barked raw notes at him, then spun and finished up in the spotlight, jammed the harp in my hip pocket and dropped down next to
him, spent.

"You should have played two or *three* songs, mahn," he said,
distressed. "You had—aw, listen to that. They put the jukebox back
on. Shit. You could have made some real money."

1976. FALL OF SOPHOMORE YEAR found me back at the Princeton Inn—haunting the stereo room, blues-crazed as ever. I hadn't
turned into Clapton or Bird yet, but neither had they at age eighteen.
Dues had to be paid. My new hero was Ricky Spillers, campus
guitar-god and chick magnet. One year ahead of me, Ricky wore
small wire-framed John Lennon glasses over his fleshy cheeks and
had a dazed inscrutable smile. When he wasn't tossing off jagged,
fusiony leads with Ismism, a jazz-rock quartet, he teamed up with a
Tex-Mex guy named Alberto, strumming and singing *Aaaa-meee,*
*what chu wanna doooo* in an acoustic group called Canyon City
Limits. You'd find lots of girls at his gigs, especially outdoors—
stripping down to voluptuous body-stockings, whirling barefoot on
the grass, chatting him up. I chatted him up, too. Guitarists love to
talk about their axes. One day, hoping his mojo would rub off, I
asked if I could borrow his black Les Paul Custom for a couple of
days, to see how it compared with my Telly. I was thinking of replac-
ing my pickups with humbuckers. He said Fine. Call him Sunday
morning.

I did that, around ten. He sounded dazed as usual but said Come
on up. He had a soft, drawly, vaguely Southern way.

I ran up from the Princeton Inn to Lockhart, a five-minute dash.
Banged on his door. There were frantic scurrying noises. He pulled
open the door with one hand and held up his pants with the other.
His bare chest was pale, speckled with black hairs.

"All riiight," he drawled.

"Hi," I said.

Over his shoulder I could see a woman I vaguely recognized
standing next to his messed-up bed. Her thick black hair was hanging loose. Her breasts swelled against her tank top, jiggling as she

swiveled. She had heavy black eyebrows and pretty eyes—dark, almond-shaped, flashing.

"Thanks, man," I said as he handed off. "I'll be careful."

"No sweat," he murmured.

Then I was out of there, heavy black fiberglass case bumping my knee as I swung down his entryway steps. Prometheus on a roll.

Helen, I suddenly remembered. That was her name. We'd met at a party freshman year.

MISTER SATAN, PROFESSOR, AND I were sitting in my car on the corner of Adam Clayton Powell Jr. Boulevard and 125th Street. It was a cold Saturday night in early February of '87. We'd kicked and stomped all afternoon, at various locations. Professor and I were drinking Romanoff; Mister Satan had recently given up liquor altogether. Professor was fondling his stack of bills in the back seat.

"I got so much money I don't know what to do with it," he laughed harshly. "Fifties, twenties."

"I *am* the Earth, Mister Adam," Mister Satan cried, inflamed. "I joke not. The Earth works in mysterious ways. I may feel a little cold coming on, mix me up a little milk and honey, drink it down, and I'm gonna wake up next morning with my health in full flower. Ain't took no doctor to cure my behind. A doctor will *kill* you, man. How's a doctor gonna help anybody produce healthfulness when he spend all day and all night studying sickness and death? Can't do it. Same thing with God. Bastard puts man and woman in the garden of Eden, shows them where the Tree of Life is, looking oh so pretty with the apple hanging down, and then go and make up some lie about how they gonna die if they go and have a taste. God *is* Death, plain and simple. Ain't no life in the mess."

"But he was right about Adam and Eve," I said. "I mean they went from being immortal to dying like we do, of natural causes."

He held up his hand, smiling fiercely. "Ain't no such thing as natural causes."

"But everybody has to die sooner or later."

"Any fool that does got what he deserved."

"I mean *I'm* gonna die, eventually."

"You damn right," said Professor. "Ain't no way out."

"The Earth got you both beat," Mister Satan countered. "Can't nobody kill me, however much they trample and dig."

"Anyway," I said, "according to Genesis it wasn't an apple on the Tree of Life, it was a 'fruit.' The text never said what kind."

He held up his hand. "The forbidden fruit is both apples *and* pears. Cut either one across the middle—sideways-like—and you got yourself a five-pointed star."

"No way."

"Wait right here." He jumped out, slammed, headed for a bodega.

Professor leaned forward. "I'm a rich man."

"I can't argue with him," I sighed.

"Motherfucker," he suggested. "I know all those words. Fuck shit piss."

"Candy dick."

"Hump jockey."

We were chuckling when Mister Satan flopped back into the front seat brandishing a glossy Red Delicious. He pulled out a penknife, bisected the apple laterally, and handed me the bottom half, grinning. A perfect geometrical figure.

"There go your star."

"Damn."

"I wouldn't tell no story, Mister."

"You a smart goddamn motherfucker, Satan." Professor laughed. "Whoo. Shit."

I cracked up, giggling helplessly.

Mister Satan sat quietly for a few seconds, his smile gone. He snapped his penknife shut.

"Goodnight Mister Adam," he barked, heaving the door open, vanishing with a slam.

Professor and I sat there.

"She'll be back," he said.

"*She'll* be back?"

He nodded. "She'll be back."

. . .

HE DIDN'T COME BACK. I felt weirdly bad all night and the next morning. The pain between us was a living thing, a shadowy negative force field radiating between my apartment up in Inwood and his tiny back room at Shakespeare Flats. Three weeks earlier, in the flush of the New Year, he'd said he loved me. It was a moment of delirious high feeling when the dream of conquering the world with our sound was being born. "I love you, man," he'd said. "I love you too," I'd said. He'd given me a black plastic folding chair a few days later, so I could sit comfortably instead of crouching on my upended Mouse. For this I'd mocked him? Conspired in mocking him?

I had an extra Mouse recharger, left over from the stolen amp. I brought it down to Harlem a couple of days later. He and Professor were on break when I pulled up in front of the New York Telephone office. He was leaning back in his hi-chair—legs crossed, cigarette dangling from his lips, tracing squared circles with a bent forefinger on one of his shellacked mandalas and lecturing as several bystanders, including Duke, looked on. I grabbed the recharger, left the rest of my stuff in the car, and got out, heart pounding. Duke caught sight of me.

"Heyyyy, Adams," he said, showing his few teeth, pivoting on his cane, "we were just talking about you."

Mister Satan looked up. Our eyes met. A flicker of nonplussedness crossed his face, followed by a gentlemanly smile and nod.

"Hello to you, sir."

"I thought you might be able to, ah, use this," I said, holding out the recharger looped with its own cord, a skinny black twinlead. "For one of your Mouses."

Our fingers brushed as he took it. He stood up, gold tooth flashing triumphantly. "Thank you, sir," he said, bowing. "I bow to you like I bow to my own people. Ain't no belief about it, ain't no Praise the Lord, ain't no collection plate, ain't no white or black. Those bastards out in Howard Beach ain't got a *damned* thing to do with you and me right here in Harlem."

"That's right," somebody called out.

Professor smiled tautly, bitterly. "Some days I wake up, I might as well be a damn Indian. My granddaddy was."

"I am a *nigger!*" Mister Satan roared, eyes raking the circle. "Can't no damn fool hurt me with a word I embrace! A nigger ain't no more than a man or woman who know and love dirt. We all come from dirt, every last one of you come from dirt. Mister Adam comes from dirt. And hear me well: the dirt is the best friend you got. Every collard green and yam and McDonald's French fry you've ever eaten was pulled *out* of the dirt, every peach and orange you've ever eaten got picked off a tree that was growing *in* the dirt, every bottle of wine you've ever drunk was made from grapes grown on grapevines that owe the entirety of their life to having roots deep down *in* the dirt. Wash off your hands and you got clean hands, but so what?" He paused and looked at us, eyes wide with furious mirth.

"What's that?" somebody called out.

"Can't grow a damn thing without the dirt you just got rid of!"

Shortly after that, while we were playing outside, he started calling me son. "Blow on, son!" he'd roar.

*1977.* FUCK THE BORDASH brothers! It was spring term of sophomore year and I was in a band. A *real* band, with some of the best musicians on campus, guys out of my league. It was like having a beautiful girlfriend you didn't quite deserve, but there she was—on your arm, happy to be with you.

Spiral. The Crusaders song we'd named ourselves after had ascending eleventhy jazz chords and a guitar-and-horns head that hurled you into the stratosphere. We were an instrumental sextet: jazzy, funky, fusiony, discoey, bluesy. I was the blues component. It was a running joke. I'd asked at the second rehearsal—everybody was exchanging band tapes—if we could throw in a Muddy Waters tune like "Walkin' through the Park." Scott, our bass player, just gave me a look. He gave Chad a look. His eyes bulged; he covered his mouth and gagged, like I'd said this hilarious thing. He had an Afro and flared nostrils but was so light-skinned that I wasn't sure he was black until I asked him, later on. He looked at me then like I was an embarrassing lovable idiot.

"Muddy Waters?" he said. "You mean, like, *blues?*"

"Primitive folk music," Chad suggested, tickling his Fender Rhodes keys. Chad was a physics major.

"I can play the harmonica part." I reached into my hip pocket, whipped it out.

"Aaaaaaaagh!" Scott howled.

They both cracked up. They might have been stoned. That was their thing. They'd toke and then rag on Bill and me for being uptight. Bill was Spiral's trumpet player and arranger: pudgy, rumpled, with glasses that slid down. Always saying Come on, guys, and nagging us to move rehearsals along, instead of just jamming. Bill's face got bright red when he blew. He'd miss every tenth high note, a sputtering clam.

Jon, on alto sax, was sixteen years old, a townie, our secret weapon. Jon could blow. Scott loved him. He'd heard about this phenom at Princeton High School and signed him up. Jon could do anything: endless blossoming strings of sixteenth notes on Coltrane's "Impressions," chuckles and squawks on Herbie Hancock's "Red Baron."

Steve, our drummer, was older, a Chem-E grad student. He smoked cigarettes, had been around. He was cynical about the college band thing. His style was freestyle: heavy on sizzling wash, light on solid groove. Scott anchored him.

Scott knew people up on Prospect Street. Suddenly, after a year and a half of being shut out of parties at Colonial and Terrace Club, I was *playing* the things—flutter-strumming the funk riffs I'd copied off Earth, Wind and Fire albums, sweating and swaying as dancers whirled in front of me, cranking up my Telecaster when Chad gave me the nod. All the Clapton and B.B. King shit I'd been working out down in the stereo room was suddenly, thrown over these new beats, *my* shit. I'd dissolve as I soloed, sucked into a six-man fluid of pure feeling. ScottChadJonSteveAdamBill. Spiral! We were beautiful and rickety, a jam band that pushed the envelope until somebody tore through. Plus I was being paid—as much for one gig as I'd made in a week of part-time bathroom cleaning. The sweetness in my heart as

I collapsed into bed at dawn was revenge on the hopeless loser I'd been. Only thing missing was a girlfriend. She was bound to come along.

One night, at the end of a late rehearsal, we all got stoned on a couple of joints Chad passed around.

"What the hell," Bill said as he took the roach, amazing everybody. He was like Lips back at the Day School: Mr. Good. Having him around made it easier on me.

Then we got the munchies and took a walk up through campus to the pizzeria on Nassau Street. We were bumping shoulders, goofing, tripping through the cool spring night. We were this floating swirling organism, a blob set free in the universe. Somebody—might have been Scott—started scat-singing the part he usually played on "Red Baron." Pretty soon Jon and Bill were coming in with their perky horn duet. Chad spluttered his piano swirls, I chock-a-chucked my guitar part. No instruments except us. Solos and everything, until we passed Nassau Hall and fell through the front gate onto lit-up Nassau Street.

BA-dump! BA-dum-dum-dum da-WHAY-you-ba-doo-be-WHA!

Six of us crammed into a booth. The pizza cheese was delicious oily goop from outer space, the best I'd ever had.

ON THE NIGHT of Valentine's Day '87, Mister Satan and I played our joint-without-a-juke gig, at the AMC Social Club on the corner of 121st Street and Seventh Avenue in Harlem. A rail-thin guy with broad shoulders and a Wild Bill Hickok hat let us through the outer and inner door after we buzzed. He was Mister Satan's age and wore trim tan slacks.

"Just call me Chick," he said, squeezing my hand. "Anything you want, you just call me."

We were the first to arrive, except for a short feisty woman in a yellow print dress arranging foil-covered trays on a pool table in the back room. The pool table had been covered with a wooden board and tablecloth and pushed against a side wall. The front room had an old white enamel stove, a refrigerator, and a bar. The linoleum floor next to the stove had been worn away in concentric parabolas, like a sand painting, to reveal layers of red, gray, and white. The refrigerator was filled with bottles of Heineken and small bottles of Bud. There were big jugs of Smirnoff, Chivas Regal, and Jim Beam behind the bar, where Chick was shoveling ice. Crepe paper streamers criss-crossed the ceilings of both rooms, under red and blue bulbs and a couple of fluorescent lights. All the windows had been bricked up.

It was Mr. Wendell Dozier's ninety-fourth birthday. By midnight he was claiming ninety-nine. A lot of people showed up, buzzing to be let in. Mister Satan and I were the only two wearing t-shirts. The place got smoky and loud. We played from seven to three, sweating out the coffees we'd started off with. During breaks the jukebox boomed Denise LaSalle's X-rated version of "Down Home Blues" with the lyrics about how her no-good husband could kiss her black ass. I had three or four conversations with older men, all of which began at the bar. Chu had a white Kit Carson hat and tinted shades, claimed to be Bo Diddley's second cousin, and knew B.B. King well enough to get us on the bill—maybe—next time B.B. played the Apollo. "I'll make a few calls," he insisted. "B and me go way back." Lanier was a trucker from Halifax, Virginia, and had the cap to prove it: "Truckers Carry Full Weight and Go the Distance." He was smoking a cigar, sipping Scotch, had a billy goat tuft under his lower lip.

"I ain't never had no trouble with white folks." He tapped the back of his hand, then the back of mine. "We both bleed red when you cut us, right? How you gonna come along after that and tell me White Is Right or Black Stay Back?"

"People are stupid."

"That's what I'm saying. A few bad apples in every bunch. Underneath we all the same."

Mister Satan sang himself hoarse, then took slugs of ReaLemon out of a small bottle to scour the phlegm from his throat. His fretting hand crabwalked across the strings, releasing showers of blue sparks. His foot cymbal clip-clopped; people clapped in time.

"You got me runnin'," he cried, "you got me hidin', you got me run, hide, hide, run, anyway you want . . . but let it roll. . . ."

When I sang "Poor Boy Blues" and whooped like Sonny Terry, the dancers in front of us patted the hand-jive on their knees and elbows. The older men were spry, self-possessed, and demonstrative; the women, answering and challenging, were easily their match but willing to be won. There were no younger men, except me. Everybody milled into the back room when dinner call came. The short feisty woman in the yellow print dress handed me a plate heaped with fried chicken, deviled eggs, potato salad, greens with pork knuckles, dirty rice, fruit salad. She yelled at anybody who went for seconds before we'd all gotten firsts.

"This ain't no soul food, this is *food*," the man behind me said loudly. "I never did understand that soul food business. This is *food*."

PART TWO

# PRETTY GIRLS

# CHAPTER SIX

# ROAMING

*Come,*
*Let us roam the night together*
*Singing. . . .*

—LANGSTON HUGHES, "HARLEM NIGHT SONG"

I KNEW THAT SOONER OR LATER, if I stuck around Harlem, a woman was bound to come along. I hoped she would. I was always secretly happy to see black men dating white women and a little jealous of white guys who'd found companionship across the tracks. Catchphrases like "across the tracks" were part of the problem. Where were the tracks, finally, except in our minds? I was a principled amalgamator: anything to dissolve the myths and misunderstandings that kept us from enjoying each other's company. I'd read Malcolm X; I understood his rage at white slaveowners who had raped their black female chattel. This was loathsome stuff, a legacy bequeathed on younger white guys—even nonslaveowner-descended half-Russian/Lithuanian Jewish, half-Dutch/Scotch-Irish mongrels like me—by generations of dead white fathers. Fathers weren't our only burden: you had idiot sons like Jason Ladone and Scott Kern doing their best to start a race-war out in Howard Beach. All the more reason, then, why redemptive action was required. Racial violence disgusted me. Why *not* try a little tenderness?

My passion was deeper than sex, although sexual hunger was

one way it expressed itself: I was fiercely, helplessly in love with the voices of singers like Denise LaSalle, Ernestine Anderson, Marlena Shaw. There was a swaggering vulnerability, a husky girlishness, a raging laugh, a despairing faith, in every belted note. They knew where to find that sweet shivery pitch between minor and major—how to tease it out of hiding, hurl it down my throat, make it swell until it choked me. Were they *trying* to choke me, or pull me deeper into their world of feeling, or both? Did they even know I was listening? I sang along with their records, shadowing their voices, struggling to make their sound mine. I imagined, in my fever, that I had something new to add to the mix—a certain tensile sweetness, innocence audibly surrendered. Others had done it: Michael McDonald, David Sanborn, Kenny G. No doubt the dead slavemaster was lurking somewhere, hovering behind the pain of an ancient lament passed from mother to daughter to he-who-would-be-son-in-law. I was strong enough to sense his presence *and destroy him in my own flesh*. Beginning today, the women and I would dissolve our differences in song and go forth to create the uncreated conscience of our troubled family. If our bodies came together along the way, that would merely incarnate the spiritual kinship I already felt with my sisters-in-blues.

This was my creed; it seems surreal and a little dangerous to me now, but desperate times breed desperate solutions. Certain elements of it, in any case, seemed to be shared. I'd already drawn scattershot female notice in the four months I'd been working 125th Street. One day, standing at the counter of the pizza place just down from the New York Telephone Company, I noticed a fragile older woman perched on a stool, eyeing me through spectacles.

"You the white boy who plays with Satan?" she said.

"Yes ma'am."

She dabbed the pizza oil in the corner of her mouth with a paper napkin. "I like the way you move your feet."

I sang five or six songs an afternoon, a determined kid who had somehow found his place among people with a knack for finding entertainment-value in talents of all sizes. The older men who idled around us couldn't get enough of "Sweet Home Chicago"—"Sing that Chicago song," they'd chuckle. "Take me back to Chi-ca-go!"—but I lived for the days when women would pause, shrewdly appraise my pitch placement and commitment, and call out, "Sing it, baby." One day I devoted the better part of half an hour to woo-ing, so to speak, a woman whose gold tooth and swirly chocolate-frosting wig reminded me of blues belter Koko Taylor. She knew what I was trying to do, she *heard* me, and she let me know how she felt. She disappeared before the set was over. Duke limped up as we broke, chuckling.

"You got yourself a fan, Adams."

"You're telling me!"

"She told me, she said, 'If that white boy puffs on pussy the way he blows that harmonica, I wanna know his name.' "

Then there was Angela. Angela, a Toledo native and Ohio State graduate, had just moved to Harlem. She had neatly brushed hair and a smooth beige open face—impossibly innocent, vaguely star-tled, doe-like. She paused to watch us, then wandered over. Angela wrote poetry and wanted blues harmonica lessons. She saw me as part of a more general self-improvement project that included cre-ative writing classes at NYU and ushering at the Met. I gave her my card, introduced her to Mister Satan. "Hello, Miss Angela," he rasped gallantly. We went out once, for a movie and conversation. Her flawless features seemed immobilized by the Midwestern flat-ness of her quiet airbrushed voice. Where was beauty without exu-berance? I couldn't see it. I couldn't see a lot of things in those days.

1977. I BREEZED BACK into Princeton fall of junior year, guitar in hand, ready for Spiral Round Two. I'd saved my gig- and bathroom-cleaning money all spring, put myself through a seven-week summer course in jazz guitar at the Berklee College of Music up in Boston. Seven weeks of finger exercises, sight reading, chord theory. Seven weeks of nightly jam sessions down in the basement practice rooms, surrounded by guys who machine-gunned sixty-fourth notes like Al DiMeola. Al was a Berklee success story, king of the jazz-fusion hill with Chick Corea and Return to Forever. Every-body wanted chops like Al, or Pat Metheny, or Pat Martino. My fingers wouldn't move that fast. I'd earned a rep anyway, as a guy who knew how to strum funky and bend a soulful note. And for being crazy.

There was only one absolute, if-you-break-it-you're-out rule at Berklee: No Practicing in the Dorm Rooms Upstairs. By the seventh week, guys were chewing on their fingernails. The next-to-last day of school I said Fuck it.

The dorm rooms—six or seven floors' worth—all looked out on a triangular courtyard. It was a sunny, muggy August afternoon. I lugged my Earth Revival amp over to the window, set it on a chair so it was hidden behind a gauzy white curtain. Plugged in my Telly, cranked everything up to 10. Gripped the creaking strings. What could they do? Kick me out with a day to go?

*Ta-da!* I screamed, hitting the nastiest, most explosively hummingbird-vibratoed note I had in me. It ricocheted across the courtyard, rattling windows. Somebody shouted. I went *off*. Forget about Al DiMeola. Ten seconds later I came out of my trance and quickly unplugged, heaved my amp off the chair, threw my guitar back in the case, shoved it under my bed, and fell onto my mattress, panting.

The courtyard went nuts. Five other guys must have done the same thing. "The Star-Spangled Banner," "Sunshine of Your Love," "Free Bird." A trumpet squealed like an outraged elephant. There were hollers and halloos. Proctors were running up and down the halls, pounding on doors.

I'd made a name for myself at Berklee. Now I was back at Princeton, ready to show the band what I'd learned. Scott had a surprise of his own, which he unloaded at our first rehearsal. He'd found Spiral a singer. A black woman named Debbie, from Westminster Choir College just down the road.

Small, slim, shy, Debbie had the kind of voice I'd only heard on Top 40 radio. Roberta Flack, Gladys Knight. It throbbed with emotion, a throat-thing. Singing at Princeton meant white boys and girls—Nassoons and Tigerlillies—harmonizing barbershop style: smooth, jaunty, a Norman Rockwell greeting card. Debbie soaring over Spiral was news from somewhere else. She'd touch her hand to her heart on "Isn't She Lovely" and you'd *see* the newborn baby she and Stevie Wonder were cuddling. She'd point at the ceiling of whatever eating club we were playing on "Shining Star":

> Shining star for you to see-hee . . .
> What your life can truly be. . . .

And I'd think, Damn. I've never backed up a singer before and here I am behind the best.

She didn't hang out with the band. If somebody pulled out a joint, she'd never toke. She came to rehearsals and gigs, did her job—shy offstage, a dynamo on—and disappeared. I knew nothing about her, except her first name and that she could sing. How could she fit such a huge, rich, throbbing voice into such a small body? How could she break my heart—call up weird aching memories of Sandra—without even trying? She was a mystery.

MY HARLEM SHIP finally came in one bitterly cold night, a couple of weeks after Valentine's Day '87. Ever since Mister Satan, Professor, and I had worked 145th Street I'd been meaning to check out a club called Carl's on the Corner—just across Broadway, cater-corner from our spot. I was filled with familiar anxiety as I drove down from Inwood, a taut swirling sense of needing to throw myself, alone and vulnerable, into a place I wasn't supposed to be. For what? The music, of course—always the music—but what else?

I stopped off at a Cuban luncheonette across the street to kill my hunger: pork, ham, cheese, and pickle slices pressed together in a warm runny steamy garlicky mass between two halves of a roll. I peeled back the top crust, slathered hot sauce and wolfed. A black guy my age shouldered through the door as if blown by arctic winds, held out a couple of screw-top wine bottles. The flaps of his Siberian-style rabbit fur hat were untied and flapping loosely, jauntily.

"Yo, check it out," he hissed. "Imported from France."

I glanced at the Sonoma County label. "Nah man, not tonight."

He shrugged, put out his hand. "Can you gimme fifty cents?"

Carl's had a jukebox just inside the tinted front window, shadowy raised seating on the left, a floodlit stage in back, a scattering of customers, a bar on the right with dangling martini glasses. Either the female bartender was giving me subtle cool standoffish looks or I was hallucinating. I ordered a Heineken and drank. Five minutes later we were sharing a rueful laugh about the bitter weather. I took a second beer over to the jukebox, losing myself in the part of this world I knew. Denise LaSalle, Lionel Ritchie, Little Milton, Ashford and Simpson.

"Opie, right?"

I looked up to see a woman with a very broad plain face and large thick glasses. "Who?" I said.

She chuckled, a little drunk, bumping me with her shoulder. "Richie on *Happy Days?*"

Sometimes it was Larry Bird, sometimes the redheaded guy in Hall & Oates. The first time at Showman's they'd called me David Stockman, after Reagan's boyish budget director.

Janice—my new friend—had other friends up by the bandstand and wondered, after we'd critiqued the jukebox, whether I'd join her. The band was swinging as we floated forward: Hammond B-3, flat-top guitar, drums, all manned by suited Ellingtonian professionals. Blowing tenor sax, improbably, was a stout older woman in an evening dress whose unblinking eyes cut through me as she honked and shrieked. Janice's sister and another woman were holding down a pair of crammed-together tables with two cologned sportcoated players in their forties. The second woman stared at me as Janice shouted introductions. She had cappucino skin, cheekbones, rosebud lips, gold hoop earrings, hair pulled up under an iridescent lime cap with a tight gray Angora sweater over curves. When she stood up a few seconds later to take a chair at our table, she turned out to be six feet tall, in faded bluejeans that fit.

Her name was Dee Dee. Grooving was not the word for the relish with which she swimmingly pleasured herself in the band's gaudy propulsive wash. She tilted back her head, snapped her fingers, shimmied in place, gloried, dwelled in the music. She leaned toward me and raved about the sax-woman. Girlfriend was playing, lord lord.

Her breath tickled my ear. I raved back, glancing at the two men who were looking elsewhere. She laughed, snorting. How could a woman this breathtaking be this free? My flesh hummed. I wanted to fuse with her liquid being and explode in aching, arching technicolor. Scrawww! screamed the sax-woman, finessing the bell of her horn smoothly around the hip-level ball mike. Bluaaaagh! Scotchitooya!

A couple more beers and I couldn't take it. I reached into the pocket of my bomber jacket and pulled out the E-flat harp I always carried when clubbing, leaned toward Dee Dee and Janice, and started jamming. The band and I were in tune. Dee Dee opened her eyes and shrieked, as though I'd made a dozen roses blossom out of a silk handkerchief.

"You have to get up there and play!" she cried, grabbing my knee. "You *have* to!"

"Wellll," I demurred, "the band has its own thing going on."

"We'll make you. We'll sit on you and make you."

"Sit on me?"

Janice slapped her hand. "What you been drinking, girl?"

"My uncle used to play the harmonica, out on Long Island." She motioned me toward her ear, grinning goofily. "I know you can make it sound like a train."

I whoo-whooed. She and Janice both screamed.

"You sound like a old black man," Janice pronounced.

The two guys in sportcoats got up and left.

"I thought you guys were with them," I said, glancing at Sister, who was staring at me with cool appraising eyes.

They'd met the sportcoats in a bar across town and been driven over. It was quickly agreed that I'd provide rides, whenever and wherever. The band swung into "Red Top," crashed home, and broke. The bass player leaned toward the organist as the jukebox came on and said something that made them both laugh. The sax-woman wiped her glistening forehead with a towel. Janice eyed Dee Dee with annoyance and nudged me, voice slurring.

"My drink's gettin' low."

Dee Dee grabbed my hand. "You gonna talk to the band?"

Janice's sister suddenly wanted to go home. *Now.* I made a

desperate case for Later. She was implacable. It was decided: Dee Dee and Janice would hold down the fort while I ran a crosstown mercy mission.

I pulled on my bomber jacket and followed Sister's furred hood out of the bar, fuming. Salted frozen slush crunched under our feet. Broadway was frigid and quiet after the hot swirl inside. We hopped in my car and slammed, our breath fogging the windows. Sister turned toward me with a sly grin.

"Let's go get us some smoke."

I stared, incredulous. "I'm taking you home, right?"

"Let's go get us some smoke," she said, covering my stickshift hand with hers, "and go back to my place."

"I'm taking you home," I said firmly, wrestling the car out past a glazed snowbank into the street.

"Come on, baby."

"I don't smoke."

"What you gotta be so mean to me for? Ain't you got a heart?"

"Mean to you?" I said. "Christ! I'm out here busting my ass and that's the thanks I get!"

She touched my cheek with her finger. "Let's go get us some smoke," she pleaded. She laughed harshly. "You got a pretty face."

She kept it up as we hurtled crosstown through iceberg-clogged streets toward the address she'd given. I swung left on Madison, sliding.

"Uh uhhh. You gotta turn around."

"A Hundred Seventieth street, right?"

"A Hundred Sen*teenth*," she slurred. "Down, not up."

Her hand found my thigh as I skittered down Park Avenue. I lifted it off. The corner of 117th and Madison, when we finally arrived, was a vacant lot.

"Here we go," I chirped as the car plowed into a snowbank and stopped.

"Come on, baby, have a heart."

"My heart's not my problem."

"You so wrong and can't even see it. Shit."

"Look, I gotta go."

She leaned toward me hopefully. "Can you give me two dollars?"

A minute later I was screaming north through the frozen wastes of Spanish Harlem, hurtling crosstown on 145th. The gold letters proclaiming CARL'S ON THE CORNER were glowing, backlit in coil-heater red. I unzipped my bomber and shouldered through. They were sitting where I'd left them, glasses empty, glum. The band was cooking; the sax-woman squealed, cresting over the sizzling snare. Dee Dee's hand went for her heart when she caught sight of me.

"Sit *down*," she said, shifting her hips in her chair. Her iridescent lime cap shimmered in multicolored light pouring off the stage.

I bought us all a round. The tuxedoed guitarist scatted along with his single-string leads, a soaring butterfly chasing his own shadow. My lips brushed Dee Dee's ear as I leaned in.

"That guy's as good as George Benson."

"You come here a lot?" Our eyes were both angled at the stage.

"My first time."

"I never go out anymore."

"You dress well when you do."

She eyed me, pursed her lips, smiled. "Adam."

We were in my car, the three of us, heading crosstown on a familiar vector. Janice turned toward me eagerly, sadly. "Where you guys gonna hang out?"

I pulled out my harp and jammed, one hand on the wheel.

"That's just like my uncle," Dee Dee exclaimed, leaning forward in the back seat. "He was this part-Blackfoot part-Cherokee Indian—he lived out in Amityville on Long Island before it was all built up, when it was just a country town without roads. He used to sit out on the back porch and play stuff like that. He'd go, 'I'm gonna catch a rabbit,' and then walk out into the woods behind the back yard and catch a rabbit with his bare hands—"

"Get out, girl," Janice said.

"—for real, for real. With his bare hands. Just sneak up on it and grab it and break its neck and bring it to the house. I could never look when he peeled it."

"Skinned it?" I said.

"What*evuh*," she said Jappishly, waving the thought away. "It was icky. But he'd always sit out on the back porch and play his harmonica like that."

We dropped Janice off at exactly the same spot I'd dropped her sister an hour earlier. I could see bumper indentations in the snowbank. Dee Dee moved up to the front seat.

"Hello," I said.

"Hello there."

I cruised halfway up the block at five miles an hour, hesitated, pulled over.

"So what the hell do we do now?" I said.

"Hmm."

We could eat. We were both hungry. We could go to another bar and listen to more music.

We sat in the idling car, silent for a moment. I gazed at my hands. "I actually have a joint back at my place. I mean if you wanted to we could go back and do that."

The air in the car seemed to tremble. She fixed me with a frank, shy smile. "I'd like to do that."

"Yeah?"

"As long as you're not some kind of axe murderer." She giggled.

"Christ."

"Sorry. I'm bad."

We sat in my living room—me on the couch, her in a chair by the phone—and got high and talked for hours. I listened to her talk. She was twenty-six years old and her real name was Desiree Dupriece Campbell and her husband's name was Esposito, he was a half-Italian Puerto Rican and they'd had two kids before he moved out. The three-year-old—who her sister thank God had taken for the night—was a blond, blue-eyed little girl. Old Jewish ladies came up on the bus and said, "Isn't she cute? You must be her nanny," and she'd tell them the girl was her daughter, and they'd pull back like Whoa! Her moms was rich. Her moms disapproved of her wanting to be a singer and was always writing her in and out of her will, depending. She'd dropped out of design school at Parsons, she'd been a model. Eileen Ford said she was too ethnic. Tits and ass. That's how models talk. Like she was supposed to feel *bad* about how she looked? She'd done enough of that all through high school. A chubby, buck-toothed little girl, except she wasn't *little,* she was always the big ugly lunk on the end when they lined up for sports. She was still ugly. It was nice of me to say she wasn't.

She'd taken off her gold hoop earrings at some point and set them on my telephone answering machine. Nobody had said anything about her spending the night. I'd been wondering when the question was going to come up. It hadn't come up, I suddenly realized, because I hadn't asked and she had class.

I asked. She was sprawled in the chair with her long legs splayed and her chin on one hand—happy, hopelessly sincere, a little goofy.

"Can you lend me some pajamas?" she murmured.

MISTER SATAN AND I never rehearsed. We played. He played; I kept up, provoking his genius. Since he was liable to take off in any direction, I was forced to go for broke as a matter of principle, shrugging off train wrecks as an occupational hazard. The groove was our one constant, the foundation of all musical sympathy: from the very first we'd attacked the beat the same way. Our shuffles swung in the jazzy Harlem style, rather than bouncing Chicagoishly.

Groove isn't a black or white thing. It's a regional thing inflected by individuals, a reflex-sharpening team sport. New Orleans musicians lag behind the beat, dragging it out into a loping how y'all doin' Nawlins drawl; New York players snap it early, like a spark-advance goosing a hot-rodded cam, Ooh bop she-bam. Within each town you've got hundreds of personal variations on the local time-feel. Some overexcited New York guys push too hard with no internal governor; there's nothing worse than a drummer who gallops after you when you swing out ahead. The tempo speeds up, the swing-feel dies. Heaven is somebody who pulls when you push, bobs when you weave, picks up what you drop—no explanations, just easy minor adjustments like the Wright brothers tightening a few guy-wires at Kitty Hawk and suddenly all resistance falls away and you're airborne. The music seems to play itself, an endless streaming glide, hard good work poured into a bottomless sweet spot.

I'd run several marathons like this, touched it briefly with other musicians, but the 125th Street groove was special. One cold windy March afternoon we were slamming hard on "Ode to Billy Joe," whirling each other in circles like a couple of dizzy square dancers. Mister Satan would belch fire and smoke, I'd lasso his cobra and squeeze. The bustle and roar of Harlem—an endless parade of dashikied Senegalese trinket sellers, blithe sexy homegirls in baggy jeans, gold-trimmed white Benzes with dark-tinted windows spewing earthshaking bass—suddenly trembled and fell away. Harlem was there and wasn't, I was here and wasn't, Mister Satan was everywhere and nowhere. We had entered the Zone. The Zone was beyond words, deeper than language. It was a flaming nuanced frenzy, fully articulated in all dimensions, sustained at the barest fraction below all-out effort.

We stayed in the Zone for an endless moment. Mister Larry, hovering on my shoulder, leaned in and shouted "Give it to me, dammit! Throw down!" I sailed through my solo like a shopper floating through supermarket aisles with an old family recipe in hand, plucking notes off shelves with dreamy rightness—dark chocolate here, turbinado sugar there, lightly salted butter from the dairy case, vanilla extract from the spice rack. Mister Satan's eyes were closed; he rocked on his hi-chair, unfurling three-octave electrical storms. Time shivered. Suddenly—*Bam!*—he gave a ferocious yank, stopped playing, fell back in his chair. I stopped on a slippery dime.

We stared at each other, naked. Wind raked my hair.

"I forgot I was *playing!*" he gasped, eyes crinkling, tickled. "I got so far into the groove my hands started moving by themselves!"

"You too?"

"Whoooo!" he squalled into the mike. "Thank y'all all. We gonna get back to the music presently because poor Billy Joe still ain't jumped!"

DEE DEE TOOK MY CARD on the morning after our endless night, gave me a delicious last kiss in the car, said she'd call. I waited and waited. Three weeks oozed by. Maybe her husband had come home, maybe she was afraid of getting involved. She wasn't listed in the phone book under either last name. I couldn't sit still in my apartment. I drove down to Spanish Harlem. I cruised back and forth 116th Street, up and down the three-block stretch of Madison Avenue surrounding the corner where I'd dropped her off. I didn't know her address. I wasn't going to ask around. If I was lucky I might catch her strolling with her kids.

The streets were clogged with dirty slush, dingy and dreary in March's thaw. The words "La Marqueta" shimmered on the cast-iron railroad overpass where the Harlem-Hudson line crossed 116th Street, an iridescent blue and white fish-scale pattern brought to life by stray breezes. No Dee Dee. After I'd made several slow passes by what might have been her apartment building, the guys sitting on milk crates outside the bodega next door noticed me. I veered down a side street and drove home, cruising back up Seventh Avenue through the part of Harlem I was beginning to know.

*1978.* BY THE MIDDLE of junior year, the no-girlfriend situation was getting ridiculous. I'd had a twenty-four-month drought. Except for a zipless one-night stand the first day of Freshman Week with a Rider College woman who was cruising the Princeton Inn and a brief abortive fling with one of the Smart Weirdos, I'd gotten no action. Spiral was it. The band was my life. And classes—I was an English major now, a Lit 151 survivor—and jogging. I'd take easy afternoon runs out across the golf course and into the woods next to the Institute for Advanced Study. It was peaceful out there, floating along dirt trails between vine-ribboned old trees. Lukewarm currents eddied and pooled, surprising you with the mellow tang of rotting leaves. I was reading lots of Keats these days, dwelling in all five senses, hungering for a nightingale to sing odes to.

There was one promising development. My occasional jogging buddy was a senior English major named Helen Toll, the Mystery Woman I'd bumped into at Ricky Spiller's fall of sophomore year. We'd crossed paths a couple of times since then. One winter night she and another guy—a noted campus politico—had been strolling arm in arm out of Theatre Intime when I'd walked by; she'd flashed me a sheepish guilty look. Next time was a sunny April afternoon when I was lying on the grass behind the U-Store grooving to

Canyon City Limits and she'd suddenly whirled up: barefoot, in shorts, with bits of grass in her thick dark hair. She grinned and held out her hand, motioning to me. Her bare thighs were huge, smooth, muscular. Her chest heaved under her sweatshirt. My heart was racing. I froze. She was too much. I shook my head no. Her smile wrinkled and broke up. She whirled away, dancing with another girl.

A few weeks later, during reading period, we'd passed each other at almost exactly the same spot. I stopped. We were both barefoot and wearing cutoffs, showing leg. We talked, awkwardly. She'd just finished her junior paper on coded desire in Kate Chopin's *The Awakening*. She had these dark striking eyes that flashed with stuff I couldn't figure out. Did she *like* me? I wasn't really attracted to her. I enjoyed talking with her. I'd never had a woman friend that you could just hang with and not worry about impressing.

Back on campus after the summer, we'd both ended up in the same Intro to Buddhism class. She sat next to me in lecture. She'd squeeze past me into her seat as Professor LaFleur droned on about Zen no-mind, giving off a tiny breeze of sweet fresh perfume. She'd wear tight cotton sun-dresses that made her look voluptuous, then smile awkwardly like she was embarrassed by her own body. Her lips were full, curved, hungry. She'd nibble on her pen and eye me.

We became jogging buddies. I lived in Henry Hall, she lived just across the courtyard in Lockhart; we'd rendezvous and cruise out around the edge of the golf course behind the Princeton Inn. Me following her, usually—floating along in her sweet damp backdraft as we talked about Keats and Lawrence and the senior thesis she was writing on *Women in Love*. Negative capability, the New Man and New Woman, the New Word made flesh in the fires of sacred blood-knowledge. She was a feminist, a horsewoman. She had broad shoulders and a flattish butt. Her mom was East Indian, London-bred, and her dad was mainline Philadelphia. I couldn't decide if she was cute. Her thighs were exactly the same size as mine. We compared them once or twice, sitting in my entryway afterward and cooling down, catching our breath. Her olive skin made mine look pale.

Intersession finally came around—a week's vacation between terms in late January—and I said Fuck it. The drought must end.

Campus was deserted; almost everybody had gone home, or skiing. I sat in my dorm room and made a list with two names of possible girlfriends. Helen Toll was Number Two. Number One wasn't in when I called. Fine. I worked up my nerve, heart throttling, then dialed. Helen picked up, surprised. I'd caught her thesis-ing. Was she free for dinner, ah, tonight? She was?

Dinner was canned minestrone in her room—warmed on a hot plate, served by candlelight with a baguette I'd brought. We talked until four in the morning. She had a way of narrowing her eyes and nodding earnestly when I enthused about Keats's synesthetic imagination. Weird sexual currents flickered. Nobody made a move. I was born chickenshit and would die chickenshit. At four I asked about dinner the following night. Since we were both around.

"I think I'm free," she said, relieved. "Sure."

The next night she'd found a bottle of white wine to go with the spaghetti and sauce I'd brought. We talked ourselves hoarse. By two in the morning we were lounging side by side on her bed. As three-thirty edged toward four, voices began shrieking in my head. Make your move, chickenshit! But she's a feminist! *She's* supposed to decide!

Suddenly the conversation was turning toward us, what was supposed to happen between us.

"Well," I heard myself musing out loud, "I've always felt there was three components to any relationship: intellectual, physical, and emotional. The intellectual is obviously there. I mean we can't stop talking. And"—I took a breath and stumbled on—"and I think you're cute, so the physical—"

She grinned. "I think you're cute."

"So the physical is there. The only thing we really don't know yet is the emotional. I mean I *like* you."

"I like you, too."

"I mean I *definitely* like you as a friend, and . . . um . . ." I paused. "My only worry would be that sex might somehow get in the way of the friendship we already have."

"I don't think it could hurt."

"You don't?" I stammered.

She reached out and took my hand, grinning. "No," she mur-mured.

Suddenly, after all this time, we were kissing. Her lips and tongue were incredibly alive. Her face looked different close-up. I wasn't sure what I was supposed to feel. The Helen I knew from jogs and talks and Buddhism class was dissolving, replaced by a quiet gentle strong body-being. Our sweaters and jeans were slipping off. We moved gracefully through a dozen small awkwardnesses in the flick-ering candlelight. Her large breasts sagged a little, changing shape as she lay back on the bed and pulled me to her. I didn't really know this person. Sex was never what you imagined it would be. I'd finally broken my drought, whatever else happened.

MISTER SATAN AND I had been playing together for almost five months and I'd never visited him at home. The day I quit my job at Hostos Community College, I drove over to Shakespeare Flats. His super, Mister Parker, was sweeping off the front steps.

"Hey harmonica, how you feel?"

I liked Mister Parker. He was always there when we loaded up my car—genial and self-disciplined, thickening around the middle of his janitorial forest greens, often sporting a Kangol cap. He, like a number of people in Harlem, had large vague plans for us involving Amateur Hour at the Apollo. He lived on the ground floor with a couple of his sons, one of whom, Cornelius, looked to be my age and had spent time at Rikers. I jerked my head.

"Mister Satan in?"

"He most likely in there, if he ain't gone out. Push on in."

The front rooms were dark with the shades pulled and seemed to be cluttered with old electronic equipment. Mister Satan was sitting on his bed in the tiny, well-lit back room, head down, strumming his twelve-string acoustic guitar. He brightened when he saw me, scratched his fluffy gray beard.

"Hey, Mister Gus, come on in."

"I quit my tutoring job," I announced, sliding onto his one chair. He'd propped my business card—a drawing of a Hohner harmonica with my phone number underneath—next to his rotary phone.

"What's that?"

"At Hostos, up in the Bronx."

He said nothing, lost in his own fluid finger flow and microtonal glories. His dingy white t-shirt hung loosely. His forearms—sexy, in a way—were those of a much younger man, tendons and muscles rippling under chestnut skin. The room was warm to the point of stuffiness. I unzipped and pulled off my bomber jacket.

"Your heat works better than mine."

He chuckled. "I always tell people, 'Welcome to Little Hell.' "

The walls were festooned with a fantastic assortment of hand-painted wooden mandalas—blue, red, and black, yellow, green, and white—which all seemed to have been jigsawed along the same general template, a densely interlocking pattern of circles and squares, trapezoids and moon slivers.

"Let me show you a few things I've been working on," he said.

I sat silently, watching his fingers skitter. I'd studied jazz guitar long enough before putting it aside to appreciate technical difficulties surmounted. He flowed back into strummed rhythms after a while, bittersweet seventy chord clusters thickened with droning open strings, and I felt a part of me dissolve and float downstream on a lazy, sun-dappled summer river, cicadas chittering in the trees overhead. He smiled at my murmured compliments.

"I got me a three-octave sound going on the world ain't never seen, Mister. That's the hardest thing a musician can do: get himself a brand-new sound."

"I've been practicing a lot," I said, reaching into my jacket pocket.

He shook his head, roused. "Practice ain't no good. You *practice* to be like somebody else. You *exercise* to be like you."

"Hell, when we're playing the streets every day I don't need to do a thing. Whatever I want is just Pow!—right there."

"Ain't it the truth?" He laughed, slapping my hand. "We be pickin' up a thousand pounds a day without realizing it."

"Ten dollars an hour."

"Shut up."

I smiled and lazed back, stretched out my legs in the gap between his knees and the near wall. "Anyway," I said, "I can come on down and play any day you want now that I quit my job."

"*Every* day."

"You should have seen my supervisor when I told her I could make better money on the streets."

"I hate money," he proclaimed. "Rent, welfare, and all the rest. Ain't no good in the mess. I pay Mister Parker consideration—maybe ten or twenty dollars on a day when the tip bucket been good—and that keeps everything beautiful. Otherwise I'm gonna let those sorry rich bastards out in the street hold onto what they got until I need me some."

A COUPLE OF DAYS LATER he called me at noon to say it was too windy to play. Then his voice suddenly changed.

"Listen to me good, Mister Adam," he said roughly. "I got something to say and it ain't good."

"Did I do something wrong?" I could hardly get the words out.

"It ain't what you done, it's what ain't gonna *be* done from here on in. When you came down and started playing with me back in the fall, we had a little thing going on where whatever bills came into the tip bucket, we split those right down the middle, fifty-fifty. That much is well and good. But then you got me into a thing where—"

"That's how I've always worked it with every other street musician I've ever—"

"Let me finish, Mister Adam!" he roared. "I don't give a *damn* what you've done with whoever! If something's goin on wrong, it's got to be corrected. Whatever was buried shall come to light. Greed ain't never gonna be a part of who or what I'm about. You blow harmonica, I ain't never had no problem with that. Split the bills, okay. Now. Somehow we done got bit by bit into a place where you end up coming away with half the silver, too, and thinking it *belongs* to you, and that is incorrect. I hold down the *bottom*, man! I am the dirt you walk on! I am the ground you stand on! The silver falls *to* the bottom, I *am* the bottom, and therefore the silver comes to me! Ain't no argument to be had."

Heart flooded, stricken, I tried to argue.

"It ain't for *me,* man!" he cried. "I give more silver away to my winos out on the street than you will ever know. People see me out there, they be calling out, 'Hello, Mister Satan, can I get a quarter for a cigarette please sir? Can I hold a dollar for a taste of vodka?' They know I'm good for that. God's people damned sure ain't gonna help out."

"No no no," I murmured.

"That's just how it is. The Bible says, 'Go to the hedges and the byways,' which is what we be doing together out there, playing for whoever come by. You blow a beautiful harmonica, I ain't got no complaint about that, but however. Greed is a mask for ugliness. I ain't just playing my so-and-so guitar; I'm laying down the time *below* what you blow and I got that silver coming to me. That's the truth. If you can't see it, you ain't got eyes *to* see it; I better dismiss myself from your sight and we ain't playing together no more. It's up to you. I'm damn sure gonna live my life either way."

I sat there after he hung up—panicked, furious, guilty, aching. Voices raged through my head. Ten minutes later, somewhat calmed and convinced he was basically right, I tried to call him back. A dozen unanswered rings.

THE NEXT AFTERNOON things were back to normal. Professor was there playing court jester, keeping things loose. "I love you, Satan," he chattered. "Don't say that, Satan. Don't." Mister Satan, fussing in the bucket after our profitable first set, whispered something to him about how I ought to get *more* than my share of change because of automotive expenses. I tried to give him back the fistful he pressed on me.

"At least take half," I insisted. "Tell the guys out on Seventh Avenue the party's on me."

"Shut up," he huffed, chuckling, accepting my donation with two warm hands.

Two weeks later, on a cool spring-leaning Thursday afternoon, the shit hit. He'd been bickering a lot with Professor but this was normal. He bickered with me. He had a girlfriend these days, a small, quiet, round-faced woman with large lavender-tinted glasses he'd introduced as Miss Macie. She leaned against his shopping cart, smoking as we played, watching the world go by. He handed her most of his share of the bills and change at the end of each set. He shook cigarettes out of his Kool pack and lit them for her off the glowing end of his own. I hadn't heard him bicker with her yet.

Professor and I snuck around the corner after our first long set—two kids escaping from Daddy's watchful eye—and bought a $1.59 bottle of Smirnoff's. I cracked it open and took a swig, he grabbed the paper bag and finished it off.

"Whoa," I said.

"Shut up," he said, lips pulled into a sneering smile. "Shut up. Shut up. Shut up."

"Fuck motherfucker."

"Shut up. Don't do it."

"Whooo!" I laughed.

"Be cool, Adams, and you'll be allllll right. Trust me now, I been there, I know."

He ducked into the store for another. My little taste had cooled me out. I strolled back around the corner, in my element. Boom boxes thumped and bragged, sullen and exuberant; an overdriven loudspeaker outside 125th Street Discount shouted, "Going out of business! Everything must go!" Harlem was an endless streaming parade of distractable, preoccupied people who seemed mercifully oblivious to my presence. Not every bumped shoulder is black and white colliding. Visible as I was, I'd suddenly become invisible, a part of daily life here. Maybe I'd finally relaxed. The minority of one had dissolved, vanished, an unneeded idea.

Three young kids—two boys and a girl—came up to me as I was sitting on my folding chair tuning harps before the next set. They stood fascinated as I scraped a smudge of brass powder off several reeds with a jeweler's file.

"Why you got so many, Mister?" the oldest boy asked, pointing at my open photographer's bag filled with white plastic cases and the jumble of harps I'd been using.

I let him hold the one I'd just finished working on. He turned it in his hands. The girl craned her neck, trying to see down the holes.

"I wish I could let you have it," I said gently, taking it back. "But I gotta use it right now, when we play."

The younger boy pointed at my mike. "I can do a beat-box. Can I do a beat-box on it?"

"Javon!" a woman yelled. "Michael! Get on over here!"

They spun away, the girl chasing after.

Professor floated back into view, Mister Satan and I retuned—his strings had a nasty habit of sharpening slightly when strummed hard, making me sound sour—and we kicked into another set. Professor was more vociferous than usual, windmilling as he plucked his clothesline, stepping all over Mister Satan's vocals. The groove came unstuck three or four songs in; a thundercloud swelled, darkening. We were making loud, ragged, clattering, tuneless noise. Suddenly Mister Satan ground to a stop, glaring at Professor.

"You are *drunk*, man!" he shouted. "I cannot play music if you gonna go and get drunk and show your behind up here like you running the whole damn show!"

Professor's mouth quivered, his voice a croak. "Leave me out of it, Satan, goddammit. I ain't in no mood to fuck around."

"Professor!" Mister Satan thundered, "you better—"

Professor jumped to his feet. "What, motherfucker? What better I do? Come on! You so motherfucking big and bad, Satan! What you gonna tell me I gotta do?"

Mister Satan glowered. "Do not use those words around me, Mister Bennett!"

"Come on, nigger! Motherfucking nigger!"

He was screaming now. I sat frozen, unbelieving. Mister Satan leaped up, the two men were grappling, Mister Satan grabbed Professor by both shoulders and, never striking a blow, pushed him violently to the sidewalk, holding him there as though he were an evil principle against which holy war must be made.

"You are *drunk!*" he roared in his ear. "Look where that liquor done kicked your mother-effin behind!"

Professor sat there, momentarily dazed. He staggered spluttering to his feet. "Fuck you, Satan! You got that?"

"Oh my," Miss Macie murmured.

Mister Satan strode quickly away, grabbed Professor's washtub and dragged it violently down the sidewalk with a loud scraping noise, tossing his folding wooden chair after it.

"You'll never play with me again!" he shouted hoarsely.

Professor was almost crying. "Fuck you, Satan! Nigger mother-fucker! Oh dammit. Shit. Take your hands off my goddamned bass!" He scooped up his stuff and limped away.

CHAPTER SEVEN

# DOWNHEARTED BLUES

*I've been downhearted, baby . . . ever since the day we met.*

—B.B. KING

ISTER SATAN WASN'T the only guy with a new girlfriend
that spring. I'd lucked into one of my own as March blew
through. Robyn was thirty-three to my twenty-nine—
shrewd, tender, with a hoarse sweet voice that caught at me and
held. She'd grown up in New Orleans and Guyana. She disliked
Harlem; the men up there "challenged" her. Her previous boyfriend
had been a blue-eyed blond. It pissed her off when black guys on the
street gave him shit.

A mixture of American and West Indian black, Scotch, Indian,
and Chinese, Robyn was proud of her French last name. It confused
people. She lived with her aunt at a rooming hotel near Macy's and
poured drinks at an African bar in the Bronx where they didn't
understand her. She had a mass of slippery black plaits—"platts,"
she corrected me—that rustled when I nuzzled her ear and felt deliciously clean sifting through my fingers. Her sparkling dark eyes
reminded me, hauntingly, of Helen's. She was in recovery; she'd
smoked crack only a couple of times, none recently. She gave blood
once a month and was certifiably healthy. She showed me her

donor's card. She had a trim dancer's body and dark smooth skin, which she babied with an exotic homemade lotion rich with jojoba and other essential oils, stroking upward from her bruised shins. The morning after we first made love she showed me a jagged scar twisting up the inside of her left arm. We were comparing bodies. Robyn's was gym-hardened and a battleground. When she was ten—a tomboy—she'd somehow gotten hooked on a fence. This was in Guyana, where the two attacks had happened. Local men. She smiled ruefully, shivering as my lips brushed the raised purplish welt.

"My aunt had a fit when I came home bleeding. 'Other girls play with dolls,' she told me. 'You had to get hooked on a fence.' "

WE'D MET AT DAN LYNCH one night back in January. She was sitting on a barstool as my friend John and I came in for a nightcap: cool and self-contained in her horn-rimmed glasses, nodding in time and munching on what turned out to be a very highly spiced lobster roll from an Indian restaurant down the block. John and I were drinking Glenfiddich—single malt, the real stuff—and talking blues as the band shuffled through "Bright Lights, Big City." Nat's ghost lingered as a sense of glittering late-night possibilities in the dusty beveled glow of liquor bottles rowed against the long mirror, the sharp sour smell of beer-soaked wood, yellowed publicity photos of black and white musicians taped to the walls—Harry Holt, the Holmes Brothers, Little Mike, Bill Dicey, guys with beards and balls and soul, guys I'd jammed with. You could plunge deep into the groove here, become what you'd always been. I pulled my harp out, tooted to make a point about Nat's tongue-blocking technique.

The self-contained young woman leaned toward me, backhanding her mouth for volume, smiling. "Don't stop."

She was wearing a jeans jacket over a sweater, both pushed up, and had strong hands with beautifully defined wrists, like a tennis player.

"We both play," I explained loudly, nodding at John.

The music surged and rolled. The young woman and I shouted happily at each other. She had the most adorable way of fanning her mouth between bites of lobster roll before dousing the flames with Cuervo Gold. After every song she glanced stageward and Indian-whooped, patting her small full lips: whoo whoo whoo whoo.

"You look like you read a lot," she said when I took off my glasses.

"I'm working on a novel."

"Really?"

The silvery daypack at her elbow was filled with sci-fi books—cover pictures of immense sprawling burrowing worms, brain lobes exposed as solid-state hybrids, orbiting space stations with bulbous pods.

I drove her home later, after John had taken off. We sat in my car across the street from the Herald Square Hotel and talked. She talked, mostly—cracked open the window, smoked, fanned her mouth. She was wearing scuffed red booties. Her troubles were multiple but conquerable and she spoke of them quietly and at length, voice edged with cheerful hoarseness, happy for my murmured sympathy. Her former roommate owed her big-time, her disabled aunt was a burden, her cousin had a crack problem. I switched off the car engine, then switched it back on when we got cold. Thirty-third Street was windswept and deserted. Midnight was hours ago and we hadn't yet touched.

"I was going to suggest that I come up to your place," she finally said, "but I've had too much to drink. I'd like your number, though."

Astonished, I gave her my card. She heaved her daypack into her lap. "Weekends are hell up at the bar. I'll call you the middle of next week."

"I'd like that."

Our lips brushed, sweetly. Her mouth was slightly smoky, warm, delicious, a promise to be redeemed.

"Take care of yourself," she said, slamming the door.

1978. ONE MINUTE I WAS a lonely horny twenty-year-old Princeton junior who'd just gotten laid for the first time in two years, with a woman I liked but didn't really know. Helen Toll? The next minute—three weeks later—I was a goner, dying with love. Every time we kissed, my dick jumped and I felt like crying. My throat ached. I'd stroke her thick black hair, choking. Her bladed nose, elegant trim nostrils, the perfumed curve of her jaw. Like a garden after a rainstorm.

Nobody had warned me. They don't warn you. It can't be described. Words fail. The sex wasn't sex, it was fusion with the Goddess. You thought she was just the slightest bit overweight, that first night? Her body has become the most flawlessly beautiful voluptuity imaginable: firm, fragrant, glorious, enveloping. Her warm throaty voice—curious, questing, perceptive—ripples with hunger for you, only you.

Music—nonblues—suddenly sounded different, as though I'd woken into a new world. James Taylor's larkish tenor called out as I was standing on line at the Student Center: "Isn't it amazing a man like me could feel this way?" My eyes blurred; I was a wreck. After all these years, life was *alive*.

Three weeks of candlelit dinners and electric sleepovers, sparks shooting through my fingertips, lips, and crotch; three weeks of drowning in Helen's dark melting eyes. Sex wasn't about bodies: it was about plunging *through* each other's bodies to get at something else. A cry, a shudder. Our twined souls.

NO CALL CAME FROM ROBYN. Two months went by. The small real disappointment lingered, then faded. I had enough to keep me busy up in Harlem.

Then she called—no explanation—and we made a date, went out to see some jazz at Sweet Basil, ended up just down the block from Dan Lynch at an alternative rock club called Nightingale where you stand no more than a foot from the band with kids surging around you, pressing into you, everybody smoking. A redhaired white guy in a black leather jacket and a black girl in a tight cute emerald green silk dress with a mass of rustling black plaits can clink shots of Cuervo Gold up front, sway in place, share a tequila kiss and sort of ooze together, no big thing if they slide into the piss-smelling men's bathroom later on and share a joint, nibble on each other's sweet-fumed lips, slide back out with his fingers cradling her silky hips and loud raw guitars arching skyward—Blues Traveller, the Spin Doctors, D'Tripp, local white boys and black boys hipping the bop hop, rapping the funk, stoned and rocking out, no parents around to say Turn it down!

We spent the whole next day in bed. Tangled, dozing. We'd picked up a small bottle of baby oil and a pint of Ben & Jerry's White Russian on the way uptown, at her request. She had endless legs and was gentle and amazingly strong, when we wrestled. I touched her lips with my index finger, tracing the sweet curve, hungering, suffused with lust. Dangling, tickling me, her plaits smelled clean and fresh, like windblown sheets. She stared in my eyes while we fucked. It poured straight through till dusk, the first real rainstorm of the spring.

A WEEK LATER I HAD TICKETS to a big downtown blues show—Homesick James, Honeyboy Edwards, Robert Jr. Lockwood—and a second date. I woke at dawn, heart fluttering, mourning doves cooing outside my bedroom window. Even shirtsleeves were too much; I wanted to be naked, flush with the new season. Grab your sneakers and go. Lavender water swirled, pooled, eddied out in the Spuyten Duyvil channel as I squatted on a shore rock breathing cool brackish air, tingling. A frog prince dreaming of kisses.

Evening arrived. I stopped by the Herald Square Hotel, on time. The doorman, a black guy my age, shook his head. She left ten minutes ago on her roller skates.

"That's impossible," I said.

I spun outside and called upstairs. No answer.

I came back with a beer, nursed it for endless minutes on a lobby chair. People of all kinds bounced and shuffled past. Nobody on wheels. I left her ticket and a note with the doorman and hurtled downtown, fresh beer between my legs. Who could sit still for old guys plucking guitars? My heart was its own song—a quivering, precious, raging thing—and needed no translation.

I called her from the lobby during intermission. She picked up.

A friend of hers had had a heart attack that morning. A second friend had gone into the hospital that afternoon. She'd put on her roller skates to visit him. She'd just gotten back.

"I'm sorry to hear that," I said.

"It was terrible."

"I must have just missed you. Tony said you left around six."

"Did he tell you that?"

She didn't want to shower and join me downtown. She didn't want to join me later for a drink in her neighborhood. She didn't want to apologize for standing me up. She wanted to stay in, by herself.

I fell back into my seat. A roadie with stringy hair wheeled a Fender Twin toward center stage as the house lights winked. I grabbed my coat and sprinted back to the phone. If she wouldn't at least come out and *talk* to me tonight, we were through.

There was a message on my answering machine when I got home. I played it three or four times:

*This is Robyn. I do not appreciate your bad attitude in talking to me the way you did just now, okay? You think I'm lying, but it's not about that. And I understand you did not enjoy having to deal with my problems and friends being sick, but I really wish you would cool it. You know? Because the impression you have of me is all wrong. I mean you can think whatever you want to, but I guess I am better off . . . alone. Just do me one little favor, okay? Send me your address, so I can pay you back the money I owe you. Because I really do not want any favors. Goodbye. (Icy)*

She was home the next evening when I called. I'd been wandering around Central Park all day, blowing and sweating in the dazed beautiful spring weather. She was cheerful, rueful, apologetic. She'd never gotten the message and ticket I'd left. Of course I'd be angry. The friend-in-the-hospital story was true, though. Some guy she'd grown up with; kidney failure.

"He's better today," she assured me.

We segued into chili recipes, for some reason. Her secret was beer; mine was cumin and fresh jalapeños.

"What's your birth sign?" she asked.

"Aries."

She chuckled. "That figures."

She met me that night at Dan Lynch. Pushed through the swinging doors an hour and a half late. I'd given up, again. She tossed her silver daypack on the bar next to my navy blue one—she'd been patching her bluejeans, spun around to show me the tight faded perfect butt quilted with a bandanna-red square, her plaits woven into twin ponytails and clipped together. She flashed her sweet restrained grin, eyes shining.

"I got carried away," she said hoarsely.

"I could kill you."

Heat flooded down through me as we kissed, mingling tongues; a flock of wild birds seemed to lift.

"I should've warned you I'm never on time."

"I've noticed."

She wrinkled her mouth. "You're mad at me."

"I'm happy you're here, let's put it that way."

Later, after the band fired up—George Worthmore and the Dive-bombers, a rockabilly trio—and we'd had a couple of shots apiece and danced in back next to the clacking pool table, she came clean. No sick friends, no hospital, no roller skates. Tony had lied for her. She was upstairs all the time—paranoid, suddenly, about being seen with me. It was nothing personal.

"Nothing personal!" I cried, hurting but euphoric. "Just a white guy thing!"

She groaned, apologized, put her face in her hands as tremoluxe guitar chords drenched and tugged us, gulped a mouthful of Cuervo Gold and beckoned me, pressed her warm lips against mine and squirted a brassy burning jet into my mouth. This was Dan Lynch; nobody gave a shit. She nuzzled my ear, murmuring.

"If I do come back with you tonight, we've gotta stop at my place first so I can get some clean underwear and my lotion."

The cruise across town was a dreamy float, a pause while she foraged upstairs, then the West Side Highway smoothly unfolding along the Hudson, a ribboned gift. She kissed my hand, nibbled on fingers. We stood at my kitchen counter as she plunked down a large mason jar of homemade iced tea with honey and limes, unzipped her silver daypack and bequeathed a cornucopia—cassettes of her favorites, Prince, Miles, Sade, George Michael; a sheaf of poems hand-scripted on lined yellow paper; apricot facial scrub with accompanying small loofah; a foil-wrapped bundle of Egyptian Musk incense sticks; red satin panties; two pairs of gym socks; a rolled joint; and a small stack of Polaroids: her aunt, a stocky woman in a flowered print dress, sitting in a wheelchair, benignly facing the camera. Robyn the bartender in a short black leather skirt and white blouse—surprised from the side, twisting a little, flashing her teeth, the professional with shaker upended above two margarita glasses. Niece behind aunt with arms around aunt's shoulders, almost cheek to cheek, dwarfed by her aunt's bulk.

Underneath it all was a sheer yellow bodystocking. We sat on my bed and smoked part of a joint. She'd found a candle in the kitchen and brought it in, lit a stick of incense. Her shoulder was cocoa-buttery against my lips as I teased off the strap. Time shivered, murmured, glided to a deliquescent stop, a dozen different nestlings, everything shot through with sweet tickling sparklers. "I'm just a softie," she whispered huskily, meshing fingers with mine. "I know," I murmured. "I know."

She switched on my desk light later, after the candle had burned down. She always slept with a light on, she said.

I GOT VERY sick soon after that—first a cold, then flu that blew through me like the weird March weather we'd been having, balmy calms followed by icy northwesterlies that lowered the temperature fifty degrees in a day. I huddled in bed, shivering.

I pulled myself together and called Robyn to cancel our Saturday night date. Her aunt answered the phone—a Caribbean lilt—and said, "She's dead to the world." It was three in the afternoon. She'd told me she'd be partying with an old girlfriend the night before. At six I called again and Robyn came on, congested and affectless.

"You don't sound like you're in much of a mood to go out," I murmured, coughing.

"I'm exhausted."

"Jesus, you sound worse than me."

She cleared her throat. "I need to do some laundry."

"I'd make you some Red Zinger if you were here."

"Yeah?"

"And tickle your fancy," I said, using her phrase.

She chuckled softly. "I can't talk now."

*1978.* HELEN HAD WARNED ME, the first night we slept together, about the other guy. He was a bicycle racer who trained at night; a little weird, to use her word. She didn't know him well. She'd been with him only once, wasn't planning on seeing him again. But she made me no promises. I'd pushed the issue aside. His name had come up once or twice in passing. I wasn't worried. What we had after three weeks was far beyond anything she could get from him. Love was its own guarantee, a holy thing. We'd burst into tears as we confessed ours for each other, bodies fused in a blinding fuck. "Fuck" was a Lawrencian word, she'd taught me. A New Word, for the New Woman and New Man.

Just before Valentine's Day, I spent a weekend at my grandparents in Manhattan, nursing a bad cold. It was the first time Helen and I had been apart for more than twenty-four hours since the night we'd come together. My bones ached, a love jones that clawed. I'd brought along my Telecaster and did my best to lose myself—snapping and hammering strings, wrenching slithery unamplified blues out of the thing. At midnight on Saturday I woke, sweating and feverish. Something was trying to speak through me. I'd never written a poem. By dawn I'd scribbled out my first:

If I cannot sing, you will sing for me

O guitar: six strings, silver nerves

Of steel that cry as do we both,

And more. Your solid maple neck

(On which our sinews wrestle finely tuned),

Once so alive, now old and stiff it hangs

In nickel-fretted splendor; yet hanging thus it holds

Our note aloft, alive and quivering
Like some iridescent moth that moans
To view its mate on tree trunk soft asleep.

Who is playing whom? Or do we rise together,
In essence met as different sorts of flesh
Are steamily united, united by the sweat
That flows from feeling fingers onto your skin
Of laquered wood? The sense of touch is crucial:
For like the Polyphemus, that loves and foodless dies
(Though pin-preserved and joyful still to someone else's eyes),
The magic note, that singing gift of feeling, often leaves
Abruptly. And what remains is no gesture
Of expression, or feeling now immediate,
But just a tic that nothing moves at all.

Yet we do sing, and I do touch with joy
Which finds response where one had earlier been.
We are each other's instruments.
And though you voice my inner pulse at last,
In one poetic burst of brilliant sense,
And lift me up, I lift you up as well;
And press us close, and lightly touch, and fly.

I knew it was derivative—Donne, Pope, and Keats, with B.B. King added—but I didn't care. My soul had spoken. I wanted my love to have it. Sunday evening I took the bus back to Princeton, walked through the slush to my dorm room, called Helen up, splashed across the courtyard to her entryway.

Total nightmare. She couldn't look at me. Her face was screwed up. "What's wrong?" I pleaded. Finally it came out. She'd bumped into the Other Guy at a Jadwin Gym dance on Friday night and gone back to his place.

"You *what?*" I whispered. "But you said he was weird."

"I know."

I couldn't touch her. I snatched my poem back, tore it in half.

The next hour was from some region beyond Hell. The whole week. She was a wreck. She'd cry, plead, then get cold and start talking about her freedom. I'd try to kiss her, then imagine her gazing up at Mr. Weird with the hungry dark moon-eyes. I couldn't do it. Whatever we'd shared was blasted, shattered, smeared in the dirt.

I broke up with her. Better to remember the perfect holy thing we'd had than hobble on with a part-time travesty. Freedom? She was free to see things through with Mr. Weird; I was out of the picture. She held my hand, eyes watering, as I delivered my tearful pronouncement. Then I walked out of her candlelit dorm room and her confused, messy life. My throat hurt, and not from my cold. Alone I'd been, alone I'd be. Alone was one thing I knew how to do.

That wasn't my last word, though. I had a plan.

ROBYN WAS DRIVING me to distraction; I hadn't been down to Harlem for a while. Mister Satan called a couple of times to check up. His early morning rings—seven-thirty or eight—had a certain majestic eagerness, the sound of a hot morning sun pressing on low-ered windowshades.

"Hello Mister Adam!" he rasped loudly, with audible cheerful-ness. Harlem street sounds—random ricocheting yells, a police siren, an uncanny open-air immanence—seemed to cradle the mouthpiece of whatever pay phone he was calling from.

"Hey Mister Satan, how you doing?"

"Just had my breakfast and doing beautiful."

His breakfast was sausage, two eggs over light, grits, toast, and coffee at a place he was always bragging about, run by Chinese with a black guy up front. Give him his works and he was set up for the day. Sylvia's was a ripoff; he'd scowl when I'd mention it.

"Ain't no damn way I'm gonna pay six dollars for the same two eggs I can get for three, just to make myself feel high-class."

"Their patty sausage is great, though."

"I don't doubt it." His scowl would suddenly dissolve into chuckles. "Hell, they can afford it—ripping off all the tourists the way they do."

He'd been sick himself. Caught a chill when the hurricane blew through, got a cold in his bones, played hard on the street to work it out, drank honey and milk every night before bed.

"Maybe I should try that," I grumbled. "My doctor gave me antibiotics but they're messing up my stomach."

"Damn your doctor, man!" he cried, voice crackling into my ear. "Can't no doctor appreciate what your own body was born knowing how to do! Get you a jar with a screw-top lid, pour in maybe half an inch of honey, pour some milk on top of that, shake it up good, pour in another cup of milk, shake *that* up and drink it on down and see if that don't kill your affliction dead."

A couple of mornings later the phone rang again.

"Hey Mister Adam, I want you to listen to this," he said, without identifying himself. There was a muffled bump as the phone changed hands; I could hear Miss Macie murmuring something about cigarettes. Then the sound of a strummed acoustic guitar was blossoming in my ear. I sat silently for a couple of minutes—drifting, floating, lost in a swirling indigo sea, cat's claws tugging at my throat and shoulders, a boogie-woogie processional under huge wide flat blue Delta skies. Fry me up a catfish in old bacon grease. Hushpuppy, hushpuppy ya ya ya. The spell lingered as the last chiming chord faded and he came back on.

"Ain't that pretty?"

"Beautiful! What's it called?"

"No name to it. I was just demonstrating the Tock-a-meanie guitar my little baby went out and bought me for three hundred and fifty dollars."

"Man, I could use a girlfriend like that."

"No you couldn't," he laughed. "She'd turn around and make your life a living nightmare for two weeks *just* to feel like she got her money's worth."

WE REJOINED FORCES on a breezy Saturday morning, at the grand opening of a Pioneer supermarket on Frederick Douglass Boulevard. Feverless but weak, I was coughing up yellowish gunk; Mister Satan was getting the feel of his newly expanded percussion setup—a second hi-hat cymbal paired with the one he'd had, both strapped down to a homemade wooden sounding-board. Miss Macie quietly surveyed the red-white-and-blue crepe banners over-head through huge lavender-tinted glasses, arms folded, at once pro-prietary and vaguely disapproving. She bent down slightly more often than needed to transfer bills from the open guitar case to the tip bucket. We weren't what you'd call tight and drew few listeners, but Mister Satan didn't seem to mind.

"It's a growth thing," he said, lighting a cigarette as we went on break. "Couldn't nobody guess in the old days with my little group—Mister Pancho and Mister Marvin—that I'd be firing myself from them to be working One Twenty-fifth Street alone. Come back to Harlem from St. Petersburg, Florida, after two weeks away and they done shifted indoors to the Lickety Split even though I *know* the club scene is dying. So I fired myself. I gotta be outside where the people are. There's your first stage of growth-upholdment. Then Mister Sonny Mo comes by, he's noticing I'm always tapping my foot when I play with Professor, so here he come bringing a sock cymbal some drummer left behind who moved back to South Car-olina. Took his drums but left that. Okay. So I get used to keeping the beat on one cymbal, by myself; I'm coming back into music with a whole new sound, including Professor on bass. My fish-flutter strum is coming along, too. Then you stop by with a harmonica and we got ourselves a furtheration of rebirth—still part of the growth-pattern, *but*."

"But?"

"Professor went and messed up."

"It's too bad you guys couldn't, ah . . ."

"Hell, I bought that no-good bastard enough wine last night to keep him drunk for a week. We were carrying on, too." He coughed—a smoker's harsh rumble—and spat. "He just ain't on the gig. Disrespectful profanilizing don't fly *no* kind of way with me."

"I'm sorry about my playing, by the way," I said, blowing my nose. "I can barely breathe."

"I'm *limping!*" he roared gaily. "My two feet been kicking each other so bad they done gave up the fight."

We crouched so he could show me his sounding-board. It was beautifully engineered, nailed pine slats fanning out to hold spreadable steel struts firmly in place. Two little docking ports for his guitar effects-boxes. He climbed back on his hi-chair and demonstrated: not just the brassy crash-crash of alternating cymbals, but a loud Slap! as his feet drove the sprung steel pedals hard against bare wood. A syncopated rattletrap: diggity-whappity-scratchity crash-a-smash-a!

"Damn," I said as we slapped, "we're gonna mess 'em up this summer!"

"Ain't it the—"

"Satan!" Miss Macie called, irritated. "Sa-tan! I'm over here, too, now."

"You know you are, Miss Baby."

"You want a coffee?"

"Yes please ma'am."

She scooted away and slipped into a bodega down the block.

"I hate that woman!" he roared, chuckling at his own outrageousness. "Ain't no love worth a damn without hate to back it up. Check it out." He spread his fingers, gleefully serious. "H-a-t-e is h-e-a-t. Correct or wrong?"

"Correct."

"Hate is the heat in the whole love mess." He chuckled again. "Jesus was so wrong it's ridiculous."

1978. THE BIG BREAKUP with Helen lasted less than a week. Desperate, I'd also gotten smart. Women, I'd figured, are like guys: they're gonna want what they can't have. If Mr. Weird was messing with her behind my back, why not just give up, let him have her, and turn *myself* into the Other Guy? Keep tantalizingly out of reach; style myself as the forbidden. Make her work to win me back.

She did most of her thesis writing, I knew, at a horse-postered carrel down on A-floor of Firestone Library. We'd rolled around on the carpeted floor more than once, gazed at by prizewinning thoroughbreds. So I planted myself at a desk just down the hall, next to the stairwell. Of course she eventually walked by, hesitating. I ignored her. This was hard—I was still in love—but made easier by the fact that part of me wanted to hurt and confuse her. Negative capability: the ability to be of two minds without going nuts. Keats had written about this. He had his own problems with women. Fanny Brawne, La Belle Dame sans Merci.

Within a couple of days we were talking. She'd pause at my desk, dally, ask how things were going. Flare her nostrils, flash me a helpless grin. I'd play it cool, until threads of pain seeped into her eyes. Then I'd reach up and brush her hair out of her face, letting my palm feather her cheek. She'd flinch a little, eyes melting—stricken, confused, hungry.

"I'm sorry," I'd say. "I guess I'm not allowed to do that."

Two more days and we were dragging each other down the hall to her carrel: hands everywhere, bodies electric. My eyes blurred as our tongues met; she chuckled, a half-sob. We pulled each other back across campus through the cold windy dark, hips fused. I hadn't asked about Mr. Weird; I'd been skating over my fear and hurt. Now, molten, I suddenly didn't care.

Back at her room, we tore off each other's clothes. I went crazy the way only a guy who blows harp and is dying for love can. I wanted to vaporize every last trace of anybody but me. Underneath, my heart was whimpering Please. She got even, once she'd come to. We collapsed at dawn, my face buried in her thick damp hair, nestling like contented gerbils.

She saw Mr. Weird later that same day, a prescheduled date. It didn't go well. What did she have left? A week later she'd dumped him. We were sitting upstairs in the Cloister Club library after Sunday brunch, holding hands on her lap. Early March sun poured in, bathing us. Silverware clattered on trays downstairs. She was mine, she said. Beloveds. She'd always chosen her words carefully. This time it was a promise.

IT SEEMED LIKE the perfect strange way to begin my twenty-ninth year. A very early Sunday morning date with Robyn.

She was tending bar at Club Djoniba in the Bronx on Saturday night. We had it all arranged. I went to bed at ten, got up at four-fifteen—alarmed awake—and fell into the shower. She called at exactly four-twenty-five from a pay phone next to the ladies' room.

The April skies were purple-black when I hit the street, the air calm and freshly scrubbed. I walked downhill toward Indian Road past a row of young leafless trees. A lone bird chirped loudly, with fairy-tale purity. Something—a breathless spirit—pulled me past my car and out across the dewy grass of Inwood Hill Park to the edge of the salt marsh, fringed with low weeds. Several ducks loitered quietly, paddling in circles, ignoring my quiet quack. The morning darkness hovered, hushed and trembling, obscurely holy. Shivering, I turned away and walked back to my car.

White Beamers and Benzes veered crazily on the Cross Bronx Expressway, windows cracked, salsa and rap blaring as they honked and flashed me, careening by. This was the first time I'd ever exited at Jerome Avenue. I floated downhill under elevated subway tracks past auto junkyards accordioned with barbed wire. Club Djoniba had a red awning stretching to the sidewalk and livery cabs idling two deep. I pulled up to the curb; several bouncers with shaved heads glared at me, or seemed to. People coming through the front doors were dressed for Saturday night—hair faded and gelled, lots of shiny black shoes—and scurried a little under violet skies suddenly lightening at quarter to five.

She leaned out, saw me, waved, ducked back inside, then trotted toward the car and I let her in.

"Do you have any money?" she asked, tossing her daypack in the back seat. "I can get us a bottle of champagne for ten dollars."

She came back a couple of minutes later, dangling it like a club. She had two little vials of coke, too. Birthday treat.

"We're the story of the night," she chuckled, swinging her plaits out of her face. "My girlfriends were curious."

"What did you tell them?"

Her tongue was alive, swirling, velvety.

"Mmm," I murmured.

"He's taken," she said, pulling my hand onto her thigh.

We were sitting on the floor of my living room later with most of the champagne gone and bright pearly light cutting under my lowered shades, snorting coke off one of the slim metal files I used to tune my harps. The day was blurring toward mid-morning. You blink after each snort, head inflated with rubbing alcohol fumes, ready to rock. Like café express followed by a chugged Heineken, my Parisian busker's recipe. Robyn was telling me about blowing her tips on the stuff, then going to Cocaine Anonymous meetings. I thought she and I had a lot in common.

"I feel funny about getting high around you," she said.

"Don't."

She snorted, half-smiling. "You're so healthy."

"You should have seen me three years ago. Total homebody."

I veered into the bedroom, pulled my Portable Blake off the shelf.

"Look," I said, flipping open to *The Marriage of Heaven and Hell*. " 'You never know what is enough unless you know what is more than enough.' "

She sighed. "My cousin Mark has a real problem." She reached into her silver daypack for cigarettes, fumbled with matches.

I looked up. "What's that?"

"Selling my aunt's television and shit. It's gonna kill her."

We were sharing fantasies as the champagne ran out. Hers was to win the lottery and relocate to a desert island with her aunt. Only come back to the world when she felt like it. Also: to go camping sometime, just the two of us. I told her I knew a beautiful spot up in Harriman Park, next to a stream.

"I'll make you freeze-dried chili," I said. "And pan-bread. You ever have pan-bread?"

"Uh uh."

"Cornbread in a pan, over the coals. And I'll protect you from the last surviving mountain lion. No wine or reefer, though. First time up there we definitely have to go clean. I swear it'd break my heart if we didn't."

"Man," she said suddenly.

"What?"

Her eyes gleamed. "I just like the *shit* out of you."

We flowed into the bedroom, shedding clothes. Her smooth brown back smelled like cinnamon. An animal musk—fruit of twined souls—rose from the sheets afterward as we settled dozily, cheek to beating heart, her plaits tickling my face.

We went for a walk that afternoon—down around the salt marsh, up along the wooded trail that circled Inwood Hill. My hand fit nicely in the back pocket of her black leather pants; we'd stripped to shirtsleeves in the yearning warmth. Gray winter woods had suddenly sprouted a brilliant green underzone flecked with jonquils: lemon-chiffon yellow, hovering on long stalks like squawky antique telephones. She followed as I left the trail and skittered downhill, ducking through a fence with chain-links ripped aside and clambering across an abandoned railroad right-of-way.

"Don't get hooked!" I joked.

This was my spot. The Hudson River was huge here, swirling and purling in the wash of Spuyten Duyvil, pouring north to the Tappan Zee Bridge—a thin beaded line—like roughened molten lavender with briny undertints. We flopped on the grassy bank. Robyn leaned back in my arms. Water sucked at the rocks below, gently rocked the rusting upended carcass of a car somebody had ditched the previous spring.

"Where are we?" she murmured.

"Upper end of Manhattan Island. The thirteenth mile."

The sun caressed our faces, warmer than you'd expect on April 3rd. Our nestled bodies seemed to melt into one drowsy delicious thing with strawberry blond hair and rustling black plaits. She stretched after a while, yawned, reached for her jeans jacket.

"I hope you don't mind," she said, smiling sheepishly as she fingered out one of the coke vials.

I hesitated, not happy, then mimed shock. "You are *so* bad."

"That's what they say."

All the colors crisped slightly, like a hyperrealist painting. She sighed as she curled back into my arms, then turned suddenly and stared hard at me, eyes impossibly sincere, searching.

"Adam, do you think we have a chance?"

"I'm scared," I said quietly, pulling her close.

She started, hand touching her chest. "I know what you mean."

Later, heading back to civilization—we'd just reached the top of the dirt bank above the railroad right-of-way—she suddenly cackled, "Let's race!"

We were neck and neck for the first hundred feet, skimming through the woods on crumbled curving macadam, laughing and cursing, playground-crazed. Then she fell away and I was flying alone, heard the thump and her grunt and yanked myself to a stop, spun to see her spreadeagled, down hard. I ran back, heart thudding. She'd gouged both palms and scraped her elbow. Her crimson blood, mixed with dirt, was already pooling. I cradled her to me, crying inside, trying to help her up.

"Oh man," she groaned, smiling weakly. "I'm such a klutz."

# CHAPTER EIGHT

# "LA BELLE DAME SANS MERCI"

*Whom do you love better than you love me?*

—SAPPHO

IN RETROSPECT, THAT was the high point. Things started to come apart a couple of weeks later.

We were in my car—it was late afternoon, I was driving Robyn home down the West Side Highway after lunch at All-American Burgers near Columbia. Cheeseburgers were our shared passion. Usually we had them late at night after too much tequila at Dan Lynch; we'd careen down Second Avenue past St. Mark's-in-the-Bouwerie and Veselka, kicking at windblown newspapers, the perfect chocolate-and-vanilla swirl of a Village couple—ignoring the looks we drew but sensing them anyway, faint shivers of resentment, indulgence, and sexual curiosity unsettling the night air. Dan Lynch was the only public place in New York where we could effortlessly be the unit we were, although nobody actually said anything anywhere else. Racial paranoia is a tricky call: either you're picking up loud and clear on a vibe somebody is radiating—Hands *off*, white boy!— or your uneasy mind is making up the vibe and projecting it onto somebody who couldn't care less. Or else both are going on, in a series of infinitely subtle recirculating blends. Robyn's term for us was a circus: "We're such a circus," said with a wry smile. She seemed to have gotten over her anxieties. I always felt a vague cringing empathic defensive stab—a kind of quadruple consciousness— when we'd stroll past a homeless black guy shepherding his sidewalk array of battered worthless paperbacks, broken clock-radios, mismatched sandals. What did he see when he glanced up? In another context—the streets of Harlem—he might have been my audience; I'd have been doing my best to entertain and impress him with gut-wrenched notes. Introduced by Mister Satan between sets, we'd have been slapping hands and bonding in shared hot-souled derision of those bastards out in Howard Beach. Becoming *realer* to each other. Now look at us: I was stealing one of his women, aggravating the blues I imagined he had. Or maybe he'd given up on the Black Woman because she'd given up on the Black Man. Maybe he preferred blondes. Which meant I was taking a potential problem off his hands. Maybe he was gay—prison-skewed—and wanted *my* strawberry-blond ass. Maybe I was hot for him and couldn't admit it and was projecting like mad. America! The whole thing was a mess and should have been called off years ago. But here we were.

We were in my car, as I was saying—driving Robyn home, in a cheeseburger-and-Cokes mood. She was warming into one more story, delivered in a tough-girl voice, about fighting. These always troubled me. I found it much easier to murmur and kiss her forehead while she told me about having been assaulted as a child in Guyana. I found it hard to relate to stories in which she deliberately inflicted pain with her hands. There were two Robyns, it seemed. The non-softie was telling me about how she and her girlfriend had torn up some coffee shop after some ugly bitch who'd been hassling her all night hassled her one too many times.

"So my girlfriend and I came back the next day, right?" she said. "We were like, This ugly bitch must be *crazy* to fuck with us. She was a crack-house whore, too. We skated on over—it was maybe ten o'clock at night and we knew she'd be hanging out, styling and profiling, 'cause that's what everybody does before the Palladium. My girlfriend had a gun in her jacket and I had a knife strapped to my leg—"

"Wait a minute, Robyn!" I cried. "I don't want to hear this!"

Her eyes, glowing with gusto, quickly cooled. She seemed puzzled.

"I mean I'm not trying to shut you up, but this shit—it's just hard to sit here and listen to you go off on somebody like . . . like you're *enjoying* fucking them up. I mean it hurts. It's against everything I believe in. I mean Dr. *King*, for chrissake—all his preaching about loving your neighbor and I have a dream. He'd say the same thing. You know? We're better than this."

She sat there silently, eyes cool and dark, not looking at me. Adam, I thought, you are an idiot. I rubbed her thigh, despairing.

"Look, I'm sorry. I'm not trying to come down hard on you, I'm just . . . I don't know. Maybe because of how nice it's been, whatever, maybe I'm a little sensitive. I'm sorry, okay? I'm sorry."

"Don't worry about it."

"I mean things have been so nice, I'd hate to, you know . . ."

She had a cigarette lit, was rolling down the window.

"Yeah," she said.

A FEW NIGHTS AFTER THAT we went to see *Lethal Weapon* and strolled out in a lovely mood. She'd had the hots for Mel Gibson ever since *Mad Max,* and I thought Danny Glover put up with more shit from Mel than any one human should. Talk about edgy comedies! New York's beaten down sidewalk trees were sprouting white buds, May Day was around the corner. Then she called home—a nervous habit—and found out her cousin Mark had gone on a freebasing binge after pawning his live-in girlfriend's stereo, punched somebody out, and been thrown in jail overnight. Robyn fell apart. My heart ached. We went on a Cuervo bender at Dan Lynch—Moose and the Bulletproof Blues Band, a funk quartet—and ended up sitting in my car across the street from the Herald Square Hotel until five in the morning. She raged, she cried; I wiped her tears away, guts coppery-sour from too much tequila. Time unfolded. She had something she wanted to tell me. I gently coaxed and it came out: she was thinking of having a kid. If she got pregnant, she was going to keep it. Our kid.

"Our kid?" I whispered, chilled. "I thought you said you couldn't get pregnant."

She sniffed. "I haven't in eight years."

We hadn't been using any protection. She'd shown me her blood donor's card; I'd trusted her, she'd trusted me. Condoms got in the way of closeness. We'd both wanted that.

"Wait wait wait," I said, feeling the ghost of frantic Woody Allen rise up. "Robyn, this is crazy. I mean, if we're still together in a year—and I hope we are—and we *decide* we want to have a kid, great. But we, we're . . ."

"I'm not seeing anybody else."

"Neither am I, it's just—I mean it's only been what, like two months? Christ, I can't support a kid! And that isn't even the point. I mean this is something we ought to do *together*, if and when the time is right."

Her eyes dulled. She reached for her cigarettes. "It probably won't happen anyway, knowing me."

We sat there in the cold, silent car. It was very late. She bit her lip.

"Hey," I said softly, taking her free hand, "there was a moment early on when I wondered if I'd met the woman I was going to marry. I really did. We still have a chance," I added. The moment the words came out of my mouth I knew I was lying, and hated myself.

She said nothing, smoking quietly. In profile she could have passed for an Egyptian queen, with her softly flared nose and bronze cheekbones, her firm jaw, plaits dangling like a beaded curtain between rooms.

"That peacefulness in bed. I know we both felt that." My throat caught. "I *hope* you still feel that."

"I do," she murmured hoarsely.

I WAS PROWLING the East Village a few days later—harp cupped, fiercely preoccupied—when I ran into Canarsie Kenny, who was just coming out of a Narcotics Anonymous meeting on St. Mark's Place, that zoo of a block between Second and Third avenues where everybody either sells, uses, used to use, or is being loudly propositioned.

"Hey harmonica!" he barked. Then he pulled his out and started wheezing. He sang ten songs in a row before letting me go. "I been clean for sixty-three days," he announced. "I was off the stuff for two and a half years before that but I slipped."

That was how we always met up. Kenny was a raw, feral white guy from the wilds of Brooklyn with a crew-cut bullet head, large thick glasses, lips curling into a friendly sneer, a case-hardened chest, a massive diaphragm clamping down over his belly, and shape-less hips. His legs were slightly bowed. Every time I bumped into him his crotch-wear had changed—white gym trunks, gray sweatpants, candy-blue Spandex cycling shorts—but his dangling penis was still there, making its gobbling turkey-necked presence felt behind every fabric. His hero was Howlin' Wolf—"The Wolf," as he called him. He sang exactly like the Wolf, insofar as a thirty-five-year-old white Brooklynite could do that. He had the same pinched huge Southern-nightmare-of-a-beast-prowling-in-the-woods kind of voice, some-thing gravelly and nasal and sexually ravenous crackling through an old AM car radio. He tilted stiffly from side to side when he sang and played, stamping his feet, cheeks trembling, sweat pouring off. "Whooooo-oooooo!" he'd howl. "I'm a Cadillac daddy, gonna riii-iide wimma baby tonight...."

Kenny disappeared from the scene a few years back. Somebody told me he was dead, but I doubt it. He knew who he was; he'd pound his chest for emphasis. He thought of himself as my *black* artistic conscience. He knew Nat and wasn't impressed.

"Nat can't sing for shit," he'd say. "He's got da tone, all right. Hell yeah. I ain't gonna take nuttin' 'way from Nat there. But I got duh *tone,* you know what I'm sayin'? I ain't got but one thing, an' dat's *it.*"

He always seemed to pull the same rusted beer-soaked old Marine Band D harp out of nowhere the moment he saw me, get right up in my face and go at it. His reeds were hopelessly flat, a jum-bled mouthful of bad teeth that would have bothered me if he hadn't meant every note. He'd stare you down through those big ugly glasses. These might be his last few notes on Earth before some motherfucker cut his heart out and they were aimed at *you.*

Once, when Kenny was blowing through an old Mouse in front

of the Astor Place Cube and I jogged across to say Hi, he stopped in mid-song and made me play for him. This was the fall of 1985; he'd kept his eye on me that summer, heard me sit in with Nat. I whipped out my harp and threw down some fast looping Sugar Blue stuff. He bent his stiff back a little and listened, hand cupped ostentatiously: give it to me, baby. Then he nodded.

"You got that high-note shit down," he said. "But you ain't got no vibrato."

"I'm doing it from my throat, the way Nat—"

"Gimme your hand."

He took it and flattened my palm against his damp t-shirt so I could feel his belly underneath. He lifted his harp with the other hand and played one strong low note. His solar plexus, warm under my hand, heaved smoothly and massively; the note quivered like an endless deep sob.

"Feel that?" he said, finally letting go.

"Wow. With your diaphragm."

"You like my tone? I got good tone, right?" He was suddenly insecure, hungry, eyes narrowing behind huge glasses.

"Aw hell, nobody hits it harder."

He grinned crazily, then cupped harp and mike. "Good mawnin' little schoooool girl . . . good mawnin' little schoooool girl . . ."

My hand tingled as I walked away.


*1978*. THE SPRING OF JUNIOR YEAR, once I'd won Helen, was as close as I'd ever come to heaven.

Princeton was thawing and budding, blossoming into a fragrant dazy garden. I had a girlfriend—brilliant, sensual, tantric—and a band. Spiral was tighter and wilder than ever, a cresting surge of heart behind Debbie's soulful throat. Scott booked us into the Student Center, then put the word out; a black-and-white dance-thing happened, surprising everybody but us. Who else on campus was covering Chuck Mangione, Stevie Wonder, Patti LaBelle, the Average White Band? We played the back terrace of the Princeton Inn one late April cocktail hour, overlooking the golf course. My old woodshed downstairs was a memory; my new girlfriend, in shorts, had kicked off her sandals and was shaking her hips, flexing her bare shoulders as I swayed and funky-strummed. Up from the stereo room! Scott thumb-popped his Gibson Ripper bass; Chad, grimacing, wrenched an ocean of spider-fingered chords out of his Fender Rhodes. Our sound swelled and poured across the velvety green, wafting toward the Grad College clock-tower, dissolving into the first lingering dusk of Daylight Savings Time. Everything was going my way.

Just behind perfection was looming heartache. I was a junior, Helen was a senior. She'd just won a fellowship to Paris, nine months at the Sorbonne starting in September. These next few months were all we had. We held nothing back. We were suicide-pact Aztecs dragging each other to the top of the pyramid at Chichén Itzá. Here's the knife, here's my rib cage. You first.

The perfect aching spring ended with a perfect aching weekend in mid-May. I'd just taken my last final—an intensive Milton course, the twelve books of *Paradise Lost*—and was through with literature for the summer. Life! I took the bus into New York Friday evening, caught a cab to Helen's aunt's duplex on Central Park West. Gayatri, away in London, had given us free rein for the weekend. Helen met me at the door—barefoot, in a diaphanous sari, braless. Our fused tongues seemed to remake the world. I kicked off my sneakers and socks. She pulled me barefoot across cool white tiles into the kitchen. She poured me chilled white wine out of a large green bottle with a French name. She fed me Brie smeared on crackers. We fed each other. The hair around her temples was soft as rabbit fur. She pulled me into her bedroom. My toes sank into fluffy white carpet. She ran a bath for us, just behind a mirrored door. We stripped off our clothes. We climbed in, awkward. We were nothing but flesh, olive and pale. Kisses made us okay. We soaped each other: thighs, calves, feet, bellies, shoulders, the cock and cunt Lawrence had renamed.

Later, still damp, we lay on her bed in the darkened room. Random taxi-honks filtered up from below, wafting through the open window. The apartment felt spacious, airy. Summer was beginning.

I'd dissolved into We. A huge beating heart had burst, perfuming the world with an invisible fluid, filling it.

Saturday morning was fruit salad and coffee in the kitchen, bare feet against cool tiles. Hand in hand we strolled down through Central Park, a sun-dappled swoon under tender new leaves. Saturday afternoon was hot Italian sausage at the Ninth Avenue Food Fair, honey-drenched baklava from the Poseidon Bakery. Miles we'd strolled, from Eighty-fifth Street down to the Port Authority Bus Terminal. Suddenly, on a whim, we were catching an early evening bus back to Princeton.

We tumbled off at Nassau Street and floated down through the darkened campus, stopping off at her dorm room for our sleeping bags. The golf course was calling. Who needed shoes? Barefoot, we padded out across lukewarm flagstones, the warmer macadam of Alexander Road, the cool sandpapery concrete sidewalk in front of McCarter Theater, more warm macadam, then back onto smooth dusty stone. The walkway curled down toward the Grad College, disappearing into clumped pines. She pulled me left onto the golf course. It was dark except for the faint glow from a spotlight on the Princeton Inn roof. Cool grass feathered my toes; lukewarm air-currents eddied, a rich fertile earth-smell.

She pulled me toward a small glimmering pond, one of the course's various traps.

"Let's swim," she said, dropping her sleeping bag.

"In the *pond?*" I said.

"Uh huh."

"Are you crazy?"

She grinned and yanked off her tank top. Her breasts splayed, free.

"Somebody'll see us!" I hissed.

"So what?"

She slipped off her shorts and panties together. I stood there—paralyzed, amazed. She turned and stepped into the pond, made a small startled sound, then waded in. Sank to her neck in dark fluid and stood up: a pale dripping vision. Her back was a complex curve. She turned and grinned. Her breasts swayed, nipples hardening.

"Come on, Adam."

I stammered. A silent sob burst through me. I stripped off my t-shirt, hesitated, then waded in. The dark water was lukewarm. Cool mud sucked at my toes. I waded toward her, squishing. Little sticks pricked my soles. The pond tickled as it flowed up past my hips. I sank to my knees, head even with her belly. Her thighs were smooth under my hands, slippery. She arched her back in the scattered dim light. Her nipples tasted pondy. I shivered as I pulled away. Her whole body was glowing.

I WAS SINGING A LOT, that first spring up in Harlem. Mister Satan, struggling with his twin stomp-cymbals, was happy for the help; I was in desperate need of outdoor unburdening as summer's warmth flooded in early, sweet and polleny and wrong, a promise flung back like a slap. Robyn was my muse, the sweet little angel who'd tumbled out of whatever sky I'd imagined her into. I'd hungered for her, thrown my heart at her; I'd certainly loved the *idea* of her, and us. I sat in the folding chair Mister Satan had given me, closed my eyes, made myself a public spectacle. The older men yelled me on. "Give It Up," "Next Time You See Me," "Key to the Highway": I'd do six or seven songs an afternoon, verses meshing like jigsaw puzzle-pieces:

Baby I'm crazy about you . . . don't like the way you do
Always mistreat me . . . say you love me too
Someday you'll want me . . . and I'll be so far from you
Then you'll be sorry baby . . . to do me like you do

Well I told you pretty baby . . . such a long time ago
If I found you with another . . . I'd have to let you go
You might call me crazy . . . but there's one thing you should know
If you want me to love you . . . got to give it up or let me go

Next time you see me . . . things won't be the same
Next time you see me . . . things won't be the same
And if it hurts you my darlin' . . . you only have yourself to blame

Well bye bye babe if I don't see you no more
Bye bye babe if I . . . don't see you no more
You know I love you girl . . . can't stand to see you go

I'm goin out walkin' . . . walkin' down through the park
I'm goin out walkin' . . . walkin' down through the park
I'm gonna walk through the moonlight . . . walk until the night is dark

I'd warm up at home before I drove down to Harlem—grab a harp and run into the bathroom to holler and wail, hone my blue notes to knifing sharpness until the old white lady on the floor below me flushed her toilet in an explosive infuriated rush. One time she pounded on my front door, then stood there trembling. "What's that smell?" she shrieked. I assumed she was referring to the heady urethane fumes wafting up from the second floor, where an apartment was being refinished. I invited her in to look around. "I won't come into your apartment!" she shrieked, backing up. A few weeks later the landlord and super showed up—there'd been a complaint—and asked if they could take a look. They found nothing and left, apologizing. Turned out the old white lady had told them I was manufacturing and distributing crack cocaine.

ROBYN HAD DISAPPEARED. I called Sunday afternoon of May Day weekend and got her aunt. "No, she's not here," her aunt said, surprised. "I thought she was with you." I'd seen her last: picked her up at Club Djoniba early Saturday morning, shared a joint at my place, et cetera. I'd driven her back to the Bronx for the Saturday night shift.

I left several messages over the next two days, when I wasn't out singing. Robyn finally called on Tuesday afternoon. She'd just gotten home and had a bad cold. Her voice sounded dead in a way I'd heard once or twice before—nullified, rather than chilly or bitter or grieving or, God forbid, sparkling with beautiful crazy dreams.

"I had to get away for a little while," she said.

"Christ, I was worried sick."

"Don't worry, I wasn't in danger, I wasn't"—she paused—"laying up with anybody."

"I didn't think you were."

She coughed. "I do plan on telling you and my aunt where I was, eventually."

She told me about the crack house later, when I came downtown to watch a movie on cable with her. Her blind aunt had gone out. She huddled on the couch, wrapped in a blanket, eyes watery. I was happy to see her; I was crying inside, a familiar feeling. I knew who I was when I felt like this. I held her hand, rubbed some warmth into her socked feet. She smelled clean and fresh, windblown, like an ad for Tide or Cheer with special brighteners. She'd always had a thing about clean laundry. Sometimes she'd take a couple of shirts or sweater of mine home with her and return them folded, sweet-smelling, perfect.

She'd watched people. That's all: smoked rock, spent her pay, kicked back in a chair, and watched. Thought about things. A couple of assholes asked her out but she didn't go there. The place was shadowy and overheated; nobody touched her. There were different rooms you could walk through. When her money was gone she borrowed a subway token and came home.

WE COULDN'T GO ON; we kept going on. But things had changed. The dream was dead, although it had a brief afterlife.

One night in early May we split a pint of Cuervo Gold in my car on badly lit Thirteenth Street, with gangly junkie-musicians skulking past in black leather jackets. Robyn was talking about her and me taking a summer road trip into the South, flaunting our affection, messing with white and black heads. "I don't know *what* we'll do to people down there," she said, eyes shining. "Which is why we *have* to go." I fell in love all over again; her musky golden breath was my heart's singing fix. We breezed around the corner into Dan Lynch, had a couple of Rolling Rocks, danced to slashing guitar blues—Bobby Radcliff, a white player who'd apprenticed himself to Magic Sam out in Chicago—and sat at the bar watching big black

Kenny, headwaiter and presiding spirit, put the moves on one more tall pretty blonde.

I never knew Kenny's last name. He was an ex-cop, people said; he had a neatly trimmed beard. Bearish as a football linebacker, yellow pencil stuck behind his ear and a swelling fistful of bills clutched in one hand, he flowed like a force of nature into and out of Dan Lynch's various smoky corners—fielding shouted orders for beers and shots, mopping up spills with a damp white rag, dovetailing his hands and slicing through the human bottleneck that invariably formed between the main bar and the little drink-ledge-with-stools corralling the band. Kenny had a fetish about keeping his center lane clear. He'd raise his voice impersonally and irritably, drop his big hands on errant shoulders and relocate people. "Keep the aisles *clear*, guys!" he'd bark. It was one of his two sacred rules. The other was his absolute right of dominion over tall pretty blondes. Every time you'd turn around, Kenny would be back near the pool table, enfolding a different giggling catch in his warm massive bearhug. Most of them had come with boyfriends, twentysomething white guys. Nobody took offense. Sometimes, when a woman was alone, he'd slip both hands in her butt-pockets and dance her slowly into the clear—swaying a little, grinding gently. There might be long probing kisses. Then—snap!—it was back-to-work time and he'd straighten up, smile, lumber smoothly away, and get uptight all over again about keeping his center aisle clear. One day, after years of steady service, he disappeared. A busy weekend's receipts had, coincidentally, been cleaned out of the downstairs safe. His credit card bill showed up at the bar a few weeks later, detailing a cross-country run to Vegas—on the lam from mob loansharks, according to the F.B.I. That was all we knew, until he dropped Karola a postcard from the L.A. County Jail, asking for his old job back. She tacked it up behind the bar. Our Kenny!

I thought he was an essential part of the place, uptight as he was. Robyn disagreed. "He wears his cock on his forehead," she sneered as we watched him home in. Her final word.

On this particular night we got back to my car and discovered that I'd left my keys dangling in the ignition. We stood there, high but descending, peering through the windows after yanking on the locked doors. Robyn knew these streets. She sprinted off to find a car thief, returning ten minutes later with six, all of whom were willing to break in and claim the twenty-dollar reward I'd offered. One white guy, two black guys, two Hispanic guys, and a butch black girl. Coat hangers, screwdrivers, ice picks. They stared sheepishly at me, not quite believing.

"Just don't break any windows, guys," I said.

All six jumped on the thing. Their ferocity and ingenuity were instructive and depressing. Nobody was having much luck when a patrol car suddenly rolled up. My crew paused; everybody eyed everybody.

"It's my car, officer," I said.

The cops were cool. "The locksmith around the corner will charge you a bill, a bill and a half this time of night," one of them grunted.

A huge Hispanic security guard from a building just down the block waddled up as they rolled away, offering us the use of his baseball bat.

"Check it out," he said, motioning at my rear quarter-panel window.

"Whoa," I said.

The butch black girl with the screwdriver finally did it. I'd given her and the white guy permission to rip out the driver's side lock. I slapped a twenty-dollar bill in her hand and another in the white guy's. She disappeared down the block. I bought a celebratory dime-bag of pot from the young black guy with the coat hanger. Robyn and I stopped off at Famous Ray's on our way crosstown—one slice each, ropy delicious Mozzarella with clear reddish oil pooling—and ended up in her living room, where we smooched while her aunt slept behind the closed bedroom door. This was Robyn's night to stay in. I worked the uptown plead, fruitlessly. There always comes that moment when the night must be rejoined, alone. We still hadn't toked. As I was pulling on my coat she asked if I could spare enough pot for a joint.

"Wait a minute," I said irritably. "You wanna kick me out and *then* get high?"

"That's not what I said."

"Nah, man, that's wrong."

Her eyes flashed cold. "What's so wrong about it?"

I was chilled when I hit the street. There was a message on my answering machine when I got home, but she'd said everything before and I listened only once. I smoked a big bowlful, lying in bed. I started shivering so badly I thought I was going to die. I shuddered into the bathroom, ran a tubful of hot water, and lowered myself, sinking down and down into the blanching, burning heat, teeth chattering.

IN THE MIDDLE OF ALL THIS, Nat suddenly decided to pay a visit. He hadn't been back to New York in fifteen months, since the shooting outside Dan Lynch. I had a pickup gig with a random guitarist at a Village club called the Speakeasy; I'd called and left a message with Esther down in Norfolk. His return call was joyously vehement, the Nat I knew.

"I *will* be there," he said. "I've already told my supervisor on the garbage truck I'm taking Friday off."

"Don't get in trouble just for me."

"They *know* me, Adam. If I've been doing good, hard work for you, showing up at the garage by quarter to seven every morning and never complaining no matter what the weather, you'd have to be a fool to tell me no. And they know it." He laughed richly, with edge. "I'll be there."

A couple of mornings later I drove out to his sister's housing project off Bruckner Boulevard in the Bronx. Angled sun glinted off my side mirrors, wiper blades, every chrome surface; lukewarm wind slapped at my dangling arm. You could feel summer about to settle in. I rolled into into a huge half-filled parking lot, pulled up next to his dented blue Toyota—the trunk was popped—and got out to see him slumped in the front seat. He glanced up as I came around. He wasn't happy. I couldn't tell what he was.

"Don't get me started," he said.

"What's up?"

He leaned back against the headrest and fixed me in his eyes. "I have the shirt on my back, the pair of pants I'm wearing, and my sandals. And my underwear." He jerked his head at the open trunk. "Kids around here see Virginia plates, they know you're carrying. I should have unloaded last night."

"Nawwwww. . . ."

"Harmonicas, microphones. Shoes. Three pairs of shoes. I don't even have a comb."

"Fuck, man."

We stared at each other. Half a dozen mingled thoughts seemed to flow. Suddenly we were chuckling.

"Well other than *that*," I said, "how the hell are you?"

He flashed his wire-retained tooth as we grabbed hands. "I'm alive and here."

"I guess it coulda been worse."

"Where's my welcoming committee?" he laughed. "You my welcoming committee?"

"Welcome to New York. Now get the fuck out."

"I love it," he said. "I told Esther I was coming the minute I heard you'd called. The timing was right."

"The folks down at Lynch's will flip when they see you."

"I mean it hurts," he sighed, creaking open the door and getting out. "I ain't lyin'. I had some nice shoes."

WE CARAVANNED BACK TO INWOOD. I gave him a small stack of t-shirts with blues themes—B.B. King's 50th Album, Blind Pig Records—and a pair of old sneakers, athletic socks, an unopened toothbrush. The comb I had to give him wouldn't work on his hair. He looked better in my t-shirts than I ever had; a natural nobility in his erect dancer's carriage. I flipped open the steamer trunk in which I'd tossed fifty old harps with one sorely flatted reed apiece and we blew through them until we'd assembled a workable set. Retired harps are musty and always taste like somebody else's. I'd been too fastidious: we found three almost new Marine Bands with nothing wrong except stiff, unresponsive reeds. Nat cradled one between his long fingers and eyed me, squinting slightly as he bore down. It yelped. It *spoke.*

"Shit," I said.

"Ask anybody," he said. "Bob Shatkin, Danny Russo. Whatever kind of trash-harp you put in my hands. I always had that ability."

"How are you getting—there's a kind of *thwup* sound you're getting on the Two Hole Draw. . . ."

"It's a tongue thing. Put your tongue on the hole."

"On the hole. . . ."

"*Against* it. Right up on it." He pulled his lips away so I could see the tip of his tongue flattened against the wooden reeds.

I did that.

"Now pull it off."

Boing!

"Damn!" I did it another five times, a kid with a new trick.

He was beaming. "Very good, Little Cricket," he rasped playfully. "Soon you will be ready to do battle."

*1979.* PLAYING BLUES HARMONICA in the Paris Metro when I flew over for Christmas was Helen's idea. She'd mentioned it a couple of times in the letters we'd been hemorrhaging all fall. Hers were sky blue aerograms—one onionskin sheet lined with scribbles, stained with tears, perfumed with a translucent spot of sandalwood, then folded into thirds, licked, sealed. Three or four a week, an accumulating stack under my senior-year mattress. Crying while writing wasn't hard, I'd discovered. All you needed was a pen, some free time between classes, and the name of the woman fate had wrenched out of your arms. Helen, Helen, Helen.

The only way I could keep our love alive while finishing up at Princeton, I'd decided, was to bleed onto the page. Reread her latest letter until I had a knotted aching throat, then let it flow. Goaded, she'd find a few minutes in her busy Sorbonne schedule to start a reply, then finish late at night. Her precise felt-tip handwriting would slowly unclot, thin out, smear into despairing adoration for her Adam. Oh God, she'd sigh. She wanted me deep in her womb. Some letters were more detached, describing the strange new life she'd been plunged into. Couscous at Tunisian restaurants in the Latin Quarter, the scarves and perfumes she'd learned how to wear like *une vrai parisienne*. An older male photographer for whom she'd posed topless, no touching allowed. She'd sent me several slides—to cheer me up, she said. One of them, with her arm curled overhead, showed a thatch of black underarm hair and flared nostrils.

If I didn't move fast, I figured, we were history. That's how the Christmas trip happened. I had nightmares about the Tunisian stud who was probably showing her the town. I told my housemate Paul Suslovic once, joking my pain away. He gave me shit every time an aerogram came after that.

" 'Dear Adam,' he'd say, air-writing a letter, drawing the words out. " 'I . . . don't . . . know . . . how . . . to . . . tell . . . you . . . this . . . but . . . his . . . name . . . is . . . François . . . and . . . he . . . has . . . a . . . very . . . big . . . dick.' "

Just before I flew over, she reminded me to pack harmonicas. She'd been telling me for weeks about the musicians who haunted the Metro tunnels: English folk singers, Peruvian combos, African drummers. I'd been blowing a lot of harp that fall, walking home alone from the library late at night. Spiral had folded—Debbie and Steve had gotten degrees and moved on—and I'd put guitar aside for academics. Helen thought I ought to give the Metro a try. Set out a little box, play a few songs. *She'd* certainly give me a tip if she strolled by!

Paris that Christmas was Heaven and Hell, an alternating current that danced me ragged. One minute we were falling into bed for the first time in months: home at last, hearts melting with an impossible tingling sweetness. The next minute—in the spirit of honesty, since I'd asked—she was telling me about the French medical student she'd been seeing.

"You *what?*" I whispered. "I thought you said you loved me!"

"I *do*, Adam. He has nothing to do with us."

"I don't believe it! I don't fucking believe we're going through this shit again."

"I've told him how I feel about you. It isn't a serious thing."

"Isn't a serious thing?" I groaned, falling back in bed.

"He's a friend."

"A *friend?* What the hell am I?"

I cried, I raged. Then my tears dried. I couldn't touch her. Everything we'd shared—every delicious nasty loving thing—had once again been smeared in the dirt. I felt icy, empty.

You go on, somehow. A stroll through snow-dusted gray streets past Tunisian pastry shop windows filled with trays of filo-dough-and-nut delicacies oozing honey syrup. Dinner at a candlelit Vietnamese restaurant where your lover gazes up from her half-eaten spring roll, eyes aching with tenderness.

Just after New Year's I made my Metro debut. I was nervous; Helen pushed me. She was proud of my playing—I'd noodle on a harp while she got dressed—and thought I owed my talent. What did I have to lose? She found me a small cardboard box. She thought St.-Michel was the station to try first, under the Latin Quarter. She gave me a Metro map, told me how to buy tickets. My French was minimal, nothing like hers. I shoved the box and a handful of harps in my daypack, kissed her, took off.

It was the first time I'd been alone on the streets of Paris. Harp riffs—"Hoochie-Coochie Man," "Born in Chicago," "Whammer Jammer"—jangled through my head. The madness we'd recently been going through fell away. I hummed and scanned, eyes laser-sharp. Everybody I passed was a potential listener, money giver, critic.

Half an hour later I was standing at the crossroads of three well-lit tunnels in the bowels of St.-Michel station, heart thudding. My pitiful little cardboard box was sitting at my feet on the hard black rubber floor. Dozens of people—businessmen, students, Arabs, Africans—had strolled by. I hadn't played a note. A first note was required. I was a Princeton senior on Christmas vacation pretending to be a bluesman. Preparing to pretend. What if nobody tipped me?

I thought about Helen. I couldn't not *try.*

It was like teetering on a diving board above a pool. The only way to get in is just *do* it: count to three, one . . . two—

Suddenly I was playing—hitting the flutter-tongued beginning of "Whammer Jammer," nailing the bent screaming high note like Magic Dick, sliding raggedly into the in-and-out chord part. I was—

Four French cops in Charles de Gaulle caps and dark blue uniforms swung around the corner. I pulled my harp away. The one with the black mustache waved his finger disapprovingly.

"C'est interdit a jouer ici, monsieur."

"Interdit?" I stammered. Forbidden?

"Interdit," he repeated as they strolled by.

That was all it took. I packed up—trembling, relieved—and left. I'd broken the ice, though. Sex was good that night; the bottle of champagne I brought home didn't hurt. Helen's little Left Bank flat could be a cozy place. By the end of three weeks we'd decided to live together when she came back to America in June.

NAT SPENT THREE nights at my apartment, out of the week he ended up staying in New York. I'd wake in the morning and wander into the living room to find him spread-eagled on my open sofabed, barely covered by a tossed sheet; his dark disarrayed limbs were beautiful, unnerving, hard not to look at. His bare chest was hairless, lightly muscled but powerful, sleek, slightly sunken. He'd wake complaining of his sinuses. I had a lingering sore throat; we'd lounge half-naked in the summery morning light comparing symptoms. He was on a health kick these days, and teetotaling. When I came out of the shower, towel-wrapped, he'd wave me toward the kitchen counter where twin pill-arrays—B-complex, bioflavonoids, chelated minerals, kelp—and a gold foil packet of ginseng tea had been laid out. "Come on, now," he'd admonish in a motherly way, pouring twin glasses of orange juice. "Take your vitamins."

I went cold turkey that week, except for one Bass Ale the night we drove down to the East Village. We sat on a Second Avenue stoop just up from St. Mark's Place and watched the punks, junkies, slumming suburban kids, and old Baltic women in babushkas flow by. He was drinking nonalcoholic Kaliber beer, basking in Downtown's hormonal mayfly-dance. Two years ago he'd been the Prince of El Cafe Street, the Little Red Rooster of Dan Lynch. Now he was singing the praises of Clean. We strolled the five blocks up to Lynch's, past the angled ancient brick walls of St. Mark's-in-the-Bowerie, talking of Robyn and crack and his own evil days with Larry Johnson, the ragtime blues guitarist he'd worked and recorded with.

"With Larry," he said, "—I mean as a *young* man Larry could play some hellacious guitar, you know what I'm saying? That's why Reverend Gary Davis took him on. We used to play Lynch's back in the early days—'79, '80—when I was still working with Odetta. But Larry had a—I mean those older guys, they don't *get* to be older guys unless they've got some meanness down in there."

"Mister Satan's chewed me out a couple of times," I said.

He laughed. "So you know what I'm talking about? It's the price you pay for all that other valuable survival-shit they have to teach. But with Larry—I mean they didn't call it crack back then, it was plain old do-it-yourself freebasing. And all the nastiness Larry had, man, every last *drop*, would come out. It messed me up, too, which is why I got out."

The Dan Lynch band—Joey Miserable and the Worms—hadn't yet started; the crowd was sparse. We pushed through the swinging doors and big blond Karola, Bavarian *Biergarten* queen and manager, looked up from her draft beer-pulls and shouted "Net Rrriddles!" The Prodigal Son had returned. Jerry Dugger, his old drummer, came waddling up, head tilted, disbelieving.

"Is that you, baby?"

Nat just grinned and flapped his arms. "Do it *look* like me?" He laughed. "Do it *smell* like me? Can't be nobody but me."

His hands were grabbed, shoulders slapped, neck wrung; he bearhugged all comers—men and women—in his embracing way, rubbed backs lovingly with his flattened palm and pulled away to take each individual in, eyes glowing. Everybody seemed to know him, even people who had never met him. He exuded glow. It was an invisible liquid you could drink and thrive on. "I feel *good*," he kept exclaiming, beaming at us. "I'm really feeling good." I kept expecting Robyn to stroll through the doors, but she didn't. I was glad. I was hurting but glad. Nat gently declined the Heineken somebody pushed into his hand, sticking with tonic water and lime. "Make that two," I told Karola. The Cuervo could stay where it was.

WE WERE LOUNGING around my apartment after a late breakfast—trading licks, getting ready to drive down to Harlem. Nat had hung out with Jerry the night before, jammed with his new band, the Sweet Tones, at a Village blues club called Mondo Cane. His hands waxed eloquent; he couldn't get over Jerry's singing.

"I've heard him," I agreed. "He has a huge voice."

"Big voice. *Big* voice. I mean Jerry is singing like a sonofabitch. He used to try to—he used to keep it in, and I'd: You big sonofabitch, get up there and *sing*, motherfucker!' "

"I know he can sing straight-ahead rock and roll. Can he phrase? Can he—"

"Blues, everything. And besides, he's one of those high-retentives when it comes to music. He was a D.J.! He remembers every song that must have ever been played on any radio any time in his life. I mean I used to go so far as to write lyrics down for him, get the songs, say, 'Okay Jerry, you're singing today, you're gonna sing this song, you're gonna sing this one, and I want you prepared to sing that one.' I used to get behind him. All I had to do was hear his voice *once,* and I said, 'That's it.' "

"That's it."

"I wish I could sing like that, I told him. And since I can't, you will."

I clicked off my Walkman with the little plug-in stereo mike—both of us now wanted tapes of our woodshedding sessions—and we headed out. The soft blowy morning poured through as we breezed down the West Side Highway, slid off the ramp at 125th Street, veered left at the Hudson View Diner, pushed across Broadway and Amsterdam, floated past the Lagree Baptist Church. Nat had a harp out and was noodling jazzy instrumentals: "Blue Monk," "Night Train," "Things Ain't the Way They Used to Be." Fifty times I'd driven this route in the past six months; this was the first time I'd had company.

Seven or eight men were gathered around Mister Satan as we

pulled to the curb. Harlem these days was an open-air bazaar: our stretch of sidewalk boasted a hotdogs and soda vendor, a gloomy caricaturist who never seemed to do any business, a one-table bookseller sporting a Kente-cloth crown, and a small brooding graying bearded guy—also crowned—who sold me barbecued meat-on-a-stick drizzled with hot sauce and delicious sweet potato pies out of a dark cluttered Chevy van parked just past the Studio Museum's maroon awning. I'd played the afternoon before; Mister Satan knew what was up. Somebody leaned in and yelled as I set my Mouse on the sidewalk next to his. He slammed to a flurried stop, grimacing, then grinned delightedly at the two of us, his face oiled with sweat.

"Hello Mister Nat Riddles!" he roared. "We're ready for you in Harlem!"

Nat was wearing the B.B. King t-shirt I'd given him. He bowed slightly as his hand joined Mister Satan's two. "It is a *pleasure*," he said. "I mean that."

"Likewise."

"Adam tells me y'all been taking care of some serious business out here."

Mister Satan widened his eyes in mock horror as he scanned the circle. "We *better* be!" he roared. "Either that or go broke!"

Everybody cracked up, fell back a little, took a breath and Whooooed as the two men let go to slap each other five. I dropped to my knees and plugged in, unzipping my daypack and handing Nat the Walkman. I sat in my folding chair—harp in hand, trembling with anticipation, shoulder to shoulder with my two masters.

"Sweet Home Chicago" went by, unremarkable; I couldn't sing with Nat watching me. A higher power descended in the middle of "Mean Old World." Mister Satan had just cried "Sometimes I wonder . . . how can your love be so cold." Suddenly, shivering, I had it—a knotted sob—and knew what to do with it. The moment he yelled Blow! I went off. I thinned my tone, got as mean as I could with maximal tongue-articulation up and down the harp, all the moves Nat had lovingly helped install. The men crowding around us shouted, "Play it!" Nat, hovering with the tape recorder, yelled, "Go ahead!" Whatever I was holding back broke out in a flood. I sobbed, cursed, raged hoarsely, flogged my own throat with the air I wrenched through it. Robyn was streaming out of me, a whole history of shitty woman-luck. Mister Satan flowed on, a steady harsh groove littered with metallic butt-kicks. People were towering over me, bearing down, wrestling me into focus. "Give it up!" somebody shouted. "Don't stop!" somebody else yelled. "That's the shit!"

When I'd said what I'd had to say, Mister Satan roared my full name and everybody roared back. I stood up and handed Nat the mike. He squeezed my arm as he took it, slipping me the Walkman so we'd have the whole thing on tape. He sat down—spine erect, legs spread in back-porch mode—and started to blow. And he did blow. His first long low note got under and upended everything I'd just played. "Go ahead, brother!" a man yelled. A current rippled through the gathered crowd. "Low down and dirty, brother!" another called out. Nat's lidded eyes narrowed as he bore down; his shoulders swiveled, feinting and parrying, a tai chi push-hands master daring you to come at him. Five, six, seven choruses. Every half-digested Nat Riddles lick I'd just thrown down—tongue-slaps, warbles, bends, glissandos—he scraped off the sidewalk, slapped around, kicked and bit back into shape, then hurled *through* the stained, oily, gum-spattered concrete we were standing on. Down they flowed into the molten core, boiling and squalling before erupting through the groaning paper cone of my Mouse. He tongued, he flogged, he chuckled, he hollered, he sighed. "Play it brother!" a woman yelled. Suddenly he was her lover and they were up in the attic getting it on; she was tender, sensuous, berry-sweet, and married; her husband was clomping onto the front porch with shotgun in hand and Nat was gone in a murmur, flown out the window and down the road, whistling. Eight choruses, nine choruses.

Mister Satan grinned. "Blow on, Mister Nat!"

The woman noticed my Walkman and leaned toward me, raising her voice over the uproar. "He showed you how to play?"

"I'm gonna have to start all over now."

She smiled a toothy smile. "I hear that."

# CHAPTER NINE

# SWEET HARLEM SUMMER

*I was born by the river . . . in a little tent.*

—SAM COOKE, "A CHANGE IS GONNA COME"

THE SUMMER OF '87 was in full swing and raw sweet Harlem was waiting with open arms. Morning birds trilled in the trees outside my bedroom window. Nat's spirit had lingered: I was drinking nothing these days except ginseng tea, and practicing hard. Listening. Trying to hear the silence behind my notes.

Technique was important, of course—you had to be able to throw down—and harps wouldn't give you full power at high speed without a fight. Ten holes, blow and draw; twenty tiny brass reeds, each requiring a slightly different positioning of tongue and jaw in order to deliver up a singing richness of tone. Bent notes—those groaning flatted thirds and fifths that mimic a blues singer's swoops—needed much more force, exerted instantaneously and released. Blues harmonica played well was a miniature tongued slalom, a tornado swallowed and contained. All that, with silence added.

Charlie Parker hunkered down in his Kansas City woodshed; I had Inwood Hill Park. I'd hike up and around through the forest with hands cupped, pausing under the Henry Hudson Bridge to fire my blue tracer-streams up and away. There was another tunnel I haunted, on the backside of the hill—dark and abandoned, littered with dried leaves and the occasional dirty blanket—where I could rub my lips raw without drawing the wrath of the paranoid old white lady downstairs. Each enclosed space had a distinctive sound, doubling my last few notes with its own brief fading echo. I'd float out into the summer woods after a while and find myself surrounded by chirring crickets, bare thighs pricked by wineberry brambles. Bouncing along the river I blew hardest of all, bathed in a glistening immensity that swirled silently at my shoulder, pumped my heart full, gave nothing and everything back. Suddenly I'd stop, hyperventilated, expectant. What was I supposed to hear? Water sucking softly at the rocks below; cheers from the dusty playing fields where Mexican soccer players tangled as their young wives, Indian-stolid, heated fresh tortillas on portable grills. All of us perched on this forgotten northern tip of Manhattan Island.

Nat's spirit lingered. One afternoon during his stay I'd returned to the apartment to find him cross-legged on the floor in front of my stereo, facing twin stacked walls of cassettes—a hundred or more, each carefully hand-labeled with his small clear printing. George "Harmonica" Smith, Kim Wilson, Louis Armstrong, Magic Dick. His ex-girlfriend—Kathy the parole officer—had let him retrieve his scholar's supplies.

"I'm in heaven," he sighed. "You have no *idea* how desperate I've been for my music down in Norfolk."

He'd made me a study tape, labeled Adam's Homework. Fifteen or twenty jazz-blues instrumentals. Saxes, mostly: Houston Person, Maceo Parker, Stanley Turrentine, "Gatortail" Jackson, King Curtis. We'd spoken often about what it meant to be a New York blues harmonica player, as opposed to Chicago or Mississippi. We had the funk, we *owned* the jazz; you had to be ready for whatever came up. I lived inside that tape for weeks after he'd left, got so I could I.D. the player by sound alone within a couple of seconds. Houston was huge, measured, playful, knowing, aching, suddenly fleet: a breathtaking gamble made with infinite relaxation in the face of every possible death. Maceo was puckish, rope-a-dope footed, the funky sky-prince. Stanley you could always tell from the spaces he left—startling, oblique, shattered by tenor hiccups, the same note played with three or four different rapid-fire fingerings. Hey! Who? Wha?!

Steal *everybody*'s shit. Always acknowledge where you got what. Can't nobody play you but you.

I HAD ONLY one enemy in Harlem that first summer—he wanted to slit my throat—and even he might have been joking.

His name was Mr. Simms. He was a small older man, slightly stooped, with a fluffy white beard over bulging Popeye cheeks and the wildest, fiercest eyes I'd ever seen. Thousands of people would stroll, walk, trot, and run by us on a typical afternoon; Mr. Simms was one of the few who always caught my attention.

"White boy!" he'd yell hoarsely.

Fused with the groove, slightly dazed, I'd glance up. He'd grin fiercely, eyes locked on mine.

"White boy!" he'd roar. Then he'd take his index finger and go *zzzzzzzip!* across his throat. Machete-style.

I'd watch him disappear down the block. He might glance back over his shoulder, he might not.

It was Mister Satan who told me his name was Mr. Simms, when I asked. He pooh-poohed my concern.

"Hell no you ain't gotta worry. That sorry old bastard liable to kill himself dead with his own finger before he gets around to you."

"He's from Georgia," one of the men around us volunteered.

"That's what happens when a man lose his mind," somebody else added. "You ain't no cracker. If he got a problem with it, oughta leave you *out* of it."

After the tenth time or so I began to loosen up. Mr. Simms could tell. He'd come closer, stand five feet away and shout, do the finger trick. I'd nod—howdy, neighbor!—and bear down twice as hard on my blue notes, doing my best to cut him back.

"Hah!" he'd bark with the same fierce grin, waving me away like I'd passed the test. He'd bounce off down the street. You'd swear I'd just made his day.

One time he came up I took direct action. He'd just hollered "White boy!" and hacked at his neck when we went on break. He was only a couple of feet away. I set down my mike, stood up, stuck out my hand.

"My name's Adam," I said.

He lowered his eyes. He couldn't quite look at me. He scratched his beard. "Punkin," he muttered.

"Mr. Simms!" Mister Satan yelled.

"What?"

"I got a dollar for you, sir."

"Hah!" he barked triumphantly, all the fire roaring back. I was feeling pretty fiery. We stared at each other.

"White boy!" he laughed.

"Come on, Mr. Simms," I said.

"Aaaah," he grumbled. He put out his hand and we shook.

After that we were cool. Occasionally he'd bounce by, sometimes even yell from across the street. I'd nod, he'd nod back. It was a greeting now, not a threat. One day I realized I hadn't seen him in a while. This was years later. I asked Mister Satan about him.

"He's most likely dead," he laughed. "All them bastards went and died on me."

*1979.* IT WAS A RARE JUNE DAY IN PRINCETON, the skies cloud-fluffed and balmy. I was lounging on the front steps of the off-campus apartment I'd held down since September. Graduation was last week; George Benson's "Breezin' " was filtering out of my—soon to be our—attic room upstairs. I'd waited, suffered, paid my dues. No more blues! Helen, just home from Paris, was driving up from Philadelphia to move in with me.

The reunion, when it came, was a dream I'd been having for weeks. She rolled to the curb in her parents' Mercedes. Slid out of the driver's seat, slammed. Trotted around the front bumper and scrambled up the grassy bank as I called out and stood, not quite believing, tingling. She grinned helplessly. Her eyes were dark melting ovals threaded with longing and relish. The last few feet were a lunge, interrupted.

"Shit," she said, faltering, falling awkwardly into my arms.

Clutching each other, we pulled apart and looked down. She lifted her flip-flop out of a ripe brown pile of dogshit.

"No!" I groaned, laughing as the smell wafted up.

She giggled and giggled, eyes wet.

It was a terrific summer, after that. We went to farmer's markets and brought home burstingly ripe Jersey tomatoes. We had long late dinners—salads, baguettes, Chablis—and watched fireflies streak through the graveyard across the street. On muggy afternoons we'd drive over to the Princeton Township swimming pool and lie side by side on our towels, books in hand, penciling notes. I'd landed a summer job at an educational publisher in Trenton, writing children's fiction; she was getting ready for an internship at a feminist quarterly out in Berkeley. We were moving to California at the end of August. I had nothing lined up but wasn't worried; I was running seriously these days—our Institute Woods jogs had turned into a fifty-mile-a-week habit—and planned on training for my first marathon while looking for work.

We kept each other happy. It was sultry under the attic roof, even with an exhaust fan. The closest we came to a fight was the day she got a letter from Paris telling her that her old flame had died of leukemia. She told me and broke down; I held her. It was a weird moment. I couldn't stay mad. I got a sick pleasure from the whole thing. *One* guy, at least, was out of the picture.

I HAD A HARD TIME for a while, as my first Harlem summer sailed onward, getting Nat's triumphant blowdown with Mister Satan out of my head. If the best I could possibly do was what he'd already done, where did that leave me?

My head stayed slightly messed until the day I bought a Bartles & James Wine Cooler from our friendly neighborhood liquor store. I'd never indulged on the job before. Mister Satan didn't drink—these days, at least—but he didn't mind if others did.

"Yes sir, Mister Gussow!" he laughed as I came back to my chair sipping from the paper-bagged bottle. "I see you got yourself a little taste goin on."

"You want one?" I suddenly felt bad for not having offered.

He shook his head. "It ain't my thing."

"I can use it today," I murmured, already feeling the slight delirious release.

"I done drunk my share, now. Whoo. Anything the Earth gets a mind to create for the enjoyment of humanity, you ain't gonna see me going around condemning it *no* kind of way. God's people will do that." He smiled. "Liquor just makes my fingers sleepy. Thank you for the thought, though."

We plugged back in after he'd finished his cigarette and clattered to life, sinking back into the deathless groove we'd hammered out over the past nine months. My body tingled; I'd fallen a half-step away from the rush and clamor, the sass and stroll, the veer and hustle of a Harlem afternoon pouring across the brim of my eyes and flooding down through. Mister Satan was singing the song about pretty girls, working his harsh rasp: "Everywhere I go . . . there's a pretty girl. . . ." I bit down hard, worked each reed, followed his vocal curves and swerves with my inner ear—doubling, echoing, urging—and felt myself sinking into a warm low free place, as though whatever I'd been standing on had suddenly softened and given way. I had infinitely more time between phrases than I'd realized. Each seemed to flow effortlessly out of the next. There was room to move down here, to stretch out your elbows and take a deep breath. Aaaaah. Feel that? What would you call it?

And then, with a small pang of disappointment, I floated back up through the music and found myself on the street, slightly high—harp and mike clasped, working hard, making functional but uninspired yowls.

A NEW GUY HAD GRADUALLY become part of the act that summer, and I didn't mind: the attention he drew took pressure off me.

James Gants—the name he used on 125th Street—was an occasional freelance singer from somewhere in the Deep South. When he wasn't working with us he hung out with his buddies in front of the liquor store next to Sylvia's, corner of 127th and Malcolm X Boulevard. They knew him by a different name, Mister Satan later told me. Sometimes I'd give him a lift up there at the end of our day. One of his legs didn't work very well; he'd yank it into the car after him. His black leather shoes were rotting internally, and smelled. He gave off a feeling of gentleness, confusion, and pride against all odds. He wore a sharp-looking Borsalino, like a Chicago gangster from another era. His skin was dark, sheened with lingering oil. There were knife scars on his forehead. He could have been my age, he could have been fifteen years older. I liked him.

He played a curious role in our evolving sidewalk show. He'd spend most of a set leaning against the wall to my right, working on a brown paper-bagged bottle of that day's fix, inscrutable behind his large tinted sunglasses. The liquor store was just behind him; I was happy to have him guarding my flank. We'd slap five when I showed up. I always gave him a dollar the moment I'd made a few.

Mister Satan would call him up just before break-time. "All right, Mr. Gants," he'd rasp cheerfully, leaning back in his hi-chair, swiveling his mike stand to the left. Mr. Gants would take a last swig, shoot his cuffs—he wore a series of cheap polyester suits—and hobble around to take his place at Mister Satan's shoulder.

"Hello," he'd mumble, dipping his head and nodding at our audience. He had a speech impediment of sorts, a habit of choking off and gargling his words, which made everything he said unintentionally comical. His most earnest efforts to sing with feeling drew chuckles, including Mister Satan's. I was uneasy at first about joining in with the general hilarity. In certain respects his entire performance was an exercise in Harlem laughing behind his back. Except the laughter was up-front, he knew it was there, and he seemed to have evolved a way of incorporating it into his act, making his ability to evoke it a part of what he had to offer.

He always sang the same two songs: Sam Cooke's "A Change Is Gonna Come" and James Brown's "I Feel Good." I quickly learned to sit out the first. As a ballad accompanist, Mister Satan was mercurial, polyrhythmic, essentially impossible to follow. He got his pleasure from knowing where the groove was and stressing every possible off-beat. Mr. Gants was nothing if not game.

"I was booooooorn . . . by the rivah," he'd belt, letting his nasal holler swell and soar on the opening strain. Mister Satan would interrupt him almost immediately with a running commentary:

"(. . . the *Hudson* River . . .)"

". . . in a little tent . . ."

"(. . . or Harlem Hospital . . .)"

". . . oooh and just liiike the river . . . I've been runnin' ever since. . . ."

"(. . . here come the police now . . .)"

". . . It's been a loooong . . . a long time comin' . . . but I knowwwww a change gonna come. . . ."

"(. . . spare change . . .)"

". . . Oh yes it will. . . . It's been tooooo hard livin' . . . but I'm afraid to diiiiiiie. . . ."

"(. . . aw, go ahead and die . . .)"

People would be falling on each other by this point, holding their bellies, absolutely torn up. Mr. Gants's intonation was as wavering as his delivery was burlesque; he had all the classic soul-crooner moves, each deployed with a flailing vigor that was either unintentional self-caricature or *intentional* self-caricature. It was impossible to figure out who the laugh was on. Were we humiliating the poor guy? Or was he secretly mocking us for being so foolish as to think that he didn't know how over the top he was? Maybe everybody was having fun and I was just uptight.

Next up was "I Feel Good." I'd picked the horn-parts off the record—Maceoooo!—and could keep up. Mr. Gants was something to watch. He had James Brown's hyperkinetic schtick down cold—dips and wiggles and shakes, hands dusting the sky. He'd spin a 360-degree circle on his bad leg. He'd sink into a partial split and scissor-snap back to full height. Mister Satan and I, for better or worse, were his tightly disciplined rhythm machine:

"So good . . ." he'd holler as we clattered toward the big close.

(Crash! Crash!)

". . . so good . . ."

(Crash! Crash!)

" 'Cause I got you."

(Crash-crash-crash-crash-crash-crash-crash-crash-crash-crash. . . .)

"Whoa!!"

Mister Satan would flail both cymbals mercilessly as he mauled his guitar's final chord, I'd wail and warble; Mr. Gants would throw in half a dozen pitter-patters and hand-quivers. Then, at the last possible moment:

"Boom!"

Sidewalk traffic would stop dead; on summer weekends we'd have a crowd of a hundred or more—Kente cloth and pinstriped suits, Bugle Boy baggies and gold hoop earrings, huge pastel pink Easter hats strewn with flowers. Harlem knew what a tip bucket was for. People would lean over and glance in first, just to be sure. Mothers would send their toddlers up with a clutched dollar.

That was James Gants. We had the big show that summer. We'd split the bills three ways after the rush had subsided—stand around the bucket as Mister Satan counted out five at a time. We were happy and rich. I'd give Mr. Gants a lift the three blocks uptown afterward.

"All right, Mister Adam," he'd say as we pulled up in front of the liquor store, putting out his hand.

"All right, Mister Gants."

"Thank you for that ride."

He'd let go, swing open the door, and ease his bad leg into the gutter, then cock his Borsalino and slide out. He had friends up there who were happy to see him. I'd round the corner past the African street vendors and drive home.

*1979.* FOR THE FIRST couple of weeks after we arrived in Berkeley, I played air-Telecaster in front of our bedroom mirror and blew my lips raw. Helen was off at her internship; I was home at our new apartment with nothing but my own anxieties. I figured I'd work my chops into shape, join a band. My panicked wails filtered downstairs; a couple of electricians rewiring our kitchen told me to check out the street musicians on Telegraph Avenue. I bounced across campus, thrilled. They turned out to be sallow-faced old hippies crooning tired Bob Dylan shit.

Whatever musical demon had been driving me since the days of Lips at the Day School suddenly faded, leaving a vague emptiness. I got a part-time job at a local franchise called Giant Hamburgers and learned how to work a rush-hour grill. I played house-husband, shopping for organic grains at the Co-op on Shattuck, cooking lentil curry out of *Laurel's Kitchen*. In my free time I tried to write adult fiction. I got a couple of paragraphs into a story about the bearded old black guy—I named him Isaiah—who used to sit on a bench outside Giant Hamburgers, sipping his heavily sugared coffee, mumbling to himself. I tried to imagine myself into his world. How did he see me and the Berkeley students who walked by? I came up with the beginnings of a believable inner voice—Damn white kids think they know so goddamn much, et cetera—but couldn't develop it into a story. I didn't know the guy well enough. We'd never exchanged more than the few words required to turn spare change into coffee. I didn't even know his real name.

MISS LILY STOPPED by one afternoon and danced a few steps while Mister Satan and I grooved. She was the dark older woman with several missing teeth who'd been doing her thing in front of him the very first day I'd stopped to watch back in October. High cheekbones, short thinning hair. I hadn't seen her since; I was afraid my presence had driven her away. Maybe it had. Maybe seeing Mr. Gants out there had called her home. She seemed shy when Mister Satan introduced us.

"How you doin'?" she said in a surprisingly girlish voice as our hands met, her smile a jagged flash, her eyes flickering everywhere but directly at me.

Her dancing was very public and very private. She drew hula-ish circles in the air with elbows and hips, patted her belly with a flattened hand—fingers spread wide, eyes lowered. She'd raise one ankle while keeping the other foot flat, hop lightly into reverse position, smile to herself. Watching her from behind, I found myself playing more simply, digging down into the groove, anchoring. Suddenly she'd slip in a quick shuffle-step and I'd scramble to double that. Her age melted away with every gentle shimmy; she was beautiful, graceful, self-contained. I felt honored to have had the chance.

"Back in the old days, in the clubs," Mister Satan told me after she'd left, "we used to play behind those shake dancers. Down in St. Petersburg, Florida. In the tittie clubs, as you might call them."

"Little Walter has an instrumental called 'Shake Dancer,' " I said.

"Same thing." He shook out a cigarette and lit up. "Guitar, saxophone, and drums—mainly saxophone. Smoke so thick your eyes be stinging with the mess. All the woman had on by the end of the song wasn't one *damn* thing except her high-heeled sneakers."

"Jesus."

"He was most likely there too, somewhere in the back with a drink in his hand, getting ready to save her behind."

A few days later Miss Lily came by pushing a one-legged woman in a wheelchair who turned out to be her mother. Mister Satan called her Miss Mama. Miss Mama had a close-cropped gray natural and a small clay pipe dangling from one earlobe. Her voice was much louder than her daughter's but she didn't talk much. She sat there watching the three of us do our thing, nodding a little. The two of them apparently had some sort of act they worked in the subway stations around Times Square. I couldn't figure out what it was, although it involved singing. I think Miss Mama was religious. She was friendly enough when we shook hands—she'd known Mister Satan a long time—but seemed preoccupied with the idea of getting downtown and back to work.

ONE SWELTERING AFTERNOON, when Kawasaki Ninjas were hornet-buzzing across 125th Street and lemonade peddlers were sloshing twenty-gallon drums around on wheeled dollies, I noticed a pack of whitefolks coming up on my right. There were white people in Harlem besides me, of course—social workers, construction workers, cops, European and Japanese tourists with cameras. The occasional husband, wife, or self-conscious lover; a couple of jazz cats I'd crossed paths with in the clubs. Since our spot was less than fifty feet from the front awning of the Studio Museum, we'd sometimes get a brief spillover when the tour buses pulled up and disgorged. White tourists in Harlem were good tippers, especially if they photographed us. I always assumed their guidebooks had warned them against stealing native souls without giving payment in return. Being treated like a native was a curious sensation. I didn't mind the money but felt, to be honest, a certain earned distance from whitefolks with cameras.

This particular afternoon there were more than Nikons coming at us. There was a film crew—two or three cameras, soundmen with headphones and shouldered battery-packs, the whole ensemble flowing down the sidewalk in our direction. Its attention was focused less on us than on the four young men following just behind, who eased to a stop and stood quietly as we played. They were skinny, unshaven, dressed mostly in black leather despite the heat; one of them was wearing a bowler hat. He nodded in time. The cameras homed in on us, then swiveled slowly toward our quartet of fans, lovingly tracking their wandering gazes. A sound guy aimed his shotgun mike at me, eyes dropping to the V.U. meters on his hip.

The song we were playing was new: recently worked up and completely out of our usual line. "Freedom for My People" wasn't a blues at all, or funky, or jazzy. It was a folk-soul ballad, a protest song without anger. Mister Satan had started singing it one day; I'd frantically shuffled through half a dozen different blues riffs, none of which fit, then stumbled into something that did: wheezing, with the harp held slightly off-mike. He called it my "frying eggs sound," approvingly. The song as sung went like this:

I want some freedom
for my people
Freedom dear Lord
for my little people

Gimme some freedom
oooooh for my people. . . .

Freedom lord
for the people
Gimme freedom
whoooooh for my people
we been a waitin'
hoping and a prayin'

something must of gone wrong
it's takin' waaaay too long
I need some freedom
for my people
freedom lord
whooooh for my people
freedom from disrespect
sayin' oh what the heck
freedom from division
causin' brotherly collision
respect for one another
for everybody's mother. . . .

uh huh
I need some freedom
for my people
freedom dear lord
whoooah for my people

gimme some freedom
whooo for my people
freedom lord
for my little people
freedom from profanity
because it's worse than insanity
freedom from confusion
falsifying and illusion
ohhh, freedom
for my people
freedom dear lord
whooooah for my people
respect for one another
for everybody's mother
freedom from division
it causes brotherly collision
I know the solution
ain't in the Constitution. . . .

Before the song was over, our quartet of leather-clad fans had moved off, continuing down the sidewalk with their film crew in pursuit. I didn't find out who they were until we went on break a couple of songs later. Somebody—not a white guy—came up as I was unplugging.

"You know who that was?" he said.

"No idea."

"You ever heard of U2?"

Of course I had—they were the most popular rock group in the world in 1987—but knew nothing about them, except that they were Irish. That was them?

A member of their entourage had taken one of Mister Satan's business cards from Miss Macie while we were playing, it turned out. Eight months later, their lawyer called. A U2 concert film was being assembled; some footage of us had been shot. The production company couldn't actually afford to *pay* us, but would we mind if they used it anyway? They'd be giving us free worldwide exposure of the sort most bands would kill for.

Mister Satan handed the matter off to Bobby Robinson. Bobby was Mister Satan's personal manager, a title which didn't seem to have much effective content these days. He was also the owner of Harlem's best-known record store—Bobby's Happy House, up on St. Nicholas Avenue—and a world famous R&B record producer, the guy who had retitled "K.C. Lovin" and made it a No. 1 hit for Wilbert Harrison as "Kansas City" in 1959. A small well dressed man with drooping Asian eyes and a small twisted smile, he had inch-long fingernails that curved like a Mandarin elder's. We'd been introduced out on 125th Street once or twice and shaken hands, gently. "I got a few things I'm working on," he'd always say, eyes darting down the street.

This particular scam he'd seen more than once, apparently. If you can't afford to pay us, he told U2's lawyers, we can't afford to be used.

A deal was quickly struck. Sterling Magee and Adam Gussow would each receive $1,000 for appearing in the movie, tentatively titled *Rattle & Hum*—and an additional $250 for the brief snippet of "Freedom for My People" that would be included on the sound-track album. There would be songwriting royalties, of course; Robinson and Magee would split those.

Bobby called me up and gave me the rundown. I was happy; any-thing I got out of the deal seemed like found money. Plus we'd be famous! I was happy until I told a friend who worked in the music business about my good luck.

"U2 is gonna be making millions," he said. "Tens of millions. If you guys are on the album, you should be getting some kind of a point deal, not a shitty little one-time buyout."

"You think so?"

"You guys are *real*. U2 is desperate for Real or they wouldn't be calling. They need you more than you need them."

I thought about this. When I got the letter from an attorney at Mitchell, Silberberg & Knupp with the accompanying Performer's Release, I called the guy up. It takes a few moments to get a Holly-wood entertainment lawyer on the phone, if they don't know you. He was friendly enough when he came on. We small-talked briefly, a couple of white guys doing business.

"Look," I finally said, "I'll tell you why I'm calling. I understand you guys aren't using much of "Freedom for My People" on the album, but you're using *some* of it, and—I mean considering the kind of worldwide distribution *Rattle & Hum* is going to have, we really oughta be talking about some kind of point deal here."

"Point deal?"

"I really should be asking you for at least a point on the album."

His end of the phone went dead with cold, pure, stunned, malev-olent silence. A point on this sort of major-label rock album, I later discovered, is one percent of total worldwide royalty sales. Figure ten million albums at ten bucks a unit net. I'd just asked for a million bucks. When he came back on he was shouting, almost screaming.

"If you think you're gonna get a motherfucking *point* on the motherfucking *U2 album*," he fumed, "then you are out of your motherfucking *mind!*"

A deal was quickly cut by which my demand was sheepishly withdrawn and had never even been theoretically raised.

*Rattle & Hum* came out in the fall of 1988. I went to see it at a theater near Times Square. The whole thing had been shot in high-contrast black and white. The big moment comes halfway through. Bono and his bandmates have just finished leading the New Voices of Freedom, a Harlem choir, through the soaring strains of "I Still Haven't Found What I'm Looking For." Slow fade to a tracking shot, on the street. You're perched on Bono's shoulder as he strolls past incense vendors and . . . What's this? A white kid in a white Western-style hat is slouched in a folding chair with his legs spread, blowing harmonica, eyeing you. There's something distinctly uncool about the way his legs bounce as his feet slap the pavement. Just past him is an old black guy with a graying beard, singing and strumming an electric guitar, eyes closed. He's sitting behind a jerry-rigged percussion ensemble that crashes and sizzles as he slaps the pedals with his feet. "I want some freedom," he cries. "Freedom for my people. . . ." Bono watches, intrigued; the Edge nods in quiet sympathy. A husky black guy in dark green Wayfarers is leaning against the wall next to the harmonica player, listening. The music is thin, keening, uncanny: a faery melody lilting through a dream you'd forgotten you ever had.

Then, suddenly, the screen begins to bleach—freezing the two Harlem street musicians in mid-gesture as their song slowly fades. Dissolve to blinding white light. You're squinting, blinking, caught in the glare of floodlights as the camera angle shifts to reveal: U2 in concert before thousands of screaming fans with lit matches and cigarette lighters held up in the darkened house. Bono is wearing a white Western-style hat. He's a rock star; it looks good on him. His legs don't bounce. He grimaces as though he feels the music. The man is cool.

*1980.* AFTER SIX AIMLESS MONTHS in Berkeley, I quit Giant Hamburgers and landed a real job. Canton, Jefferson & Berk was a San Francisco firm specializing in management labor law. I'd wanted *labor* labor law—something socially conscious—but none of those firms were hiring paralegals. Suddenly, at twenty-two, I was commuting by bus with my fellow office-drones, wearing starched white button-down shirts and a Brooks Brothers pinstriped suit. Doing my best to fit in.

The job sounded good, until you actually did it. Canton, Jefferson & Berk was currently representing the University of California system in unionization hearings before the National Labor Relations Board. It was a massive, mind-numbing case. In order to keep wages down, U.C. wanted all its employees represented—since unionization had just been legally mandated—by a handful of huge, systemwide unions. Dozens of small pesky locals, on the other hand, wanted to negotiate their own contracts on behalf of various subsets of U.C. employees: maintainance machinists at the Davis campus, for example. Our job was to prove that maintainance machinists on all U.C. campuses did exactly the same thing; the pesky locals were trying to prove that maintenance machinists at Davis did wildly different things from maintenance machinists on other campuses. Each side had been calling maintenance machinists to the witness stand and asking them to describe what they did. Steamfitters were next, then two hundred other job categories from the bowels of the modern academico-industrial complex. My job was to wear my Brooks Brothers suit and summarize the printed transcripts of these hearings—orally, with the help of a hand-held dictaphone. Eight hours a day, day after day, in a sunny twelfth-floor office with a window that opened onto a dizzying view of the sidewalk below. At the end of each day I'd stand up, stretch, and walk out front to give the tapes to Geri, the firm's Chinese-American office manager. She'd send them out to be transcribed; in the morning they'd come back, neatly typed up.

This was an actual job in the so-called real world. I functioned normally for the first three weeks. Then signs of stress began to appear. I'd burst into tears in the morning while walking toward the bus stop. My tie began to choke like a noose.

I started speaking in voices. Nobody had specifically instructed me that the voice in which I summarized transcripts had to be my own. What was my "own" voice, anyway? Musicians hear a pleasurable sound, they figure out how to make it. I'd always loved and mimicked accents: Boris and Natasha, Yosemite Sam, Inspector Clouseau, Minute Mouse and Courageous Cat, Edward G. Robinson as Little Caesar. My homeless black friend Isaiah. I'd sneak in a portable radio, dial up some bebop, and do everything hipster-smooth and angular, like Kerouac at the Village Gate. Epiphanies of apprentice steamfitters in the Frisco afternoon! Suddenly I had a palette, a range of choices. "Tongues" was my middle name.

Geri out front couldn't get over it. She'd preview each day's Dispatch from the Far Side, gazing at me with wonder when I emerged to drop a fresh tape on her desk. Poor crazed boy in the corner office! I was much happier as my polymorphous self. The transcripts came back every morning in standard English, revealing nothing. Geri kept it our little secret.

I quit after five months. Just before I did, as I was walking back to the office with my jacket slung over my shoulder one lunch hour, I came across some street musicians surrounded by a small crowd. The shriek of slide guitar cut through a part of me I'd forgotten about. I shivered, craning my noosed neck. A black guy whacking a snare drum, a white guy in a cowboy hat strumming guitar. The singer's mouth was contorted under dark drooping aviator shades as he hollered, "Wake up, mama . . . turn your lamp down low. . . ."

People were tossing bills and change into a half-filled cardboard box at his feet. His fretting hand was a stainless steel hook, like Long John Silver. He'd slipped a hollow steel slide on it and was making the shrieks with that.

MISTER SATAN AND I never did make a Southern getaway that first Harlem summer—our pilgrimage through Mississippi would come later—but we did manage a couple of expeditions to Times Square. Four miles due south on Manhattan Island is worlds away. How would the cops down there treat us? Police and street music generally do not mix. The Beaubourg in Paris, Centraal Station in Amsterdam, anywhere I'd ever worked: you were loud, visible, the most public of nuisances, and they had all the power. Harlem was the first place I'd busked where the cop factor was zero. No shutdowns in ten months. By this standard alone, Harlem was street-music heaven. Times Square was the East Coast's Wild West, downtown Gomorrah, a calculated risk. The spare-change capital of the world.

We picked the kind of early August dog day when any shirt you put on is drenched within five minutes. Mister Satan was leaning against his loaded shopping cart when I pulled up in front of Shakespeare Flats that morning—puffing on a cigarette, fluffy graying hair bisected by a green terrycloth headband.

"Let's get on downtown and collect from those money-throwing bastards!" he roared gaily.

Mr. Parker was puttering around as usual in his janitor's greens, sweeping, kibbitzing, pausing to lean on his broom. The crab guy on the corner was unhinging the slatted wood cover of his day's catch and digging down into crushed ice. We heaved Mister Satan's Mouses into the back of my car, careful not to add new dents to the ravaged wire-mesh covers. We'd just heaved his shopping cart up onto the roof, settled it on the strip of carpet, and begun lashing clothesline through the rear windows when a squad car rolled to a stop. A young white cop on the passenger side jerked his head.

"Where'd you get that shopping cart?" A blue plastic sign dangling from the side of it suggested Waldbaum's.

Mister Satan flashed his gold tooth. "I stole it from Waldbaum's."

The officer glanced at his partner, then smiled as the squad car slowly rolled away. "Just don't let them catch you."

"You know I won't, Mr. Officer!"

Mr. Parker chuckled as we briskly looped and knotted. "Yessir, Sterling. You got to have a good relationship with your po-leece."

We breezed down Amsterdam Avenue with elbows out and the radio at cruise volume, Bobby Watson's alto sax shrieking in a lifting chromatic surge of suspended fourths. My car was amazingly comfortable with just the two of us up front—no Miss Macie overseeing operations—and the shopping cart creaking overhead. We drifted, squeezed through bottlenecks, flowed past the Lincoln Center fountain as Broadway sliced left and away. We parked in a Ninth Avenue lot, loaded out, and heaved the shuddering, cymbal-clanking contraption across Forty-third Street, past porn video emporia and an endless row of loading bays filled with New York Times trucks. My Uncle Mel, a drama critic, worked upstairs; I suddenly wondered what he'd make of us.

Mister Satan glanced back at me as we passed a braless woman in a lemon sundress.

"She's gonna have trouble wherever she goes."

"Mm mm."

We set up against the south-facing marble wall of One Times Square, at the foot of the Marine Recruiting Station. Our only competition, already hard at work, was a duo of Bible thumpers—a black woman in a straw hat and a white man in a suit—at the building's far corner. They had one Mouse; we had five, plus percussion.

"I played this exact spot with Bill Collins last spring," I said, setting down my daypack and stretching. "The rockabilly guitar player I went over to Paris with last summer."

"How much you make?"

"Ten bucks each in about fifteen minutes, before the cops came."

"They'll leave us alone." He smiled as he set a cymbal stand on the wooden sounding-board, steel legs splayed. "God's people got us covered."

We thrashed out four long sets in the hot sun. The brim of my Stetson did what it was supposed to do. Our audience was everybody: dreadlocked black bike messengers in purple Spandex shorts straddling battered one-speeds, a trio of Japanese girls in black leather skirts, office drones with shoulder-flung suit jackets and gelled thinning hair, Macy's shoppers, Minolta owners, dollar crumplers, change scatterers, five-dollar-bill droppers, a contortionist in grimy sweats and Knicks singlet dragging a filthy strip of cardboard who pretzeled himself not far from us, a tall red-skinned guy with a scarred craggy face who knew Mister Satan from Harlem, a couple of sniffling street people in laceless sneakers who stared hungrily at his open guitar case, young black boom-boxers with turbo-bass pumped down so they could hear us, construction workers with Igloo coolers in bluejeans powdered plaster-white, token tossers, discount drugstore leafletters, a professional harmonica player I vaguely knew who leaned in between songs and asked for my card, one large boa constrictor draped around somebody's bare neck. More quirky soulful beautiful women of all shapes, sizes, and tints than I could possibly hunger for at the same time.

Several cops gave us the thumbs-up as they strolled by. Whenever we paused you could hear the voice of the black woman in the straw hat rising and cresting just down the block, an unending crescendo of admonitory thunderation: homosexuality was evil, AIDS was God's punishment, Dave Winfield and Ricky Henderson and crack and smack and every other worldly good weren't going to help you when the time came to walk through those pearly gates.

At the end of our third set Mister Satan finally got pissed off.

"God's people got a little racket going on," he roared, waving his hand, "preaching the same old tired mess they *done* been preaching since Jesus was a baby! All that love-your-neighbor bullcrap ain't done a damn thing but drive Christians around the world to start wars and tear the mess up! And for what? Love your neighbor? Hell, if you got to *kill* me to *love* me, you might as well go on and hate my ass!"

"Damn!" somebody called out. "They gonna mess with you!"

"I'm deadly serious," he laughed, eyes ferocious. "I am Satan—Mister Satan to you. Ain't no Jesus told me this and that! I speak for my*self!* Everywhere I go I preach respect. I say Hello Mister, Hello Miss, Hello Little Man. Ain't no damn love *required* if you got respect for your neighbor! Ain't that right?"

"You preachin' now, brother!"

"Listen good: Forget everything they told you about me. Satan this, the bad apple that. They done lied to you so long they got you dazed and confused and backwards-bamboozled. When you die, they say, you gonna go to heaven. Hell no! You gonna be stone cold dead, in the ground, and we all gonna be sitting around drinking, having us a beautiful time remembering your black ass."

People howled. The red-skinned guy he knew from Harlem held out his hand for a slap. Satan was glowing.

*"All you got is your life!"* he roared. "That's it! Next time God slaps a plane out of the sky, next time Jesus makes a promise he can't keep, you remember what Mister Satan told you: All you got is your *life!* You want to take a drink, you want to smoke a little reefer, go right on ahead and take you a little taste. Creation put the mess here for your enjoyment! Worst thing you can do is condemn what you do. All *that* gonna do is tear you up inside. But just remember this. . . ."

"What's that?"

"The end of your money is the end of your addiction, no ifs ands or buts." He winked at me. "And while you're meditating on that, Mister Adam and I *damn* sure could use a dollar to feed whatever we got going on back home."

It was like a butterfly migration coming straight at us, all the fluttering and rustling, crumpling and flowering. The fourth set was a lagniappe, our gift to the seized day. We folded our tents at six— grimy, flush, deliciously spent.

"First thing we gonna do is let the bucket take care of the car," Mister Satan said, squatting next to it, skimming fifteen singles off the top, smoothing and folding them into a little wad. Then payday.

I sat on my Mouse and watched him after I'd packed up. He carefully threaded his cymbal-stands through the loops of picture wire he'd twisted into the back of his shopping cart. His hands knew their way. Each piece of equipment—Mouses, bucket, microphone, hi-chair, small brown bag filled with pliers and cables—had its earned place.

We heaved and pushed ourselves back across Forty-third Street, past the Times loading bays and porno video emporia. The cymbals crashed loudly every time we came down off a curb. He growled at me once or twice for pulling too hard. The sidewalks were crammed with Friday rush—impatiently pushing past us, veering toward bridges, tunnels, the Hamptons, upstate. We were chuckling when we got back to my car, pockets bulging. Eighty sweet bucks apiece.

. . .

TWO DAYS LATER the harmonica player who'd taken my card called. He was glad to see me working. Could I use another gig? He'd been out with the bus-and-truck tour of *Big River*—Broadway's version of *The Adventures of Huckleberry Finn*—and needed a sub. Three months on the road, late September through Christmas. Ohio, Kentucky, Mississippi. The pay was pretty good.

"How good is pretty good?"

"Eight hundred a week. Plus four-fifty a week for hotels and meals."

"For playing *harmonica?*"

"You'll be onstage, too, with Tom Sawyer's gang." He chuckled. "You'll need to bone up on your country licks."

PART THREE

# BIG RIVER

# CHAPTER TEN

# LABOR DAY

*I wanted to get them out to one side, and pump them a little,*
*and find out who I was.*

−MARK TWAIN, *THE ADVENTURES OF HUCKLEBERRY FINN*

NEXT THING I KNEW, Labor Day '87 had come and gone and I was on the bus with the pit band, bound for Hartford, Connecticut. Huck, Tom, Widow Douglas, Pap Finn, the King, the Duke, Silas Phelps, Aunt Sally, plus Jim and the rest of the singing slaves were already up there. Our leg opened in three days. The trumpet player running out muted scales in the seat next to me was Richie Vitale. Dressed entirely in black—shirt, pants, socks, shoes—with a shaved white head and tinted glasses, he was short, spare, so hip it hurt. He flipped open his trumpet case to show me what he'd brought along: a toothbrush, a spare pair of black under-wear, some sheet music. I'd brought two flight bags and a garment bag, plus my daypack full of harps and blank journals and a boom box. Loop everything around my neck and I could barely waddle.

"That's it?" I said, staring.

He stroked his soul-tuft and chuckled. "What else do you need?"

"Pussy," volunteered Rick Molina, the guitar player, leaning over Richie's headrest.

"You don't gotta bring that with you, babe."

"If you knew what my wife looked like, you'd know why I'm holding my own for the next three months."

"Sick Farina." Richie squinted at me. "And Madam Pussow."

"Hey," I complained.

"Fatum Guss."

Molina fell back. "So where's the hang in Hartford?"

"They had some kind of a Monday night thing going on at the Bourbon Street Cafe last time I was out with Sadao."

"You played with Sadao? Fuck, man, I hate you."

Richie tossed off a dizzying muted flourish—a suppressed scream—and lowered his horn. "Sadao is *bad*, man. Cat used to practice in his sleep. Walk around the hotels and shit."

"Riiiight, I heard that."

"Sadao?" I said.

"Watanabe," he said. "Ka-pow What-a-knobby."

I'D GONE ON TOUR with Mister Satan's blessings, and something like a lover's anxiety. I did not want to lose him, or us. No amount of money could replace what I had always considered the greatest gig a blues harmonica player could have. Still, I was young and hungry for experience; this seemed like too good an offer to pass up. He agreed.

"Ain't nobody gonna replace you," he said the day I told him. "You might as well dismiss that worry from consideration."

"I wouldn't blame you if you gave Professor a holler."

He made exaggerated big eyes at me, his gaze veering quickly away. "I'll bet you I don't."

"We have a good thing out here," I said, gazing off at the Apollo Theater. Our stretch of sidewalk was beginning to feel like home. "Anyway, the fall months aren't as good for what we do."

He puttered—fiddling with his various cables, lifting the mike stand so the few dollars he'd made before I came down settled onto the change underneath. His way of helping sticky-fingered street-people avoid temptation.

"We'll live through it," he shrugged. "I ain't worried about the fall too tough."

I stared at his back as he turned to sip at the cup of coffee-light-

and-sweet I'd brought him. His t-shirt was drenched. His jeans were dark with sweat where his butt-bones hit the hi-chair. He'd made do all those years before I'd come along. So why did I feel like shit?

"I mean I'll definitely be back," I murmured.

"I hate promises!" he declaimed to nobody in particular. "A promise is a lie until corrected."

"Well, I'll be correcting the whole danged thing around Christmas time, and that's a promise."

Suddenly he was chuckling. "You'll be back. Creation has a hand in the mess. Ain't up to me to say Stay or Go. We gonna get bigger than you ever know." He glanced up, stroking his beard: one journeyman to another. "The pay is good in the *Big River* show, you were saying?"

"*Very* good. Hell, they're giving me some kind of extra union rate for doubling on tambourine."

"Go ahead on, Mister Percussionist!"

"Of course the union gets it all back in dues and initiation fees. And I gotta pay taxes."

"They got a million ways of taking away what you ain't even made," he said. "And sound reasonable doing it! The streets can't be bothered doggin your behind for no ten cents on the dollar. You make a dollar out here, you got a dollar in your pocket and no hand on it. Correct or wrong?"

"Correct."

"And I got Miss Macie. Ain't that right, baby?" he called out. She was sitting in a folding chair next to the curb, smoking, enjoying her afternoon. She was a part-time nurse's aide at Harlem Hospital.

"Ain't what right?"

"Ain't you got a hand on every dollar I make?"

"Oh, I'm gonna *get* my money."

He elbowed me and cracked up, tickled. "You see what I got going on? My baby is a *money snatcher!*"

I SPENT THE next couple of weeks learning my part from the Broadway cast album, flying out to California to get a look at the show on location, and trying to think of a going-away present for

Mister Satan. Summer ended the way it always does in New York, with one long cool rainy night that silences all but a few of the katydids and cicadas who've been swelling the trees with a restless, clattering, late August surge. The blanketing haze has been washed away; the skies are tight, blue, earnest, promising, disciplined. All your dreams are freshly scrubbed.

The last time I saw him, two days before taking off, I brought him a pair of six-volt burglar alarm batteries from a place called Abco down on Canal Street. He'd turned me on to Abco; it was the place you went whenever an overworked Mouse needed fresh blood. They were compact—each battery the size of two packs of cigarettes—and comfortingly weighty, the density of rolled quarters. He beamed when I pulled them out of my daypack.

"I figured one of your four babies was due," I said, "after the summer we had."

"Thank you, sir! Most definitely."

Later, after we'd played and I'd packed up, we shook hands. We only did that on special occasions; most of the time we slapped. We were both sweating now in the mild September afternoon.

"There's no way I won't be back," I said.

His gold tooth flashed. "I'll be here forever."

"I'll tell you," I added. "As tricky as *Big River* is gonna be with all the different cues I have to remember, we work a hell of a lot harder out here."

"We *got* to!" he cried. "A hundred percent always gonna seem like nothing next to a thousand percent. Right here," he said, pointing at the sidewalk, "you have a river of music and people and admiration, and *our* music keeps on cutting deeper and deeper and flowing along, where if you're playing a show everything's fixed, the boundaries of what you be doing are fixed, it's a *lake*"—tracing a closed loop with his hands—"and there's nowhere *for* it to flow because a lake is a lake no matter what."

"Huh," I mused.

"That's the truth. You may not see it yet but you will."

"I'm starting to."

"Good!" he proclaimed. "Flow on, young man!"

*1981.* I FIRST BEGAN to have something like an ongoing relationship with street musicians when I was an editorial assistant at the Viking Press. I thought of them as my better half, sometimes. The wild outdoor part I'd given up in order to have a career.

I'd gotten the job by chance—a friend of a friend—right after Helen and I moved back to New York from Berkeley in the fall of 1980. Helen was a first-year English grad student at Columbia now, a feminist Americanist preoccupied with patriarchal oppressors and the free-range madwomen who challenged them. I was still searching. Law I'd ruled out, after my paralegal fiasco; publishing seemed a good bet for somebody who loved stories. Viking had made its name as a classy, edgy house: Thomas Pynchon, Nadine Gordimer, Jack Kerouac. Malcolm Cowley, chronicler of the Lost Generation and grand old man of American letters, still came in once a week from Connecticut to edit the Viking Portables. A smaller crumpled Hemingway at eighty-three, with his shock of white hair and mustache, he'd hobble past the reception desk and halooo down the halls at people he knew. I was in awe. I stood next to him once in the men's room, frozen to my urinal. The guy had brought Faulkner back from obscurity in '46! I'd sneak into his empty office on rainy days and eat lunch—pulling open desk drawers, staring at trays of ground-down old pencils and dried-up pens, inhaling used-eraser smell. I wanted to be a *writer,* suddenly. A literary man. I was twenty-three and had no idea what to write. I started keeping a journal, hoping stories would happen to me.

At lunchtime, when the weather was nice, I'd take my journal downstairs and walk one block across Fifty-ninth Street from Madison to Fifth. Sherman's statue was there: a bearded bronze guy with a sword on a rearing horse in the middle of a small plaza, bracketed by marble benches.

A jazz combo—four or five players—seemed to have the midday franchise. The ringleader, a trombonist about my age, had a largish nose and mouse-brown hair cropped tight. His pants sagged. He wore a corduroy coat over old t-shirts. He looked Russian-Jewish, like my immigrant cousins out in Williamsburg. He'd escaped from

Andropov's clutches, I imagined—jazz, the sound of freedom—and was trying to make a new life in the Big Apple. He'd rock front to back as he blew, wristing his slider, cheeks puffed. His lips were reddened when he pulled the mouthpiece away, squeezed into a rounded point. Diddlyotten-woodyotten she-bop-sha-*bam!*

When my hour was up, I'd slap shut my journal, chuck my brown bag in the trash, brush off the butt of my Brooks Brothers suit, and toss a couple of quarters in the large black fiberboard kickdrum-case the band used to collect tips. It was a good deal, on a sunny day. The music and fresh air blended into a sweet new thing, spicy and diaphanous. Upstairs in my small office, refreshed, I'd get back to work—processing box after box of unsolicited manuscripts, sending all but the occasional gem back with a form letter.

Years later, after my life had changed, I ran into the mouse-haired trombonist again, playing a subway platform in the bowels of Times Square. He was still bouncing, still wristing. I told him, tenderly, what his music had meant to me. He smiled, gave me his business card. Weddings, parties. His name was Alex LoDico. From Rome, he said.

I'D BEEN TO ONE *Big River* cast rehearsal at a sunny, airy Union Square dance studio just before Labor Day, where a famous fight director was giving the actors a brush-up course on how to slap, punch, and wrestle somebody to the ground without actually hurting them. William, the guy I was subbing for, thought I ought to see how a traveling Broadway musical was put together. Show people spent a lot of time kissing, hugging, and stretching, I noticed. The prettier the women, the rattier the sweatpants. The musicians wore black jeans, slapped hands, talked shop, made snickering oblique remarks about the male actors all being gay. I sheepishly corrected the first couple of people who welcomed me on board, since the gig was obviously contingent on some sort of audition with David Westlake, the conductor. You didn't just *walk* into a show like this, off the street. I don't know when it suddenly dawned on me that pit musicians were a self-governing guild and William's word was gold. I was in! I kept my mouth shut and eyes open.

The five black actors were shouldering bales of stage-cotton and shuffling through a scene, doing a halfhearted job of pretending to be beaten-down slaves. They exchanged sly smiles while the white actors walked through their lines. One of the two women—Jacqui, a slim pretty Ariel with astonishingly large eyes that bulged—couldn't control herself, breaking suddenly into a wobble-kneed Charleston with scatted accompaniment that broke everybody up, included the testy white director.

"Go, girl!" somebody called out.

"Whoooo!" she groaned when the fit was over, holding herself. "You gotta excuse me, everybody! It's in my *bloooood.*"

She'd been in *Little Shop of Horrors* and *The Tap Dance Kid,* I found out later. Her friend Gail ended up slouching next to me in a row of chairs against a mirrored wall while two slavecatchers in t-shirts and faded bluejeans called Jim nigger and wrestled him into a make-believe flatboat outlined on the floor. Gail was taller than Jacqui, heavier, and moved like somebody who thought of herself as ungainly. Her voice was soft, rich, knowing, creamy, sad, mirth-filled, and direct. Something about her made me wonder if my heart was in trouble again.

"You're William's sub," she said.

"That's what they tell me." I stretched my arms. "I can't quite believe it."

"See. When they called me back in April I was like, Get out, you want me for *what?* 'Cause I hadn't ever done the touring thing."

"Welcome to the club."

"Watch it, nigger!" barked the brawnier slavecatcher, in character. The fight director showed him how to grab Jim in a choke-hold and apply visible force without collapsing his windpipe.

"This play is weirder than it looks," I murmured.

She wrinkled her mouth. "Don't get me started."

OUT IN CALIFORNIA I GOT A LOOK at the show in the final stand of its previous incarnation, with the new actors worked in. My first couple of nights at the Orange County Arts Center I shadowed William—sitting next to him in the darkened pit amid a forest of spotlit music stands, tailing him down to the dressing room as he exchanged one set of silk-lined rags for another, watching from the wings as he skipped onstage with the guitarist and fiddle player at the beginning of Act II to blow his big solo, soon to be mine. The first night, after we'd lingered too long in the performer's lounge, he suddenly overheard his cue on the piped-in P.A. and made a mad dash upstairs. The fiddle player had recently been let go, or quit; he cornered me after William had fled.

"The *only* thing that counts is how much cash you send home. Westlake's an asshole, man. I hate this fucking show."

The conductor was nobody's favorite. He had a close-cropped reddish beard over residual baby fat, a lagging baton few could follow, and a repertoire of exasperated eye-rolls and saddened head-shakes. Groove was a problematic concept. The drums and electric bass were on the far side of the pit, hidden by his raised podium. The horns were back there, too, and invariably tuned a quarter-tone sharp. Westlake was the ski-lift, relentless as bundled steel cable; the musicians were the gondolas: idling, hesitating, then grabbing hold—yanked into the clear, swinging wildly before settling down. Between cues everybody except Westlake flipped idly through old magazines, one ear cocked for whatever telltale strain signaled their fifteen-second warning. Two nights of this and I felt as though I'd fallen into the works of a malfunctioning Swiss chronometer. I still hadn't seen the face of the thing, or helped move the hands.

The harmonica part, as William played it, did allow you a certain freedom that none of the other musicians enjoyed. On "Guv'-ment," Pap Finn's drunken diatribe against the sorry sons-of-bitches who had their hands in every pocket of his britches, you got to wail bluesily for twenty-four bars. On "The Crossing" you got to fill in behind Gail's keening lament as she and the other slaves were poled across the Mississippi by ruthless overseers. On "River in the Rain" you got to play sugary country licks as Huck and Jim, lazing back on their raft, intertwined reedy and throaty voices. You got to slap a tambourine on the gospel number, boing a Jew's harp while the fat bearded King—a thoroughgoing rogue—danced the Royal None-such costumed as a bare-tit-chested half-ape. You had eighteen other cues, some as brief as five seconds, and several long breaks where you could dawdle downstairs and shoot the shit, or flirt, with whomever. You could laze back in your pit chair and gaze up at Gail, Jacqui, Huck, and Jim as they pleaded, voices soaring and arms outstretched, for the love of darkened auditoriums filled with nobody you knew. Your harmonica, which opened the overture and soared above the orchestra, was the audience's first taste of the delights to come.

Westlake pulled me aside after the second night's show. He still hadn't heard me play. He wasn't happy.

"I thought you ought to know," he said. "William's been fired. I realize you're only contracted through Christmas, but I hope you'll stay through next June."

"Wow. Thanks. I'm sorry. I mean he brought me on as his sub."

Westlake smiled through his teeth. "That's right."

WILLIAM HAD BEEN ready to quit anyway, but still. It was an awkward situation. We handled it by taking a bus to Laguna Beach the following afternoon with Gail and two of her fellow slaves, Belle and Ivan.

Ivan was new to musical theater and seemed to be suffering through *Big River* with excess sensibility, like a pair of Ferragamo loafers worn through mud season. Fluent in Dutch, German, Italian, and French, he'd worked in the intelligence section of the U.S. Air Force before leaving to join the Dutch National Opera in Amsterdam. Belle's background, like Gail's, was in the church. Stocky and solid, with a hard laugh and natural hair buzzed short on the sides, she was friendly but took nobody's shit. She had no last name, either—was listed in the Playbill simply as "Belle," with quotation marks.

"It's all about getting paid," she told us. "Waiting around for the phone to ring don't pay no rent."

Gail inspected her nails. "I'm serious."

"You want me to play a slave, show me the money and I'm gonna slave you up *good.*"

"Don't *even* go there," Gail chuckled richly.

Belle lifted her arms, shimmied in place on the bus seat. "I got me a *big* old catfish on *my* raft. Hey Huck!" She waved out the window at a blond surfer dude on a bicycle. "How you doing, baby? Looking good! Gimme a call sometime. Wait a minute. You swing *what* way?"

"Uh uhhhhh."

William and I were sitting behind the two women, harps out, deep in the woodshed. He'd just shown me a mind-blowing new technique. Overblows were a way of playing three extra notes in the middle octave by reversing direction on a draw-note bend so the pitch popped up. The notes literally *weren't there;* you made them happen with shrewdly applied tongue-force. The tone went glassy for a split-second, then broke into clear usable higher ground. Suddenly boogie-woogies were possible, jazzy blues heads like "Blue Monk" and "Night Train," all the sax riffs I'd been fudging. A new world swims into view! Blues harmonica players had barely touched this stuff yet, William told me, but a jazz cat out of Chicago named Howard Levy had already perfected it, blowing any song you gave him in all twelve keys on the same ten-hole harp.

"That's impossible," I grimaced.

"No it's not," William corrected me, always matter-of-fact. "It's just hard."

Gail glanced over her shoulder as we noodled. "You guys gonna give me lessons?"

William smiled. "I didn't know you played."

"I guess I gotta learn."

"I guess we gotta show you," I said. "Talk to me in a few weeks."

"Talk to him," William sighed. "I'm unemployed."

"That's right. Shoot." Gail narrowed one of her almond eyes at me, nostrils flaring, smiling playfully: a Hollywood startlet. "I'll talk to you later, darling."

*1991.* MISTER SATAN TOLD ME about the Illusions That Create Confusion much later on, when we were driving up to Saratoga Springs for a gig. The road was beginning to open him up.

"Okay," he said, tapping the ash off his Kool. "I had me a little

Posing with my first harmonica for the Rockland County Day School yearbook, class of '75, at age sixteen.

Nat Riddles leading the Richmond Blues Society's weekly jam session at the Stonewall Café, Richmond, Virginia, February 1990. Note the Futurist curve of his favorite harp mike, a midfifties Turner originally designed for taxi dispatchers. Courtesy of Beth Horsley.

The author, Mister Satan, and Professor Sixmillion (Bobby Bennett) in the fall of 1986, a few weeks after I had started sitting in. Mister Satan was using only one hi-hat cymbal at this point.

Mister Satan kicking and stomping in our usual spot, the New York Telephone office in Harlem, with Mister Danny and Mister James Gants looking on. Note the work gloves with plastic-tipped index fingers crowning Mister Satan's cymbal stands, above the tambourines. Courtesy of Danny Clinch.

The cover photo of *Harlem Blues,* March 1991. One of Mister Satan's mandalas, reassembled to make a necklace, is propped against the window behind us. Courtesy of Cynthia Carris Alonso.

Mister James Gants, Harlem sojourner. Courtesy of Danny Clinch.

Another *Harlem Blues* snapshot: Mister Gants, in sunglasses, putting it on for the cameras and several unidentified onlookers as I catch my breath. A cup of coffee and scattered harp cases are hiding behind my Mouse in the foreground. Courtesy of Cynthia Carris Alonso.

We feel good! Mister Gants going to town, backed by the Uptown Rhythm Machine, May 1991.

Homer, Joshua Magee, and Bo posing in front of Joshua's truck in Mount Olive, Mississippi. Highway 49 is in the distance, level with the truck roof. I took this photograph in June 1998 on my way home from Fort Worth, Texas.

The *Big River* pit band '87 in motel-room hang mode. *Left to right:* Jeff Potter (drums), Jason Forsythe (trombone), Rich Vitale (trumpet), Brian Hamm (bass), me, Ann Patterson (saxes), Ernie Reed (fiddle), Rock Molina (guitar).

"We are *stars,* Mister!" Miss Macie and Mister Satan relaxing near the SummerStage bandshell in Central Park on the day we opened for Buddy Guy, June 1990. Courtesy of Cory Pearson.

The Nat we all loved, enjoying Nat Riddles Day at Dan Lynch, April 1991. *Left to right:* Frankie Paris, Chuck Hancock, George Worthmore, Nat, Andy Story. Courtesy of Larry Ghiorsi.

The thirsty apprentice and his master working a Mort & Ray street fair at the corner of 104th and Broadway on New York's Upper West Side in September 1989, a few weeks after Yusuf Hawkins's murder in Bensonhurst sent race relations spiraling to a new low during the summer of Spike Lee's *Do the Right Thing*. Copyright Jack Vartoogian / FrontRowPhotos.

El Café Street redux! Charlie Hilbert and I are grooving in cramped quarters during one of his famous champagne-soaked holiday parties, December 1990. Courtesy of Larry Ghiorsi.

A playful moment during the photo shoot for the Satan and Adam cover story in *Living Blues* magazine, May 1996. We are posed in front of Mister Satan's "throne," an abandoned stoop on Adam Clayton Powell Jr. Boulevard between 122nd and 121st Streets. The star sculptures hovering above our heads are Mister Satan's gift to the neighborhood. Courtesy of Paul LaRaia.

group back in the early seventies, we used to play clubs up in Port-chester, Newburgh, wherever. Black clubs. Me on guitar. I was the leader, you know. Had me a little apartment up in Newburgh I might sleep in overnight, if we came up.

"We got in behind this group of three men—sissies, you might say. Dressed all up in women's clothes and I mean mister, those bastards were looking *good*. Shake their behind in your face, do the Boogaloo. You couldn't tell. And the clubs we played, it was mostly *men* coming backstage afterward, to the dressing room! Bringing the ladies—the whatevers!—gifts. Perfume, champagne, wrap up a little box and give it to your favorite Illusion, or maybe you already went on a date with one, last time they came through town.

"Now, quite naturally a musician is gonna keep his eye out after the show, for the overflow fan-ladies the star don't want. Rap with 'em, buy 'em a drink. Most of the time they don't want you if you *ain't* the star, but then again: Marvin Gaye only got two hands. Maybe you played a pretty solo that night, that tickled somebody's ear. Only problem is, what if she's a she-*he*? The Illusions That Create Confusion messed my thing up!"

THAT NIGHT I SAT in the house and saw *Big River* for the first time. The show's basic shape was familiar—who hadn't read Twain's novel?—but the addition of twenty-one musical numbers and singing slaves gave it an unexpected subtext.

With the exception of Huck, white guys in *Big River* burst into song as a way of expressing how much fun it is to cuss, brag, and prank-play your way through the Slave South. Tom Sawyer leads his boy-gang in a circle-sing; an Arkansas simpleton lisps the praises of his home state; the Duke and King—Laurel and Hardy on the lam—strut and hoof and mutilate Shakespeare before clapping chains on Jim. The slaves even the score in their songs, or try to. The difference between Pap Finn drunkenly lambasting the dad-gum tax-man in "Guv'ment" and Gail pleading for deliverance from slavery in "The Crossing" was the difference between burlesque and whatever deep feeling burlesque was afraid of. When Jacqui—the wispy black girl with the big eyes—stepped forward at the funeral of her dead white master and belted out "So Blest We Are" with gospel bravura, a hand seemed to seize my throat and squeeze. What cruel history had produced such smoldering heart, such disciplined ferocity? Then her moment was over. Time for the next series of pranks! *Big River* seemed to have been designed to corral the slaves, wring every last drop of singable soul, then shunt them aside for more burlesque. No sooner has Jim brought the audience to its feet with his triumphant rendition of "Free at Last" and been clapped back in chains by those pesky slavecatchers than Tom is carried in on a stretcher, wounded and feverish. He and Huck have just "freed" Jim after weeks of invented delays by digging the poor guy out of his backyard prison with a spoon.

"Turn him loose!" Tom cries, waving his hand. "He ain't no slave. He's as free as any creature that walks this earth! Old Miss Watson died two months ago, and she was ashamed she ever was going to sell him down the river, and *said* so; and she set him free in her will."

"Then what on earth did *you* want to set him free for," asks Aunt Sally, "seeing he was already free?"

Tom grimaces. "Well, that *is* a question, I must say; and *just* like women! Why, I wanted the *adventure* of it, and I'd a waded neck-deep in blood to get it!"

The audience chuckles; Jim shakes his head. What *will* those white folks think of next? Poor Huck would have done things differently if left to his own devices, but Broadway musicals are Tom Sawyer country. *America* is Tom Sawyer country: cheerful, shallow, violent, oblivious. Was I the only one who saw this? *Big River* was the story of how America refused in the end to take the pain of black people seriously, even while grooving to the sorrow songs.

I'd worked myself into a state by curtain call. I was shivering as I pushed through the stage door and ran into Gail, just coming up the stairs in her bulky slave gowns.

"Gail Gail Gail."

She glanced up, brightened. "Hey, what's up?"

"I am so. . . ." I trailed off in a visionary trance.

Next thing I knew we were holding hands—hers was warm—

and I was pouring out my heart: the show said more than it knew about who we were. It made me hate white boys like Tom Sawyer. It was about nobody, even Huck, finally taking seriously what the slaves wanted, the *only* thing they wanted, which was freedom.

Gail was gazing softly at me, wonderingly. "If I can make one person see . . ." she murmured.

I was borne aloft on a cloud. Jacqui swung around the stairwell in the tight black gown she'd been wearing since her solo showcase at the funeral. I'd watched her swaying during the closing bows, convinced, in my trance, that she carried the groove in her body with as much soulful effortlessness as she sang. Some day, with luck, I'd come close to both.

"And you," I said, turning, "were the only person during the closing bows who was really *moving.*"

She stared at me—blank, incomprehending, irritated. "What are you talking about?"

I struggled to explain as the cloud dissolved with sickening, plunging suddenness.

"I was moving too," Gail said coolly, letting go of my hand.

"Of course you were, I—"

She spun and disappeared down the stairs.

Jacqui was standing there, proud and irritable, staring at me. She did not understand. I stammered, lost.

"I have to apologize," she finally said, yanking the stage-mike clip off her dress. "I have an attitude problem, it's late in the tour and I want to go *home.*" She turned and disappeared down the stairs.

I SAT IN MY ROOM UPSTAIRS—aching, grieving. Condemned by my own words. I'd blown it. I wasn't worth the ground Gail and Jacqui stood on. The blues I had right now couldn't even be dignified with that word.

I wandered down to the hotel bar later and found William, who let me buy him a beer. In his quiet way, William was a remarkably soulful guy. Sometimes when I hated white people, or myself, I needed to be reminded that we had better in us. William was a gifted jazz player who had spent time in Brazil and was prone to falling into mystical trances that sometimes compromised his ability to show up for gigs on time or make every cue in a Broadway musical. Guys in the pit liked to joke about "William Standard Time." It was easy to joke until you heard him fronting his Brasilio-funk quartet— eyes closed, music writhing through him, endless breathtaking lines that blossomed like doves cooing to life under a magician's draped handkerchief. William wasn't "cool." When other members of his quartet were soloing he'd pick up a tambourine, sinking so deeply into the groove that his mouth would fall open as his eyes rolled skyward: a death mask in the service of life. His show clothes—the St. Pete costume, the River Rat rags—fit me with no alterations. Secret sharers of the golden harmonica chair. He did his best to calm me.

"Gail likes you," he said. "She was probably jealous."

"I'm such a fucking idiot." I gulped my beer. "The last thing anybody needs is me flying in and playing drama critic when they're busting ass every night. Jacqui, man. Fuck."

"I wouldn't worry about Jacqui. Jacqui is moody."

"I would be, too, if I had to deal with assholes like me."

He smiled. "You may need to chill out."

"I may need to shut up."

We picked up our beers, swiveled on our stools. "Shake Your Booty" by K.C. and the Sunshine Band was thumping the jukebox. That's the way, uh huh uh huh, I like it, uh huh uh huh.

"The show's been fun," he sighed. "Even if Westlake hates my guts."

"The whole thing sucks, man."

"It does suck and it's also partly my fault. I can't blame him for doing his job."

"Why not?" I laughed. "Everybody else does."

"His job is to be an asshole and make sure the show happens. The rest of us just go through the motions and get paid. It's easy to bitch when you're not in charge of anything."

"Let me get this," I said, signaling for the tab.

He emptied his beer, swallowed. "You'll do better than me on the road. I never did figure out how to live out here."

.   .   .

ALL WAS FORGIVEN, remarkably. William gave Gail a harmonica and told her how sorry I was. *Big River* thrived on this sort of back-stage tête-à-tête, like a tiny incestuous high school. Tom was Danny Lee from Baton Rouge, Louisiana: great-great grandsomething of Robert E. Lee, the Civil War general. Raymond Kimbrough, who played Jim with Magic Johnson's visible warmth and Mike Tyson's confused fury, had run with a rough crowd back in the Black Power days. His show-nickname was Wreck. Married but willing to party. His favorite pickup line, overheard: Baby, you just *happen* to be talk-ing to the highest-paid runaway slave in America.

Departure day was a warmly luminous September Saturday afternoon in Costa Mesa. I was leaning against the railing outside the stage door—waiting for an airport shuttle bus, tooting my harp—when Belle pushed through, also tooting. The matinee had just ended.

"All right Belle!" I laughed. "I didn't know you played."

"Two whole days." She cradled it playfully between opposed pairs of fingers. "It ain't right you and William having *all* the fun."

"Check it out." I cupped my hands and flapped. "You'll get a better wah-wah sound if you hold it like this."

I was just showing her how to purse her lips to make single notes with a tight seal when Gail came out. She had on a summery pink dress and dark sunglasses with luscious red lipstick and she was standing tall. She'd relaxed her curls with oil. She seemed to float in a halo.

"Hey," she pouted. "What you doing giving Belle lessons? You were supposed to give *me* lessons."

Jacqui, right behind, put a hand up to shade her eyes, then saw Belle. "Ooooh girl, you look so country with that thing."

"Thank you, baby." She honked and they both shrieked.

"Gail," I murmured pleadingly. "She has the first thing any har-monica player has to have: she's crazy about the instrument."

Gail suddenly grinned, outrageously flirtatious. "I might be crazy, too."

"How crazy is crazy?"

"You'll just have to find out."

"Nawwwww," Jacqui warned. "Don't go there."

Gail said she'd spend her week off practicing so she'd be ready for me. I said I'd see her in Hartford. I shouldered my flight bag.

"You're leaving?"

"Here's my bus," I nodded.

"Oh well," she sighed. "Then I have to give you a kiss." She leaned forward to hug me, planting a big lipsticky smack on my cheek. Her oiled hair had a delicious smoky scent.

"Whoa," said Belle as we pulled apart. "She's marked you up, Adam."

I turned to eye myself in the building's mirrored gold facade.

"Don't rub it off," Gail said. "Wear it proud."

Jacqui shook her head and smiled, tut-tutting. "Girl, I'm gonna tell your mama on *you*."

CHAPTER ELEVEN

# GOING SOMEPLACE

*Look out for me, oh muddy water. . . .*

—ROGER MILLER, "MUDDY WATER"

THEN WE WERE IN HARTFORD, all of us: conductor and pit musicians, overseers and slaves, older women down in Wardrobe who smoked cigarettes and purred as they folded freshly laundered costumes, a bearded stage manager named Starling who gazed hungrily over the tops of his half-moon glasses at any young man in tight jeans with a nice butt. Two massive eighteen-wheelers were idling behind Bushnell Memorial Hall, ready to swallow Huck's servo-driven plywood raft and Jim's four-foot rubber catfish. A bus-and-truck tour is a circus. Ringleader Mark Twain was there with his walrus mustache and creamy white suit; the guy who played him reappeared later in the show as a doctor, lawyer, slavecatcher. I pored over our first Playbill as opening night loomed. We were Broadway veterans, commercial actors, opera singers, soap opera walk-ons, up-and-comers who'd beat out wannabes. Everybody was a refugee from somewhere else: *Amadeus, Peter Pan, Bubbling Brown Sugar, All My Children, Romeo and Juliet, Hee Haw, Porgy and Bess, Best Little Whorehouse in Texas.* We were a *Whorehouse* alumni club, in fact: three actors plus Ernie Reed, the replacement fiddle player from Nashville.

I saw a lot of Ernie during rehearsals, as they worked us into the rotation. Ernie had played *Whorehouse* a thousand times on Broadway, smoked several million cigarettes—most with a drink in hand—and was currently on his fifth wife. He was forty. His hair and beard were gray, his eyes narrowed, his face pockmarked, his hips trim. He had Tennessee on his tongue: bluegrass, aw shit, and mountain honey. He'd forgotten more about his instrument than I would ever know about mine. Rick Molina was there, too, with his thrusting incisors and dangling pair of hardshell guitar cases. Colombian-American but accentless, pale, dark-eyed, a jazz-fusion player from Brooklyn with witheringly fast chops, Rick had been a ladies' man in an earlier life, before marriage.

"You ever been with an older woman?" he asked me one night.

"Thirty-six is about it."

"Much older. Fifty-five, sixty."

"I'm missing out, huh?"

"You have no idea, man. Sweet. Slow. So slow and sweet you can't even—and grateful as shit, too, because most guys are like Hmmm when it comes to older women. Trust me: if you ever get the chance, go for it."

Rick, Ernie, and I were the pit band's elite fighting unit, the only three musicians who wore costumes and appeared onstage. These appearances were scattered—two minutes here, five minutes there—and culminated in the Entreacte, where we strolled out from the wings into a spotlit circle and let rip as the band bluegrassed at our feet. Ernie was first out, sawing and Orange Blossoming like a devilish gray billy goat; he'd been suckled on this stuff and would occasionally throw in a burst of Paganini to keep things fresh. Then Rick, who was fond of playing way outside—substituting whole-tone scales and bebop runs for the blue-sky triads you were supposed to play, all with such string-snapping fluency that nobody could tell what harmonic rules he'd broken. Westlake, gazing up from his raised podium, would cock his head: Whaaaaa? Then my turn. The two-step tempo was faster than anything Mister Satan and I had played—it burned rather than swung—but the streets had trained me well. Professor Sixmillion, Mr. Simms, James Gants. I gazed out across the darkened rows and fired from down under, hurling our Harlem blues into the mix.

An hour later I was waiting in the far wing, preparing to hand a shovel to the sheriff in the gravedigger scene. Wreck was standing there in Jim-costume with his wrists bound, ready to be dragged onstage: tall, brooding, shadowed. We'd been introduced once by William. He was the star; I'd been gazing up at him from the pit. I'd been slapping the tambourine on "Muddy Water," his first big duet with Huck where the raft they've just leaped on pivots downstage, tilting South toward freedom:

> Look out for me, oh muddy water
> Your mysteries are deep and wide
> And I got a need for going some place
> And I got a need to climb upon your back and ride

Nine thousand a week, William had told me. Sing with a voice like that—huge, resonant, consistent—and you could name your own price. He glanced up, saw me loitering, smiled.

"Hey man, nice playing," he said in a stage whisper. "Welcome to the show." He reached out his knotted fists and we improvised a handshake.

"Thanks."

"Check it out." He slid something off the wooden locker just behind him, held it out. An economy-size box of Trojanenz condoms.

"Oh shit," I laughed.

"Union stagehands." He rotated it cautiously, wonderingly. "I could use a few of these."

OPENING NIGHT WAS a series of countdowns: half-hour (all actors in the house), five minutes (all musicians in the pit), one minute (all eyes on Westlake). The house lights slowly dimmed, the audience hushed like fowl roosting for the night. Westlake was staring at me, baton raised. For weeks I'd been woodshedding the show's catchy little theme song: not a blues but bluesy bluegrass, the high lonesome sound with edge. You're perched in front of a live mike, out of sight of your listeners, trying not to cough. Westlake had warned me against foot-tapping and other excess motion. I could empathize with Huck; the pit was already beginning to feel a little cramped up and smothery. I played from that—an exuberance born of frustration—as Westlake's baton jerked down, hauling me on board. We slid away from shore and eased into the current, creaking slightly.

Disaster loomed briefly, spectacularly, in Act II. Relaxing in the pit after blowing our wad on the Entreacte, Rick and I gazed up as Jacqui, trim and resplendent in funeral black, stepped forward and prepared to belt "How Blest We Are." Stage and house quieted; her dead white master lay motionless in an open casket, inches from her clenched fist. She raised her eyes—large, beautiful, bulging, astonishing—to the heavens. Suddenly they welled with tears. Tears were rolling down her cheeks, she was opening her mouth *and fumbling the first few notes:*

How blest we are. . . .

The auditorium and pit went pin-drop silent; some great, collective beating heart seemed to seize. She paused for a split-second, filled her lungs, then cut loose—mouth quivering, shoulders trembling:

As children of a God so good and true
To understand his moving hand
And love for me and you

The ascending line from "children" to "God" was a rocket's red flare bursting in air; the God-note was a wild note, razoring through. Her voice, a timbral cornucopia, formed and re-formed as the song poured out: a torn shroud, a gasping birth-scream, a quivering new life. Time, baptized, began to flow. The collective heart sighed with relief. Rick grinned over his shoulder, gave me a thumbs-up. Somehow, amazingly, the thing had come together. The show was flying.

*1992.* MISTER SATAN AND I were cruising up I-95 North one afternoon toward a gig at House of Blues in Cambridge, Massachusetts, when the subject of his parents came up. His daddy, I knew, was a super-deacon in some church down in St. Petersburg, Florida; his momma was a church lady. He'd just spoken with them by phone for the first time in years. I asked him if his mother called him by his new name.

"She *definitely* ain't gonna call me that," he barked. He pushed in the cigarette lighter, shook out matching Kools, offered me one. Chuckled as he lit his and exhaled.

"I was an abused child," he complained. "I'm deadly serious. They ain't gonna let you play no blues at home. I used to play piano in the church back in Mount Olive, Mississippi—that's okay, God gonna *loooove* you, boy, if you play that gospel song. So I come home, sit at the piano we got. Make sure Momma and them is out, quite naturally. And then I'd go off on some blues—Lloyd Glenn, Louis Jordan, Big Maceo. I could play, too. Next thing I know, Momma done snuck back in the house *while* I'm playing, come up behind me and *Blam!* Right in the back of the head. I'd sit straight up on the bench and start up with 'Nearer My God to Thee' and all that ugly mess." He shook his head. "Ain't that pitiful?"

I SAW LITTLE OF GAIL in Hartford, offstage. I'd crossed paths with her and Jacqui the first afternoon, coming through the hotel lobby.

"Gail," I said, heart fluttering.

"Hey Adam, whassup?"

"Not much." I kicked at the carpet. "You been practicing?"

She made a face. "Naw."

Her boyfriend was in town, Jacqui told me a couple of days later. My heart fell. I'd seen her hanging out with a quiet black guy in corduroy slacks outside the stage door on opening night. After that, I'd really only seen her at work: her on stage, me gazing up from below. Her big spotlit moment was when she screamed "No!" as a heartless slave-trader yanked Jacqui—her slave-daughter—away, seconds after the finals bars of "So Blest We Are." Crouched over my mike, I couldn't see her during "The Crossing"; our blending was subtle, invisible; intertwining lines of cadenced grief. She did sound sad. Was that only because she was paid to?

I WAS HANGING in the hotel bar with Ernie one night after the show—we had eight in Hartford—when Walker Joyce and Michael Calkins strolled in: the King and the Duke.

The King, as Walker played him, was *Big River*'s answer to W. C. Fields, Falstaff reinvented as an Arkansas snake-oil salesman: no lie too big, no profit too small, no perfidy too perfidious. Sell off Mary Jane Wilkes's beloved house slaves after promising her you'll do nothing of the sort? Hell yes, bubba! Walker was bearded, balding, talked out of the side of his mouth, and waddled across stage as though pulled by his beachball of a belly. The Duke, as Michael played him, was Walker's antipode and foil: a failed Shakespearian tragedian, emaciated and antic, with a faceful of wildly expressive creases. These were often aimed in the King's direction, signifying wincing distaste. Michael was flamingly, delightedly gay; his Duke had a conscience but was willing to make a buck.

"What say, Ernie?" Walker bellowed, waddling up. He was freshly showered; his potbelly heaved under a white t-shirt and sky blue polyester slacks.

"Not a whole hell of a lot."

"Did we kill tonight or did we die?"

Ernie pulled at a cigarette. "Shit."

"Hah hah." He clapped his hands. "Gentlemen, I hadn't realized until last night's performance, when I was forced to sit out with my"—he coughed, fist to mouth—"terribly sore throat, just how *good* we are."

"We are," I agreed.

"I mean I knew we were good, but I didn't realize we were *this* good. We're *magnificent.*"

Michael's face creased as he turned toward me, leaning against the bar. "Have we officially met?"

"I'm the guy who boings the Jew's harp in 'When the Sun Goes down in the South.' "

"Ahhh. And a wonderful job you're doing, boinging that . . . that . . . What *do* they call that little metal strip?"

"It doesn't have a name. Jew's harp prong-thing."

"Jew's harp prong-thing. Right." He showed all his teeth as he turned and signaled the bartender. His stonewashed jeans were bun-tight.

Walker, a man of many talents, had recently produced his first Nashville recording session; he'd heard about Ernie—the cream of the crop—and was thrilled to be around him. Ernie lit up a cigarette and told good ol' boy stories about Vassar, Jerry Jeff, and a dozen unknown studio greats. Most involved perfectly executed sight reading, excessive beer drinking, and collapsing late at night on the floors of each other's living rooms.

"Hello everybody!" Jacqui cried. All heads turned. She'd drifted into the bar and was standing next to Walker. Her hat was leopard-spotted fake fur; her coat had a lavender ostrich-feather ruff that matched her lipstick. Her eyes were huge, sparkling, mischievous.

"It's the Diva," Michael called out.

"Girl," she hooted, flapping her hand, "don't even *try*."

"Diva incoming."

"Hey Walker, how's your throat doing?" she asked, tilting toward him.

"Close enough for bus-and-truck."

" 'Cause I was thinking I could give you my throat secret, if you want."

He rubbed his hands, eyes suddenly roguish. "I'd, ahem, like that very much."

"Every night before you go to bed, right? Whatever motel or hotel or wherever you're staying at, go into the bathroom, close the door, turn on the hot water and let it run till it's steaming, then turn it down about halfway and pull up on the knob so the sink starts to fill with all that steaming hot water. And then stand over it and breathe and I mean *breathe*."

"Inhale?" Walker said.

"Inhale the heck out of it, so it gets all up in your sinuses and cleans you *out*."

"That's what you do?"

"Cross my heart."

"Amazing. And if I do that, every night, will I be able to sing just like you?"

She batted her eyelashes. "You can die trying."

"Ahhhhhh," Walker roared. "I love yah. You wanna beer?"

"I don't drink. Or smoke," she added, waving Ernie's clouds away with her hand.

Ernie smiled. "Your life must be boring as hell without any vices."

"Well I do have *one* vice," she said, grinning.

"Ice cream," I suggested.

"That too." Her eyes locked on mine. "I don't know you well enough to tell you."

Ernie snorted. "Aw shit."

"Tell *me*," Michael demanded, stroking her lavender ostrich feathers.

"Night everybody!" she hollered cheerfully, pulling away and flouncing out of the bar.

RICHMOND, OUR SECOND WHISTLE-STOP, meant a brief reunion with Nat. He'd moved out of Esther's place in Norfolk over the summer, lost his sanitation job, gotten very sick, moved North, been taken in by a woman named Cheryl. The precise order of events was unclear; we'd talked once back in July. I called the new number from my Hartford hotel room. He sounded weakened but resilient—energized, like Job, by furious astonishment at the disasters that had befallen him.

"You should have seen me right after I got sick," he said. "I looked like a Biafra baby. My ribs were literally pushing through the skin on my chest, and my . . . my—I mean I was sick as a *dog*. Couldn't work, couldn't do shit." He laughed. "I'm still skinny. Twenty-five pounds down."

"What the hell was it?"

"Nobody knows. The *doctors* don't know. I was like Boom! boom! boom! Gimme this test, gimme that—because I knew from my days at Bronx Lebanon what the various indicators we oughta be looking at were."

"That's right, weren't you some sort of a—"

"Hematological technician." He coughed. "After my mother died."

He was working two shit-jobs now: making window displays in a FarmFresh convenience store by day, pumping gas at night. Even he couldn't pretend they were part of a master plan. I was embarrassed for him—the great Nat, my hero—and didn't know what to say. He hadn't touched his harps in a couple of months.

"I *couldn't* play," he said when I protested. "I barely had enough strength to lift a glass of water to my lips."

" 'Cause I've been playing a lot. I mean I just wanna make sure we're still in this thing together."

"Oh we're still in it." He chuckled. "I get lazy without you and New York and Charlie Hilbert and that whole Dan Lynch crowd around to—"

"Wait," he said, interrupting himself.

I could hear a radio babbling behind him. Suddenly the *Big River* theme—solo harmonica fronting an orchestra—came on. A teaser from the cast album.

"You're famous," he laughed into the phone. "They're letting everybody know you'll be here."


*1981.* I'D BEEN WORKING at the Viking Press for about a year—returning unsolicited manuscripts by the wagonload, when November's chilly rains blew in and I came down with a low fever that lingered. After three weeks I saw a doctor. Diagnosis: mono.

You feel like near-shit for six months: punky, slightly dizzy. I kept the job, barely. I gave up running, which hurt. I needed that fix of inhaled space. I curled inward, crawled into bed, drowned myself in words. I typed up lists of Great Books, then mowed them down. *Anna Karenina, The Magic Mountain, Their Eyes Were Watching*

*God*. I read everything Malcolm Cowley—my hero, the Viking patriarch—had ever written.

Cowley obsessed me. He'd made his living back in the twenties and thirties as a freelance literary journalist in Paris and New York, peddling reviews to newspapers, magazines, quarterlies. This suddenly seemed like the most romantic possible calling a young man could have. Live by your wits! Homebound, I began to write reviews on spec and send them out, modeling my critical style on Cowley's no-nonsense homespun. Hart Crane's poems, he'd once written, "were solidly built and clumped on heavy feet, like Hart himself." What synesthesia! Cowley's theory of art—that singer and song couldn't be separated—was an aging editor's creed, not a younger professor's. He'd spent decades at Viking and *The New Republic* working with living, breathing writers, with the poems and novels they'd sweated out. He respected the creative process. Younger professors, in thrall to Roland Barthes and Jacques Derrida, sneered at it. The Author was Dead; texts were no more than raw material for deconstruction. Neither singer nor song had a chance in today's theory-mad academy.

I knew what younger professors were up to because Helen and I socialized mostly with her grad-school friends from Columbia. She was moving more deeply into feminist theory these days: Tillie Olson on the silences that plagued the careers of women writers, Hélène Cixous on *l'écriture feminine,* the "female sentence," which supposedly flowed in accord with a woman's languid, diffused sexuality rather than stiffening into crisp, phallic, Hemingwayesque thrust. I thought Cixous was full of shit. I knew Cowley would have agreed.

Helen and I got into lots of fights over this stuff. She had a habit of taking our intellectual disagreements personally, as though I was attacking *her* and not her theories. "I'm a feminist!" I'd shout. "My mother's a smart woman! I *like* smart women! I just don't think you can reduce women's writing to sentences spun out of mother's milk!"

One night, when I was dizzy and feverish, the shit finally hit. I'd rolled over without kissing her goodnight, bugged by some stupid argument we'd just had. She touched my shoulder. I feigned sleep.

"Adam?" she whispered.

Nothing.

She got pissed off. She heaved herself out of bed and stalked off down the hall.

The spare bed we used during fights was in my study. I'd covered it with books—Cowley, Hemingway, Kerouac—over the last couple of weeks. I heard her throwing my stuff onto the floor. There was a crash that sounded like a notebook splattering against a wall.

Shivers of black rage warped through me. I leaped out of bed, ran barefoot down the dark hall.

"You shouldn't have done that!" I yelled as I flew by.

Her study was just past mine. I whirled into the shadowy room, reached down into her bookshelf, shoved my hands behind her god-damn Women's Books—Cather, Chopin, Nin—and heaved. A whip-like stream of volumes flew off the tips of my fingers onto the floor. A few more strokes and I'd emptied three shelves.

THEY FLEW THE ENTIRE *Big River* cast from Hartford to Washington, then bused us down. I had a wallet thick with crisp new hundred-dollar bills after my first paycheck, even with hundreds in taxes taken out. I'd received union scale as my base pay, plus bonuses for doubling on tambourine, tripling on Jew's harp, and appearing onstage. I'd made as much in one week with *Big River* as I'd made the whole summer with Mister Satan. Wreck, I supposed, had made as much in one performance. He could sing.

Nat came to opening night—I'd comped him—and looked better than he'd led me to believe, although thin. His eyes burned as we grabbed hands: fiery, pained, exuberant, liquid, distinct. He wore his blackness casually, effortlessly, a man who knew no enemies until they made their presence felt. After the final bows I pulled him back-stage toward the reception, where our stars were expected to drink champagne with local arts patrons.

"You heard that shit I was playing on the Entreacte?" I said. "The weird stuff in the middle octave?"

"I heard something fishy in there."

"Those are the overblows I was telling you about."

"I prophesied this a *long* time ago," he said, flashing his wire-retained tooth, voice suddenly gone aged and Southern. "All us ooooooold-timers gonna get pushed out the way by you younguns."

The patrons who belonged to the Benefactors' Circle were mostly red-faced white guys in tuxes escorting blond trophy wives and fiercely cheerful unaccompanied older women in expensive smocks. One of these—wandering, sipping—swiveled suddenly and beamed at Nat, touching his hand.

"You sing *marvelously.*"

"Thank you, darling." His smile was dazzling. "You're too kind."

"And you were . . . ?" Pulling back slightly, squinting at me.

"The harmonica player."

"Wonderful! My granddaddy used to play that on the Foth of Jew-lah."

She showed her teeth and wandered off.

He clinked my glass. "We're moving up in the world."

Gail came through the door, saw us, and drifted over. She was wearing the uniform—navy blue show jacket over t-shirt and jeans, white Reeboks—and glowing. I'd mentioned her to Nat.

"You gonna introduce me to your friend?" she teased, bumping me with her shoulder.

"I thought somebody around here already had a friend."

She made a face. "Somebody around here had a rough time up in Hartford with somebody who isn't around here anymore."

"Well *somebody* around here thought you were just ignoring me."

Nat chuckled. "You must be Gail."

She rolled her eyes as we all laughed. Her smile was sideways-pulled, sheepish, absurdly cute. "See," she said, drawing the word out into a richly inflected mixture of resignation and complaint.

"This is Nat," I said. "My harmonica teacher."

"Get out," she said, impressed.

"He's my boy," Nat beamed.

Her right eye narrowed. "So like, if I take lessons from him, I'm really taking lessons from you?"

"That depends on what kind of subtleties he shows you."

"Subtleties?"

I sipped my champagne. "I haven't even showed her how to hold the thing."

"Hey, Wreck," she called out as the star wandered into view, "don't be a stranger."

Towering over us, Wreck juggled a small paper plate of cocktail food as he and Nat shook.

"I'm a local guy," Nat joked. He nodded at a nearby cluster of patrons. "They already got me mistook for you."

Wreck glanced up from his chicken fingers, gaze flat, giving nothing away. A fleeting tension seemed to hover. Then he smiled. "Don't do anything I wouldn't do."

CHARLOTTE WAS OUR NEXT STOP: a five-hour doze in twin motor coaches, with lunch at a cafeteria in a nameless North Carolina mall where the fried chicken came with sides of collard greens, green beans, mashed potatoes, and candied yams, plus huge tumblers of sugarless lemonless iced tea. The weather had grown mild; we'd caught up with Indian summer, after Hartford's cool blowy rains.

Gail had no idea what she was starting to do to me. The show was a womb in which we floated, a relentless low-level swirl of lust, gossip, and petty gripes. I'd gaze up at her longingly from the pit, dawdle backstage in her general vicinity before striding out to blow the Entreacte, flop into the nearest available bus seat as we were ferried between auditorium and motel. She'd already punched my shoulder once or twice in a playful way; I'd shoved her back. Her speaking voice—murmurous, sensible, chiding, tickled, raucous—kept me fascinated and off balance. Little bits of her pre-show life had emerged: She'd worked for five years at an international organization responsible for placing college kids for a term or two with interested families overseas. She could pass for white on the phone; some people who'd known her that way were surprised when they first met her. She'd weighed 200 pounds until losing 40 last year. She passed snapshots of her old self around the bus, putting the fat girl down. She'd been hurt—somewhere, somehow—and carried it with her as a knowing wryness that drove me nuts. She expected disappointment and knew how to survive it. What would it take to destroy her expectations and make her wildly happy? I thought she was infinitely more beautiful than she seemed to know.

Our third and final night in Charlotte, after the Sunday matinee, Jacqui and I were hanging out in Gail's motel room, watching her iron a skirt. Some local guy helping load out the show—a black guy, I gathered—had asked her out on a date. We were waiting for him to call. It was getting late; Gail had gone over the skirt a couple of times, carefully pressing out every last wrinkle. She and Jacqui were giving me a singing lesson, setting me straight on the difference between a head voice and a belt.

"See, your head voice," Jacqui explained, lifting the back of her hand against her lower jaw, "is strictly from your vocal chords up. It's not about supporting the note with your diaphragm, it's about visualizing the note and *feeling* it, up inside your head while you're singing it." She demonstrated with a single clear bell-like tone that suddenly skipped, darted, and swooped, a butterfly in a summer meadow.

Gail snorted, smiling. "Go on and riff, girl."

Jacqui showed all her teeth, like Little Richard hamming it up. "Can I do my Minnie Riperton, y'all?"

"Isn't she the one with like a three-octave range?" I said.

"Looovin youuuu," Gail crooned, "is eaaaasy 'cause you're beau-uuutifullll. . . ."

Jacqui flapped her hand. "Minnie Riperton is *sick.*"

"Seriously," Gail agreed.

"Four octaves, five octaves. I mean up in the oh-*zone*. Can't Whitney do nothing but *cry* when Minnie blows her dog whistle." Jacqui opened her mouth wide, strained her neck muscles, and produced: silence.

Gail stopped ironing and cracked up, backhanding her mouth. "Uh uhhh," she groaned. "That's *wrong.*"

"Thank you very much," Jacqui chirped in a saccharine-sweet, little girl voice.

"So a belt is what—lower and stronger than that?"

"Your belt," she said, "is as high as you can go with full power, supporting your voice from underneath."

"With your diaphragm?"

"Totally with your diaphgram. Like if you wanna really *project,* step out in front of the band or whatever, you're gonna dig down into your belt and come up into it as hard as you can."

"I mean this is what I think of as a belt." I sang the first line of "Sweet Home Chicago," straining, a self-conscious bush-leaguer among pros.

"All right, Adam," Gail said, chuckling richly.

A smile tugged at Jacqui's mouth. "Definitely a belt, with some other stuff mixed in."

"Aretha belts," I suggested.

"Aretha *sings,*" Gail corrected. "It's like Sarah Vaughan as far as her having pushed it to the point where it's not about how high can you belt or how pretty can you riff, it's about you can do *anything,* so what do you wanna do?"

"Exactly," Jacqui agreed. "I gotta know it's your *own* voice when I hear you on the radio, not you trying to sound like Aretha or Patti or Whitney or whomever."

"It's the same thing with harmonica," I said. "A lot of guys just want to sound like Little Walter."

Gail glanced at her watch, sighed. "Somebody's standing me up."

"Girl," Jacqui murmured. "I feel for you."

Gail said nothing, pushing her iron in slow patient circles.


*1982.* HELEN AND I didn't really know any black people, except for characters in books and voices on records, which was strange since we lived right on the border of Harlem. The Columbia University community was curious that way. Well-meaning white folks scared you when you moved in with stories of grad students getting mugged and shot. How were you supposed to feel about the neighborhood after that?

We tried hard to keep a balance between constructive paranoia and fruitless hysteria. It certainly felt risky walking the three blocks north to 125th Street, past the projects. We did that a few times, to have dinner at a cheap Indian restaurant up there. You'd pass loitering young black guys with chrome-plated boom boxes on their shoulders, laughing and yelling at friends down the block. Who knew what they were capable of? I'd feel vaguely protective as we strolled by. I had no idea what I'd do if they came at us. I envied them a little, for all that. Enjoying the hell out of themselves, outdoors, while the rest of us slaved away inside.

Every now and then we'd get really daring. We'd discovered— thanks to a grad-student tip—that you could buy pot from seedy little walk-in establishments, "candy stores." There was one of these just across Broadway, a couple of blocks from our apartment. When the urge hit, almost always at night, we'd take a little stroll up into Never-Never Land. Pot was an aphrodisiac; it turned us into voracious animals. I'd been an occasional toker since Spiral days and had introduced Helen to the stuff early on, one of the few times I'd actually led the way in our relationship.

Hunger laced with danger hurried us past the projects on 123rd Street, ducked us under the subway tracks. She'd usually wait outside while I went in. The smallish front room, postered with malt liquor signs featuring shiny motorcycles, voluptuous women, and ravenous jungle animals, was empty. Centered in the back wall was a small thick plexiglass window. You walked up to it and waited; a young black guy's face appeared after a moment. He'd stare at you— bored, sullen, nonplussed. You'd slip out the five or ten you'd been clutching in your hip pocket, stick it through the slot under the window, ask for either a nickel or a dime. He'd take your bill, disappear briefly, then reappear and push a small bulging envelope—like a tiny brown paper pillow—through the slot.

Drugs! It seemed safer than buying off the street, which we'd never done. The candy stores couldn't give you oregano, or angel dust, because you might come back and raise a stink. Which was not to say it was great shit. We always assumed, in fact, that the guy behind the window kept a small stash of lower-quality nickels and dimes for guys like me, who weren't likely to complain. White-boy mix. It was our running joke.

The stuff did get us high, though. We'd slink home, strip, light up, feel as though we were doing something slithery and evil. One time we brought back a bong that Helen had selected from a head shop next to the candy store while I waited in the car. The glass stem was decorated with a red-and-black decal of a furious lunging rattlesnake, fangs erect and dripping.

The only problem with mixing sex and pot, we agreed, was that your feelings weren't nearly as engaged as your bodies. More lustful than loving. That was okay, as a change of pace: lust was an improvement over yelling, crying, freezing each other out. Our relationship had always been schizophrenic. More often these days, perhaps. I'd wake the morning after—ravished, fog-headed, filled with vague guilt—and wonder where the hell I'd been.

JACQUI AND I HAD ADJOINING ROOMS—a suite connected by doubled locking doors—at the Radisson in Spartanburg, South Carolina. The show had become routine; our new friendship was anything but. We'd pause at various points during the day, open our door, and knock on the other's.

"Hey Aaaad-um," she'd call out. "You there?"

I'd jump up, unlock, and pull mine open; she'd be leaning against hers, giving me her baby-of-the-family grin.

"Whatcha got goin' on?" she'd say in one of her many voices. She could do dozens, from Dracula to Buckwheat; she'd broken up the bus more than once by combing her hair out into clumps and lisping "O-tayyyyy."

"Not much," I'd say.

Were *we*, then, supposed to have an affair? But each of us had a heart set on someone else. Hers was a guy she'd grown up with back in Hollis, Queens, also twenty-one. We sat cross-legged on the carpeted floor one afternoon and told all.

"Wowww," she said after I'd confessed my feelings for Gail. "That's so sweet."

"What do you think I should do?"

"The only thing you really *can* do is go by what your heart tells you. And keep a positive attitude."

"I mean I'm not trying to break up whatever she already has going on back home. That's one reason I've been hanging back."

Her eyes were bright. "I know you respect Gail, right?"

"Absolutely."

"So you gotta respect her enough to allow her to make up her *own* mind about what she's gonna do."

"You think I oughta come right out and just tell her how I feel?"

"I think if it was me, I'd rather know how somebody felt about me than not know."

"I just think she deserves to be happy."

Jacqui smiled. "We're all working on that."

Suddenly, out of the blue, she was telling me about losing her virginity—blindingly sweet, like nothing she'd ever experienced outside of church.

"I envy you," I sighed. "My first time was at college with somebody I didn't even know."

"Uh uhhh. I couldn't do that."

"I don't know why I did. It took me two years to find somebody I really cared about, and it was almost like you're describing, at its best. And then she left me after five years for another guy and I flipped. That's when I got back into music, whatever it was—like three years ago."

"I can tell by the way you talk about her she's still on your mind."

"Nah."

"Positive attitude," she chided, wagging her finger.

I smiled. "Hey, do I look unhappy?"

"I didn't even *tell* you what Gail said about you."

"What?"

"Catch you later," she laughed, jumping up.

CHAPTER TWELVE

# CATFISH ON THE RAFT

*We are pilgrims on a journey . . . through the darkness of the night*
*We are bound for other places . . . crossing to the other side*

—ROGER MILLER, "THE CROSSING"

AT THIS POINT in the tour a guy suddenly fell in love with my sound. He was the replacement sax player: Arkady Kofman, Russian Jewish emigré and king of the Long Island bar mitzvah circuit. To him, *I* was the real blues.

Arkady had joined our pit band in Spartanburg after Ann Patterson, a hawk-mouthed altoist from Texas by way of Venice Beach, had finished her promised two weeks and flown home. Ann was quietly professional; Arkady was the unquiet kind. Rick had warned us before he arrived.

"The guy's a madman," he said. "Killer sight-reader, *monster* chops, plays three hundred club dates a year."

Nobody was quite prepared. He showed up one night, a small wolfish guy with a mustache and brown mane, rock-star length. Ten years he's been in America and his accent was still Cossack-thick, Boris Badunov calling Natasha. He'd just blown a thousand bucks on a video camera; he had one month on the road to get it *all*, everything he'd been missing back in Brooklyn: Waffle Houses and Shoneys, 7-Elevens and Kwik-Stops; the salad bar at Hardee's with six different dribble-on dressings; a series of puzzled but smiling gas station attendants, fireworks salesmen, front desk clerks, and motel cleaning ladies; and every other random American he could buttonhole, including the entire *Big River* cast. He'd race up and down the aisles of our motor coach with the viewfinder jammed against his eye socket, homing in on people tying shoelaces, napping, staring blankly out windows. He spun around when Belle pulled out a pick and started working her top-heavy Afro into shape.

"Fascinating!" he exclaimed, wristing his zoom lens. "What are you calling this device?"

Belle eyed him. "Ain't you never seen a pick before?"

"Beautiful, beautiful. You must smile, so whole world will be saying, 'Aha! Big American movie star.' "

"This one's for you, baby." She fluttered her eyelashes, teeth showing. "You want another shot of me doing my black-hair thing?"

"Yes pliz!"

"Mm mmm," she moaned. "Dimitri, you sure do make me feel *goooood.*"

"Arkady," he corrected, pulling the camera away and shaking out his mane. "No Dimitri. Arkady. Good Russian name."

"You drink vodka, Arkady?"

"See me later, we will discuss this."

He latched onto me his first night in town, as I was leaving the pit with harp in hand. I'd just tooted a couple of notes.

"Hey!" he called out.

He strode toward me, a tiny proud grizzle-faced guy with long thick hair—head tilted, eyes lit with amazement. He grabbed my free hand and pumped, jerked his chin at my instrument. "Ever since I was small boy in Kharkov, I want to learn this. You'll teach me?"

"You like blues?"

"Ohmygod. I'm huge *huge* fan of this music! Sonny Boy Williamson, Muddy Waters—excellent!"

We never actually got around to a lesson, although he repeatedly made me promise we would; he was too busy cramming America into his videocam. I felt an uncanny sympathy with his crazy energy, the way he bounced and davened while blowing sax in the pit. I, too, had relatives in Kharkov and was one-quarter Russian Jewish. We had cantors in our tribe, mournful demonstrative Asiatic blood. My grandfather had spent the first ten years of his life in a dirt-floored shack, then wandered the Baltics for five more with his mother, fleeing the pogroms. Amerikanski! she'd cried at strangers who pointed guns. We're Americans! You can't touch us! My father, born here, collected old jazz records: Louis Armstrong and Bessie Smith, grooves filled with daring, finesse, and squawk. I read Holocaust literature and played blues harmonica. What did that make me? A white Russian negro? A blue half-Jew?

Arkady didn't care. His eyes gleamed: I was the real thing, the American sound.

"We will make videotape," he said, pulling me into the Radisson parking lot. "You're playing harmonica, I'm cameraman."

I blew and sang a Sonny Boy piece called "I Know I Had a Wonderful Time Last Night," about drinking, womanizing, and forgetfulness. It was cheerful, bouncy; a lot of squawk. Arkady faced me, camera perched on his shoulder, free hand motioning me gently onward to new heights.

"Marvelous!" he cried after my final wail. "Come look at playback. You'll have out-of-body experience."

He wasn't far off. The sound was there but my eyes wandered as I played: a soul lost in the music.

"I can do better than that," I said, shaking spit out of my harp.

"One more merry-go-round?" He grinned wolfishly, patted his camcorder. "You're becoming addict for pictures already, like me."

This time I made love to the lens, caressing it with my gaze. He circled, wristed the zoom, panned away toward the bright yellow Waffle House sign, the Jeep Cherokees and Nissan Sentras, the rusted green dumpster filled with ripe trash, then swooped back down on me. I finally got tired and stopped.

"You got what you need?"

His eyes danced. "I'm on Mississippi River right now, with old black man and bottle of whiskey!"

. . .

*1994.* MISTER SATAN AND I were at the beginning of a ten-day road trip that would take us from New York to Miami and back by way of St. Petersburg, Florida, where his parents lived. He was driving my Honda; Miss Macie was dozing in back, hemmed in by amps and percussion gear. I was outlining the tour: the TV appearance in Charleston, dollars we'd pick up, number of sets per night. He was with me, then suddenly not. He waved his hand, irritated.

"You and my daddy, taking me out to the woods and pointing out *each tree* we gotta chop down. All those trees I gotta get through in order to get my last one and be through with the mess. That's a holdback, man."

A few minutes later, lighting up a Kool, he told me more. His daddy had a little lumbering business in Mount Olive, Mississippi, back in the old days. Fifty-two miles southeast of Jackson. His sisters and them worked at various things.

"You might catch a bus the farmer sent down, take a ride up into the Delta and pick cotton for a dollar a day, give half to Daddy and Momma when you get home." He laughed harshly. "They gonna *get* that, now. Whip some God into you if you try and hold out. Grandmama, too."

He let the tip of his cigarette stream out the cracked window.

"When my Daddy was a boy and done wrong, Grandmama used to put that bastard in a croaker-sack and hang him up over a smoky fire, talking some mess about 'God *looooves* you.' Smoked the righteousness back into him."

OUR BUS-AND-TRUCK TOUR OF *Big River,* I'd learned, was not the national tour, which had already finished up. Broadway shows are reincarnated as traveling versions in two slightly different ways. The national tour had spent a month in each of half a dozen major markets: Chicago, Dallas, San Francisco, Miami Beach. Their cast was flown from city to city; their road crew had plenty of time to transport and reinstall the set, troubleshoot the raft, and fly the four-foot rubber catfish from whatever pulleys were provided. The flown catfish was a crucial prop: Jim had to be able to reach up during his first encounter with Huck on Jackson's Island and haul the thing down out of the sky, as if by magic. "Look what I'se caught, Huck!" he'd say as it flopped heavily toward the stage.

On our tour, as it turned out, Jim's catfish was a disaster waiting to happen. Bus-and-truck operations are tightly scheduled, with big and small towns alternating: a week here, three nights there, a couple of back-to-back one-nighters. The itinerary we'd been handed showed twenty cities in ten weeks, Massachusetts to Mississippi. Our road crew began striking the set the moment the final curtain had fallen—rolling up canvas backdrops, sectioning and stacking the false floor across which Huck's raft pivoted and tilted. There were spotlights to be repacked, music stands to be collapsed, endless roadcases from Props and Wardrobe to be filled, latched, and kicked. Load-out into the pair of eighteen-wheelers took six hours, start to finish. Then our roadies would diesel through the night, blow into the next town, and reverse the process. Load-in and setup took seven hours. Sometimes, no matter how fast the crew drove, only six hours were left. Corners had to be cut; the first was always Jim's catfish. Instead of being flown from a nylon fishing line—the better to drop into his hand—it would be laid out near the rear of the raft. A union prop man supplied by each house was responsible for doing this during the pre-curtain scramble. The nightly cast memorandum would have a small announcement: "In tonight's show, the catfish will be on the raft." Which meant trouble.

Union stagehands were an overpaid, humorless bunch—tough white guys who'd inherited their jobs from fathers and grandfathers—and they had a thing about Jim's big floppy rubber catfish. They couldn't seem to remember to put it out, so Wreck could find it. "Look what I'se caught, Huck!" he'd say, reaching behind him on the raft, feeling around. Patting the wood boards. Nothing!

Wreck was a class act. Without missing a beat he'd slap his head. "Lawd amighty, Huck, I 'most fuhgot I done *hid* that big ol' daddy catfish ovah thataway in the bullrushes!" Then he'd step off the raft *into what was supposed to be the middle of the Mississippi River,* look both ways, and creep slowly toward the wings. This gave the frantic prop guy a few seconds to scramble, find the thing, and set it in a nook just out of audience view. Wreck would triumphantly snatch it up. "By *golly,* Huck, ain't she a beauty!" he'd cry, beaming as he held it out, flopping it in the spotlights. The way he made it flop—like it had a life of its own—always drew chuckles. Then, kneeling on the raft, he'd slice it open with a knife and pull a tarnished gold coin out of its belly.

OCTOBER WAS IN full dress when we hit Toledo: maples flaming red and yellow, green grass stiff with morning chill. I paused in midrun next to a highway guardrail and plucked a bunch of dusky purple fox grapes, wasp-fragrant and sweetly tart.

I had no idea whether Jacqui had reported back to Gail; I'd been claimed by Arkady, in any case. The Great Midwest was his latest fascination—impossibly broad streets and lawns, the Bob Evans country-style restaurant next to our hotel—and he played video paparazzo to the pit band as we headed out to VIPs, a local club, on our first off-night in a week.

"You must push together," he directed, backpedaling just ahead of us. "Makes for much better picture."

Trumpeter Rich Vitale laughed short and hard. "I don't gotta do shit except blow my horn, babe."

"The cat's insane." Rick Molina shook his head. "Yo Arkady! You wanna do us a favor and chill?"

He laughed. "Beautiful! We are walking through back alley Toledo with real American jazzmen having heated discussion about music."

"I'm gonna fuck you up," Richie warned.

"No violence, pliz! I'm small person, easily broken."

A Top 40 band called Touched was playing—we'd been invited down by the guitarist, who knew Rick—and all of us sat in except Arkady, who acted out the part of MTV cameraman. When I sang "Sweet Home Chicago" and blew harp, he fell to his knees just in front of me, shooting upward into the rainbow glare, swiveling away to get the mirrored disco ball and dappled crowd. He collared me later, on the dance floor.

"Amazing! You could be a movie star, truly."

"I can't act."

He patted my arm. "I have friend in Hollywood. We'll make you next Bruce Willis."

The following night I was back with Gail, whom I'd asked out on a post-show date. She met me in the Ramada lobby, freshly perfumed, wearing a burgundy dress and heels, clasping a small purse.

"Hey there," I said, heart fluttering.

"Sunglasses or not," she said, slipping them on and voguing.

"You've definitely got the look."

Her mouth wrinkled into a smile. "You ready to go dancing?"

"I'm gonna get left in the dust."

"Don't even *try.*"

Arkady bounced out of the elevator and spied us. "Famous American disco singer with blues musician escort," he crowed, squinting into his viewfinder. "Where's your big party tonight?"

Neither of us had the heart to blow him off. We entered VIPs tailed by our own celebrity videographer. It was Fuzzy Navel promotion night so we sipped a pair of those, swaying in place on the dance floor as Arkady circled breathlessly, trying to get it all: the Top 40 cover band fronted by a Gloria Estefan lookalike in purple sequins; the latticed swirl of lights; the throb, humidity, and promise of a Friday midnight. I held Gail's hand and faked a jitterbug step, then let go.

"If I step on your toes, kick me," I joked.

"You hear me complaining?"

"You've heard of two left feet, right?" I shuffled in place.

Her fists were crossed at the wrist as she worked her elbows. "I can show you a couple of moves."

She showed me half a dozen. The person who snapped, floated, locked, and released in front of me bore no relation to the slavewoman I had been gazing up at for the past three weeks, hulking across stage in her bulky gowns. Here was a power that seemed to remake the space around it. She never flailed or gyrated wildly; she did it all with fierce little shoulder-shimmies—lips pursed, as though humming to herself. She moved eloquently, beautifully. I echoed her weakly, humbled. I'd forgotten about Arkady until he came darting through the swaying bodies, videocam shouldered, a terrier nipping after mice.

"Guitar player is excellent!" he yelled over the frantic phase-shifted solo-in-progress. "Sax player is"—he flapped his free hand—"Tom Scott clone."

"Bye, Arkady," Gail said with a smile, waving at his viewfinder.

"Bye, Arkady," I echoed.

He pulled his eye away and looked wistful. "I was thinking maybe of returning to hotel."

We slow-danced after he left. The fluid beautiful spirit I'd glimpsed was also, I discovered, simply Gail: a firm back under smooth fabric, slightly damp; the vaguest stiffening self-consciousness as my hand brushed the residual thickening at her hip. Her hair, misted with a smoky light oil, pillowed my cheek. We eased apart as the song ended, gazed at each other's mouths. Her eyes slid away as I slowly leaned forward; my kiss grazed her cheekbone. She was brooding, suddenly. Lost to me.

"You look sad," I murmured.

She sighed. "Thinking about nobody I wanted to be thinking about."

"Your boyfriend."

Her gaze was frank, almost despairing. "I don't know what we are these days."

"You wanna head back?"

The band was thumping now, the music a swirling fluid that teased and pulled.

"No." She wasn't smiling, or frowning. She took my hand. "I'm not trying to rain on your parade."

"Nah, I've had a great time."

"I mean you're cool with me being confused and whatever?"

I smiled. "I'm confusing you?"

She chuckled, a rich deep sound. "Yes."

"How am I confusing you?"

We were still holding hands. "I can't even *begin* to explain," she said.

THINGS BEGAN TO MOVE QUICKLY NOW, in a kind of slow-motion flow-state spread out across the next couple of days. We went jogging before the Saturday matinee—both of us, alone, had dreamed restlessly—and had lunch at a yogurt shop. We talked blues music, which she knew almost nothing about, and R&B, which was her thing. She'd grown up near Trenton, a church girl in love with Chaka Khan, Luther Vandross, Freddie Jackson. I'd never heard of Freddie; she called him "the riff king" and demonstrated, drawing the word Baaaaaaaaby out across a soaring, cascading ten-pitch phrase. I told her that "The Crossing" was straight-ahead blues—and not hard to double on harmonica—the way she sang it. She had no idea; she'd learned it by ear, from the cast album. I told her how much I'd learned from Nat and Mister Satan. She thought Mister Satan was a strange name for anybody to take voluntarily. I tried to explain but realized I'd have to write a whole book.

Between shows we played video games in the hotel bar. Gail played; I sipped beer and watched, awed. She was a Pac-Man expert—slamming the control rod to rotate the relentless voracious little monster, nailing the button to spew unending torpedo rounds at all would-be devourers. She put her whole body into it, shoulders and tongue, eyes fiercely focused. She offered me the controls; I pleaded incompetence.

She grinned. "Stick with me and I'll teach you."

That night, after the show and more rounds of Pac-Man, we watched *Return of the Jedi* up in her room. Hers looked pretty much like mine—suitcases flung open, clothes exploding across the carpet. We were lying on her bed; she'd changed into a knee-length white t-shirt and had no socks on. Her bare feet and legs and the gentle rise of her ass under the t-shirt were beautiful and I tried hard not to look at them and couldn't not. Her smooth brown forearms were beautiful and I couldn't not look at them, either, although the movie was absorbing. I'd never seen the *Star Wars* trilogy; Gail, amazed at my ignorance, provided running commentary. The Emperor, an evil white guy who commanded most of the universe, wanted to bring Darth Vader over to the Dark Side. Darth—dressed in black, with James Earl Jones's menacing voice—was actually a white guy who'd gotten his lower jaw blown away during an earlier war and had to wear a helmet and face mask. Darth was *actually* the father of Luke Skywalker, the white-boy hero, although Luke didn't discover this until the end. Both Luke and Darth were masters of the Force, an invisible power handed down from older to younger men that took lots of training to master. Gail murmured, "All right, girlfriend," whenever Princess Leia, the cool, self-assured young white heroine, blew away one of Darth's bad guys with a ray gun.

I left her room at four in the morning, dizzy. We hadn't done more than hold hands. Eight hours later we were having Sunday brunch at McDonald's and talking show-talk. She wasn't happy to be a slave, although the pay was good and she did get her chance to shine. The pit was wearing on me, too—nothing like the excitement and uncertainty of Harlem's sidewalks—but trying to keep up with Ernie and Rick on the Entreacte was a challenge.

"I mean I live for the moments when everything's clicking and I'm on top of the world," I said, sipping my Coke. "That's the nicest thing about playing the streets."

She gazed down at her pile of salted fries and half-eaten Big Mac. "I've never felt like that."

"Never? Even when you sing?"

She shook her head.

That night we lay on her bed with the TV off. She'd changed into the same long t-shirt. We spent hours, as though hypnotized, watching my fingers softly stroke her forearms and wrists and hands. At a certain point my fingers became my lips. I had never in my life wanted so badly to make a woman feel good. She chuckled wonderingly, incredulously when I told her how beautiful she was. I kissed her cheek. Our lips still hadn't touched. Hers were full, glorious, a wonder. I didn't dare.

"I know this is gonna sound weird," she murmured, "and I know

you're gonna laugh, but I've never been with a white guy before."
She hid her face behind her hand.

"I'm not gonna bite you."

She was smiling as I teased her fingers away. "Not even a nibble?"

"Oh shit."

"See," she laughed.

Her breath was sweet. She let me stay.

COLUMBIA, SOUTH CAROLINA, was an endless day's drive south
from Toledo, a plunge back into summer, balmy and fragrant. We
dawdled outside my second-floor motel room after the show, soaking up the cricket-soft night. Lights were glimmering on the swimming pool down below; Gail, leaning against the railing, seemed to
half-dissolve into the shadows. Her bent splinted pinkie glinted.
She'd broken it in Hartford three weeks earlier and the splint—
foam-lined aluminum and adhesive tape—made it stick out like a
tiny wounded wing.

"I'm worried about that pinkie," I said. "You're gonna need to
rehabilitate it after the cast comes off."

She swiveled her wrist, gazing at it. "I guess harmonica lessons
are out for a while."

"Just make sure you flex it a lot once the cast is off, or it's gonna
stay bent."

I reached out and gently ran my finger the length of it, skating
across patches of textured white tape.

"That tickles," she complained happily.

I leaned in and found her lips, brushing them lightly. "I gotta get
to sleep."

"You gonna kiss me and run away?"

I chuckled as I eased away. "It's been a long couple of days."

"I was gonna give you my demo tape." She jammed a hand in
her jeans and pulled out a boxed cassette, dangled it between two
fingers.

"I didn't know you had one."

"A girl's gotta do something beside pay the bills."

"Did you get a record deal out of it?"

She sighed. "Still waiting around for the phone to ring."

I listened to it a few minutes later, lying in bed with headphones. Her voice bathed me like an impossibly sweet liquid; I seemed to have fallen, dreaming, into a shimmering aquamarine grotto:

If I came to you . . . and you came to me
Would we find the love . . . that was meant to be
Would you hold me up . . . would you squeeze me tight
Would you keep me warm . . . on those winter nights

If I came to you . . . and gave you everything
Would you teach me joy . . . make me laugh and sing
If you trust in me . . . then I'll trust in you
My looooove

At two-thirty she called and woke me. "You busy?"

When I pulled open my door she lingered for a moment on the threshold. "You gonna invite me in?"

"I love your tape," I said, moving aside.

"It's getting a little old."

She slipped off her jeans and lay next to me in bed in the darkened room, our bare thighs grazing. "You made me feel so good last night I was really buggin' out and I—" She paused, lips pulled into a sly grin.

"What?"

"Well, I wanted to return the favor."

WE WERE BARNSTORMING THE SOUTH, running ourselves and our road crew ragged: nine shows in seven days, Columbia to Roanoke to Raleigh to Huntsville to Jackson, Mississippi. The poor catfish was having a tough time finding his way onto the raft. Actors forgot lines and made up new ones on the spot, laughing about it afterward over stiff drinks. The first Huntsville show went off an hour late as frantic stagehands wrestled behind a puckered curtain, trying desperately to cram the sectioned false floor into a substandard auditorium; Richie Vitale muted his trumpet and played cocktail music with the rhythm section to keep the audience from walking out.

"What the hell kinda show these New York folks think they runnin'?" somebody muttered.

I peeked over the pit wall: a roomful of crew-cut Bama boys in white patent leather loafers and their hoop-skirted wives. When Walker, the King disguised as a bereaved visiting Englishman, was in the middle of preaching his "funeral orgies" speech to the quietly sobbing Wilkes family—which got him laughs every night—somebody onstage cracked a huge blatting fart. Earlier, when Wreck had gone hunting for the missing catfish, a prop guy hidden in the wings had *tossed* it at him. "Lawd amighty, Huck!" he exclaimed as the whiskered rubber projectile flew into his hands, "That big ol' cat done sprung back to life, same as you!" I bumped into Walker after the show, bellying out the stage door. "At least nobody got killed," he muttered.

Everybody was getting punch-drunk. Jacqui leaned over the back of her seat in the motor coach and did her *Alien* imitation: eyes swollen to bursting, lips finger-hooked away from teeth and gums like a slobbering rabid dog: "Waaaaaugh!" Danny Lee came into the performer's lounge one night with falsies pushing out the front of his Tom Sawyer tunic and did Patti LaBelle for Gail and Jacqui, his thin reedy Louisiana twang ravaged into a gospel growl, face contorted by mimed effort: "Voulez-vous couchez avec moi . . . ce soir. . . ."

Jacqui clapped him on. "Go *Dan*-ny! Go *Dan*-ny!"

"Well *shoot,*" he whined happily when it was over, "I'd have to be good, raised up by the mammy I was."

The next night Gail and Jacqui went off on a Grandmaster Flash version of "Tar and Feather," the dirge chanted by the Bricktown yokels before they lynched the King and Duke in Act II. Gail had on dark green sunglasses and Rich Vitalie's little black porkpie hat; Jacqui kept flawless beat-box time on a table top as they jumped around, fisting their chests like rappers.

"Tar and feathuh . . . we're gonna *tar* and *feathuh* y'all, tar and feathuh. . . ."

By the time we made it down to Mississippi I was wiped out, running on caffeine and a heart blown wide. Gail and I had become an item but nobody except Jacqui knew. I hadn't said a thing to Rick or Ernie, anybody. Then I ran into Ron Layton payday afternoon at a local bank. Ron was the smaller of the two slavecatchers and played his role with authentic roughneck panache. He had a bushy black mustache over jumbled teeth; his eyes twinkled mischievously. The world had been good to him. He'd guested on *Hee Haw,* he'd played bass in a country band. He had a wife and kids back in Long Island City. He pronounced the word *nigger*—onstage—like a north Florida cracker born to the task.

We were shooting the shit while waiting in line. I didn't really know him but was willing to make conversation. He'd just said something about the previous day's nine-hour bus ride being a drag.

"Man," I said without thinking, "if you think that's bad, you should try it on two hours' sleep."

His eyes twinkled lasciviously. "Sounds like somebody's been burning a little midnight love oil."

My skin crawled, suddenly.

He leaned in, grinning. "Would she, perhaps, be a reader of *Jet?*

"Come on, Ron," I said.

"A user of Afro-Sheen?"

I got out of there as quickly as I could.

THAT NIGHT GAIL AND I were sitting in a small park across from the Holiday Inn, my arm around her shoulder, our faces caressed by lukewarm breezes. The next morning we'd be heading north to South Bend, Indiana, leaving the South behind. Downtown Jackson was a generic cluster of marble and steel skyscrapers, a pint-size replica of Hartford. The only authentic Mississippi experience we'd had so far was the pond-raised catfish for dinner—cornmeal-dipped, bacon-grease fried, tasting faintly of mud. We were talking about God, whom Gail believed in and I did not. We'd been watching Jimmy Swaggart preach that morning on TV.

"It's not that I don't believe in *anything,*" I said. "I just don't believe in some old white guy sitting up there in the sky, watching over me. The whole Judgment Day thing. It's not how I was brought up."

She seemed troubled. "Church isn't like that for me."

"I didn't think it was."

"It's about having somewhere you can go no matter what else is going on and don't have to worry about work, your money troubles, *whatever*, just sing and worship and get back to who you are inside. You might of had a terrible week and church lets you wash it off. I mean you can't just say Forget about religion, because a guy like Jimmy Swaggart goes and gets stupid in God's name."

"I'm not saying forget about religion. It's just not connected for me with worshiping God in a church. It's more about honoring creation—being outdoors, in nature, with a clear head—than worshiping a creator."

"More of a by-yourself thing."

I sighed. "I lose touch out here, blasting around from town to town."

"See. Jacqui was like, 'Girl, I gotta find me some organized religion one of these Sundays or I'm gonna bust.' "

"I envy you guys, having that."

"I don't really have it, these days."

"I thought you said you believed."

"I do, I just haven't been going for a while." She traced a finger across the back of my hand, sighing. "Blame it on the show."

"Don't worry, be happy," I murmured, putting on Bobby McFerrin's put-on West Indian lilt as I kissed the side of her head.

We sat quietly, soaking in the mild, pine-scented October evening. Mississippi wasn't so bad. Gazing up, I could see the stars: Orion's three pinpricks in a row, the Big Dipper, a much brighter dot not far from that.

"Is that the North Star?" I asked.

She gazed up. "I wouldn't know."

"I think it is." It doubled and wobbled as I squinted. "I'm never sure."

CHAPTER THIRTEEN

# A GENTLE,
# FUMBLING THING

*The wind was trying to whisper something to me and I couldn't make out*
*what it was, and so it made the cold shivers run over me.*

—MARK TWAIN, *THE ADVENTURES OF HUCKLEBERRY FINN*

JUST AS THE SHOW HAD become routine, I got a nasty cold
sore on my lower lip. Every six months this particular curse hit,
a harp player's nightmare: first the faint scratchy tingling erupting into a small cluster of pus-filled blisters, then, after two or three
days, a scab easily ripped off by anything more than the gentlest
playing. Gail was cool; Westlake was not. I'd told him I could do
everything *except* the Boys' Song, the Entreacte, and the Chase for
the next couple of days, during our stay in South Bend. He smiled
tightly.

"You can't sit those out," he said. "They're part of the show."

"Just those three—there's no way of playing them softly and if I
hit them hard I'm gonna have blood running down my chin."

"It can't be that bad."

"I'll do the Boys' Song," I pleaded. "You can have Ernie take two
choruses on the Entreacte."

"I can't do that."

"I'm gonna *scar* myself, for chrissake."

"No."

We stared at each other. The small amount of real concern in his eyes was masked by frozen astonishment at my chutzpah. Desperate, I went out and bought a small bottle of New-Skin, a toluene-based liquid bandage. You were supposed to paint it directly on your open sore with the tiny applicator brush, like clear nail polish. It certainly stopped the bleeding. For the next few days, as my lip struggled to create a workable scab out of dried platelets mixed with airplane glue, every ragged solo I blew was a curse directed at the conductor's podium. Slavedriver! I was picking tiny shards of plastic out of the mangled shrinking wound for weeks. Mister Satan, harsh as he could be, had never told me I *had* to do anything—except rid my vocabulary of words like "fuck" and "shit." I'd made a deal with the devil, taking this gig. The streets were beginning to haunt my imagination as the most delicious sort of freedom, which for some foolish reason I'd surrendered.

*1982.* SUDDENLY IN MAY, after six endless months in a mono-and-pot cloud, I'd blossomed back into the world. I was working at the Curtis Brown Literary Agency now, biding my time. In September I'd be entering Columbia's English Ph.D. program, two years behind Helen. The academic theorists were in trouble. Malcolm Cowley and I were coming after them.

Shortly after leaving Viking in March, I'd dared to send Cowley a long essay I'd written over the winter of my discontent. "Whatever Roots We Had in the Soil: Malcolm Cowley and the American Scholar" was a fan's impassioned defense, an exploration of Cowley's insistence on anchoring his critical vocabulary in rhetorical figures drawn from the American landscape. It also reflected the fact that mono and pot had messed up my head. I missed nature. The thing came back a few weeks later with a hand-typed letter, signed by God himself. "Thanks for sending me your essay," he'd written, "which is, I think, about the best one that has been written about my work." I flipped. Every freelance review I'd sent off—to *The Village Voice, The Soho Weekly News*—had been rejected. Suddenly I'd been baptized, sanctified. Cowley's heir! My ambitions were infinite and unquenchable. Life had begun again at twenty-four.

I'd grab a harp in the morning as I headed off to work, filled with a careening joy my tweed jacket and tie couldn't hold back. People stared, white and black. Messing with heads was my secret pleasure. You thought you knew me by my skin color and clothes? Here was this *other thing* I was—this spring song in my brimming heart—and I was giving it away for free.

Instead of getting off the subway at Columbus Circle and walking across Fifty-ninth Street, I'd get off at Lincoln Center and cut past Tavern on the Green into Central Park. Loosen the tie, shrug off the tweed jacket. Cup a harp and blow myself breathless as I trekked overland, past vacant ball fields, huge gray boulders, the circus carousel rimmed with poled wooden horses, iceless Wollman Rink, the long gentle downhill next to the zoo. Central Park in May was Eden on a good day, a buzzing polleny dappled tangle. Sometimes I'd detour through one of the tunnels, letting my sound swell around my head. At Sherman's statue I'd pause, panting—shirt damp, harp full of spit—and cinch my tie tight. Office drones were trotting past me toward the Plaza Hotel and Midtown. I'd be joining them in a moment, but that was cool. The music was in me. The world was glistening.

GAIL AND I HAD NO IDEA what to make of each other, and made what we could: a teasing, raunchy, gentle, fumbling thing, shot through with glimmers of deep feeling that never blossomed into love, hard as we tried. Home was a series of Holiday Inns in Kentucky, West Virginia, central Pennsylvania, upstate New York. We'd retire to one of our two rooms after the show and stay up late: talking, smooching, watching MTV, drifting night after night into the endless slow whirlpooling hours before dawn. Freddie Jackson was our muse. She'd pop his cassette into her portable deck, flick the "endless loop" switch; I'd lie there afterward as she dozed, bathed in a voice that cooed and groaned with an unbearably sweet yearning that wasn't quite mine. Mine was Little Walter crying, "I'm gonna find my baaaaby . . . I declare I wouldn't lie. . . ." as he stomped off down the street chased by his own squalling harp. Where was my loneliness now, my demon restlessness? I'd found the baby I claimed I wanted and lost touch with my song.

During the week *Big River* played Philadelphia, we roomed together at the Warwick. The good life! Our wallets were thick with crisp hundred-dollar bills; you could stay up all night and sleep all day, as long as you did your song-and-dance every evening. Gail woke at noon, ordered room service, hummed along with MTV dance videos, enjoyed herself mightily until bus call. Her spirit thrived indoors, mine clouded. I'd stagger onto the street after my wakeup shower, blinking in the raw cold Philadelphia sunlight, a stranger to myself. I'd fallen away from something that lived only out here. Sometimes, after walking several blocks with a harp cupped against the wind, my throat would suddenly ache. This is who I most was, this yowling animal under lashing skies. Mister Satan was right: Creation knew where I lived. Black and white, even as lovers, couldn't tell me that.

GAIL AND I FOUND OURSELVES IN HARLEM—briefly, incongruously—with a month left in the tour. We had a free day between Philadelphia and Boston; we caught a gypsy cab at the 125th Street Metro North station after our train let us off in late afternoon. It was strange to be back in chilly, dirty New York, a fugitive sneaking home in mid-flight. We cruised west across 126th Street, past Madison, Fifth, Lenox. A few African vendors were working the corner of Lenox, peddling purple-gold dashikis and carved wooden masks from a stretch of chain-link fence. The State Office Building rose up on our left, a blocky beige monolith, familiar as a lover's face after the months I'd spent gazing at it from our spot next to the Studio Museum. A year ago Mister Satan and I would have been working with Professor on a day like this. I glanced across the plaza as we came into the clear, hoping beyond hope.

"Hey!" I yelped. "There he is!"

We slowed but did not stop, a ten-second glimpse. Mister Satan at 200 yards was no more than a tiny fuzzy ball of grayish black hair, a furious clatter of elbows and knees half-hidden by loiterers.

Nobody was playing with him. The New York Telephone building, four stories high, dwarfed him.

"That's him?" Gail asked.

"That's him."

I cracked the window just as we passed behind the State Office Building. A faint whiff of sound tingled the mid-November chill—a briny ragged squall hissing with cat's claws: thrashing, relentless, alive.

"That's him," I repeated, shivering, rolling up. "That's what he sounds like."

Should we have stopped? I wondered as our cab sped across Adam Clayton Powell Boulevard and past the Apollo's battered stage door. How was he doing? I could feel my soul rustling inside the cocoon, suddenly.

Later that night, back at my Inwood apartment, Gail and I had one of our rare fights. We'd rolled apart, happy, and were pillow-talking about Freddie Jackson. Over the past month she'd made me keenly aware of how many techniques and inflections blue-eyed soul singers like Michael McDonald had borrowed from guys like Freddie.

"Freddie is *bad*," she murmured. "The first time I heard him go off on a riff I was like *damn*, Luther better watch out, 'cause up till then Luther was definitely my ideal."

"It's so funny to hear you talking about riffing in terms of some-body inventing a melodic line with their voice," I said, "because when I was learning guitar I always thought of a riff as a *repeated* line, like the theme to 'Sunshine of Your Love,' not a fancy embell-ishment."

She made a face. "Riffing is just riffing, whether you're gonna get pretty with it like Freddie or from the heart like Shirley Caesar. It's a church thing. That's where we all learned it."

"It carries over into blues, too," I said. "I have a book called *Deep Blues* by Robert Palmer where he talks about how what B.B. King did was bring gospel melisma into blues singing."

"Gospel *what?*"

"Melisma. I mean that's the technical term for riffing—carrying one word through a whole series of pitches."

Her eyes clouded. "Why you always gotta do that?"

"Do what?"

"Get so technical with something that ain't about technical?"

"I don't *always* get technical, I just happen to know the word."

"Maybe you read too much."

"What are you talking about?" I laughed, angry. "Hell, maybe you don't read enough."

"You think *I'm* ignorant about music just 'cause *you* went to college?"

"Gail!"

"I'm serious. Don't go there."

I took her hand. "Look, I think *I'm* ignorant about music every time *you* open your mouth and sing."

"Riff," she corrected in a small voice.

"Riff," I echoed.

She said nothing. We lay there for a moment, side by side. She rubbed the back of my hand with her thumb. "What's that word again, that Freddie's doing?"

"Melisma."

"Melisma." She rolled it around in her mouth, drawing out and stressing the second syllable. Then she sang it like a lover's name—working her throat and lips, unfurling the final "a" like a musical whip that struck my heart with a stinging snap as it rose and fell. "That's what I'm doing?" she said.

"I don't know what the fuck I'm talking about," I groaned, pulling my pillow over my face.

"See." She was stroking my arm. "Now we can have a conversation."


*1982.* THREE YEARS OUT OF COLLEGE and I'd scuttled back into Columbia for the fall term like a starving termite determined to eat libraries. Five grad courses and a master's essay on *On the Road* weren't enough; I was reviewing books for the *Spectator* and

*Saturday Review,* finishing up essays on John Cheever and Alice Walker—*The Color Purple* had just been published—and worrying, suddenly, about nuclear war. Reagan was threatening the Evil Soviet Empire with Armageddon; cruise missiles were being shipped to Europe. Jonathan Schell's *The Fate of the Earth* had just been published, explaining in lucid detail precisely how the world would end when the bombs went off. I was suddenly beginning to wonder whether the white men who'd been in charge of Western civilization since the days of Odysseus hadn't perhaps fouled things up irretrievably. *Black people* certainly hadn't invented nukes. Women hadn't. My tribe had. Hypertrophied brain-tools with dreams of world domination. It was enough to give an ambitious young white guy pause.

One afternoon, in a rare free moment, I pulled a box of old blues records down off the closet shelf where I'd stowed them when we moved in. Little Walter, Muddy Waters, Paul Butterfield, B.B. King. Helen preferred sweeter pop-jazz—George Benson, Chuck Mangione, the Crusaders—and I was cool with that. Today, though, I wanted raw.

I put on Little Walter, keeping the volume down. I had a harp out and was trying to jam along. The guy was amazing. Sonny Boy's licks I could copy; Walter was light-years beyond me. Was he even using the same kind of harmonica? He seemed to find twice as many warbling, whistling notes.

"If I get you . . . in my sights," he sang. *"Boom! Boom!* Out go the lights. . . ."

Helen was lying on our bed, underlining a paperback copy of *Their Eyes Were Watching God.* "I really don't like those lyrics," she said irritably, glancing over her shoulder.

"What lyrics?" I was focusing so hard on the solo that followed I hadn't actually heard them.

" 'Boom boom, out go the lights.' He's talking about hitting a woman—shooting her, really."

"Little Walter," I groaned, "is a black guy telling the truth about his situation in the language *of* his situation, which happens to be Southside Chicago."

"So his blackness excuses his violence against women?"

"It's a *song*, for chrissake!" I laughed incredulously. "You're gonna tell me we oughta stop listening to Little Walter?"

"If he's violently misogynistic, we ought to call him that."

"You really *don't* want me to be happy, do you?"

She turned back to her book and said nothing.

My heart flared. I felt like screaming. I'd never hit a woman and never would. I'd drive a thousand miles in any direction before I did that. I leaped up, wrenched the tone arm off with a grating *sssss-cratch*.

"You wanna hear some *fun* stuff," I said, slipping Muddy out of his sleeve. "Check this out."

I spun up the volume and kicked back. "Oh Yeah" came on, with Muddy and Walter intertwining on the guitar-harp intro:

> Whoa yeaaaah . . . someday I'm going to cut you, Sue. . . .
>
> Whoa yeaaaah . . . someday I'm going to cut you, Sue. . . .
>
> Whup you in the mornin' . . . I'm gonna cut you in the afternoon. . . .

"Go ahead, Muddy," I said.

She got up off the bed and walked out.

I GAVE WESTLAKE NOTICE IN BOSTON. Come Christmas break, I'd be gone. Gail had decided to stay on.

The show, by this point, had become no more than a comforting and familiar daydream, the game we all played to put money in the bank. We were slave traders and slaves, widows and drunks, boys and rogues. The days of 600-mile bus caravans and ragged one-nighters in Danville, Kentucky, were long past; we'd made it back to civilization, a three-week stand at the Colonial Theater.

Now that I was about to move on, I began to see our cast in a new light: neither stars nor pawns but fellow professionals, self-disciplined troupers who gave all every night. We musical ground-lings were our actors' most discerning fans. Lazing back in the pit between cues, we'd watched the same tearful monologues and wise-cracking dialogues dozens of times; we savored inspired perfor-mances for what they were. Bad performances were rare, and let go of the moment the curtain fell.

The biggest surprise was Wreck. It was hard to see him clearly at first; I'd heard so much from Gail and others about his shadowed past, his carousing. He played Jim, I now realized, with a note of veiled sexual menace, pride deferred but never extinguished. He was willing to put up with Huck's boyishness; willing to love him as a brother, cry with relief at his narrow escapes, blend voices with him in song. He was willing to be yanked around and called Nigger by the slavecatchers. He was even willing to play along with Tom Sawyer's idiotic plot to dig him out of prison with spoons. Whatever he'd given away he got back with interest when he sang "Free at Last" with a slave chorus just before the final curtain. He was seated as he began, wrists chained:

> I wish by golly I . . . could spread my wings and fly
> And let my grounded soul be free for just a little while
> To be like eagles when they ride upon the wind
> And taste the sweetest taste of freedom for my soul

He built slowly, working his rich, winy baritone up through the middle registers—pleading, whispering, placing each of his soul's desires on the table. His heart was hurting. He rose to his feet, unbent his back, held his bound wrists out like an offering:

> Then I'd be free at last, free at last
> Great God Almighty I'd be free at last

Gail, Jacqui, Belle, and the other slaves had suddenly appeared on a riser behind him. They, too, were holding out their hands. The orchestra swelled—Rick strumming, Ernie sawing, horns blaring, kettledrums thundering—as Wreck stood tall. Twain's patient gentle Jim had been shed like a snake's clear papery skin; he was proud, angry, took nobody's shit. Gail's hands, everybody's, were balled into fists. Things had suddenly gotten hot and loud. Free at last! the slaves roared, Gail's contralto surging upward and supporting Jacqui's diamond-hard belt. The black actors seemed to boil off the stage into our laps, a furious collective roundhouse punch; if they'd had guns they would have murdered us all.

GAIL HAD A HARD, CHALLENGING SIDE—a residue of old wounds—but she could be romantic too. It took a while. One cold windy night near the end of our Boston run we were walking back to the hotel. She slapped my butt playfully, then racewalked ahead; I'd never seen her so bouncy.

"Come down to my room in fifteen minutes," she said as we pushed into the lobby.

I showered and changed, with Ernestine Anderson's "Never Make Your Move Too Soon" playing on my boom box. I flicked on CNN to kill a few minutes. The stock market had crashed back in October—the night we came together in Columbus—and trade futures were still shaky.

I took the fire stairs one flight down. She pulled open her door. The lights inside were low and the air wafting toward me smelled like warm spiced apples.

"Entrez," she said, stepping aside. She was wearing a lime green silk teddy and not much else. The former fat girl triumphant.

"Whoa," I murmured appreciatively.

She fell back against the closed door after I'd slid past, hugging her shoulders. "If you say *anything*, I'm gonna kill you."

"Am I allowed to say you look cute?"

"Yes."

"Swan-like?" I pecked her neck.

She shoved me playfully, then bit her fingernails and stroked my hair. Turning, I saw the spread she'd set out: a block of Cheddar cheese, sesame seed crackers, a large bunch of seedless green grapes, two red delicious apples, and a bottle of something icing in a champagne bucket.

"For me?" I murmured, floored.

"If I left something off the list, I don't wanna know."

"It's perfect."

"Yeah?" she said, eyebrow arched, waiting for my joke.

"Yeah." I kissed her forehead, savoring the oil-smoky scent of her hair. Our fingers intertwined. Her broken pinkie, recently un-splinted, was still skewed outward, away from the flock.

"Well," she purred, "that's what friends are for."

We kissed, tongues sparring and mingling, something more than friends. What we were remained an open question.

"I'm gonna miss you," I murmured, an ache tweaking my throat.

"I'm gonna *see* you," she said, her voice suddenly husky. "I know that much."

THE LAST WEEK OF THE SHOW—Toronto, Syracuse, Elmira—was a frozen blur, endless dozing bus rides across featureless gray wastes followed by the George Washington Bridge and Manhattan's glitter-ing holiday skyline. I was a professional now; I'd made the gig. Ninety-one performances. I slipped away at Columbus Circle after hugs to Gail, Jacqui, Rick. Gail and I had a New Year's Day date.

My apartment smelled strange when I first pushed through the door, as though the life I'd lived before hitting the road had an accu-mulated tang I'd never noticed. The big local news—I flicked on the radio as I took a shit—was the Howard Beach trial. The verdict had just come in: John Lester, Jason Ladone, and Scott Kern had been found guilty of manslaughter in the death of Cedric Sandiford. Ten-sions had eased in the black community, although Al Sharpton was still crying Murder! Race war, it was felt, had been narrowly averted.

I plugged my Mouse into the wall recharger and dialed up Mis-ter Satan, ready to burst back into his world and get to work.

"Hello?" he rasped when he picked up, slurring a little.

"Mister Satan!" I whooped. "It's Adam! I'm home!"

"Hey Mister Adam, hello to you sir." He sounded strange. "I been expecting your arrival."

"I'm home for good," I said. "Jeez, it's *cold* out there. You been playing much? I saw you out there back in November when I—"

"I ain't playing no more," he cried. "How can I? My numbers never lie. Nineteen eighty-seven is the last one we got. The whole damn world ain't got but ten days left to go!"

# CHAPTER FOURTEEN

# BALL OF FIRE

*I was in my room and I bowed down to pray—*
*then the blues came along and blowed my spirit away.*

—SON HOUSE, "PREACHIN' THE BLUES"

L ATER ON, AFTER WE'D BEEN THROUGH the cycle a few
more times, I'd learn to have a sense of humor about Mister
Satan's annual Countdown to Apocalypse. This first time all I
could do was drive down to Shakespeare Flats, heart pounding,
wondering what I'd find.

We had a surprisingly cozy visit, the three of us. He pulled me
into his tiny overheated back room, heady with cigarette smoke and
a jangle of women's perfume. Miss Macie was lazing back on the
bed, Kool in hand. He'd anointed himself, I gathered—blended half
a dozen different scents from bottles guys had sold or given him on
the street. He showed me the collection, rowed on his dresser:
Opium, Obsession, English Leather, Charlie.

"Get you a little dab of my rainbow cologne," he said, holding
out the bottle.

I hesitated, then submitted, trying not to wince as I sniffed the
back of my hand.

"Good," he chuckled. "I like that."

He had something important involving numbers to show me. Before doing so, he reached underneath his bed and pulled out a half-filled mason jar, clear liquid slightly wisped with impurities.

"Back in Mount Olive, Mississippi," he said, fumbling with the two-piece screw top, "we used to send over to my cousin Joshua Magee's when we ran low. Corn liquor." He poured half an inch in a smudged glass and handed it to me, then topped off his own.

I hesitated, sniffed. "Strong stuff."

"Got to be!" he cried. "Hell, the times done got so effed up and messed up, Creation might as well go on and have a drink."

Miss Macie held out her paper cup. "You could pour me one too, Mister Sa–tan."

I ventured a sip. It tasted like paint thinner mixed with fermented hangovers. "Wow," I murmured as the heat flushed downward. "I'm amazed you can get this kind of stuff up North."

His eyes blazed. "Creation bless me with that. Ain't nothing I gotta have can't be produced on time, in time, every time."

"Yes sir," I murmured, suddenly tickled. "Hey everybody, Merry Christmas."

"Merry Christmas," Miss Macie echoed distractedly.

Mister Satan's smile faded. "I got a *very* big surprise for my evil little world and Christmas ain't no part of it."

"You talkin' a lot of damn mess now, Satan," she huffed.

"Mister Satan," he corrected briskly.

"Aw Satan, shut up."

His frown suddenly melted into glee. "Whoo," he sighed. "Hey young man, welcome home from the *Big River* show. You enjoyed yourself, I gather?"

"Oh man, I had a great time. The road wears you down, though."

"Ain't it the truth?"

Miss Macie lit up another cigarette, whipping out her match. "I might have to play guitar myself just to make the damn rent."

"Ain't gotta pay no more rent," he boomed. "That's out."

He took out a pencil and proved to me, on the back of an envelope covered with scribbled numbers, how it was theoretically impossible for Time to move past the last second of the last day of 1987. His calculations were dizzying and relied on repeated transformations of one integer into another—sixes become sevens, fours blossoming out of nines. You had to take him on faith; that done, the Doomsday scenario made sense. He'd certainly convinced himself.

"I got something I want you to hear, Mister Adam," he said excitedly, reaching for an old Panasonic tape recorder next to his bed. "I'm very serious. Two nights ago I got high—*whoo* I got so high! That white lightning kicked my behind clear into next week and threw away the bus ticket home."

Miss Macie held out the ashtray; he tapped his cigarette, cleared his throat.

"Thank you, baby. So as I was saying, Creation snuck up on me and spoke through me. Wasn't nothing could I do except turn on my tape recorder and let the mess come out. I call it my God Tape. Check it out."

He pressed the play button and we sat there as it rolled. His voice was slow, measured, fierce, implacable.

---

### MISTER SATAN'S GOD TAPE

Oh Mister and Miss Lady. Mister Man, Mister Woman. Miss and Mister Man. All you are crossed up and carrying on with your disrespectful aggravations amongst each other. You better listen to the words of Mister Satan.

Every one of you know me. You damn sure know me. Oh yeah you know me. I play the guitar up there by the Telephone Company. You come by, you see me. Some of you stop up your ears as though my music is so deplorable. Those of you that enjoy it, it's a blessing. Those of you that stop up your ears, it's also devastation for you because guess what? *You don't like my name!* A bunch of you come by and tell me, "You know, you were kicked out of heaven." Well so was your black ass! You ain't in heaven. You walking around here. You can't doo-doo in heaven; God wouldn't let you have a commode up there! So what are you doing? You're playing against your existence.

I don't address you otherwise than Mister and Miss, Thank you ma'am or Thank you sir. Be you small or be you middle-age, elderly or what. I don't know how you wrapped up this mess, to think that I'm so terrible, when at the same time you can see the result of your God every day. His trophy yards are your tombstones.

Let me tell you a story.

Back in the late seventies, maybe '78 or '79, right at the transition period of the decade, there was a Pope called Alexander. Maybe John Alexander, Henry Alexander. I don't care what it was, he's dead anyway. They asked everybody on the television—the whole world—to pray against his sickness. So. The Methodists prayed, the Baptists prayed. Had he got healed, they would have said, "Jesus did it." The Jews don't go for Christ; *they* prayed. Had he got healed, they would have said, "Messiah did it." The Muslims prayed. Had he got healed, they would have said, "Allah did it." The Indians prayed; they would have said, "Buddha did it." So God said, "All this praying got me confused." He killed the bastard.

Now you gonna tell me you're praying? If your prayers are worth a damn, why can't you get a blessing from the authoritative source? You are wasting your time. You are spending your money for nothing.

In my Bible, I got written there, Let the dead bury the dead. Nobody buries anybody but the churches. The funeral homes are *hired* by the churches; they are the gateway to the grave. Think about it. There's always in a movie, whether it's a western or whatever, there's that worthless church with a cross up top. What you call a cross is really a sword. Lay it down sideways in your mind, you got a good sword. And it's stabbing you with death. Walk by your churches and see if don't a lot of them are rich enough, from your deposits, to have the funeral director's name out front. Yet I challenge *anybody* to go to a nightclub with a funeral director's name on it. They'll say, No no no, I don't wanna go there, I might die in there. But they'll go to church. And God's people will bury them. God's people will teach them how to die. They'll say Booooy, you get killed, we gonna send you to heaven. They don't send 'em nowhere but down into the dirt.

First thing you must learn is that the Bible came not from heaven. I wrote it, I oughta know about it. I was kicked out of heaven. So are you. You're right here on Earth. Also in that Bible I wrote to you that man can endure if he have respect. You didn't read that. I'll go over to a better scripture: Heaven shall come to Earth. Now, if heaven shall come to earth, that means Earth is the boss. Let your astronauts, as you might have them, go all out there in space. Where you gonna find a tree out in space? I'm a greedy person, yet I'm a giving person. I'll put it better: I am a greedy jealous god but I will give all I got, right here. I will not share it with anywhere else. I am the Earth. You ain't got any water up in space, no air. Nothing! I am He that is responsible for you being made from nothing.

I am Mister Satan. Were it not for me, you wouldn't even be here. I'm the Earth, I'm the dirt, I'm nothing. You come from nothing. A drop of juice that you leave in a condom sure can't be called a baby thrown away. You discard it as nothing. Yet you come forth and act like you're so much of something. You ain't *nothing!* You better try to project some beauty and respect for one another, *then* you will be something! Otherwise I will damn you into damnation beyond consideration. Check me out. And guess what? You have to acquaint yourself with nothing. You build a great big house, it's rising up around a nothing called space. So you can move your somethings therein. They all come from nothing. You don't build a house to put seeds in. The seeds that grew your furniture, that made the lumber it was built from, that made the surrounding which you call a house—every bit of it come from the Earth. And you'll get something and denounce nothing?

I can't blame you for hating these homeless bastards out here in Harlem. They had something, once upon a time. Because of their disrespect they got exactly what they deserve: nothing. And don't know how to deal with it. But *you* got everything and gonna lose all you got, because guess what? I'm gonna take it from you. I'm gonna take it from you. I'm gonna destruct—not destroy, destruct—your holdings. Then I'll decide what I'll do with the remainings of you.

I *am* Mister Satan. I am the god of all gods, whether you like it or not. You must die because of it, or live with it. Whichever way you choose is up to you. You won't harm me. No no no. I will not allow one pistol to fire on me, not one knife to stick in me, not one harm to come to me, because hey: I am that which controls whatever you got that you depend on to protect you. My powers will do that. God is the one who's damning you.

Tell you a little story.

I had a young lady, I gave her a dollar. I'll not call her name so I will not inflict harshness on anybody. And when she got my dollar, she said, "God bless you."

I told her quickly, "Why should you tell him to bless me, or tell me he's blessing me? He's damning you the whole time! You shoulda said, 'Thank you Mister Satan for blessing me.' "

"I believe in God," she said.

"God never says thank you!" I said. "He's the one got you into this hardship." And I said, "He's gonna kill your ass because you got no respect for me."

So finally she walked away and said, "Fuck you."

I said, "See how He got you cursing?"

I ain't seen her too tough since then.

I have to speak on a tape such as I am now. My children, you all listen to me real well. It is very imperative that I speak on a tape, because so many people think they in touch with God. Ain't *nobody* in touch with God. God never said Huh?, never wrote a book, never said Thank you, never answered a damn prayer! It was always somebody saying, "God told me." That's an eternal copout y'all got: God told me, God told me. Well I'm Mister Satan. I speak for myself. Jesus can't play no damn guitar! Think about it.

God is my protection and your destruction. You better read the last of my books in the Bible, J-o-b. Not Jobe. *Job.* There it is written, "The day you see God, you'll die." Why should you seek death? You were born to live. Babies that are born dead are showing you I'm for real. Babies that are born dead are those that *I* want to supplicate me in my devastation on your living asses that disrespected me. *I am the Earth!* I grow every tree, I grow every damn thing you got. I make flow every ocean, I give over every stone. I'm the flesh and blood of that. I can't wave my hand and stop the mess, but I know I'm that much. You got money in the bank and you can't get it out, because guess why? Most of my black-ass people up here in Harlem got their money taken away, because Freedom National Bank was shut down by whitey. They couldn't get their money, so how could I command my powers? My powers command me. And guess what? I must wait a few days to reveal myself. You jump off of a building because your money defaulted in the stock market, you can't get your life back. Hell no. You ain't got but one. All you got is your life! You ain't got your life, you ain't got a damn thing. I ain't got nothing but a sweet little lady called Miss Macie Mabins, my wife.

I'm the only person you'll ever meet that graduated from Sunday school. You know how you graduate from Sunday school? You don't go to it anymore. Pray all you want: God, Jesus, none of 'em ever said Thank you. I level myself with you. I'm the only God you got.

The one thing you must realize is, ain't nobody take me serious. They think I'm a joke. They expect a god to come on great big flying wings and ships of angels, as they have been shown by ignorance. Were I to show you an ignorant projector, an ignorant light, those will burn out. Notice my sun hasn't ever burned out yet. The bulk of your films burn out. And they show you violence, that make the screen ignorant and the projector ignorant. And you go and fight war and wanna be a soldier. Look at the G.I. Joe games, look at the killer this-and-that games. Never no respect. Never no game with Mister and Miss. There's not one game in this whole damn toy thing that. . . . You might call it a society. But I call it a devastation. Barbie Dolls. Her and her boyfriend must curl their hair and blah blah blah. Think about it. While you're thinking I'll keep talking. You better listen because you can't think anyway.

Since my tape is probably being played to fools, you won't hear me. But you damn sure gonna see me. You gonna see me. You have seen me. But you haven't really seen me. You gonna see me in my ungratification of your disrespect for one another. Disrespect! I see dogs with more respect than mankind. I've never seen a dog rape a little baby girl dog, or a pregnant girl dog. I've never seen a boy dog fight a girl dog. And all the aforementioned, Man does. And he's in jail right now for doing it.

I find it hard to love you. The littlest person out there, which you thought was a wino, a junkie, a crackhead: I call them Mister and Miss. You discarded me when you put them in jail, and did them as nobody. They wouldn't have broken your home had you helped them. Your black and white ass was born without *anything*. How you gonna get so damn much of what you call something, tell everybody it is something, when I know it's nothing? I'm gonna dismiss it all. Even your carcass. But however.

The richest of you beg from the poorest of us. That's the worst calamity in the world. Rich bastards asking money from poor rejects. How in the hell you gonna put a movie star on a damn TV station, asking for fifteen dollars from me? Let's go with Mister Jerry Lewis. He got the sickle-cell or whatever. Muscular dystrophy—it's ain't worth a damn. His kids still got it. He ain't gonna heal nothing. You ain't never heard what kind of money this bastard gave to his own cause. When he's showing me how much he's *giving,* then maybe I will match it. You all use him for a smokescreen for your conscience. I'm gonna burn out your smoke, your screen, and your conscience. I'll burn out your asses. Because there won't be nobody to bury you.

I don't like you at *all.* Now my displeasure's in you. You should give my orders and my wishes to your God. He will smite you with AIDS, syphilis, claps, overdoses of damn drugs, *everything.* He will disavow your desires for an answer and cater to my wishes for your dismissal. Check it out. 'Cause I got my day of destruction coming up. This month. This month!

I'm *glad* you can't answer back, 'cause I'm on tape.

I am God. You're not. I'm not just a man, I'm not just a god. I'm God and man. I am He that made everything. I walk amongst you. I will make you shoes and go barefoot. I corrupt everything my way. Why? I shall look *very* good, when you recognize me. And the least you can say is, Thank you Mister Satan. Because everybody was taught to hate me. You'll never catch me in a hospital or in a cemetery. My name will not habitate with death. God got that.

You're a bunch of pitiful people. I'll leave you with pity. I shall speak no more in behalf of you. You must correct yourself. Then I will see improvement in your behalf.

HE REACHED OUT AND PRESSED STOP. His eyes gleamed merrily, as at a terrific joke. "I might just send that tape down to my daddy in St. Petersburg, Florida, one of these days. The super-deacon."

"Super-deacon?"

"The man what stand behind the preacher while he's doing his thing, mumbling, 'Yessir, Mister Preacher, you right about that.' I might just do that around New Year's. Him and Mama both." He laughed. "God's people damn sure gonna kick my behind now."

ON THE SECOND DAY of the new year—his numerological forecast having gone down in flames—Mister Satan gave a solo recital at Lincoln Center's Alice Tully Hall, the third of four acts in a Community Arts Festival devoted to homegrown uptown talent. Miss Macie had called the day before, inviting me. He was sleeping off his failed prophecies, I gathered.

"He's okay," she sniffed. "Satan ain't gonna show his behind like that again or I *will* move out."

He was listed in the Playbill as "Mr. Satan, Guitar Man of Harlem" and followed the Mount Moriah Baptist Boys Choir. Three or four stagehands slid his spider-legged hi-chair, wooden sounding-board, and cymbal-stands into place. The brass cymbals had been buffed to a gleaming finish; the dented, birdshit-streaked Mouses were gone, replaced by a pair of Fender Twins with silvery pristine grill-cloth and no missing knobs.

He bounced onstage to scattered applause, solid oak Ampeg Superstud dangling from his neck—catching and holding the lights, burnished with hard street use. Miss Macie had undone his tight cornrows, fluffed and combed his hair back into a regal mane.

"Hello everybody!" he roared, smile blossoming as he leaned toward the mike they'd given him.

The sound he produced—a thrashing, flurrying bone-groove—was as familiar to me as the crashing surf at Jones Beach, as whisper-close as my own dreams. My toes tapped, helpless. I knew him in a way nobody else did, as a full-body pull crying, Fall at my feet! Stand on my shoulders! Exalt me and be exalted! His voice, here at Lincoln Center, was a revelation: no longer muffled by weather-savaged speaker-cones, it was outrageously large, microtonally playful, raging from a hot core. His guitar playing was an endlessly unrolling Persian carpet with gristle and clanks added. No matter how well I played my sideman's part—how deeply I listened, how fiercely I blew—I would always be a younger Salieri chasing old Mozart's tail.

Creation had put me here to do that, I realized with a shiver. The measure of his genius was his ability to step outside the circles we drew around him. Somebody had to grab hold and live to tell the story. I could and would.

I tried to get backstage after the fourth and final act, an African dance troupe, but he'd already split. He called me the next morning, asking if I'd seen him.

"It was great!" I raved. "They were screaming!"

"I couldn't hear myself through the monitors too tough, but however." He chuckled. "Take away the streets, you *bound* to mess us up."

Miss Macie come on after he'd made me listen to a loping new guitar rhythm he'd worked up.

"He's a genius," I told her.

"Well now we've been talking to some people," she said. "It's gonna be our year, Mister Gussow. You in it, too. We *all* in this together. I got Bobby Robinson talking about recording contracts this and that, maybe even a European tour. You watch. It's gonna be a very good year."

"Preach on, Miss Baby!" I heard him call out joyously behind her.

*1983.* HELEN HAD ALWAYS been two years older and a little more adventurous than me, freer—except when she kicked into prim-and-proper WASP mode and talked through clenched teeth. I admired her wild side, the horsewoman at full gallop; I'd told her that more than once. It pulled me out of myself, helped me get in touch with my own wildness. But this time she'd gone too far.

She'd needed a fantasy to carry her through Ph.D. qualifying exams, some juicy reward for months of scholarly self-discipline. One day she sprang it on me. I'm taking a little vacation over in Europe this summer, she said. By myself.

I was cool with that. She'd been to Europe solo before—the nine months in Paris—and knew the ropes better than I did.

I want my freedom, she said, while I'm over there. An open relationship. Of course I was free to "explore" while she was gone.

We argued for days. I was not happy. The monster had risen from the grave, jaws dripping with gore. Three years we'd been living together since her year abroad; three years of workaday monogamy. Sure, we'd had problems. What couple didn't? But *this?* A knife in my heart, twisted.

She was adamant. She had the *right,* she insisted. I had the right to end our relationship, of course. She hoped I wouldn't. She really did still love me. If we were to continue growing as a couple, this solo flight was something I'd have to accept. She was planning to write her dissertation, I knew, on renegade desire and domestic revolt in modern American literature: Chopin, Wharton, Hurston, plus Mary Austin's *Woman of Genius.* But those are books! I wanted to cry. This is our *life!* It never occurred to me that she was taking my theory about the indivisibility of singer and song to its logical conclusion. Embodying her ideas, as it were. Field research!

We bickered for months. She breezed through her qualifying exams, June came around. Time for Helen's Great Adventure. What could I say? We were bound by a sacred Lawrencian blood-knot. I really *really* don't want you to do this, I said. She murmured sympathetically, refusing to back down. We kissed goodbye at JFK; our tongues did a little dance, squeezing tears into my eyes.

Five weeks dripped by like water torture. Each day alone was edged with panic. I could only imagine what kind of field day the Tunisian studs were having over in Paris. June was humid, muggy; I tossed in bed. Having the collective young womanhood of New York at my disposal was an intriguing idea, but my heart wasn't in it. I'd never been a pick-up artist. I tried to lose myself in books—I'd been chained to my reviewer's desk for the past nine months—but my mind wouldn't stay put.

One weekend, blowing harp as I wandered dazed through Central Park, I came across a white guy in a cowboy hat and jeans sitting on a bench inside the zoo, near the seal pool. He had a mustache and droopy eyes, was strumming a guitar and singing country songs: Jerry Jeff Walker, Hank Williams, Jr., the big-hearted whiskey-dust stuff Ricky Spillers had done with Canyon City Limits back at Princeton. I watched him nod and flash his beaver-teeth at little kids who paused and stared from the safety of mama's clutched hand. He seemed to like kids.

He took a break after a while, glancing in the paper tip-bag next to his cracked yellow lizardskin cowboy boots. I introduced myself. He sprayed spit when he talked. Marty Quiteman, from Brooklyn. Nah, he didn't mind if I sat in. Did I have a harp? *Four?* He flashed his teeth. A real pro we got here, folks. Stick around for the show.

I played with him that afternoon, and the next, and the following weekend. It was like high school all over again—trying to figure out his chord progressions, feel his grooves, stay out of the way when he was singing. He seemed anxious when we took breaks, like he'd forgotten something crucial and his mind was working on it. My playing seemed to please him. He'd nod at me to take solos. He'd smile when I showed up, each afternoon. We had a good thing. It got tighter as I learned his stuff. He kept all the tips, since I was only sitting in. He wasn't a real cowboy but sang the songs like he believed them. "Hey Hey, Good Lookin'," "Your Cheatin' Heart," "I Can't Get You off of My Mind."

The third weekend I went down there, he never showed up. I had his phone number at home, so things were cool. Helen was flying in from Paris the next day. I played for hours in a tunnel near the zoo, working out my country licks. Getting reacquainted with my axe.

GAIL AND I DID SEE EACH OTHER, briefly, before she went back down to Memphis and New Orleans with *Big River* after New Year's. We met at her sister's apartment in Jersey City on an icy, wind-scoured afternoon. I had business in the neighborhood but still felt, by the looks I got from three young guys slamming hoops in a driveway across the street, as though I'd crossed somebody's idea of tracks.

Charysse was out; Gail and I huddled in front of the TV watching Oprah Winfrey and Whoopi Goldberg in Steven Spielberg's film version of Alice Walker's *The Color Purple.* I'd written admiringly, if naively, about the novel; Gail had seen the movie ten times, memorizing every moment in which her heroes, black women all, spoke truth to power. She talked back to them—applauding Shug's blues singing, warning her girlfriend Celie when male evil was about to strike. "I may be poor," Celie declares tearfully as she's carried away on the back of a wagon, "I may be black, I may be ugly, but I'm here. I'm *here.*" Eyes on the screen, I heard Gail murmuring, doubling Celie's words, speaking and spoken by them. I'd never quite be able to do that. All I could do was squeeze Gail's hand. Neither of us was poor, thanks to the show. We'd managed to find and embrace something real in each other. Wasn't that enough?

The dream we'd shared, or tried to, lasted long enough to fly me out to Pittsburgh for a weekend in late January. She'd invited me willingly—was there with the show—but our not-quite-magic had vanished. Her boyfriend had eased back into the picture. We couldn't seem to touch. We lay on her Ramada Inn bed watching Michael Dukakis drone on C-Span, puzzled by the nothing that hung between us like heavy invisible fog. I took a long walk by myself out along the Susquehanna during the Saturday matinee, inhaling the big river, reviving. We kissed goodbye after the Sunday matinee. She seemed vaguely embarrassed that I'd come, relieved to have me go; I felt the same. We said we'd talk. We didn't for a long time.

SINCE EARLY OCTOBER, when we'd touched base in Richmond, Nat and I had been making huge plans for the spring, blues plans involving total conquest of the club scene out in Chicago. We'd talk by phone every couple of weeks from wherever I happened to be with the show. Nat was my secret weapon; I was his protégé, the guy who helped create his Riddles-aura by feeling it so intensely. Most of our idols—the first Sonny Boy, James Cotton, Little Walter, Big Walter—were Chicago players, but we'd honored them by jazzifying, funking up, smearing, bruising, adding noise to, stepping all over, and otherwise seriously messing with the music they'd left us. My overblows had excited Nat; he was beginning to treat me like *his* secret weapon, a force of nature he'd unleashed and couldn't wait to aim and fire. Chi-town had suddenly become the target: blues harp Mecca and the O.K. Corral rolled into one.

"We'll need transportation when we get out there," he'd say.

"Ain't no ifs or ands. We're gonna kick some serious Midwest bootie."

This thrilled me. A longtime Kerouackian, I'd always secretly hungered to do the soulmates-hit-the-road thing; fold in the black-and-white buddy-thing and I was gone. Of course we would drive. Both of our cars were aging Japanese tin cans that refused to die and had reclining front seats that could be slept in. We'd done that one night down in Virginia back in August when we'd had too much to drink while jam-sessioning at several clubs. Nat, instead of driving us home to the apartment he shared with his new girlfriend Shakurrah, had pulled off into a dead-end street. We'd cracked our windows, sighed, turned back to back, and settled in, dozing fitfully. At some point he'd stirred, creaked open his door, and—rolling slightly on his reclining seat—let loose what sounded like an endless drenching piss onto gravely macadam.

"Hell yes," he'd chuckled when I'd asked him the next morning. "I'm always gonna select the most convenient option."

Falling out of his dented blue Toyota, unkinking my spine in the bathwatery August dawn, I felt as though we'd bonded in some new way. Now Chicago beckoned. We'd bring my Mouse, Nat's tool kit, all our harps, the Panama hat. Maybe I'd bring my guitar and we'd reconstitute El Cafe Street; I'd back Nat up Charlie Hilbert-style as we busked Wabash and the Loop. Maybe we'd find Junior Wells holding court at the New Checkerboard Lounge and Nat would rap with him between sets, get invited up to blow, and tear the house apart. Anything could happen; I wished it would:

I'm ready . . . ready as anybody you'll meet
Well I'm ready for you . . . I hope you're ready for me. . . .

Nat himself was in great shape these days, healthy and fit. A good woman made all the difference; he owed his entire Richmond base of operations—clothes, meals, cash, and a job—to Shakurrah. Much younger than Esther, Shakurrah was cinnamon-skinned with freckles and dreadlocks, a dreamy slow-talking New Age businesswoman who wore loose, flowing, purple and black tie-dyes and sandals. She sold vegetarian patties, Jamaican honey, and nutritional supplements from a booth at the Richmond Mall; Nat was her help. He seemed committed to her and the work—nobody was a more dedicated, creative, believable salesman than Nat—but he also reserved the right to lavish his attentions on other women. He had a little black book filled with phone numbers, each with a complicated story attached. The morning after we'd slept in his car he spent half an hour paging through, making calls, seeing—unsuccessfully— what he could round us up. He knew, if he could be believed, more remarkable, luscious, fine, deep, beautiful women than one man had any right to. The enjoyments he described taking from their combined company were exquisite, multileveled, and guilt-free. He genuinely *appreciated* women—each an irreplaceable individual with delightful quirks, generosities of spirit, demands to be met. His affections were color-blind; skin came in a hundred different shades, each delicious.

I listened to his stories in awe, unnerved, wondering how he pulled it off. Crises did occasionally strike—one woman finding out about another, the wrong man's woman messed with—but Nat always seemed to land on his feet. He'd never done anything wrong to anybody involved; the problem was invariably the small-souled Southerners who surrounded him. Maybe this was true. I loved Nat too much to judge him without knowing the full story.

He called me one night in late January, stricken. Shakurrah was throwing him out. I listened for three hours. Everything was collapsing—his relationship, his livelihood, the roof over his head. He loved Shakurrah, he'd *always* loved her, he'd made that clear from the beginning. He'd helped her organize her inventory, he'd personally renegotiated her lease with the Richmond Mall, he'd put in long hours, *endless* hours, talking up her products, doing everything he could to build her business, making contacts. Of course, some of those contacts were women who talked. Shakurrah had gotten jealous; she was taking vicious lies as gospel truth.

"It sounds fucked up," I murmured.

"I've *told* Jeannette not to listen to the sort of backbiting bullshit her girlfriends try to lay on me," he fumed. "It ain't none of my business until it becomes my business, at which point I will *make* it my business to find out who and what is behind the various distortions you're trying to propagate about me."

His outrage had a shrill new edge of evaporating cool. His options were limited. He couldn't go back home to his stepmother and father in Norfolk; he couldn't deal with Esther. He'd sold his car and spent the cash, so New York was out. Maybe he'd work things out with Shakurrah. I was worried about him and said so; he promised to keep in touch.

He called a couple of days later, collect, from a pay phone. She'd put him out.

"I'm on the *street,* Adam," he cried. "I ain't lying. I got the clothes on my back and five dollars in my pocket. The woman was so cold to me I can't even—I'm speechless. Speechless. My own mother never even in her worst moments would've pulled some cold-hearted bullshit like this."

Panicked, I tried to calm him down. "Isn't there some sort of shelter or whatever, a place you can . . . where they serve meals or . . . I mean where you can at least crash for the night?" I couldn't bring myself to say the word "homeless." "I mean there must be somebody down there you know, a blues musician or somebody who can—"

"It's cold out here, Adam," he said, his voice choking. "I'm afraid, man. This is some serious shit."

My hand chilled on the receiver. If I didn't do something he might simply disappear—fall off the deep end and never come back.

"Look," I said, "maybe I can write you some money or something. Maybe there's a way of doing that. Just to get you through the next couple of days."

"I've never asked you for a cent, I—"

"I know that."

"That's not what we're about."

"It's not," I said.

"I mean I don't deal, *ever,* in that kind of bullshit. That's not my way."

"No no no. Look, I can do that. I want to do that. It's the least I can do."

"Thank you." He seemed genuinely relieved. "Thank you."

He called me three more times, collect, in the next thirty-six hours, while we worked out arrangements. Wire transfers were expensive—thirty dollars on top of the two hundred fifty I was sending him—and I'd have no definite confirmation of his receipt unless he called me after picking up the money at the Western Union office we'd agreed on.

"Just do me one favor," I pleaded after we'd agreed on a plan. "Call me when you've got the money in your hand. Let me know things are cool. Otherwise I'm gonna assume something fucked up."

"I *will* do that," he assured me. "You know I'm gonna do that."

"At least we've still got one car in the family," I added, trying to sound lighthearted. "We're gonna make it out to Chicago if it kills me."

I wired the money that afternoon. I thought about him alone on the streets of Richmond. New York was freezing, too, in early February. I hoped he'd call that night.

A day went by. No call, collect or otherwise. Two days went by. Three days. Four. Seven.

I carried on a long silent conversation with the ball of fire in my chest. If he *hadn't* received the money, one had to assume, he would have called and asked where it was. Therefore, one had to assume he'd received it.

A month went by. Either he'd blown me off without a backward glance or he'd been killed. Or both, in sequence. He was dead to me either way. I had no way of reaching him. I doubted he'd been killed. So this was how Shakurrah felt. All his women. Nat Riddles was a fucking asshole. I raged and grieved, saying many different silent goodbyes that leaked into and electrified my playing.

1983. HOW MUCH WAS ONE GUY supposed to take? That's what I wanted to know. Helen had come back to me after her European escapade, but home was hardly the word for where we now lived.

I'd met her at JFK as arranged, we had our usual tearful reunion, everything was peachy for the first ten minutes. Then I had to ask. Did she, ah, experience her freedom over there or not?

She lowered her eyes. Nodded.

"You wanna tell me about it?" I said. Not wanting to know, needing to know.

Hesitating, awkward, she began to talk. Two. The second, Brian, was some Canadian she'd met at the Uffizi in Florence.

I leaned back against the headrest. And the first?

She hesitated, stared at her hands. You know him, she said. Vince. It's not what you think.

"*Vince?*" I whispered.

Vince was a friend of ours, an assistant editor at *Partisan Review*. We'd had dinner as a threesome several times. He wasn't a bad guy. He was over in the South of France researching an essay on Hemingway's *Garden of Eden* phase. Helen had taken a train down from Paris; they'd met up in Arles. Seven days on the Riviera. He'd be back in New York any day now.

"You hooked up with *Vince?*"

"It's over when he gets back. We agreed on that."

I raved for a week, heart flaming. This was freedom? A guy we both *knew?* She cried. We both cried. She swore that nobody had ever come close to the secret chamber of her heart devoted only to me. Oh, Adam. She reached out, aching. I walked the streets in a daze, torn apart. I wavered. I wanted to believe. How could I? Most men had a girlfriend; I had Aphrodite crossed with Kali the Destroyer, She of infinite ravenous limbs.

MISTER SATAN, WHO'D BLOSSOMED BACK onto 125th Street the moment February tossed him a thaw-mild afternoon, held no truck with the way Nat had treated me. We'd just gone on break after knocking back "Tequila" by the Champs, a tune we'd recently worked up; his eyes darkened as I fumed, both of us blown wide by the driving funk-groove.

"In all the time we been together," he barked, "I ain't *never* tried no effed up bullcrap like that, talking about 'Hey Mister Adam, lemme hold a dollar till payday' and all that sorry-assed mess."

"It isn't even about the money, it's about asking me for the money and not caring enough to—"

"I hate money!" he interrupted, scooping cool air chestward with his cupped hands. "I got to *have* it, no doubt—a dollar here and there always gonna help out with a pack of cigarettes or paying Mister Parker consideration—but you ain't never as long as I live gonna find me *begging* no damn body."

I took a swig of the paper-bagged Heineken I'd picked up and set it on the sidewalk, happy. "Hell, you know you'd get a dollar from me if you needed it and I had it."

"Likewise me!" he cried, slapping my hand. "We got to be watching each other's backs! Miss Macie got mine pretty well covered these days but however." He chuckled. "Thank you, sir, for that kind thought."

"I mean it."

"I don't doubt it. Can't none of us buy friendship worth a damn, but you got to make payments on it. Correct or wrong?"

"Correct." I rubbed my grimed hands on my jeans, crouched next to my photographer's bag, raked through the jumble of loose harps. Thin hard sun fought with shadows in the furrowed concrete face of the State Office Building across the street. My months with the show seemed to have fallen away like melting fog; we were doing it again, tighter than ever—master and journeyman, ready for the new season.

Mister Satan smoked, coughed, spat toward the gutter. "Mister Nat Riddles gonna be very sorry he showed his ugly behind on this money thing, you watch what I'm saying."

"Ahhh," I sighed, the pressure in my chest suddenly lifting, "considering how much he showed me about playing, all he really did was collect what I owed him. You know? Pay up for the blues lessons. I can live with that."

Mister Satan scowled. "He's gonna *die* with that, and broke, too!"

"I hope he doesn't."

"Your hope ain't worth a damn next to the disrespectfulness he's already projected against your friendship and the condemnation Creation gonna bring down against him. I'm very serious. You watch don't his own greediness trip him up."

BOBBY ROBINSON HAD scheduled a recording session; we were going to be stars. Miss Macie called with the news one morning in April.

"I got everything under control," she said. "I *know.*"

I knew little about Bobby at that point, except what I'd been told. He was a producer, he owned a Harlem record store, he'd negotiated on our behalf with U2's lawyers. Strolling across 125th Street, he'd paused a few times to watch us play, then come up to shake hands and linger—a small dapper man with hooded Asian eyes that darted restlessly, noticing and calculating. He gave Mister Satan money from time to time up at his store, I gathered. Mister Satan had bragged about the convenience of the arrangement. I wasn't sure who owed whom what. I'd never been in a recording studio before and owed nobody anything except cooperation. This was our big break, not to be blown.

I picked up the two men outside Shakespeare Flats on the sort of limpid bursting April morning I'd probably have been drowsing with Robyn the year before. This year, tasting my memories in every caressing breeze, I was touched with poetry, ready to blow. We heaved Mister Satan's Mouses, cymbals and wooden board into the back of my car, where they kept my lone Mouse company. Bobby eased himself into the front seat and slammed.

"How you feel?" he asked, eyes swiveling toward me under droopy lids as we pulled away.

"I'm ready to kick A and stomp D, young man," Mister Satan called out from the back.

I ran my hands through my hair. "Mister Satan probably told you about me being new to the studio."

"All you gotta do," Bobby advised, "is forget about everything except music. Whatever you and Sterling been doing, as far as the kind of sound you've been developing, it's just a question of bringing the street sound *inside.* You see what I'm saying? Nothing really gotta be added, it's more a matter of staying out of the way, as far as the recording goes. We did the same thing with Elmore James, Buster Brown, King Curtis, you name it."

"You recorded Elmore James?"

He glanced at me, then laughed long and slow. "Elmore James? Oh man, we was in the studio with Elmo—that's what they called him, Elmo—back in the late fifties, doing "The Sky Is Crying," everything, the whole ball game. I was the first guy to put James Cotton out on record. He came through here—Sterling would remember, one of those all-day shows at the Apollo, six shows a day."

"Hell yes," Mister Satan agreed, lighting up. "Six shows a day, and might be seven on Saturday."

"Well now, Cotton came through on one of those Chicago bills—Muddy Waters, Junior Parker, might be Big Maybelle, Big Maceo. That's how I got Cotton. Wasn't none of the Chess Brothers got their hands on him yet, so we got him up here the next morning after the Apollo, before the bus pulled out, in the little studio I had put together in my office. Roll the tape with "Cotton Crop Blues" or whatever he did, I don't remember. Oh hell, man they *all* came to me after Wilbert Harrison hit with 'Kansas City' back in '59."

Mister Satan leaned forward and tapped my shoulder. "That was a very big song on the jukeboxes, Mister."

"Mister Satan mentioned you had a hand in that," I said.

"Oh man," Bobby chuckled, warming. "First thing about it was, they had the title of the song wrong in a way that, I mean I couldn't see *myself* buying a record called 'K. C. Lovin',' which is what Wilbert come into the studio thinkin' he's gonna call the record. No way. So that's out; I told 'em change that title to 'Kansas City.' And on the rhythm guitar—first time through, Wild Jimmy Spruill got too fancy on me, I told him, 'Cut it back, man! Give it to me simple!' So Spruill—and he was a very good guitar player, too. Sterling, you remember Spruill, up at the Apollo?"

"Whoo, do I! Man could play it between his legs, behind his back, duckwalking all that mess like Chuck Berry."

"That's it. So I told him, 'Spruill, give it to me simple!' That was his thing, too, in the studio: straight fours, on the beat. He liked to do that. Chuck, chuck, chuck, chuck. So we had that on the recording. I threw a little reverb on Wilbert's voice, you know, for the smoothness of his voice, to make it come out a little smoother. So now, okay: I got my recording. I sent my master tape off to the record plant, I got my first batch of—we always had a thousand records made up real quick, to send 'em out to the D.J.'s and see what kind of reaction we gonna get as far as how many of the *main* run, you see, are we gonna pay to press up? 'Cause obviously if nobody at the *radio* stations like the record, we're in trouble with the people. So I got my first thousand and I sent 'em out, over the weekend. Back in those days, back in 1959, the mail *worked,* see. Send it out Friday afternoon, it's there Saturday morning. None of this getting lost in the Bronx for two weeks. Okay. So that's where we are. Give everybody a little taste and see what we got. Then on Monday morning I come back into my office, I get to the front door of my office, I got my key in the lock and I'm turning the knob and *my damn door won't even push in!* I'm saying What the heck is going on? And I can hear the phone jumping off the hook inside there, too! Turns out I got about a thousand and fifty-three telegrams piled up just behind the mail slot, from the D.J.'s, telling me Bobby, you got a hit! The listeners is going crazy, the record stores is going crazy, we gotta have us about a million more records *right now!* Seems like everybody in America knew I had a number one hit except me."

"Yes sir!" Mister Satan laughed.

Bobby coughed. "So that's how the whole thing worked. Might none of it never happened, too, if I hadn't of told Wilbert, 'Man, we gotta change that title.' 'Cause I just couldn't see no Number One hit called 'K.C. Lovin',' even with exactly the same music behind it."

The studio Bobby had booked us into was somewhere in the wilds of Brooklyn and run by Plinky and Mitch, a pair of young white guys who seemed competent enough. Mister Satan and I set up street-style, side by side; Mitch slouched around the room angling mikes at our Mouses while Plinky sucked on a Bud longneck and fiddled with his mixing board behind the control room window. Every note we played would be preserved and critiquable; this terrifying fact suddenly hit home. Working the streets, I'd never worried about mistakes, masked as they were by Mister Satan's phase-shifted guitar wash and deafening clatter. Often out there I'd play one backing pattern for five minutes, then try something else. Should I select a particular riff this time and stick with it? My musical mind—which liked to drink, screw, hum, groove, and otherwise dissolve itself in pleasurable flow—was easily spooked by such questions. My musical mind decided that a Bud longneck was in order. Mitch obliged; flow was quickly achieved.

My musical mind was beside the point, it turned out. After we'd recorded three songs, lengthy jams all, Plinky rewound for playback and discovered that Mister Satan's vocal track had somehow vanished. Bobby grumbled as Mitch retraced each line through a snake's nest of mike cables slithering past our ankles. Plinky put down his Bud longneck, scratched his five o'clock shadow, did whatever cocky engineers do with their faders and V.U. meters when things inexplicably crash. Mister Satan sat back in his hi-chair and smoked, legs crossed at the knees.

"Ain't nothing we can do but try it again," he finally sighed.

We threw ourselves into Round Two, fighting inertial doubt. Tensed looseness had tightened into straining push. This time on playback—impossibly, mercifully—Plinky had lost Mister Satan's vocals on two out of the three redone tracks. The one good track, "Cry to Me," revealed us in all our thrashing sidewalk glory, but nobody was in the mood to appreciate that. Bobby fumed quietly, grumbled, but did not yell. Ashamed of my own people, I packed up my harps while Mister Satan disassembled his cymbals, folded up his wooden board. The three of us loaded out and left, grumbling.

"That's a damn shame," Bobby muttered more than once as we cruised home to Harlem. "A *damn* shame."

"We'll live through it," Mister Satan sighed. His window was down, mild breezes blowing through. He chuckled, scratching his beard. "I damn sure ain't gonna let it ruin my day."

WHEN DAVID WESTLAKE CALLED and asked if I'd like to go back out with *Big River* for three weeks—mid-May through early June—I made quick calculations and said sure. Utica, Columbus, Cincinnati, Indianapolis, Fort Worth; three thousand easy bucks and I'd end up in Texas. The Chicago trip with Nat had fallen through, but I had a new blues plan now. Buy a used car in Fort Worth and drive home by way of Mississippi. Check out the juke-joints, get my first look at the Delta. Visit Mister Satan's people down there. He'd mentioned a cousin, Joshua Magee; I was going to be traveling through. Why not look the guy up?

I'd need Mister Satan's permission, of course. I wasn't sure he'd give it. He was skittish about his Christian name the few times it had come up; he seemed to have shed an old self along with it in becoming who he was now. I was curious about that old self—a mystery to be solved, plainly—but aware of the need to tread softly. Mister Satan's story was *his* story, not mine, however much our musical souls had intertwined; he'd tell it at his own pace. His cousin Joshua, of course, might also have stories to tell.

The afternoon before I flew up to Utica to rejoin the show, Mister Satan and I got a rare chance to conversationalize at length, indoors. He and Miss Macie had just moved from their cramped back room at Shakespeare Flats to a big second-floor walkup on the corner of Manhattan Avenue and 116th Street, at the foot of Morningside Park. He made me a cup of instant coffee after I'd creaked up the steps, then showed me around. I'd always known he was a visual artist of sorts—a constructor of shellacked wooden mandalas filled with arcing trapezoids governed by obscure numerological principles—but had no idea how busy he'd been. The grimy lime-green walls of his bedroom, living room, and kitchen were hung with a glittering, particolored menagerie, an endlessly permutating profusion of deconstructable five-pointed stars and jigsawed isoceles triangles. What I'd thought at first was a small fold-out Art Deco bar in the living room turned out to be a three-dimensional mockup: a mandala reconfigured as a chest-high plywood coffee table.

"That's my altar," he proclaimed when I asked. "What used to be in the back of my step-van. Hell, my altar was the first piece I ever did. I didn't *ask* to be given no artwork, you know. Creation bless me with it. Couldn't nobody square a circle before it came on me to do that."

The polleny May afternoon poured through open windows, filling his living room with soft light and the siren-punctured drowse of Harlem street life down below. We got lazy and comfortable in our tilted chairs, basking in dreams of the summer we'd have when I got back. He wanted us to drive out to Long Island some Saturday afternoon and play outside a stadium on rock concert day, serenading the queued-up fans.

"You know those bastards gonna be throwing money," he laughed, slapping my hand. "Waiting on the Who or whomever. Ain't no doubt."

We'd had a decent spring so far: scattered afternoons on 125th Street, an excursion to Times Square, half a dozen new songs. I'd paired the Mouse I'd been blowing through with a second one fresh out of the box, greatly strengthening our surround-sound. Bobby Robinson had been talking about another recording session; Miss Macie had promised nothing would be done while I was out of town. He reiterated that promise now. Sensing an opening, I mentioned my planned drive home through Mississippi and the possibility of stopping off in Mount Olive.

"If you thought it was okay," I suggested, "I'd maybe, you know, go around and pay my respects. Find some folks who knew you way back when."

He made a face, reached for his cigarettes. "They done forgot me. I been keeping in touch with my mama down in St. Petersburg, Florida. But all the friends I had that would—" He paused. "Are dead. They died."

He puffed on his lit cigarette. I said nothing. A Kawasaki Ninja buzz-bombed the street below.

"See," he continued, "because I was there back in '77, '78, '79. My Aunt Donna, she died. My Uncle Elohu, he died. And the younger generation, they into the crack thing and the drug thing. All my people are down in Florida anyway. I got one cousin there, Joshua Magee and Clara Mae Pittman. I don't even have their telephone number. We don't keep in touch until somebody die. Hell, they wouldn't know me with this beard anyway. I didn't have no beard when I left out of there, after my wife got killed. They all— with their graveyard thing, really. That's what they gonna believe, can't nobody tell 'em otherwise. I come on talking about living my new life after the change come over me, they look at me like I'm a fool!" His eyes burned; his laugh was hard. "Can't nobody down there accept what Creation done without a *damn* bit of help from their worthless-ass God."

He smoked his cigarette down to the filter and stubbed it out.

"How you coming on your coffee?" he asked, fluffing his beard around the throat-part with one hand.

"I'm fine."

He coughed into his balled fist. "Creation is the biggest bastard you got, Mister. Ain't no God of the Christians or Jews got Creation outdone on the size issue. Creation get a mind to whip your behind, you might as well let the bastard go on ahead. Whoo!" He laughed, suddenly merry. "I ever tell you about how my change come over me?"

"Uh uh."

"Back on May 10th, 1979, I was out in—this was down in Mount Olive, Mississippi, in the backyard of my mama's place down there. The cancer got to my wife and killed her dead, I had me a few drinks. Okay. So—and the spot where I'm standing in the backyard is *exactly* the same spot where I buried my dog Fuzzy, that had stars in his eyes and got run over by a truck when I was five years old. Five-pointed star in one eye, six-pointed star in the other. You ain't never seen such mess in no dog's eyes! So I'm standing there, on that same graveyard spot. And then this power—a hand came out of nowhere and dropped down on me. The bastard grabbed my hair by the roots and yanked me *backward*, onto the ground, rolling me around for a second, maybe two. Couldn't see a thing! Wasn't nothing *to* see, really. And then the hand or whatever yanked me back up onto my feet and shook me around like a little rag doll. That's when the voice—I ain't never talked like that before, I ain't ever heard no preacher do it either. It wasn't my voice but it was damn sure talking through me. It was *damn* sure talking through me. About a year later I found out who I was."

He paused, chuckling. "Hell, if you pass through there, might as well drop off and ask where Joshua Magee live. Tell him you play with me. Sterling Magee. He might be somewhere in a hospital trying to die, you know. They all busy doing that and can't see it."

CHAPTER FIFTEEN

# BACK DOWN YONDER

*Way back down yonder . . . where I come from*
*We worked for a living, . . . we got up way before dawn*
*We lived our dues . . . we did it with those sanctified blues*

—STERLING "MISTER SATAN" MAGEE, "SANCTIFIED BLUES"

THIS TIME, HAPPY to be a mercenary, I packed light.

My old familiar show costumes were waiting in Utica—freshly laundered and folded, two complete sets of handmade rags designed to make me look like either a lovable waif (St. Petersburg Boy) or a mud-spattered roustabout (River Rat). *Poor,* above all. There was something strangely comforting about slouching around backstage in the same silk-lined Wookie-fur pants I'd worn all fall, as though the pants and I had earned our right to a second go-round. Gail and I, on the other hand, failed to reconnect as anything more than fellow showbiz survivors; the romance was gone for good. She had a cold when I arrived and seemed drained of vitality, as did the entire cast. A series of cities—New Orleans, Miami Beach, Houston, San Antonio—had been opened and closed in since Pittsburgh; some had been "fun," some had been "downers." The show itself had ceased to provide anyone inside it with more than fleeting highs, like a voluptuous *Playboy* centerfold jerked off to a few times too many. Who gave a fuck about Huck and Jim and their quest for freedom? The high point of the week was Dollar Friday:

You wrote your name on a greenback, tossed it into Mark Twain's stovepipe hat, and hoped you won the sixty-buck pot—to go along with your fat paycheck—when the winner was called out over the backstage P.A. during intermission. A little extra drinking money always came in handy.

There was one exception to the general malaise: Wreck and Rick Molina had gone fish crazy. They spent every free moment before and after the show paging through tattered copies of *Angler* and *Bass Fisherman*, debating the merits of neoprene hip-waders and lined wicker creels, whip-casting their carbon-graphite poles in hotel parking lots, lazing around the back of the bus dreaming out loud about fishing holes they were going to descend on in the next town, the largemouth bass and catfish they were going to catch, clean, and fry up. They'd rise before dawn and take a cab out to whatever local body of water the kitchen staff at our hotel told them was biting. Hours later they'd fall onto the bus, loud and spent and happy, talking trash.

"I'm the man, baby," Wreck crowed in Columbus, stretching his endless limbs in one of the back seats, angling his fishing cap pimp-low over his eyes. "Ten pounds three ounces *without* the head."

Rick's delighted sneer showed lots of teeth. "Your shit stinks, Wreck."

"Oh Mister Fisherman, can I trade you for that boot you caught?"

"Your mama's shit stinks."

"You what? You gonna *wear* it? Dag."

"Fuck you. Blow me."

"You Colombians, man, with your freaky tastes."

"Don't go there, babe."

"Hey, I'm cool. To each his own. Just keep that Deliverance shit away from me."

"Your wife called me up last night, man. She was lonely."

Wreck grinned. "Just 'cause I'm smiling don't mean I won't fuck you up."

. . .

CINCINNATI, OUR THIRD STOP, was perched on rolling hills next to the Ohio River. Reconstructed paddle wheel steamboats from the days of slavery—wedding-cake white with black trim—were docked at the foot of the levee, promising leisurely excursions down to New Orleans. Kentucky was just across the way, lit up with billboards hawking cheap bourbon. The hometown blues hero, I discovered, was H. Bomb Ferguson: a skinny old piano player, nut brown, who wore a long silky purple-tinged blond Barbie wig with bangs. His haunt was Cory's, a small club up in the hills that I taxied to one night after the show. He shook his head like a Muppet as he pounded the keys and hollered, gossamer hair shimmering in the spotlights. His bearded all-white band, the Medicine Men, followed every wig-flick. The music and several cold beers flooded down through and reviscerated me, a needed gift from familiar gods.

I called Shakurrah's number in Richmond from my hotel room the next morning, fierce with sudden whimsy. Maybe she'd have a new listing for Nat. Maybe I'd call the bastard up.

Nat, of all people, answered.

"*Hel*lo," he said. Familiarly, like I'd caught him cooking breakfast.

"Nat," I said.

"Yo."

"It's Adam."

"Adam!" he yelled. "I was just telling Shakurrah about two days ago I oughta give you a call."

"I didn't expect to get you, ah, in."

He laughed. "It's a long story. Hey, how the hell are you?"

The ache I'd struggled to bury suddenly blossomed in my chest. "How am *I*? I sent you some money back in February and never heard a word."

"Money? Oh, the money, the Western Union. Thank you. I got that, you really saved my—I was in a bad way when that came through, man. I mean a *bad* way."

"You never called me, Nat," I said, choking. "That's all I asked. Just give me a call when you get the money so I'll know you're okay.

You never called. You panicked the fuck out of me, I came through with the cash, and you disappeared. You *hurt* me, Nat."

He was silent. The line hissed softly.

"I'm sorry," he finally said, huskily. "I couldn't call."

"Why not?"

"I couldn't face you, given my situation at the time."

"Couldn't *face* me? What's so hard about a lousy phone call?"

"I was eating out of garbage cans. I owed some money, I was emaciated, going without food two or three days in a row. I was *low*. You have no idea what I've been through this whole spring."

"I guess not."

"What was I gonna do?" He gave a hard short laugh. "Call you up again and beg for more? I got my pride, same as you."

"Well, you worried the shit out of me, man. Needlessly."

"You woulda been *seriously* worried if you'd talked to me later on, which is why I had to lay back. I had to."

"Christ, I figured you'd been killed."

"They ain't got me yet." I could hear him smile. "The situation had me so fucked up I couldn't *think* straight enough to be sorry about what I wasn't able to do. I was lost, I ain't lyin'. You gotta believe me."

I felt myself softening. "Well, I'm glad I called to check up."

"I was planning on calling you when I had my own place. I'm on a waiting list." He coughed. "Shakurrah's letting me stay here until my apartment comes through."

"We missed out on Chicago, you know. Our spring trip."

"Says who?" He laughed richly. "Last I heard, Chicago was still out there."

How could I hate the guy? The best masters teach hard lessons; I wrestled with my pride, struggling for clarity. We talked. He was driving a school bus these days, getting back into shape, blowing harp with the Blues Defenders, a Richmond quartet. He played snatches of their demo tape over the phone. The joyously strident yelp I knew so well seemed to burst out of the mix, a sergeant in command of his troops. I'd forgive anything for a sound like that.

When I mentioned my Mississippi plan he perked up. Did I want company? His car was out of hock; he just might be persuaded to drive down, or catch a bus.

FORT WORTH, AS THE GREGARIOUS God-fearing natives made a point of telling us when our Broadway hootenanny came to town, was *Texas.* Dallas was phonies like J.R. Ewing, the western outpost of the decadent East, and crawling with homosexuals. Fort Worth, thirty miles west, was the West: the one and only Cowtown, its other name. Fort Worth was the foot of the Chisolm Trail, the gateway to Kansas City's slaughterhouses and meatpacking plants. Stagger out through the swinging front doors of Filthy McNasty's, the best little blues bar in Texas, and you'll come smack up against a split-rail fence surrounding a big ol' holding pen on three sides. That fourth side raht air, with the desert opening out behind? That's where the cows come home—or did, back in the good ol' days, after the cowboys had driven 'em a thousand miles, down out of Laramie and Dodge City and across the West Texas plains. The Fort Worth Stockyards. Texas swing, the Texas two-step. *Texas,* goddammit! Yiiii-haaaah! Praise the Lord.

I'd never been in Texas before, or Cincinnati, or most of the towns we'd played. *Big River* was my ticket to America, it turned out. All I had to do was lift my head and inhale. The Land of the Free was out there, waiting: all singable promise and endless swoopable space stretching to the horizon, with Harlem and Mister Satan waiting just past that:

> Come onnnn . . . baby don't you want to go
> Come onnnn . . . baby don't you want to go
> Back to the same old place . . . sweet home Chicago

Sweet home, hummed, was anywhere my hungry heart drove me. This time it was a Mississippi dreamscape of my own imagining, a series of hypericonic, blues-drenched, mud-caked, kudzu-covered, devil-at-the-crossroads place names I'd pieced together from Robert Johnson songs, *Living Blues* magazine, and scattered passionate reading about the civil rights years: Rosedale, Clarksdale, Greenwood, Tchula, Tutwiler, Yazoo City. Maybe I'd meet an actual white

Southern racist—a bull-necked, nigger-hating, lynch mob–forming redneck—and confront Evil for the first time. Mister Satan had said nothing about the role such monsters might have played in his own Mississippi childhood, but I'd heard they still roamed free as late as the mid-sixties. I'd seen *Mississippi Burning;* I knew all about the murders of Chaney, Schwerner, and Goodman. The heat in my heart told me which side I was on.

My Mississippi plan required wheels. The mere idea of a Texas used-car salesman terrified me. With two shows left and Jubilee approaching, I dragged Ernie Reed out of bed one morning to go shopping. Surely Nashville had seen every trick Forth Worth could throw at me. Still recovering from his hotel bar bender the night before, Ernie coughed and grumbled his way through Marlboros and takeout coffee. Our taxi lurched; high plains winds whistled through my blood as we cruised out Azle Boulevard into blanketing early heat, last week's pay thickening my hip pocket. The bossman at Jenkins' Used Cars took his feet down off the desk when we wandered in. Adjusted his cigar under his scrub-brush mustache, pushed back his Truckers Go the Distance cap.

"Mornin'," he drawled. "Kin I do fer ya?"

The big gas-guzzling Lincolns and Monte Carlos were cheapest. Every coat of paint in the lot had been scoured by wind-driven grit. Jenkins was proud of and confident in his stock.

"She blows lotsa cold air," he'd volunteer each time we strolled around a possible sale. "Take 'er fer a drive."

Ernie was stuporous. I kicked a few tires. The mud brown '77 Nova Custom I liked had a V-8 and dual exhausts that seemed to yearn, when you floored it out on Azle Boulevard, for stock-car Saturday nights in Rebel-held territory. The brakes worked.

Ernie slumped in the passenger seat as we pulled back into the lot, lit another Marlboro, tugged his gray billy goat tuft. Tomorrow, after our final show, he'd be flying home to his fifth wife in Nashville.

"Might as well," he sighed. "Cain't see no reason why not. I mean she runs."

"Blows lotsa cold air," Jenkins reiterated as I climbed out. She did, too, until the split-second I'd throttled out of the lot a second time. I rolled down the windows, let the Juneteenth swelter pour through with Ernie passed out beside me. Yiiiihaaah. She was mine now.

*1997.* BITS AND PIECES of Mister Satan's military background had come out over the years: his stint as a U.S. Army paratrooper back in the fifties, stationed near Munich; the white German fellow who'd saved his life one night when a fight broke out at a U.S.O. club. He'd bought himself a gleaming white Mercedes and cruised the autobahns, ruined it by neglecting to change the oil. He'd started playing guitar back then, too, after hearing about a white fellow named Elvis making lots of money.

He'd never told me the story of actually *getting* his first guitar. One day I asked. We were driving up to Portsmouth, New Hampshire, for a gig at a bar called the Press Room.

"I got it in the army, over in Germany," he said. "I had me a bad conduct discharge because I couldn't go with carrying a gun and killing no damn body. They'll make you do that, you know. And I was selling cigarettes from out the back of my Mercedes, that I brought in from outside the base. Direct competition with the bastards *on* the base, so they definitely gonna get rid of Sterling Magee. They found some white woman—she happened to be white—to say I'm selling. So I'm not gonna fight that, and let somebody tell a story about Magee done this and that. Leave the mess behind will do you better."

He pushed in the cigarette lighter, reached into his Triple Fat Goose jacket for his Kools.

"When did you actually get your first guitar?" I asked.

"That was Danny Boy O'Donnell—Dan O'Donnell, but everybody called him Danny Boy. A fellow on the army base. Had him an electric guitar plus an amp and didn't want it. And I *did* want it, to chase down Elvis Presley. Care for a Kool?"

"Sure."

He lit his, passed me the lighter, blew smoke out the window. "So okay, I gotta have me a guitar, and Danny Boy *damn* sure gotta have his money. So we made a trade."

"O'Donnell and Magee."

He chuckled. "Bastards told me, 'You out, Magee,' like saving *my* life is supposed to depress me! So I made this agreement—Danny Boy and I did—that he's gonna wait until a few days after I left, give me a chance to catch my boat, and then report the guitar stolen. Not by *me*—hell no. I paid him the two hundred fifty dollars he's asking. It was an insurance thing. Something get stolen off the base, from your room, those army bastards gotta pay you for a new one. So that's the deal we made, that got him double-paid, the army effed up, and me the guitar I want. He was happy to give it over, too."

VICKSBURG WOULD BE my point of entry into Mississippi, after East Texas and northern Louisiana had been taken. I scanned Rand McNally's two-page American grid as I blew down the highway. It was a question of translating a couple of inches of blue line into relentless forward motion with the help of high-octane musical fuel. European orchestral works, I'd found, couldn't cut through wind-slap and tire-sizzle at a steady seventy. I cycled through my handful of blues and bluegrass cassettes, an equal opportunity groove-hound in search of endlessly cresting euphoria. The words being sung scarcely mattered: it was Telecaster screams and clawhammer twangs that sailed me along, t-bone shuffles and high lonesome breakdowns; black and white moans smeared together like resin and hardener that kept the Chevy's pedal epoxied to the metal, eight cylinders humming, white-lined blacktop unfurling toward the horizon even as I reeled it in, an exhaustless supply. Here was America. Been there and gone.

When my cassettes had been played out I switched to radio. Today's Country was upbeat rather than downmarket, rock-and-roll guitars framing the view through tinted front windows of paid-up Blazers and Broncos. Good men still drank too much whiskey on Friday night, cheatin' hearts still cheated, but faithful dawgs no longer died—not on these playlists—and urban cowboys were too busy line-dancing to bother murdering anybody, not to mention doing time at Folsom Prison. The groove, too, had been streamlined: *bim* ba-da *boom* ba-da *bim* ba-da *boom* ba-da, an eighteen-wheeler on deadline under caffeinated hands. The whole thing was sponsored by Bud Light and Godfather Pizza.

The Nova seemed to billow slightly as we blew across I-20, past Shreveport and Monroe. Just this side of Mississippi, the right rear tire let out a terrific BANG! I veered onto the shoulder, made a quick tour of my steed. The thing wasn't flat and looked okay, for a retread. Later that evening, at the Motel 6 in Jackson, I discovered the missing slab of black rubber—three inches square, as though the macadam had reached up and torn it off.

CENTRAL MISSISSIPPI IN mid-June was drought-dry, according to the TV weatherman. A ghostly image from some old black-and-white movie flickered through my head as I packed for the day trip: skinny white women in cat-eyed Flannery O'Connor glasses with tight disapproving mouths fanning themselves in sweltering court-rooms while fat white men with greasy cowlicks chewed cigars and leered. I pulled out a harp, wailed at the chattering TV until the cat-eyes and leers faded.

Mount Olive was fifty miles southeast of Jackson. The proper soundtrack would ward off evil spirits, I decided, shuffling anxiously through cassettes as I headed out. Howlin' Wolf and I were gonna get up in the morning and ride out Highway 49. Divided by a grassy median, the four lanes rose and fell as they skirted Richland, Piney Woods, D'Lo. I stopped at a roadside stand for a quart mason jar of comb honey—present for Mister Satan—and a box of sun-warmed blackberries, which purpled my fingers as I ate them and drove. Ten miles past D'Lo signs for Magee started popping up. Sterling's ancestral plantation? Robert Johnson was goin' to the crossroads, falling down on his knees, crying Lord above have mercy. Just before Mount Olive I bought a disposable Kodak at a Winn-Dixie. Come back, the checkout girl twanged cheerfully.

Main Street of Mister Satan's hometown had a white water tower at one end; downtown was Napa Auto Parts, Carr's Discount

Drugs. All I had to go on was a name. Directory assistance showed no listing. I stood at a window in Town Hall and told the pleasant young white woman who I was looking for. Town Hall was being renovated and smelled of fresh paint; behind me, side by side, were prefab wooden doors marked "Mayor" and "Police." The pleasant young woman eyed me, expressionless, then picked up her phone.

"George," she drawled matter-of-factly, "this is Jo Beth down at Town Hall. I have a young man here who says he works with Sterling Magee up in New York City. Uh huh. Passing through town. And he wondered if y'all—Sterling Magee, that's raht. And he wondered if y'all might know where Joshua is. From New York. To pay his respects. Kin you do that? I'll tell him. He'll be waiting out front. Thank you, George. Bye now."

She hung up.

"George'll be bah at one-thirty," she said. "He'll bring you on over."

I killed three hours. At one-thirty a late-model Pontiac pulled up in front of my Nova and a slim black guy with a mustache in a pale yellow polo shirt and navy slacks got out. He was older than Nat and had prominent cheekbones angling down to a taut trim jaw. His eyes brushed past me, then flickered back. He hesitated, eyeing my Texas plates.

"Are you George?" I said.

"Uh huh."

I smiled, stuck out my hand, told him who I was. I felt myself performing a role, suddenly: the gee-whizzing Yankee white boy come to bring tidings of great joy. He didn't smile or frown. He was cool, unresponsive, but not in any way that could be interpreted as disrespectful. I was a creature from another planet; I might yet prove to have fangs. Finally, desperate to connect, I reached into the car and set my boom box on the roof.

"Everybody up in Harlem calls him Mister Satan," I explained. "I made this tape of us out on the street a couple of months ago."

I punched Play. We stood where we were as the voice I knew well came on—hoarse and enraptured, a rapid-fire scat cresting over the top of our clatter. I'd cued up "Mother Mojo":

I went through Mississippi . . . trying to get to Florida, USA

I made a bad turn in Mobile Alabama don't you know I ended up in
Atlanta GA

You can bet your bottom dollar Sister Woman I doggone sure was lookin'
for my mama mojo every day

Out on the highways and the byways of the boondocks of Savannah
Georgia . . . people didn't understand

Every grocery store and supermarket thought I was a crazy man

They'd say "What can I do for you, sir?" and I'd say "I wanna get a
dozen of your mojo hands"

George was gazing at me with something like quiet wonder.

"That's Sterling," he murmured. "Mm mm mm." He cleared his throat as my solo came on. "That you?"

"On the harmonica, yeah. He's playing all the percussion."

I reached into my car and pulled out a proof sheet checkerboarded with shots of us working 125th Street, backs to the New York Telephone office. George turned it in his hands as the boom box clattered and roared.

"Y'all got it together," he finally said, giving his pronouncement the slightest questioning edge.

"It's a good gig. We make a little money, too."

He laughed as our hands met for real. "That's Sterling."

He walked over to a pay phone, placed a call, and within five minutes a slim self-contained woman in a magenta blouse with a cross around her neck appeared, on foot. Annette was Joshua's daughter, which made her Mister Satan's first cousin once removed. I caught a fleeting whiff of her hair relaxer as we shook hands—the same light, smoky-oil scent Gail had used.

"We ain't heard a word from Sterling, really, since whenever it was he left out of here," she said as the tape played on, more quietly now. "Maybe seven or eight years."

"He's doing okay. Better than okay. Everybody up in Harlem knows him."

She turned to George. "Ain't his mama and them gonna be surprised?"

"Joshua too, most likely."

"Lord, I can't wait to call *somebody* up." She stared at the proof sheet. "He ain't had the beard back before. He look just like Sterling, though." She beamed at me. "This is some kind of big day for a Monday, ain't it?"

They got in George's car and had me follow them across town into what they'd called Southside. Gravel suddenly spit up under my tires, as though we'd crossed some invisible boundary, but the houses here were neatly kept on shaded, winding lanes. Stray breezes cooled me in the baking heat. We pulled into the driveway of a brick ranch house set a hundred feet back under leafy trees and stopped next to an old Ford truck.

There was a lot of yelling and laughing about how cousin Sterling done taken over New York City as Joshua Magee rose from his porch chair and came out to meet me. He was slab-solid under slight thickening and either of his hands could have crushed both of mine. He shared Mister Satan's burnished bronze complexion but was clean-shaven except for a small gray soul-tuft, which made him, when he smiled, the spitting image of Dizzy Gillespie. His pink Oxford cloth shirt and jeans were rumpled and dirt-smudged. He pushed back his trucker's cap, worked on a cheeked wad of gum, and giggled—a high, gentle, incongruous sound—as we were introduced. Two other men who'd been sharing his porch also wandered over. Homer had thick glasses and a squint; Bo had a brown plastic leg sticking out of his cutoff shorts along with the real one.

"He told me I oughta look you up if I came through," I said as we stood in a loose circle, the four of us plus Annette. George had headed back to work.

Joshua giggled. "Is that a fact?"

"He said nobody down here except you would remember him."

Everybody whooped.

"Now *how* he gonna go and say something like that?" Annette laughed in a complaining way.

"Can't *nobody* forget Sterling," said Bo.

"Ain't no chance," agreed Homer.

"Ain't that something?" Joshua chuckled, as though I were an angel from the Land of the Dead.

"He's going by the name of Mister Satan now, up in Harlem. Everybody calls him that."

Bo, tickled, slapped Homer's outstretched hand. "Sterling still bad, ain't he?"

"Whooo. Lord have mercy."

Joshua giggled. "Sterling always gonna do his own thing, now."

"Couldn't never tell that man too much he didn't wanna hear," Bo agreed. "He liable to jump in his car and *sshooom!* Just take off."

They pointed at the red split-level house across the street—just off Highway 49—when I asked where he'd grown up. Annette frowned.

"He was back in there around 1979–80, after his mama and daddy had moved down to Florida and left it empty. 'Cause his wife Betty was very sick, you know. It wasn't no happy time."

Bo swiveled on his plastic leg, elbowed me gently. "Sterling's wife?" he said. He made exaggerated *Playboy* centerfold curves in the air. "Break your heart."

Homer shook his head. "Break your heart, a woman that fine."

"He spent near about a year up in there," Annette said. "With her, you know. At her bed."

"She had the cancer," Homer said.

"He mentioned," I said.

"He ain't never been *nowhere* near the same after she died," Bo said. "Talkin' about graveyards and shooting stars."

Homer pushed his glasses up. "Remember when his mama and them came up, that took him back down to Florida?"

"Whoo damn!"

"Scairt the heck out of her."

"Daddy," Annette said, nodding at me, touching her cross, "the young man come all this way and we ain't even offered him a drink of water."

I was relocated with great alacrity to the front porch, where I replayed "Mother Mojo" while we all sipped tall glasses of sweet lemony iced tea. Joshua replenished his wad of gum from time to time with sticks from a pack of Juicy Fruit in his breast pocket and stared at the proof sheet Annette passed around. Time unfolded as in a dream—fluid, dazed, dawdling in the strange fullness of perfection.

"That's Sterling, all right," Bo called out, slapping Homer's hand as the tape clattered away. "Shoot. That's *damn* sure Sterling messing around on that."

"He'd play anything," Joshua said. "Give him a bucket, he'd play it."

"Piano, whatever you got lying around," added Homer.

"He plays piano?" I asked.

*"Piano?"* yelped Bo. "That was his main thing."

"Far as I'm concerned, it always was," said Joshua.

"In the churches," Annette explained. "With the gospel groups and all that."

"Ask him about it," Bo said. "He'll tell you."

After an iced tea refill, I walked back to my car and got a harp. The one concrete achievement I'd taken away from *Big River* was my own arrangement of Scott Joplin's "The Entertainer," worked up during idle motel-room hours with the help of sheet music and those overblows William had shown me. Falling back into the chaise I'd been sharing with Annette, I played a few minutes of it for her and the three men. It owed nothing directly to Nat or my recorded blues masters, but of course traces of their sound—a flapdog eagerness shadowed by knowing sadness, a certain tongued kick—had flowed through various openings, molding and firming every note I played. I wasn't aware of my tapping feet until Bo pointed them out.

"Sterling rubbed off on you already," he laughed as the others joined in. "You movin' just like Sterling."

Speaking of Sterling: Annette hoped both of us might drive back down in mid-August for the second annual Magee family reunion, a large event which had debuted, with her help, the previous summer.

"I mean Adam," she said, "you ought of *seen* some of those older people carrying on, partying to beat the band. Hadn't nobody never done something like this before, for them. Calling everybody back from Alabama, Tennessee, wherever they got spread out to. Connecticut. And some of these elderly people got stories! This one brother and sister—couldn't they both of been less than ninety years apiece, they got up and talked about how back in slavery-times the master had sold off one of the slave Magees' daughters, Tom and Easter Magee's daughter. That's the parents of Sterling's grandfather, Tom and Easter Magee is. So the master had gone and sold off one of their little girls, just because he could. But this old brother and sister had gone and renamed themselves *into* Magees, even though their grandmother—that little girl who got sold—had been baptized something else by the new master, that bought her. So this old brother and sister were now calling themselves Magee, instead of Hanson or whatever. Just to keep alive the memory of the people they came from. Wasn't no dry eyes at the picnic, after that." She sighed, played with her cross. "So y'all can come down this time, I hope. Shoot, y'all can *be* the band, if you want. You think cousin Sterling might do that?"

I promised I'd relay the invitation. Before I left, Joshua found a pair of scissors inside and I cut the black-and-white proof sheet filled with on-location action shots of Mister Satan and me right down the middle—keeping one half, giving the other to Annette. This way she'd have something to send Mister Satan's parents, along with news of how their son and a young man from New York were beginning to make a name for themselves as a musical act on the streets of Harlem. I took snapshots of everybody before taking off, with my Winn-Dixie Kodak. "Don't show my leg," Bo called out as he, Homer, and Joshua posed in front of Joshua's truck, meaning the one he didn't have.

"I won't," I said, squinting.

And didn't. I angled the camera up instead, catching the shade tree behind the truck and the three smiling men. Highway 49 is level with the top of their heads, a hundred yards away across a drought-parched field.

PART FOUR

# HOT TOWN

# CHAPTER SIXTEEN

# DO THE RIGHT THING

*Oh, she was pretty . . . pretty as a summer day*

*Oh, I'm so sorry . . . that I let her get away*

—STERLING MAGEE AND JESSE STONE,
"OH SHE WAS PRETTY" (1966)

THE NEW YORK SUMMERS of 1988 and 1989 blur together in memory, or rather melt: an endless bruising string of steam-bath busking days and fan-raked nights under my rooftop apartment's simmering tarred ceiling. Growing up in the suburbs, I'd always thought of June, July, and August as a succession of berry seasons: mulberries, wineberries, blackberries. Summer in Harlem began and ended with the Lemonade Man—a young man, invariably, pulling a dolly through the strolling crowds on 125th Street. His large plastic garbage pail was a sloshing potpourri: several huge blocks of ice and bags of smaller cubes, composite lemonade—powdered mix, canned concentrate, squeezed real lemons—plus floating slices of peach, apple, and watermelon. He'd pause and ladle Mister Satan and me large oversweet Styrofoam cups, a dollar apiece. It felt good to be working hard outdoors, sweating, quenching a bottomless thirst. But there was such a thing as too hot, even for us.

A few days after I got back from Mississippi, New York was scorched by the worst heat wave on record, forty-three continuous days of ninety or hotter highs. TV weathermen spoke of "global warming," when they weren't blaming ashes heaved skyward by the previous year's eruption of Mount Pinatubo. Mister Satan, wiping dead finger-skin off his strings with Lemon Pledge and an old washcloth one torturous July afternoon, thought they were full of shit.

"It's too damn *hot* is what it is," he laughed harshly. "Can't no scientist second-guess Creation. God—G-o-d, that's the Growth of Death, he's got a good thing going on with all those old people dropping dead out in Chicago."

I wiped my forehead on the back of my arm. "More tombstones for his trophy yards."

"I'm gonna *snatch* those bastards!" he boomed gaily, putting on God's voice. "Just to show the whole world how big and bad I am!"

Mr. Oscar, one of our longtime fans, got up from his folding chair and wandered over. A small, solid, round-shouldered man in his sixties with a shaved brown skull, he always wore the same yin-yang t-shirt—black and white teardrops curling into each other to make a perfect circle—and palmed the same two polished steel exercise balls, rotating them in his hand like oversize bearings while he gazed at us and the variously unencumbered women who strolled by. I was working on one of my harps as he came up, massaging a sticky reed with a bank ATM slip.

"Hot weather got to it, huh?" he said, gazing down.

I glanced up from my crouch. "We play so damn hard these things are always flatting out."

"I never could play the harmonica. Saxophone, maybe. I always figured if I put my mind to it I could."

"Get on over here, you bastard!" Mister Satan yelled at Mr. Danny, one of many older wine, beer, and vodka drinkers our tip bucket occasionally subsidized.

Mr. Danny veered toward him and accepted the crumpled palmed bill. "Thank you, Mister Satan."

"I'm basically a frustrated sax player myself," I admitted, giving the reed a quick buff with the jeweler's file I'd pulled out.

"Is that a fact?" His steel balls swirled hypnotically.

"Gene Ammons, Houston Person, Gatortail Jackson. That's the stuff I love. Organ-sax trios."

"Huh. Ever listen to country music."

I smiled. "When I'm driving through West Virginia."

"Hank Williams, Merle Haggard?"

"I've heard of 'em."

"Man," he chuckled. "That's all we *had* back in Tennessee."

A Kawasaki Ninja screamed by like a large furious hornet—engine wound tight, lifting into a wheelie that turned our heads. The next moment a white mag-wheeled Benz spun by, thumping the sidewalk with angry MegaBass drum-talk, a sulking boastful tirade about *Fuck the police don't be steppin on my toes, 'cause I'm down with my niggaz and my Tec-9 hoes.*

Mr. Oscar made a face. "I never did go for no rap."

"I like the beats," I said, pressing the harp's coverplate back into place. "It's the 'kill-whitey' part I have a tough time with."

Mister Satan had swaggered over in his damp t-shirt—cigarette dangling, face gleaming with heat and hard work. "Hell," he boomed, "all I hear is misery and complaint. Every last one of 'em sound like they need a kick in the behind."

"You can't tell 'em nothing," Mr. Oscar agreed. "They liable to shoot you."

"Our music ain't about complaining *no* kind of way. People got the blues-thing all wrong, talking about 'My baby left me' and all that mess. Hell, if you treated her right, with respect and admiration, she ain't *gonna* leave you for no other man. Ain't that right Miss Baby?" he called out to Miss Macie, who was leaning against his shopping cart and smoking, unreadably cool behind large violet sunglasses. She ignored him.

"You see what I'm dealing with?" he cried, delighted.

1983. THINGS WITH HELEN HAD TURNED OUT surprisingly well, after the fiasco back in July. Her feelings for Vince had *never* gone deep—he was a fantasy, not a relationship—and she knew now where home was. Oh, Adam. After hurting like shit for a week, I'd melted. We'd renewed our commitment, struggled to open our hearts. Things had settled down into a kind of exhausted detente with pockets of tenderness and sex.

It had been a jittery fall, politically. With Reagan's finger on the button, everybody was anxious about nuclear war, accidental or intentional. One night in November, Helen and I had walked up the block to Riverside Church, sat in folding chairs with a crowd of a thousand, and watched "The Day After" on a projection screen TV. Mushroom clouds over America! The walking wounded, skin blackened and peeling. A hundred million had tuned in, according to *Newsweek*.

The only thing you could do in the face of such madness was insist on lucidity. I'd redoubled my efforts on the review-front, Cowley's avatar gone prophetic. Men had constructed a pathological, death-driven civilization? *Reweaving the Web of Life: Feminism and Nonviolence* is the answer! I'd cried in the *Village Voice*. Neoconservatives like Hilton Kramer and Norman Podhoretz were poohpoohing the nuclear threat? I'd mugged them with reality in *Boston Review*. Helen knew better than to disturb me at my desk. I had a world to save *and* seminar papers to write.

We were getting along well, I thought, as Christmas approached. It was time for the English Department's annual holiday party in Philosophy Hall. My only worry was that Dear Vince—friend of several in the department—would show up. Helen assured me he wouldn't.

He didn't. The party proceeded as those parties did. You'd hear animated booze-chatter about Kristeva and Derrida somewhere high over your head as you trudged up six marble flights. You'd pour down a couple of strong vodka-tonics, toothpick a few cheese cubes. An hour later you'd find yourself trapped in a pointless argument about phallologocentrism with a Lacanian feminist wearing bright red lipstick. I considered all poststructural theory of a piece with the nuclear scenario spinning of Edwin Teller and Herman Kahn: evil abstraction in the service of apocalypse. What we needed was *less* theory, not more! Listen to the life-instinct! Reroot yourself in the concrete! Sometimes I wanted to deconstruct my own overloaded brain. We all did; that's why we drank.

I hung out briefly with Helen—she had her own crowd—and

took off with Peter Herman, a bearded Jewish Renaissance specialist in the class behind me who hated theory, loved John Lee Hooker,
and swore by Glenfiddich single-malt. We were quickly becoming
buddies. Helen I'd see at home. She seemed cool with that.

A couple of hours later I showed up on our doorstep, high, a blues
album under my arm. Peter and I had been sipping and listening at
his apartment. The cover of *The Original Sonny Boy Williamson* was
a glowering-buzzard-in-the-barnyard picture I remembered from
*Blues Harp*, the instructional book I'd started off with back at the
Day School. Sonny Boy himself I'd somehow bypassed; his sound
now came as a revelation—a swingy, sharp-edged little sob that
nailed you in the throat.

I heard live music, suddenly. Staggering, I put my ear to our front
door. Helen was strumming a guitar and crooning in her girlish singing voice somewhere down the hall. This was strange. She almost
never played, or sang.

I twisted open the locks, shouted something about being home.
Slammed and relocked. She was sitting on the sofa at the end of the
front hall, her nylon-string guitar cradled, hair fanning like a small
black cape across her shoulders. She glanced up, embarrassed.

I tried to smile. "I'd forgotten how well you play that thing."

She shrugged.

I hesitated, held up the album. "Isn't this cool? Peter just lent it
to me."

"Sonny Boy Williamson."

"The guy's one of the great blues harmonica players of all time
and I never paid any attention to him when I was learning."

She was gazing at her hands.

"Helen," I murmured.

She sat without answering, dark sheets of hair draping the side
of her face.

"Look," I groaned, "this is crazy, you gotta talk to me. Is it
Vince? What, did Vince come to the party after I left?"

She lifted her eyes, slowly shook her head. My heart leaped, then
faltered. Something in her gaze had nothing to do with me—a

strange cool flatness, as though certain key liquid places had suddenly hardened.

"Is it somebody *else?*" I whispered.

THE NEXT TIME I CAME DOWN TO HARLEM it was so slambastingly hot Mister Satan had left his musical equipment at home and was giving a lecture-demonstration at our usual spot, explicating one of his mandalas to a circle of onlookers. This mandala, like most, was a kind of jigsaw puzzle: the nestling, painted wood pieces could be exploded and reassembled into a dizzying array of pictograms—swords, eyes, a penis-with-balls.

"Damn 360 degrees!" he roared, winking at me as I came up, tapping his chest with a scimitar-shaped sliver. "I got that Nobel Prize for mathematics coming to me! Mister Adam was telling me some joker at Columbia University got his medal last week for proving the circle *can't* be squared. Now ain't that the biggest mess you ever heard? I been squaring, quintuplifying, and double-refrying *my* circles going on ten years, right here in Harlem, and educated ignorance gonna tell a story like that."

Each of his, he explained, had three billion, three hundred and thirty-three million, three hundred and forty-five thousand, three hundred and ninety-nine degrees in it. His proof involved seven dimensions and a dizzying spiral inward through proliferating quadrilaterals.

"Go on, Devil!" somebody laughed.

"No sir!" he barked. "You got that incorrect. I am Mister Satan! Ain't no D-e-v-i-l in S-a-t-a-n, that's a story God's people gonna propagate to sow confusion. The *Church* is the Devil! God's people got a monopoly on death and destruction! Spell me D-e-v-i-l backwards, you got L-i-v-e-d, lived. Lived means you ain't alive no more! The Bible is a book about dead people! That's all you got in the graveyards, which the Christians care so damn much about. Check it out: I had a church lady walk by last week, Mister Adam and I were out here and this church grandmama hobbles by and tosses one of her Praise Jesus flyers in the tip bucket. And she's holding her ears as she hobbles away, like Mister Satan's music is corrupting her enjoyment of the day. Now, how you think Jesus gone and rewarded her?" He paused and pointed off down the block, brimming. "Three days ago, that same church lady was walking past McDonald's when the front of a building came down—*Blam!*—right on her head. Jesus loves her so damn much he killed her dead! Bastard couldn't say Thank you ma'am not *once* in all those years, but he's waiting right there with thunderstorms, loosening bricks and throwing the mess down on her beliefs. Ain't that pitiful?"

I sipped lemonade and watched, drifting away after a while into a conversation with a guy my age named Tony. Very dark in his stained white Nike singlet and cutoffs, with a small delicate mouth and sharp chin, Tony had sat in with us a few times on electric bass, slapping and thumb-popping, a virtuoso. Other afternoons he'd drifted by, eyes glassy, barely noticing us. Today he'd paused to smoke a cigarette, setting down a suds-filled plastic bucket and squeegee. He had a new gig as a self-employed window washer.

"Mister Satan and I go way back," he said. "*Way* back. Like in the studio—maybe ten years ago I was on a session with him and George Benson, with Gatortail Jackson on sax."

"Benson is *great,* man."

"You oughta seen him next to Sterling. Shut *down,* man. Ask anybody. Sterling was all *over* the motherfucker, running circles around Benson's shit. Benson couldn't do nothing but watch him go."

"Damn."

"I was *there,*" he insisted as we grabbed hands. "You gotta get him out of Harlem so the rest of the world knows what we *been* knowing for a long time."

Before he left he leaned in, breath tickling my ear behind his hand. "You got a dollar I could hold till next Friday? Business is down."

"Sure." Glancing around, I pulled out my wallet, extracted a one without showing off other bills, shoved it back in my pocket, and palmed him the buck, all as inconspicuously as possible.

"Cool," he said, cigarette bouncing.

"Any time."

We sat for a moment, lost in the flow of Harlem's sweltering July. Heavy sweet incense wafted by.

"Where's your bass?" I asked. "You oughta sit in next time."

He turned thumbs down. "Sold it."

1989 WAS THE SUMMER OF *Do the Right Thing*. Spike Lee had, it was rumored, made a movie that would literally set New York on fire. White folks were anxious. Lee had loosely based his fable on two of the city's most infamous recent murders of young black men: Michael Stewart's 1983 chokehold asphyxiation by the cops; Michael Griffith's 1986 beating and death in Howard Beach. He'd upped the ante, reviewers claimed; turned the beat around. His black Brooklynites, infuriated by the "accidental" police murder of Radio Raheem—a hulking, confrontational, boom box–toting Voice of the Community—trash and burn Sal's Famous Pizzeria while Sal, played by Danny Aiello, looks on in helpless rage. Public Enemy's "Fight the Power!" was Radio Raheem's hip-hop anthem, and the anthem's bellowed refrain: "Fight the Pow-ah! Fight the Pow-ah!" I'd already noticed the phrase popping up on Harlem t-shirts and baseball caps, as "X" and "By Any Means Necessary" would a few years later. Some collective pulse had been fingered, or created, or both. So where were the fires? Where was the fight?

I was anxious that summer. I'd known for a long time that my Harlem visa was provisional, subject to communal pressure. The Howard Beach verdict in December 1987—manslaughter rather than murder for Lester, Ladone, and Kern—had infuriated black New York; Mister Satan had called me a few days after his Lincoln Center recital, troubled but firm.

"This Howard Beach mess got my people up in arms," he'd said. "I think you better stay away from Harlem for a week or two and let things cool off."

"*I* didn't do anything," I'd protested.

"It ain't about you *or* me. Hell, we gonna be together forever, anyhow. I just can't take responsibility for every no-good bastard out there. My people got a right to be upset, you know."

I *did* know. I was upset, too. I'd always viewed what we did—in

Harlem, near Columbia, at Times Square—as principled opposition to New York's chronic undercurrent of violent racial antagonism. Certainly that was how we had been embraced uptown. Our regulars—Mister Oscar, James Gants, Mister Larry—were the tip of the iceberg. Dozens of times over the past three years I'd been pulled aside, a hand laid on my arm.

"It's *good* to see y'all getting it together," one person would say. "Pepper and salt. Y'all got it goin' *on*."

"He plays harder when you come down," another would confide in me. "You push him. That's good."

Once, when a wine cooler had sunk in and a long, hot-hearted solo was in the process of erupting through my clenched hands while Mister Satan flailed in five or six dimensions, I'd noticed one of our onlookers—older than me, glasses and dreadlocks—grooving with serious toe-tapping joy. Or was his extreme agitation something else? The moment my solo had played itself out he bounced toward me, reaching a hand into his half-unbuttoned shirt, pulling something out, lifting it from around his neck.

"You've *earned* this, brother!" he'd cried, looping it around my neck and hugging me, eyes burning with righteousness. His dreads were scratchy; I'd caught a whiff of musk-spice cologne. "You've *earned* this! When you come down to Harlem, you *wear* this!"

He'd backtracked and beamed, clapping his hands in jubilee-time as Mister Satan roared on. Heart racing, I'd gazed down at his blessing: a green-black-and-red silhouette of Africa painted on a hand-stitched black leather medallion.

I'd worn it a few times after that, self-consciously. Africa, glorious as it might be, wasn't mine to claim; I felt no need to parade a solidarity with liberation struggles I supported in principle but had little detailed knowledge of or personal investment in. I was a New York blues musician with a Harlem gig. I was grateful for my brother's gift. I hung it up at home, on the bulletin board next to my typewriter, a talisman.

DO THE RIGHT THING WAS THE SUMMER'S BIG HIT; late July was high lemonade season. I jumped in my Honda and drove down to 125th Street, ready for one more afternoon's hard good sweat and the twenty-five crumpled dollars it usually netted me. I parked in front of the same hydrant I'd been illegally blocking for almost three years. Slapped hands with Mister Oscar—he kept lookout for traffic cops, warning me—and leaned back against a fender, catching Mister Satan's eye, glorying in his sound. As they had since the first day, harp lines began percolating through my head, tugging at my shoulders and hips. Responses to his call.

Somebody crossed my field of view, sneering. "Don't you smile at me, white boy."

Startled, I looked up to see a man in his mid-thirties—strong, young, neatly dressed in a striped sport shirt and tan slacks. He had on a pair of half-black-framed Malcolm X glasses; his eyes were filled with cool, bruised, seething hatred. For me.

"I wasn't smiling at you," I stammered. "I didn't even see you."

He'd already swung around the car behind mine, was striding purposefully away down the block. I stood for a moment, heart weirdly sick. Glanced at the young woman in shorts and sandals who'd claimed an adjacent portion of my car's fender. She shook her head sadly, with what seemed like compassion. Mister Satan finished up his song with whirlwind strums.

"Get on up here, Mister Gussow!" he roared happily, falling back in his hi-chair.

I'd just finished unpacking and plugging in when the Malcolm X guy returned. The accomplice he'd brought was taller, older, and wearing a knit skullcap. The Malcolm X guy planted himself in front of Mister Satan, folded his arms, jerked his head.

"Why are you letting this white boy play with you?"

Mister Oscar and a couple of the other older men rolled their eyes. Mister Satan pulled at his beard.

"That question is incorrect," he said. "I will not be challenged as to the correctivity of who I do or do not choose to have play with me."

"I asked you a *question*," the man hissed, jabbing his finger at the ground. "Why is it when a black man goes to a white neighborhood out in Howard Beach he gets *lynched,* but white people can come into *our* neighborhood any damn time they please and nothing is supposed to happen to them? Huh? You tell me that."

Mister Satan hesitated. The sidewalk seemed to open up beneath my feet. He grimaced, cast his eyes to the side. "No way does that mess out in Howard Beach have anything to do with what me and my harmonica man trying to do right here in Harlem."

"Your *harmonica man?*"

"That is correct."

"You know what you are, old man?" the Malcolm X guy sneered, working his shoulders like a boxer. "You are a *Nee-gro.*" The syllables were separated, elongated, dripping with irony. He glanced at his friend in the knit skullcap, shook his head. "Giving me all this bullshit about playing with some white boy. Damn, we got us a *Nee-gro* right here."

Within a minute he had called Mister Satan a nigger and a motherfucker and offered—stabbing the air with his hands—to take the whole thing down the block and settle it. Mister Satan, flustered, offered no real reply. Then he spun away abruptly and came toward me. I was frozen to the black plastic foldup chair Mister Satan had loaned me several years earlier.

"Why are you here?" he demanded.

"Look," I began, "I—"

"What, do you love black people?" he sneered.

The faces, bodies, and sad chuckles of Gail and Robyn flashed through my head, trailed by guilt; then an image of Nat in his Panama hat, blowing through cupped hands. "I'm here to play with him," I said levelly, nodding at Mister Satan. "I'm a musician."

"You're no *musician,*" he spat out, rocking back as he glared down. "You're just one more white boy come to rip off the black man's music."

I was rising to my feet; we were suddenly in each other's faces. It happened in one slow, dreamy, almost delicate motion. I wanted to do nothing that could be perceived as aggressive. My heart was hot; I needed him to hear me. We stood at an oblique angle, eyes flickering.

"I'm a musician," I said quietly, "and a music teacher, and you're probably not gonna meet a lot of young white guys who know more about the history of white ripoffs of black music than I do. My people have a miserable record. I *know* that, I teach it to my students, I make sure they know who created the stuff we're trying to learn. It wasn't a bunch of white boys, it wasn't Elvis or Pat Boone or the Blues Brothers with their minstrel-show crap. When people ask me where I learned to play, I *tell* them: I bought every record I could get my hands on, I listened to and learned from the best blues harmonica players in the world, and ninety-five percent of them were black. The best in the *world*. And all I'm trying to do—you asked me why I'm here and I'm trying to tell you . . ."

He nodded, eyes flickering. Leaned in a little, head bowed.

". . . all I'm trying to do is play the music I love, from my heart, as well as I can. I've been coming down here for the past three years and playing with him"—I pointed at Mister Satan—"because he's the best gig I'm ever gonna have. I *know* how lucky I—"

"You leave that young man alone!" Mister Satan yelled, suddenly fierce, waving his hand. "It wasn't *him* swinging those baseball bats and making all that mess out in Howard Beach! *Those* are the mother-effers you should be picking on!"

People had started to gather. The Malcolm X guy flashed me a strange look—angry but no longer hateful—and backpedaled toward Mister Satan, launching into a loud, face-saving retraction. The shouting was heated but the tide seemed to have turned. The guy in the knit skullcap slid toward me. He was taller and older than his friend; his chocolate brown face was pitted, scarred, grave. He seemed burdened.

"It's not like I just started coming down here," I protested. "We've been playing this spot for almost three years."

He couldn't look at me. "I've seen you."

"Then you *know*. You've seen how people feel. I'm not trying to make any trouble."

"Be that as it may, the fact remains that this is a black neighborhood, not a white neighborhood, and black people gotta be watching out for their *own*. Now when a white person comes in, shows his face. . . ." He shook his head. "Like it or not, we got a problem."

"*I'm* the problem?" I touched my chest. "Christ, if it was up to me we'd hang those guys out in Howard Beach for what they did. They make me ashamed to be white."

He looked distinctly pained. "All that may be true. I'm not talking about that. All I'm trying to say is, you may be innocent. See. You may be. But so was the brother who got killed out in Howard Beach. So was Michael Griffith. So was Eleanor Bumpurs. A whole lot of innocent black people been killed by the white man in this city. So all I'm saying is, just because you may be innocent don't necessarily mean you *safe*."

I stared at him, speechless.

"Like me," he said, almost apologetically. "I may not have any personal complaint with you one way or another. You know. I may or may not. But there's a lot of young brothers out there who may not see things the same way I do. That's all I'm saying. People in a lot of pain these days. Can't nobody tell when somebody might do a crazy thing that gets some innocent person hurt."

He and his friend in the Malcolm X glasses spun away a moment later, disappearing down the block. Mister Satan and his crew huffed and puffed. I sat down on my folding chair, gazed at my clasped hands. The air had a shattered feeling. My hands were pale. I looked up. Afternoon traffic roared by on 125th Street. Gleaming white BMWs with gold mag wheels and fluffy raccoon tails dangling from rearview mirrors. Shiny black Jeeps with padded black roll bars and wire-covered headlights. Rap music thumping out of everything that moved. *Fuck the police don't be steppin' on my toes, 'cause I'm down with my niggaz and my Tec-9 hoes.* Lots of young gangstas and gangsta wannabes. Would one of them be willing to drive by and pop a white boy, if the price were right? For *free*? The thought had never occurred to me. Not once in three years.

I STAYED AWAY FROM HARLEM for the next couple of days, brooding. Consciousness hurts. I'd been huddling under Mister Satan's wing for the past three years, dreaming my way down into the music I loved. Nothing would ever be the same now.

So what was the right thing? I was determined to do it, if I could reason it out. Agree, in solidarity with my black nationalist critics, that I had no legitimate business in the neighborhood? Pack up, get out, and never come back? Save my own skin, since Mister Satan obviously no longer could? Abandon him and the two-man sound we'd worked so hard to create? Or be brave and stick it out? Disrespect two guys who plainly meant business? Refuse, as a matter of principle, to be driven away from a gig I'd earned with my own sweat? Play the blues for real, as if my life depended on it?

My eyes suddenly opened; shivering, I saw my situation in a new light. For the past three years I'd been making more noise in public, arguably, than any other white person in Harlem. Blowing my own horn, literally. Why had I blithely imagined that Mister Satan's aura could protect me against all possible resentments? My pale skin would always retain the capacity to symbolize Evil Whiteness in certain eyes, no matter how many others had taken pride in listening *through* my skin to the soul whistling underneath. The color-and-culture game was trickier than I'd realized; I'd been so preoccupied with proving my musical right to play with Mister Satan—mastering and elaborating the "black" sound Nat had passed along to me—that I'd missed the point. The more soulfully I played, the deeper I blew from, the more seamlessly our sounds meshed, the *more* I was an affront to those who insisted that black and white were warring opposites, that hatred and separation were the only solution. Mister Satan and I had found common ground. I hadn't understood this until seeing U2's *Rattle & Hum* the previous fall. Joined at the hip on "Freedom for My People," projecting one hybrid sound and look, we *worked*. A couple of skinny, intense New York guys, the oddest of Odd Couples. If we could get it together, different as we were, then America might be able to do the same, given time. Which was not what any black nationalist wanted to hear. Satan and his Red-Headed White Devil are misleading you, my brothers! We were more dangerous than I'd realized. I was a sitting duck, quacking loudly.

Maybe I should get a gun. I thought about that, briefly. I'd heard one story about a white guy with a gun in Harlem. Danny Draher, a blues guitarist from Chicago who'd been on the New York scene for years, had a black wife—Dodie, a singer with a bleached Afro—and used to work the uptown jazz clubs. I knew Danny vaguely; he was built like a linebacker, had a deceptively relaxed smile and a snapping turtle's jaw. One night, after a dispute about pay, he'd pulled a gun on Jimmy "The Preacher" Robbins in Showman's Cafe. Preacher, who I'd jammed with more than once, was an old-school organist from the Deep South: brilliant, oily, hard-drinking, a master manipulator of foot pedals and stops. The story, as it came down to me, had no content—except for the fact that Danny, a white guy in an all-black club, had pulled a gun on Preacher, who was nobody's fool. And walked out of the club untouched. And was still alive, to this day.

DISCRETION IS THE BETTER PART OF VALOR. I stayed away from Harlem for four or five days. I practiced a lot, feverishly. Took several long walks up through Inwood Hill Park—chewing on sassafras twigs, making blades of grass moan and scream. Went for a swim in nearby Spuyten Duyvil, the brackish channel that connects the Harlem and Hudson rivers and flows, according to Dutch legend, "in spite of the Devil." Did some reading: Malcolm X, Claude Brown, James Baldwin, Ralph Ellison. I realized now what a precious gift Harlem had given me—taking me by the hand, filling me with music, hollering at me to work it out, slapping a dollar in my hand when it was over. Refusing to hold me accountable for the sins of the fathers. Fair enough. I wasn't going to hold Harlem accountable for the first harsh words to come my way in three years.

Mister Satan thought I was grossly overreacting for being worried at all. "Those ignorant bastards ain't worth a damn," he'd barked when I called him up. "Talk a lot of mess about the white man is the Devil, and ain't done one so-and-so thing to make the world a more beautiful place."

Suppose they did return and kill me? I was beginning to wonder what his reaction would be. Would it cut him to the quick, kill his groove for good? Would he die a bitter, broken-hearted old man? Or would he treat my death the way he'd treated every other, as something to be laughed at harshly, cast off, rejected? I could imagine him puffing on his cigarette after they'd buried my white ass. "Bastard got himself killed. Ain't that a mess? I'm *damn* sure gonna live through it, though."

The next time I went down to Harlem, I was strapped. I'd hooked that black leather Africa-medallion off my bulletin board and around my neck, under my t-shirt. I wanted to feel the rawhide against my skin. Never again would I snicker at the idea of someone actually *believing* in mojo. When your ass was on the line, mojo was real. I was scared. But I was going down there. We had deeper music yet to make.

"Hey, Mister Gus!" Mister Satan roared delightedly when I got out of my car, the first day back. "Get on up here and *work,* young man!"

He went on break almost immediately, as he usually did, to harvest bills from the tip bucket and retune. Mister Oscar came up as I set down my twin Mouses. His palmed stainless steel balls circled each other smoothly, endlessly.

"Good to see you back," he said. "We was wondering where you got to."

"I thought I'd give things a chance to cool off after last time."

He waved his hand dismissively. "Outside agitators, the whole bunch. That one loud guy, with the glasses? He was from Brooklyn."

"Brooklyn?"

"Satan found out. The guy ain't even seen Satan *play,* and he's trying to mess with his business. That ain't right. He knew it, too. That's why he and that other fellow left out of here so quick."

We had an okay afternoon. A residual uneasiness fevered the early August swelter as we got going. I eyed the sidewalk traffic— dozens of exotic sculpted and braided hairstyles, lithe pumped shirt-less teenaged boys, t-shirts blaring "It's a Black Thing, You Wouldn't Understand." How could I possibly have thought I *belonged* here? Still, here I was.

Drenched with sweat, working hard without quite grooving, I jogged off after the first set to get a beer from a corner deli. Most of the Harlem delis seemed to be run by Arabs. Indians had the drug-stores, Koreans had the produce stands. Sylvia still had Sylvia's, hopefully. When I floated back into view a few minutes later, Mister Satan handed me a note somebody had tossed into the tip bucket.

"My people be driving me crazy," he laughed, "asking about you when you ain't around."

It was scrawled on the back of a Public Office Memo Bill from the New York Telephone office just behind us: We missed you white man when you do not come. Signed, Harlem.

YUSUF HAWKINS WAS SHOT TO DEATH a couple of weeks later. You couldn't get away from the story; it was splashed across all the New York papers and local TV news shows. The basic outlines were familiar. A sixteen-year-old black boy and three of his friends take the crosstown subway from their home in Brownsville to the Benson-hurst section of Brooklyn—a tough, close-knit Italian neighbor-hood—in search of a used car they've read about in a want ad. They're set upon by a group of local hoods who mistake them for the young black men that a "nigger-loving" girl named Gina Feli-ciano has reputedly been dating. The hoods have been drinking; things get very rough very fast. One of the hoods pulls out a gun and points it at Yusuf's head. Yusuf sees it, staggers backward, falls to his knees. Pleads for his life. He's not the guy they want, he hasn't done anything. Please.

The hood shoots him anyway. Twice, in the chest. He's dead on arrival, half an hour later.

THAT WAS THE END OF HARLEM FOR A WHILE. I stayed away as much on principle—respect for an aching fury I shared—as out of fear. New York was coming apart at the seams; death was every-where. There was only so much two street musicians could do.

# CHAPTER SEVENTEEN

# BILLED OUT

*I got the key . . . to the highway*
*Billed out, I'm bound to go*
*I'm gonna leave here running because*
*Walkin's most too slow*

—BIG BILL BROONZY, "KEY TO THE HIGHWAY"

ONE THING MISTER SATAN and I did as the streets began to heat up was set our sights outside the neighborhood. Harlem was the source of our sound and would always be home; the open road, in whatever form, remained a teasing possibility, a vacation from the racial pressure cooker. "It's *hard* to get me out of Harlem," he'd insisted more than once, but he'd told me stories that suggested otherwise. Such as the time he'd jumped in his '59 Cadillac at six o'clock one morning—in Harlem, this was—and showed up at his mama's front doorstep in St. Petersburg, Florida, at five the next morning.

"Thirteen hundred and eighty-five miles in twenty-three hours," he'd laughed. "I was drinking vodka, too. Liquor will make you a *very* good driver, Mister. You can't afford to be stopped by no police."

New York's Finest had been surprisingly supportive during the past few years; more than once they'd given us a smiling thumbs-up as they swaggered by. We'd developed, by this point, a profitable circuit of sidewalk stages spread out across the city. First choice after 125th Street was One Times Square, corner of Forty-second and Broadway. We'd played there on St. Patrick's Day—a balmy post-parade afternoon—and had been recognized by several people as "those guys in the U2 movie." Tips had been heavy; thirty-eight seconds of worldwide exposure give you the juice. Second choice was the corner of 145th and Broadway; a bus stop out-front, a liquor store to your right guaranteeing a receptive crowd. Third choice was Columbia University: either the Chemical Bank on 113th Street or Broadway Presbyterian Church one block up. Ann Douglas, my former graduate advisor, always seemed to wander by and pause, trans-fixed at the sight of Mister Satan and me joyfully flogging each other in public. Willowy, with a fixed hard smile and a brilliant voracious mind animated by Marilyn Monroe's breathless Yes!, she'd scribble a note to herself and pocket it, drop a dollar in our bucket, wave goodbye, float away. I found out later she'd been working on her magnum opus during those years—*Terrible Honesty: Mongrel Manhattan in the 1920s*—and evolving a theory of black-and-white American art. One day in 1993 I called her up. Ten years earlier we'd read Kerouac, Poe, Dickinson; I was thinking of coming back to school to work out my own ideas about interracial apprenticeship.

"Adam!" she said breathlessly. "We *do* need to talk. I'm working on Sonny Boy Williamson."

BIT BY BIT OVER THE LATE EIGHTIES, Mister Satan and I had eased into another lucrative Manhattan hustle, the weekend street fair scene. Late spring and early fall were high season; the Upper West Side was particularly fertile territory. An organization called Mort & Ray Productions had the franchise. I spent more than a few Saturday mornings chasing down Mort Berkowitz, who patroled each week's ten-block domain in a chauffeured golf cart, bearded and irritable, barking into a cellular telephone. Mort was no more ham-fisted and arbitrary than the job—as he defined it—required. New York was a loony bin; people who spent their weekends frying up zeppoli and peddling Five-in-One Slicer Dicers probably had a

nut loose somewhere and needed to be watched closely. And the
street musicians! Meshuggener, the whole bunch, and they didn't
even pay you rent.

Mort tolerated us. He'd give us a spot if we showed up at exactly
the right moment, after every last trinket peddler and funnel cake
sugar-powderer had been allocated space and duly charged. Immediately after the right moment came Too Late. Mort would shrug:
the few remaining feet of unleased macadam had just been given
away to a bunch of thumping and pennywhistling Peruvians or some
disco-dancing kook wrapped in aluminum foil. Or, more likely, to
Russell Scott Donnelon, the god of gutter-funky classical guitar.

Russell *owned* New York's street fair scene during the late eighties and early nineties. I admired the guy, envied his awesome portable
sound system, couldn't figure out why he'd never made it big. One
year he had a deal with Columbia Records; the next year it collapsed. His handicap may have been that he wasn't pretty, like Kenny
G. or Yanni. He was a short seal-faced guy in an old tux and black
sneakers, frizzy blond hair tied back like a mop. He always looked
harassed, enervated. His talent, like Mister Satan's, was outsized
and demanded regular open-air ventilation. He had a generator-
powered P.A. that produced shatteringly clean sound.; he'd set his
massive speakers in the middle of whatever Broadway intersection
he'd been assigned, plug in his nylon-string Ovation, and go. He was
John Williams, Paco DiLucia, and Robert Johnson crammed into
two blistered hands. He'd cycle through oceanic chord clusters, spat-
ter notes with percussive fingernails. He'd flog and thrum, bedaz-
zling you with rough beauty. "Classical Gas," "La Luna en Mi
Bosillo," "Desire's Bones." He'd pace restlessly, bracketed by Italian
sausage vendors and Pennsylvania Dutch Pretzels, master of his own
small universe. Every note was attacked and *meant*. He and Canarsie Kenny had that in common.

In person, surprisingly, he was somewhat nebbishy, a soulful
complainer. I couldn't blame him; he should have been playing the
Beacon Theater. So should we, I was beginning to feel. I'd already
asked Mister Satan if he wanted to play Amateur Hour at the
Apollo, just for the hell of it. We were on break one afternoon on

125th Street; you could see the red and yellow marquee from where we stood.

"Hell no," he barked. "I already backed up James Brown over there one time, with my little group, and ain't got paid."

*1991.* A FRIEND AND I HAD GONE DOWN to the Village one night—a Mississippi-themed bar called Crossroads—to check out a blind black blues guitarist named Jay Owens. He was sitting at a table next to the stage, seemingly brooding behind dark sunglasses, when I uttered the words Sterling Magee.

Owens jumped like he'd been stung awake. "Does somebody here know Sterling Magee?"

"I play with him," I said. "Up in Harlem, on the street."

He leaned in my general direction, beaming. "Maaaaan, when I was coming up in St. Petersburg, Florida, Sterling Magee was *it,* as far as guitar players. Young cats like me couldn't get enough. Sterling still playing, huh?"

"He's doing great."

"You ask *anybody* in St. Petersburg, man, they'll tell you. Sterling Magee! He had a thing he did—way before Michael Jackson—with gloves, white gloves. Sit up on a stool in there, white gloves on both hands, in the spotlights, and play! Fast, too. Ask him, man. That was his thing."

"White gloves?"

I asked Mister Satan next time we played.

He grinned, almost sheepishly. "He ain't telling no lie. They called me Five Fingers Magee, on the marquee."

ONE THING WE HADN'T DONE, for all our talk of Florida and Mississippi, was actually leave Manhattan Island. In May of 1989 we finally broke out, crossing the George Washington Bridge to play a weekend gig I'd landed us on the boardwalk of Jersey City's Liberty State Park. Miss Macie had stayed home; suddenly it was the two of us at seventy miles an hour with six Mouses stacked in back and road wind slapping our faces. Mister Satan smoked, preached, corrected my driving—"Please don't be tailgating no trucks, Mister

Adam!"—and told me he'd just had a birthday. May 20, 1936, which made him fifty-three to my thirty-one. His gray beard was, I'd come to suspect, a disguise adopted by his inner volcano. Saturday we hammered out four long sets in the spring sun; his ferocity increased exponentially—a kind of demonic possession—as hours elapsed. He drove me like a circus pony, stropped my groove into shape. By late Sunday afternoon he was unstoppable. Showers had threatened that morning, scattered drops as we were setting up. He'd beaten them off.

"It ain't gonna rain," he'd laughed. "We ain't gonna let it."

He'd kicked into "Mother Mojo," hurling fish-flutter strums out to sea. Manhattan's skyline loomed over his shoulder—twin stainless monoliths of the World Trade Center, reliable thrusting old Empire State Building, all the street-level madness invisible from this distance. The clouds had broken up by the time we'd finished the song; the sun pressed down, an equal-opportunity heater-upper.

"You thought I was joking," he chuckled, forehead rilled with sweat. "I can do that, you know."

"We sound great," I panted. A breeze suddenly kicked up, flicking one of the dollars we'd just made out of his open guitar case and across the boardwalk past our scattering of listeners. I dropped my mike and ran it down.

"Chase after that dollar, Mister Business Manager!" he roared happily.

I'D FIRST HEARD about the International BuskerFest in Halifax, Nova Scotia, that spring, from a friend who'd read about the second annual staging of it the year before. Here was Mecca, surely: the forty greatest street acts in the world, by invitation only, convene for seventeen days in a small clean coastal Canadian city. Tens of thousands of tourists; endless days and nights of outdoor musicking, juggling, magic-making. Clear blue late-August skies. No police interference at any time. A People's Choice Award for Busker of the Year on the festival's final day. The organizers paid most of your travel expenses, threw in hotels and food; all you had to do was play your heart out and cash in.

"We're *going,*" Mister Satan had barked when I first told him about it. "Ain't no ifs or buts."

We were New Yawk's secret weapon: the loudest, the wildest, the most outrageously in-your-face. We *had* to go. I brought my boom box down to 125th Street, taped an hour of our best jams, sent in an application with a Polaroid snapshot. The organizers were intrigued by our *Rattle & Hum* cameo. We made the final cut.

Mister Satan had already worked out the details. I'd attach a trailer hitch to my Honda; we'd rent a little two-wheel clamshell for our Mouses, strap his shopping cart to the roof. Miss Macie would come along to pass the hat. Our third summer was suddenly shaping up, the best so far.

That was May 30th. The next weekend was my tenth reunion at Princeton. My classmates had gone on to become doctors, lawyers, investment bankers, published novelists, parents. Of the three '79ers in Spiral, only Chad—the keyboard player—had come back. He was a physics professor at Cal Tech and still gigged occasionally. Scott, I knew, was an A & R man at Arista Records; Bill, who'd put down his trumpet and been born again, was a specialist in Soviet computer systems. I'd called all three before the fifth back in '84, floated the idea of a band reunion, almost pulled it off. This time I didn't have the heart. I staggered through a wilderness of beer blasts, cocktail parties, and class dinners. Everybody had a "line," a career description that made sense. What was I? A grad school dropout, a literary journalist who hadn't published in years, a Harlem street musician. I tried to communicate Mister Satan's genius—breezily, with vividness and intelligence, in the fashion we'd been taught. People smiled as indulgently as they could. Mister Satan? International Busker-Fest? I was a freak. There was one in every class. My example, I sensed, cheered people up. I made them feel better about life choices they'd made. There but for the grace of God.

I came home in a panic. Street music was a noble calling—Harlem was a priceless gift—but enough was enough. I needed stability, income, something I could build on. The next afternoon down on 125th Street I broke the news to Mister Satan. It wasn't a question of not playing with him anymore, but of easing off a little once the cold weather came, something we'd always done anyway. It was a question of getting a part-time job, beginning to think about some kind of career. Of course we were still going to Halifax.

"You *got* yourself a career," he said, reaching for his cigarettes. "A musician always gonna be a musician, one way or another."

"It has nothing to do with you," I murmured.

"Hell," he boomed, "I gave up guitar for seven years in the late seventies and came back into the mess twice as strong as I'd been." He blew out a cloud of smoke, rocked back on his heels. "The one thing I ain't never done is be no kind of a slave to my guitar."

The next afternoon I came home to find a message on my answering machine. He'd been thinking. Give him a call when I got in.

I dialed his number, heart pounding.

He cleared his throat after coming on. "We ain't going to Halifax," he said. He didn't sound angry.

"Why not?" I said, staying calm.

"I can't argue about it. We just ain't going. The wind went out of my sails after we talked yesterday." He paused. "About the money, you know."

I'd told him the Halifax folks were giving us $480 toward the $780 that three round-trip tickets would cost on the Portland-to-Yarmouth ferry.

"Four hundred and eighty bucks isn't bad," I said.

"It ain't *enough*," he said. "Hell, if they want us bad enough, they got a way of finding the other three hundred."

We talked for a while, pulling ourselves back together. He wanted me to see things his way, which I was finally able to. He never said a word about my career plans.

THEN CAME *Do the Right Thing*, Yusuf Hawkins's murder, and the rest of that long hot summer. We tied Mister Satan's shopping cart to the roof of my car and roamed Manhattan Island, profiting off racial polarization by offering ourselves as its in-your-face alternative. My reunions anxieties faded; this seemed like vital work, a task

I was born for. We got back into something of a Harlem routine that fall, after September's cooling breezes had blown through; each time I plugged in on 125th Street, I half-expected the Malcolm X guy to come striding up with his pistol drawn. I began to smoke an occasional Kool now, when Mister Satan proffered one. Nicotine helped float me down into the deep fluid groove where our best music was made. Cigarettes, like wine coolers, were a temporary fix. The shattered feeling lingered for months, a faint bitter aftertaste. My innocence was gone—not a bad thing but a change nonetheless. I felt noticeably freer in my own body these days when we played outside Harlem.

One day in October, after a decent afternoon's work in Times Square, Mister Satan and I hauled his shopping cart into the parking lot on Forty-fourth Street and began loading Mouses and percussion gear into my Honda. Getting the cart itself up onto the car's roof required both strength and finesse. Once we'd spread out the large square of old carpet we kept in the trunk, I'd crouch, grab a pair of wheels, and heave the upended cart toward the car at chest height while Mister Satan guided his side forward. We'd pause after setting it on the carpet, make sure no bare metal edges were digging into the roof, then slide it forward into position and tie it down with looped clothesline.

Mister Satan could be an impatient man. I could be fiercely protective of my car, battered as it was. This particular afternoon we had a little problem. It came as we paused after the initial heave, with one of the cart's welded steel ankles resting heavily on maroon roof-paint. I was struggling to slide a strip of carpet between the two. Mister Satan, with no warning, began to drag the cart into position.

"Wait!" I screeched, watching bare steel cut an inch-long gash in my car's finish. "Stop!"

He stopped.

"God dammit!" I moaned. "Look at that! You scratched the roof!"

"I didn't scratch a damn thing," he grumbled.

"That's a *lie!* I was watching as it happened. Look at it, right there." I pointed at it as he came around the car. "See that scratch? I asked you to wait. Fuck, man."

"Mister Adam," he warned.

"Didn't do it," I fumed quietly. "That's a goddamned lie."

His face was flat. He said little as I drove us home up the West Side Highway. He said little as we unloaded back at his apartment, lifting the shopping cart briskly but carefully down off my car's roof. He said nothing after I said goodbye.

A weird fluttering agitated feeling pervaded my apartment that night. Silent was something he'd never been in the three years I'd known him. The next morning I dawdled at my desk, feet restless. I'd been too harsh—sweated what was, after all, very small shit. I needed to apologize. Drive down to Harlem and apologize.

I got in my car and drove around, wasting time, circling through the Upper West Side. It was a breezy overcast October Saturday. Cooler than the day we'd first played, way back when. I was getting this very weird feeling, a direct atmospheric transfer. I drove across 110th Street, cut left up Adam Clayton Powell Jr. Boulevard. The feeling got weirder. I scanned the streets as I cruised slowly uptown, caught sight of his bright red ski cap and gray beard a couple of blocks up. I could hardly breathe. He was hanging out with the guys near his throne. Mister Larry, Mister Danny, Mister Marvin.

I rolled up to the curb, tooted the horn, waved. He caught sight of me, scowled, put his hand up—as if to ward me off—and turned away.

I shut off the car and jumped out. "Mister Satan!" I called out.

"You ain't playing with me no more, Mister Adam!" he cried roughly, turning and glaring. "I dismiss myself from your sight!"

I floated toward him as though sleepwalking, my bones and belly gone hollow. Tears sprang into my eyes.

Mister Marvin backpedaled toward me. "Be cool," he murmured, backhanding his mouth under his trucker's cap.

"I'm sorry, Mister Satan," I said. "I made a mistake yesterday and I'm sorry."

"*Damn* sorry!" he roared, face contorted. "I ain't never stood for

318

no disrespect up here in Harlem and I damn sure ain't gonna start downtown!"

Mister Larry pushed his tinted glasses up on his nose. "You got the master very upset."

"Mister Adam ain't done nothing wrong," Mister Danny insisted, his mouth a jumble of slurring teeth. He touched his chest. "If it ain't wrong in his heart, he ain't meant it."

My eyes were wet. We were five men clumped on a stretch of dirty sidewalk, shivering. Mister Satan wasn't looking at me. This was horrible.

"Look at me, Mister Satan," I pleaded, desperate. "These are tears in my eyes."

"See?" Mister Danny said triumphantly. "He ain't meant it about you lying, Mister Satan. He ain't meant it. Y'all been doing this too long to mess a good thing up."

Mister Marvin stroked his goatee. "Seems like everybody got a right to make one mistake."

"That's the truth," agreed Mister Danny.

"I made about four or five and the master ain't kicked my butt out of Harlem yet." He winked at me.

"Okay, Mister Adam," Mister Satan barked sternly. "Listen to me real well. I said we ain't playing together no more, and that still goes. *But:* I got my people's wishes to consider, too. Mister Larry," he commanded.

"Yes, master." He was standing with his arms folded across his chest, feet squarely planted.

"I'm going to displace the matter into your consideration, sir. You been knowing Mister Adam going on however many years he's been working out here with me."

"That's right."

"Okay. I'm deadly serious about this now. I submit myself and Mister Adam to your judgment. If you say it ain't working out and we oughta end the mess right here and now, we gonna do that. If you say the young man has put forth adequate compensation and apologies for whatever disrespectfulness gone down in Times Square, I gotta live with that and we will play again. You got that?"

"Yes, master."

"Good. I'm walking over there by my throne and smoke me a cigarette while you work it out." He turned and strolled away.

The four of us stood in a circle where we were. Mister Larry was wearing sunglasses; I couldn't see his eyes. Breezes blew and I shivered.

Mister Marvin resettled his trucker's cap. "He likes you, Mister Adam."

"Hell, I like him," I said, my voice catching.

"He's always bragging about you when you ain't around. I mean brag-*ing.*"

"Mister Adam," Mister Larry said firmly, with a sigh, "the master is a wise man."

"He's wise," Mister Danny agreed, winking at me. He and Mister Larry were brothers.

"And he definitely has your best interests at heart."

I wiped the tears out of my eyes. "I know he does."

"We gotta come to some kind of decision about important things, 'cause his cigarette is gonna burn *down,* you see what I'm saying?" He held out his hand for my grip. We shook. He didn't smile.

"It's a damn shame," Mister Danny slurred, finger poking my shoulder. "Y'all should be playing together like you *been* doing. He don't mean it about *any* of it, the whole goddamned thing."

Mister Larry scowled. "You out of order, my brother."

He pulled back, taking exaggerated offense. "I got a heart too! I got a heart too! How you gonna tell me I gotta—okay okay okay." He put his hands up, warding off his brother's imaginary blows.

"Now," Mister Larry continued. "I gotta know one thing, Mister Adam. Because I know you're sorry . . ."

"I am, man, I really—"

He held up his hand. "I know about that. So my question is: *if* my judgment ends up in a favorable direction to continuing the whole musical thing, do you think you and the master got a chance at pulling it back together? I'm talking about *you* and *him,* now. Forget about everything else. Is that gonna happen? 'Cause I gotta know"—suddenly a smile tugged at his mouth—"I gotta know whether a favorable judgment is gonna lead to a continuation of my drinking music or not. You see what I'm saying? Otherwise we're talking about a corruption of justice, and you *know* the master don't want that. I'm talking about some serious goddamn drinking music. We gonna come through on that?"

We were holding hands again. "Mister Larry," I said, "I got a bottle of Guinness waiting for you every time I see you for the next year."

Mister Marvin curled his arm around my back, proudly. "Like I said, be cool."

"Master," Mister Larry called out, "I think we ready to go with a judgment."

Mister Satan blew out a cloud of smoke. "Thank you, sir," he said, tossing his butt and walking toward us. He glanced at me as he came up—quickly, with no evident feeling one way or another.

Mister Larry cleared his throat, rose to a properly ceremonial height, took a deep breath. "We've been talking over the problem."

"Top to bottom," Mister Danny agreed.

"And I believe we finally got down into something like an understanding."

Mister Satan's head was slightly bowed. "Mister Adam and I submit to your judgment, sir."

"Okay. Now, we got us a problem, obviously, being that Mister Adam is a young man and got carried away with some downtown disrespectfulness. And spoke out of his head. No doubt about that. But that can happen. Especially with a young man who's gonna blow the blues from his heart and tell you how he feels with whatever's coming out of his horn, it makes sense he's gonna get *too* loud at some point, with his mouth, and say the wrong thing. That's part of doing what he's *supposed* to be doing, only he *over*did it. You see what I'm saying?"

"I'm listening, sir. Continue."

"So that's understandable. And it gotta be said that he *knew* he did wrong. That's how come he's standing right here, today, and not off with his friends somewhere drinking champagne or whatever. He ain't like that, Mister Adam ain't. He knows he did wrong, and he's trying to rectify the situation. And not waste any time letting the wrong *stay* wrong. So as far as my interpretation, I would have to say that he did the right thing—driving up here, to your throne, and getting down to business."

Mister Satan smiled. "Preach on, Mister Larry."

Mister Danny elbowed me. "You okay, man. You back in."

"The whole point being"—he paused, flexed his muscles, took the four of us in—"the whole point being that y'all got way too much *good* going on to let the *bad* step all over your thing. Y'all should be playing with each other, making a dollar here and there, whatever, and not . . . not . . . I mean look: Y'all *belong* together. Ain't no mystery!"

"I'm serious," Mister Marvin agreed.

"So my question to you, Master, is: Are we all gonna put the bad behind us and get on with the good? Make us a little more music and whatever else?"

Mister Satan shrugged, bemused. "Ain't my choice, really. I *got* to submit."

"Are y'all gonna shake hands on it?"

We both stuck out our hands. They met as our eyes met, with some tentativeness. Mister Larry cupped them warmly, like a softball.

"I'm sorry," I said.

Mister Satan made a face. "Ain't no big issue."

"There we go," said Mister Larry.

"This is what I been trying to say!" Mister Danny huffed, brow furrowed. "Y'all ain't had *nothing* going on wrong!"

Mister Satan elbowed me, chuckling, and shook out a Kool. "Shut up and smoke, young man."

*1984.* WE WERE IN THE MIDDLE of a paradigm shift, clearly: either about to break through into deeper love than we had yet known—with marriage and kids to follow—or the other unthinkable option. Helen was perched on the mountaintop, wavering. I was down on the killing floor. Albert King's song had never really made sense to me back in college. Now it made me shudder. I'd been listening to my old blues records lately, while Helen was up on campus teaching or having coffee with Jack. She'd been trying to forget about him, she claimed, ever since the departmental Christmas party, when they'd exchanged a few drunken kisses. This was proving to be difficult. Jack was smart, articulate, soft-spoken, intense, a tall dark-haired Shakespearean who'd entered the program the same time she had. Platonic coffee dates were Helen's way of figuring out how she felt. What harm was a little friendly conversation, staring hungrily at his dazzling smile? She wouldn't go further than that, she insisted, as long as we were still together.

"I should have quit you," Albert would sing, "a long time agooooo. . . ." He'd whip off an icy guitar-fill, jagged as cut glass; my eyes would blur with gratitude. As long as I could feel, I wasn't dead. As long as I was alive, there was hope.

I knew I should kick her out or move out myself. Five long years. What if we were just about to turn this thing around? The world was a sickening uncertainty that hovered over me, leering.

I was scared. There'd been one very bad night in early March. Helen had gone out alone to a party; I'd stayed at home, relaxing in bed with Malcolm Cowley's *Exile's Return*. All my writing these days was about nuclear war—the role of Walter Benjamin's storyteller in the nuclear age, nuclear numbing in *One Flew Over the Cuckoo's Nest*—and I needed a break.

Cowley's words blurred, suddenly, as the truth hit me. Who was I kidding? This was how relationships ended. My girlfriend was leaving me for a guy I knew. He and I had been sharing a seminar table once a week in Postcolonial Lit. He wasn't a bad guy. Self-contained, slightly arrogant, but not the sadistic type. He probably had no idea how much pain he was causing me. I had some idea of the pleasure Helen was giving him. It was nice to have the full force of her hunger and tenderness turned on you. I'd had that for a while. It was his turn now. I'd blown it, hadn't I? This was how love ended. Any fool could see that.

323

I put down my book, rolled toward the wall. Suddenly the whole thing imploded. I couldn't cry. This was past that. This was my life shattering in slow motion, melting, flowing into the solar plexus, gripping my throat, strangling.

I tried to think of a book I could pull off the shelf that would help me. Books were my reason for being. I couldn't think of one. I couldn't do anything. I lay there, holding myself. It was over. The whole house of cards came crashing down.

A FEW WEEKS AFTER MY RECONCILIATION with Mister Satan, in November, David Dinkins was elected New York's first black mayor. We played 125th Street the morning after; there was a palpable feeling of jubilee. Blacks had come together, whites had pitched in. Mayor Koch had been booted; a new beginning was at hand. Mission accomplished. The long hot summer of 1989 was finally over.

Relieved but exhausted, I was suddenly starting to feel like I'd had enough. Where was the joy I'd brought to Harlem on that long-ago first day? The streets of New York were too damn *raw*, uptown and down. I needed a job. An indoor job, with a paycheck and a future.

My harp students tried to help out. Telephone sales? Catering? Johnny Mills suggested the Post Office, where he had a couple of years left until retirement. The pay wasn't bad, and you couldn't beat the job security.

Johnny was somebody the Malcolm X guy might have wondered at. He was one of three black men—along with an aspiring actor and a Harlem father—who paid me for blues harmonica lessons. Tall, trim, graying, he had more than enough enthusiasm but a tough time learning new licks. Tongued rhythms were particularly hard; he couldn't keep a steady beat with his foot. I'd get impatient and have to rein myself in. All I wanted from each of my students was a reasonable facsimile of the sound I'd just made—a sound that was a transformed facsimile of the sound Nat had once made for me. I was an equal-opportunity encourager. Johnny presented me with a paradox. What could I possibly teach this man about the blues? I'd learned how to produce a sound; he'd lived the life. Wasn't the life of a black man who'd come of age during the pre–civil rights era necessarily a study in blues feeling—sadnesses and violences, humiliations and euphorias I could hardly imagine? Yet the wah-wahs and moans that actually escaped from his cupped hands were no deeper or more subtly inflected than mine had been before Nat. His was the white boy's sound; mine was the older black guy's sound. He was visiting my apartment to reclaim himself, in a sense, to carry home a gift I'd borrowed, husbanded, added traces of my own song to. I was here to give Nat's gift back. This was the purpose of our blues lessons. The twenty bucks he paid me when our hour together was up was his way of saying thanks for taking care of my music while I was away.

That was how my first line of reasoning went. My second line of reasoning went: Why should I assume that Johnny Mills had *any* intrinsic claim on the blues? He was a clean-cut New Yorker, an Upper West Sider, an ex-military officer. I knew little more about him than that; we'd respected each other's privacy. To connect him "naturally" with the blues made about as much sense as connecting me "naturally" with Aerosmith or Pink Floyd. If anything, his interest in blues harmonica was a curiosity. What would Johnny—who'd moved on up, become more respectable in certain ways than me—possibly have to gain by digging back down into the devil's music? Suppose he played in public some Sunday afternoon, noodling by himself on a park bench. I often did that; white boys have less at stake. Wasn't he risking the possibility that he'd be seen, by whites and blacks alike, as somebody who'd *never* moved up, who'd stayed down in the alley? Unless he was more of a race rebel than I'd realized. Maybe he didn't care *what* people thought. Maybe the sound of the instrument had simply grabbed him, as it had me. Or maybe an older relative had played when he was a boy and he was trying to get back to his roots. Maybe the sound I made reminded him—as it had reminded Dee Dee—of his own grandfather.

Or maybe both lines of reasoning were pure fantasy. Maybe, as a street musician, I'd lived more of the blues life than Johnny had. Maybe he looked at me—a manic younger white guy—and saw an image of something worth bringing into his own life: some aliveness,

some freedom, some ability to feel what you're feeling *and get it out.*
Maybe what he hungered for was what Nat and Mister Satan had
pulled out of me. What Bob Shatkin—a brainy Brooklyn Jew—had
pulled out of Nat, when Nat was starting out. What an old black
guy out on Ocean Parkway had pulled out of Shatkin when *he* was
starting out, according to Nat. An endless chain we'd forged. Masters and apprentices, a labor of love. Pass it along.

So where had our gifts gotten us? One more white boy come to
rip off the black man's music. Yusuf Hawkins dead. Bensonhurst the
new Mississippi. Fight the pow-ah. Fuck the police. Fuck the niggers. Niggaz with Attitude. Fuck you white motherfucker.

THE DECADE WAS ENDING; I felt trapped, stymied, burned, brit-
tle, restless. New York had finally gotten to me. Boston was beckoning, a friend with a spare room. Mister Satan could take care of
himself. I had to get out.

CHAPTER EIGHTEEN

# ANGEL SOUND

*I don't care what people are thinking*
*I ain't drunk, I'm just drinking.*

—Albert Collins, "I Ain't Drunk"

MISTER ADAM'S First Annual Countdown to Apocalypse ended not with a bang but with a long-distance call to Mister Satan—a fit of inspiration—on New Year's Day 1990. Miss Macie came on; I heard a toilet flush in the background.

"It's Gussow," she called out.

"Miss Macie," I said, "how do you think Mister Satan would feel about going into the recording studio again, if I paid?"

She snorted. "Bobby Robinson ain't done a damn thing in months."

"Well, you can hardly blame him after what those two recording guys did, losing Mister Satan's voice and—"

"Satan's ready," she declared. "We *all* ready."

"Ready for what?" I heard Mister Satan rumble. He coughed. The phone changed hands.

"Happy New Year," I said.

"Hey, Mister Gus," he murmured, lower key than usual.

His number mess had fallen through, again. One-nine-eight-nine should have been the last one. Wasn't nothing he *could* do except live through it. We small-talked. I floated my modest proposal. For more than three years we'd been playing our hearts out on the street; except for a few boom box bootlegs I'd made, every note had vanished into thin air. Someday, with luck, I was going to be a grandfather. I wanted my grandchildren to know what their grandpa had done when he was a young man. What *we* had done. If I paid for the studio time, would Mister Satan help me lay down a few of our best tracks? At the very least we'd have a demo I could use to get us some gigs.

"Ain't nothing happening up in Harlem, in a club way," he said. "The bastards all gone into a graveyard situation."

"I know a few places downtown. Dan Lynch, Nightingale. We could sell cassettes on the street."

He laughed. "Hell, we might as well. Give the little Gussow grandbabies something to worry about."

HE DIDN'T EVEN KNOW I'D BEEN AWAY. It was strictly a test-flight. I'd lasted a week up in the frozen northland—camping out on my buddy Ed Slattery's sofa, Guinnessing at the Plow & Star, running around to jam sessions at Harper's Ferry and the Cantab Lounge. Work was available, if I wanted to stay. A harp blower named Vinnie—Boston Baked Blues, a jump quintet—said he'd introduce me to Magic Dick, who was alive and well. Pierre Beauregard, founder of the Cambridge Harmonica Orchestra, was looking for fresh talent. Watermelon Slim, "Earring" George Mayweather, the Radio Kings: Boston blues players had an Austin groove—big Texas kick-drum, Stevie Ray circle-strums—and a Chicago gangland style, draped slacks and hair gelled back. Nothing gutter-funky or dirt-smeared. That was our New York difference. I missed it already. Boston was vintage Fender amps, tweedy, pedigreed; New York was my buddy Mason Casey, the granite-jawed upstate stonemason, who'd muscled through the swinging front doors of Dan Lynch one Sunday afternoon during the jam session, lugging a reissue Fender Bassman that barked, woofed, and cawed like a rabid dog with a shrieking raven stuck in its throat.

"Check it out," he'd grunted, flipping it around and tilting. Each of the four speaker cones had been slashed in twenty different places. "I took a fuckin' steak knife and went at 'em."

My city in a nutshell. I couldn't stay away. My road novel wasn't going anywhere; maybe the immortality I secretly hungered for could be achieved on magnetic tape. Recording sessions were a kind of indoor job, weren't they? I had a crazy idea and a producer's phone number. I packed my bags and drove home into icy sunny January, heart singing.

HER NAME WAS RACHEL FARO, pronounced "Pharoah." She was a striking Jewish redhead—all cheekbones and jawline, the slightest gap between perfect large front teeth. I found out later she'd had a big career of her own back in the late sixties, a singer-songwriter in the Laura Nyro mold. She'd handed me her card one afternoon back in the fall when Mister Satan and I were working Times Square and told me to call her when we were ready.

Rachel was, in retrospect, the only one who could have made it happen. She believed in astrology as fervently as Mister Satan believed in Earth's supreme governance. She was a practicing Tibetan Buddhist; she chanted and lit candles. Her life was scattered between a small apartment in the Village and Cologne, where she produced salsa records for a German label, lived on an expense account, and was taken seriously by men. In New York, men—record industry people—didn't quite take her seriously. She complained often to me, once we got to know each other. I took her very seriously. We were both Aries. This was the sort of detail I learned to notice much later, after the endless phone calls and shouting matches. Rachel loved our sound passionately and knew what should be done with it. She blew her hair out of her eyes at random moments. She was the smart, pretty, goofy big sister I'd never had. Her natural voice was a rich smooth purr, phone sex the way it ought to be.

She knew tape. She booked studio time and gave me a shopping list. This was my first exposure to midtown New York as capital of the recording industry. Angel Sound, a block down from the Brill

Building and three blocks south of *Cats,* was filled with duplicating decks and stacked cassette jewel cases—tomorrow's No. 1 hit on Hot 97, fifty copies at a time off the studio master, for whoever at Arista or Columbia needed to preview Whitney's rough mix. The smell of acetate and other chemicals wafted through, pricking my nose. I handed over Rachel's list; the tape tech stacked flat foot-square boxes of Ampex Grand Master 456, each reel as heavy as a ream of Hammermill bond. Time was gathering to a head, suddenly.

RACHEL, CONSULTING STAR MAPS, had scheduled the recording session for February 8th. Our fourth January outdoors blessed Mister Satan and me with one more rebirth, a falling away of husks that left the fire-born core intact. We'd driven down to Times Square one cold gray afternoon, set up, been shut down by the cops after fifteen minutes. This was new. A Dinkins administration policy shift? We unplugged, repacked, hauled, reloaded, drove uptown, and rolled to a stop in front of the Broadway Presbyterian Church. We were already in the hole five bucks each after the Forty-fourth Street parking lot; Mister Satan reached into his pocket and pulled out the one crumpled dollar we'd made.

"Mister Adam," he said. "Please go and buy us a taste of Georgi vodka or whatever they got. I *swear* I'm gonna kill off this dragged-out mood."

I ran off, intrigued. We hadn't shared a taste since the last time with Professor three years earlier, when he'd sliced an apple in half to show me a five-pointed star. Except for my occasional wine cooler and that one toast of New Year's moonshine after *Big River,* alcohol had played little part in what we were about. Lately he'd eased back into drinking: small bottles of Listerine, which seemed to leave him with no side effects except aggressively fresh breath.

I tossed in a couple of bucks and brought back a half-pint of Stolichnaya. We broke the seal and passed it—sitting in my car, eyeing the fading winter afternoon. He couldn't get over how smooth it was. Too smooth, really.

"Cheap vodka is *better,*" he insisted gaily. "More of the fire aspect is gonna come through, quite naturally. If you ain't got but one dollar for a taste, it better do the job or my poor people ain't gonna buy it. The Georgi folks know that."

"I always liked Stoly, myself. I had a girlfriend once, after Helen moved out. Maaaan, Debbie and I used to get so—"

"*Take* yourself a drink, Mister Gussow," he said, bumping my hand with the half-empty bottle. "And shut up."

"Shut up," I echoed in Professor Sixmillion's breathy cartoon voice.

"Shut up," he chuckled, echoing my echo.

Fire spread pleasantly through my belly. I sighed. "I miss Professor."

"Ah, that old bastard's still around."

"You ready to kick and stomp?"

"Just as sure as you are handsome."

We fell out of the car and threw our shit into place, plugged in and kicked, church at our backs. The sidewalk scene dissolved; I was wandering in a garden of earthly delights, hands cupped against the sweet cold fluid air. Every bent note was a pitch-perfect arrow puncturing the gray dusk. You only live now. Blue notes danced and spun, lines endlessly unfolding like so many wrapped gifts laid bare. Mister Satan, seated behind flurrying twin hi-hats, was a voice in my head crying See! See see rider! Aw See! What you have done. . . .

We veered crazily, in tandem—thrown, falling, catching a foot in the stirrup as our horse galloped. Holding on, inches from the blurred dirt. Smelling the dirt. Flying along under everybody's radar. All the way outside.

Miss Macie fed us later, back at the apartment: pork chops, greens flecked with salty bits of ham hock, mustardy potato salad with hardboiled egg, warm buttered cornbread. She was happy for the small sack of change and bills Mister Satan thunked down on the kitchen table. She could have the silver. We finally had us.

*1984.* THE SUNDAY HELEN MOVED OUT—a polleny May afternoon—I ran a half-marathon up in Yonkers and drank a six-pack of

Dos Equis Dark with my cheese sandwich when I got home. What used to be home. That got me through the first night.

At eight-thirty the next morning I called her friend Cynthia's apartment, where she was theoretically staying until her new lease came through. Nobody answered. I had to give her credit. She'd promised she wouldn't do the Freedom Jazz Dance with Jack until our breakup was official. They were probably having a sweet time now, back at his place. The Happy Couple. I wasn't sure what I was, except alone and twenty-six. Everything else was up for grabs.

Our apartment without her books and clothes looked violated, raped. I sat on our bed—my bed, the one I'd just made—and stared at the phone.

I called nine more times before lunch. When I wasn't counting unanswered rings, I was hovering next to my turntable jamming along with an old double LP called *The Great Bluesmen*. Well I'm moanin' and groanin', my baybeee's gone and left meee, I ain't even got train fare out of town. My yelps and wails fit right in.

By the middle of Monday afternoon our empty apartment— mine now—was threatening to become a chamber of horrors. I'd read Poe; I knew what happened to unleashed minds. Telltale hearts, huge velvety tongues inching downward toward helpless victims.

Monday evening I fled, a handful of harps in my shouldered daypack. I'd made a date with my new blues buddy Bram down in the Village. Bram was a Columbia senior who also blew some harp, wore rimless spectacles, had bushy black hair, and was annoyingly, refreshingly sure of himself. We met outside a folk club called Speakeasy, on MacDougal Street. Monday night was jam night. We sat on a brownstone stoop across from the club after we'd signed up and warmed into a two-harmonica boogie. A skinny junkie in black leather pants paused to watch. Bram waved over a young guy with a dulcimer and a wispy Zen goatee. The boogie became an Irish jig. Bram's friend Marty fed us from a bag of freshly baked whole wheat rolls he'd picked up. Sunset had dissolved into nightfall, soft and fragrant, apple blossoms mixing with incense from a head shop up the block. Anything, suddenly, seemed wildly possible.

"Let's play the arch," Bram said, pointing at the half-size Arc de Triomphe on the north side of Washington Square Park.

He put out a waxed Coke cup he'd found in the trash. We wailed for a couple of hours, notes echoing off the curved, engraved marble and spiraling out toward various groups of strolling girls we hoped might notice us. Several did, none lingering. We'd made sixty cents apiece. It was almost nine o'clock.

"Give me your watch," Bram snapped.

I put it in my daypack. A plan coalesced. We were going to find a bar and get smashed and find women who would do us.

I'd never heard of McSorley's Ale House, established in 1853. He pulled me through crowds of drunken frat boys into the back room, past cobwebbed light fixtures and walls hung with faded photos of Babe Ruth and Jack Kennedy. We drank eight small glasses of dark beer each—they came in pairs—and washed down ham sandwiches. The mustard made my sinuses bleed.

"I should have warned you about the mustard," Bram said.

We were wandering through the Village. Buildings swayed and careened; the sweet May air was streaming with poems. The only thing missing was nubile young women.

"I hope he breaks her fucking heart," I said gleefully. "She'll have to fucking *beg* me to take her back."

He snorted. "Never complain, never explain."

"Whoo!" I hooted, stubbing my toe and glorying in the smeared circus night.

We were sitting on the stoop of a St. Mark's Place brownstone, hearts naked, harps cupped, dancing madly around each other's best stuff. My raw scraped lips had earned their pain. Oh bay-bee . . . you don't have to go. . . .

"Take your time," the black guy who'd paused to kibbitz called out, black wingtip cocked against the bottom step. "Work with it."

Flattered, I slowed and dug down. Bram eased off, grooving.

The guy's tux shirt was unbuttoned to the breastbone. His tails had seen better days. His singing voice lifted gently, effortlessly into position, a brandied incantation spun out of nothing:

Wellll . . .

We're sitting here this evening

Two white guys and a black

We're grooving on St. Mark's Place bay-bee and you

Know it is a snap

His name was J. T. "I do Nat King Cole," he said. "That's what I do."

A guy in a muscle shirt with tatoos and a girlfriend on his arm tossed a dollar at our feet during "Route 66." We stared at it. The groove tautened. Bram reached out and handed J. T. the bill. J. T. waved him away.

"Wrong."

"It's yours, man."

"How you gonna pay me and not pay you?" He got right up in our faces. "You on the gig too, ain't you? *Never* sell yourself short."

When we'd made three I ran off and bought beers. I clinked J.T.'s through our matching paper bags, tilted my head back. What a fucking night! I was a bluesman.

"Later on, gentlemen," J. T. chuckled richly as he slid away, heading toward Second Avenue. "Don't do anything I wouldn't do."

"You got it," I called out.

Bram didn't say a word.

THREE WEEKS AFTER Miss Macie's greens-and-cornbread dinner, just before Valentine's Day, Mister Satan and I wheeled his clanking shopping cart through the doorway of Giant Sound, 1776 Broadway at Columbus Circle. A sunny temperate morning, silky with spring hopes. I veered into a liquor store and bought two pint bottles of Stoly. "Glasnost" was Mister Satan's term, a nod to Gorbachev. We'd glasnosted a few times recently on frigid breezy busking days, burning through our set opener until fingers and lips thawed.

I was quivering like a racehorse as we spread our amps out across the hardwood floor upstairs. Behind the control room window, ponytailed engineer Matt—just up from Sun Studios in Memphis—

spent ages recalibrating his thirty-two-track mixing board. Rachel had just breezed in from Cologne and was wearing pink-rimmed cat-eye glasses and bright red lipstick, like a Hollywood starlet from the forties. I handed her the bag of boxed tape as we brushed cheeks.

"I have a *very* good feeling about this day," she said breathily.

She'd never met Mister Satan. I brought her over. He was looping the legs of his hi-chair to the wooden sounding-board with a piece of clothesline.

"Mister Satan," she said, "I've heard so much about you. I *love* your cap," she added. It was a reddish knit with small earflaps, hung with various trinkets and costume jewels.

His smile morphed into wide-eyed cartoon outrage. "You out of order on that. This is my *crown.*"

"Your crown." She blew her hair out of her eyes, self-consciously ditzy. "Cool."

"Thank you, ma'am," he beamed.

"Mister Satan, Rachel was wondering about some kind of set list for the session, apart from the couple of songs we already—"

He held up his hand. "Ain't no need. We'll feel them as we go."

A moment later I'd stepped into the control room for a brief consult. She was thrilled.

"His energy is so *amazing,*" she raved. "He's so—I mean it's *aristocratic.* He's a tribal chieftan. We just need to totally relax and go with it."

I slouched back into the studio, cracked open the first bottle of Stoly, and took a slug, muttering. Eighty-proof spirits precipitated sudden and remarkable levels of concentration combined with hints of superhuman euphorias to come. Gods would be striding the planet shortly.

"You want a taste of glasnost?" I asked, holding it out.

"Yes!" he roared.

Matt was dancing around us, placing microphones over the hi-hats and in front of each Mouse. A stereo room-mike hovered somewhere behind my head, ready to capture the "ambience" already crackling off the foam baffles hedging us in.

We brought everything up to speed for a test take, like copilots tweaking their jet engines in that last trembling moment before takeoff.

"Rolling!" Matt called out through our headphones.

Mister Satan's eyes met mine; we kicked into "I Want You," same as we'd been doing in the freezing winds uptown. We seemed to float above the polished hardwood floor, suspended in crashing spew: a fusion flux in the reactor's belly. I couldn't make out his words through his overdriven Mouses but was carried along anyway by the sound of his voice, surging heart-melodies compelling my yelped responses. We finished up slam-bam, the usual killer flurry.

Rachel called us into the control room for a playback. I grabbed the Stoly bottle and we flopped into chairs.

"That was *wonderful,*" she gushed. "I'm really thinking record, if we keep this up."

Matt punched buttons; the Frisbee-reels blurred, served to a stop, then smoothly traded tape.

"I get everything I want!" cried Mister Satan out of the studio monitors, his voice a river of aching pent-up glee. "Guess what? I want *you!*"

I sat dumbly, in a trance. Mister Satan bent forward slightly, intently, eyes closed. All had been revealed. His words, our sound. *What we were about.* The mix needed tinkering, but still: some ferocious two-hearted creature had just blown through the studio doors and was glaring down at us, panting. All we had to do was set the bastard free.

Matt made the necessary adjustments as we ran back inside.

"Glasnost!" I yelled, handing my deathless master the bottle.

"Thank you, sir." He upended it, danced a little jig, then ripped it away. "Whoooo!"

I grabbed it back. The liquid fire slid all the way down, hit bottom, flared up and out. We stared in each other's eyes for a split-second with amazed holy love and shared nastiness of purpose.

"You ready to be famous?" I said.

"I already am!" he roared gleefully, falling into his hi-chair. "Hell, they *got* me in every damn Bible around the world!"

We hurled ourselves at each other and did it again. The rest of the afternoon was a streaming blur. We caught the wave and rode it, naked to the endlessly unspooling blank tape. Later, after I'd gotten back from the ATM downstairs and paid Rachel, Matt, and the studio off with fistfuls of hemorrhaged cash, we plunged into the maelstrom of "C. C. Rider." We were working for free, this time. Glasnost—"openness"—had prevailed; furies flapped shrieking from our blown hearts and spontaneously combusted in midair.

Rachel, wise lady, left us alone.

MISTER SATAN'S WORK WAS THROUGH. Rachel's and mine had begun.

We drank coffee and sat with Matthew in a small editing room at Giant Sound, three or four sessions over the next couple of weeks. The streets—and vodka—had encouraged Mister Satan and me to play long, spurring endless versionings and codas. Rachel and I were the cleanup crew. Analog editing meant razor blades and splicing tape. We diagrammed each cut, parsing verses, choruses, harmonica solos. Almost every song needed a trim; several needed severe prunings. This suited my poetic temperament just fine. Drunken inspiration was then, rigorous selection was now.

Rachel's method was intuitive, instinctive; her one-woman production company was called Shambhala Music. I favored streamlined perfection; she favored inspired flow and had an ear for emotional logic, the story being told within and between songs. She changed the way I heard. Accidentally bumped mike stands and popped Ps were okay: traces left by our bodies, signs of soulful life. The occasional vocal flub might turn out to speak our superheated hearts. Ugly-beauty is deeper perfection.

"I Want You" was pared from eight minutes to six. "I Create the Music" needed weeding and fading.

"Freedom for My People" was our chance to get right what U2 had teased the world with a snippet of. Mister Satan, in his messiah's trance, had preached for ten minutes; here the story Rachel heard required excision of needless repetition. Matthew gamely sliced and diced the master, taping each deleted section to the side of the editing deck like a dangling brown noodle. None of our edits worked; we came out of our own trance to find the song hopelessly spaghettied into unmarked parts. Matthew, perspiring, slowly hand-rocked the deck's reels.

"Gwrrrraachinggggollllaawwwwwrrraaach," drooled Mister Satan's catatonic basso out of the monitors.

"We're fucked," I groaned. "He'll kill me." I stared at Matthew. "He'll kill *you*."

"This guy a friend of yours?" he grunted at Rachel, meaning me.

Rachel blew her bangs out of her eyes. "I think we all just really need to re-*lax*."

Somehow we managed to reconstruct the freedom struggle as Mister Satan had envisioned it, at seventy-five of my dollars an hour.

"Sweet Home Chicago," the only song I'd sung, featured Mister Satan on background vocals—his chocolate rasp behind my vanilla tenor. Shadowing me, supporting me, gently mocking my fevered earnestness. All this time he'd been doing that, out on the streets?

We ended up with a six-song demo, edited and sequenced. All we needed now was a group name. We'd never had one, amazingly. Never needed one, since we'd never worked a club, solicited a record deal, been advertised or publicized or sold. We'd always just been the two people we were, our Harlem street-names: Mister Satan and Mister Adam.

Satan and Adam.

I HAD THE SENSE THINGS were about to break for us in a big way. I wanted some final blessing from Nat. One Sunday at the end of March I threw my Fender SuperReverb in the car and blew down to Richmond, a six-hour shot. I didn't tell him I was coming. This was the point. I knew he was running a Sunday jam at a place called the Stonewall Cafe. He'd told me this last time we talked. His life had come back together, miraculously. He was married again, to a dancer and radio DJ named Chandra. He was working steadily with a band called the Fan Blades. I wanted to surprise him, flip him off his feet.

I got to town at seven Sunday evening. Just around the corner from Robert E. Lee's bearded statue on Monument Avenue, the Stonewall Cafe was jumping like a Civil War blockhouse in frathouse mode—good ol' boys and girls dangling longnecks, mugging along with James Brown's "I Feel Good," leaning out of floodlit third-floor windows, talking trash. This was either as far as you could get from the streets of Harlem or eerily close. I eased my way in past the Bud banners and spring break tans. The jam was about to start. Nat, back to me, was bent over his amp at the end of the half-filled room, Astatic mike in hand, fiddling. Framed by his guitar player on one side, his piano player on the other. They were young and white, had mustaches, were gazing at him with a love I knew, masquerading as respectful patience. Nat's boys! The chosen few.

I stood grinning in the doorway. Nat stood up, unkinked his spine, lifted his head, glanced at me, turned back toward his amp. Froze. Lifted his head a second time, ghost-struck.

I nodded. Uh huh.

He whooped. He ran toward me, squeezing through tables as his band stared.

"It's you!" he yelled. "I don't believe this!"

We bearhugged. He smelled like spiced limes and looked healthy and strong—a Timex clinging to his wrist, dark slacks that fit, a lizardskin belt, the "B. B. King's 50th Album" t-shirt I'd given him. His eyes blazed; his smile seemed to pour out of deeps where great pain also lived.

"I figured I oughta check up," I said, grinning helplessly. "See what you're putting down," I added, echoing the Junior Wells song we both knew.

"Oh man." He cackled. "Oh man. This is just too—"

"Hey Nat!" a young guy with a shouldered padded guitar case called out from up by the stage.

"Yo."

"You got a jammer's list goin' on, buddy?"

"Talk to Kevin," he called out, nodding at his own guitar player. I let go of his hand. "You gotta get to work."

"Always."

He beamed, taking me in—basking in my unexpected, undeniable presence. Suddenly I wanted to kick the shit out of him, musically. I'd driven three hundred and thirty miles on a whim. I had stuff in me as fierce as *anything* he'd ever blown. I was a man now, not one of his boys. His equal. He needed to see that.

"My amp's in my car," I said. "If there's space left on the list."

"Oh, you're *gonna* play." He laughed. "These guys think I'm talking trash behind my bullshit when I brag about the quality of harmonica players coming out of New York as compared with down here."

He put me up first, had me blow my wad on "Sweet Home Chicago" while he sat in a front-row chair and whooped me on, sunning himself in a glory he'd helped create. Good as the band was, their groove wasn't Mister Satan's; without his metallic butt-kicks chasing me, I wasn't quite myself. This audience responded as though they couldn't hear the difference; Nat made me blow another. Then I sat down and he got up and sang a slow blues. Didn't touch a harp. His vocal technique was skimpy—I could hear that now, in a way I hadn't before—but he knew how to tell a story: how to pause, close his eyes, summon the next phrase, create each line as an inevitability:

When I need my baby . . . she can't be found

I get up early in the morning . . . and she's Tin Pan Alley bound

Whoaaaa . . . what kind of place can this alley be?

Every woman I get, boys, you know this alley takes away from me . . . takes
away from me

I slouched back as he sang—sipping beer, brooding, exhilarated. I felt foolish, suddenly, for thinking I could blow him off the stage, or needed to. Nat was Nat, for better or worse. An identity. He'd reached that point. That had always *been* his point. He'd never tried to hold himself over me. He wasn't interested in producing a clone. He was a teacher. He'd summoned up blues power—he knew I was in love with him and his sound—and done his best to share it, demystify it, help me take it on. He'd blown a brilliant iridescent bubble that first April night, held it quivering in his cupped hands, knowingly enchanted me, then guided me to the source. Equals? We'd always been that in his eyes, I suddenly realized. The Riddles-Is-God thing was my creation. All he'd ever been trying to teach was Be *yourself!*

He got me up on the next tune, Big Walter's "Have a Good Time," and we did the dueling-harps thing. His through the house P.A. wasn't nearly as loud as mine through my Fender. I wanted him to be heard. We traded mikes, at my insistence. He sounded huge through my rig—bobbing and weaving, flutter-tonguing and thwapping, the Nat I'd worshiped for five long years. He tore the house apart. My shit sounded weak through his beat old Astatic, but so what? My master lived. His glory was ours.

THE SATAN AND ADAM DEMO WAS COMPLETE. A hundred duplicate cassettes had been spun off at Angel Sound. Mister Satan and I replayed our new toy more than once on my car stereo in front of his Harlem throne, a bricked-up stoop on Seventh Avenue where he and his crew gathered. We'd fan the doors wide, pump up the volume, toast our limitless future with clinked plastic cups of Georgi vodka or Midnight Dragon malt liquor. We wanted to fill the world's hungry ears with our huge raw perfect sound. Every band goes through this stage. It had taken three and a half years. The streets would be our springboard.

The winter of 1990 gave way to cool breezy March nights. I prowled the Village, dropping off cassettes and press releases with a dozen skeptical bartenders and club managers. Two guys who sounded like a band? Progressive gutbucket blues? Our track record as a club act was a tough sell; except for Wendell Dozier's juke-joint birthday party back in 1987, we'd never actually played indoors. I preached, pleaded, sold. The gigs came in, miraculously, a sprinkling through June and July: Dan Lynch, Nightingale, the places I used to haunt. A former D.J. from WKCR who remembered us from the Columbia neighborhood called up, wondering if we'd open for blues guitarist Buddy Guy at a free June concert in Central Park.

The summer, our fourth, suddenly hovered before us like a glimmering, careening promise—all pent-up frustrations about to melt, all dreams about to come true.

Our ascent began in late April, on Earth Day: a Mort & Ray street fair in Midtown Manhattan, the first time our demo cassettes were offered for sale to the general public. We sold out the sixty I'd brought during our first set, a seventy-five-minute feeding frenzy. Cash flew into my hands from all sides, cassettes tumbled off; Mister Satan steamrolled along as I juggled helplessly—dropping harps, breaking off in mid-solo to make change, our groove mangled into pure profit. Satan and Adam! I'd taped a schedule of upcoming gigs to a lightpost behind me, a blank sheet marked "Mailing List"; people shouldered through the crush to sign up. Suddenly we were a band with a name, an itinerary, a fan base, all without having yet made our club debut.

That came in early May, at a Tenth Avenue tavern called Chelsea Commons. John Guitierrez, the tavern keeper, had taken my card on Earth Day, invited me down to check the place out. It had the right look—smoke-filled, shadowy, with polished brass rails and a heavy ancient slab-wood bar from Tammany Hall days—and the right smell: whiskied good times mixed with stale fry-grease. Jimmy, John's partner, vetted me in the basement office when it was time to talk terms. Jimmy was the Irish half of the operation: sandy-haired, boyish, with a big soft gut. He wanted a blow-job, so to speak.

"Play for me," he said, closing the door behind him, smiling mildly.

"Right now?"

His breath was beer-soured. "Play for me."

"John didn't say anything about—"

"Paul Butterfield played here one New Year's," he interrupted. "You like Butterfield?"

"He's great."

Jimmy grimaced. "Got here at noon and drank all day. Guy was the fucking best. He died two months later."

I played for Jimmy. He closed his eyes, tapped his foot.

"You're okay," he chuckled, coming out of his trance. "May 3rd—I'll give you a C-note each. Drinks and dinner on us."

We were wildly, extravagantly too loud on opening night, a hurricane wrestled indoors and released. We'd replaced our matching pairs of five-watt Mouses with pairs of fifty-watt Randalls and Fenders, trying to mask with sheer volume the fact that we had no bass or drums. I worried about that, and everything else. I worried that people outside Harlem would laugh at Mister Satan when he asked to be called Mister Satan. I worried that our extended street-jams would bore people. I worried when Mister Satan's thrash-groove devolved into grooveless thrashing after his fourth or fifth vodka. I drank to kill my worries. That was the summer I learned how. Mister Satan was an old pro, it turned out, and helped me along.

"I don't drink to get *high!*" he'd roar, toasting everybody from the bandstand with a shotglass. "I drink to get *drunk!*"

We glasnosted our way straight through the summer, our big summer. Drinking kept us close—blended us, in a sense—except when it made Mister Satan suddenly flare up, barking or roaring at me for imagined transgressions. I had dared, for example, to count out the hundred bucks in tips John had collected for us in a beer pitcher on opening night, then pay Mister Satan at the end of the gig. He'd seemed happy enough with this business procedure at the time. Two days later we were wandering down St. Nicholas Avenue, passing a paper-bagged pint, when he suddenly stopped and glared furiously at me.

"No sir!" he thundered. "I don't like that Chelsea Commons tip mess one bit."

"You *saw* me count the bills out," I protested. "Right on top of the piano."

"I ain't seen a damn thing except *you* paying *me,* and that ain't right! Not at *all.* We ain't worked that way with the tip bucket up here in Harlem, we ain't gonna start downtown."

A minute later, after my chastisement had been smoothed over with another vodka go-round, he was grinning almost sheepishly.

"Hell," he chuckled, "I never even *expect* to get paid on a gig. In the old days, some of the clubs I worked, you couldn't. I'm always amazed when I do."

Up on 125th Street that summer, our beverage of choice was Midnight Dragon, which came in cheerfully decorated forty-ounce bottles featuring an open-mouthed rattlesnake with dripping fangs and the corporate motto, "Get Bit!" Mister Satan would send me or Mister Danny off on a beer run. Three plastic cupfuls of that and a Kool and Mister Satan and I were in our zone; three more and we were holding nothing back, including various stray musical grunts, coughs, chuckles, murmurs, and paranoid delusions that didn't subscribe to any known rhythmic or melodic logic. We were free. We'd pushed past outside-playing into something else, centripetal clattering mind-melt. *I* was free, at least. It was a relief not to have to worry about being executed at gunpoint by the Malcolm X guy. If he came at me now, he'd be shooting the empty white husk of the uptight guy I used to be.

We drank our way through our Dan Lynch debut and managed to fill the place. Nat, who'd recently split up with Chandra—that bitch, he was now calling her—had driven up from Richmond.

"You thought I was gonna miss this?" he laughed incredulously, gesturing at me, the night, the scarred brown walls papered with posters for gigs days and years gone by. "I gotta get my batteries recharged, too."

Later he told me the story of how he'd helped inaugurate the Sunday blues jam back in 1979, when Dan Lynch was a run-down Irish bar with a biker clientele. How Bill Dicey—an older white harp player we both knew—had gotten in his face one afternoon and Nat had called him on it, warned him, then decked the motherfucker with one punch.

"Bill *knew* me, man. He knew where I'd been, he knew what I was about, and he's gonna disrespect me behind all that?"

After years on the spectator side of the bandstand, I was suddenly holding down the gig. I half-expected Robyn to wander in with some new blond boy-toy on her arm; my stomach swirled with sickening epic motions that three or four shots of Johnnie Walker

Black only intensified. I'd seen her once, fleetingly, since we'd broken up; nothing in more than two years. I had no idea if she was even alive. I threw up later, back at my apartment, wrecked and overwhelmed. I was a blues pro now, so help me God.

SATAN AND ADAM HAD burst onto the scene, after a fashion. We knew we'd arrived the day we opened for Buddy Guy in Central Park in front of ten thousand people. Mister Satan had lately descended into a fury of mandala construction; this particular afternoon he was sporting a huge heavy necklace made of shellacked five-pointed stars, fifteen or twenty, braided with strings of costume pearls.

"We are *stars*, Mister," he insisted, pointing at his hung neck. "I got the whole mess spelled out right here."

In the summer of 1990 Buddy Guy was the blues guitar-player's blues guitar-player, a Chicago legend beginning to catch fire with the young white audience Stevie Ray Vaughan had helped create. His whole band—bass, drums, second guitar, keyboard—was young and white. We sat around in the backstage trailer, the seven of us plus Miss Macie, sharing his bottle of Rémy-Martin cognac before our opening set. The keyboard player, a busty blonde in a tight black skirt who could barely play, ran her fingers through his oiled Jheri-curls. Buddy was a beautiful, sexual man: drenched in relaxed confidence, exuding explosive prowess, with a pleading edge in his voice that made his whisper-shrieked singing irresistible. He was exactly the same age as Mister Satan, it turned out. The two bronze kings faced each other as the rest of us stood by like awed courtiers. Mister Satan, a couple of shots down, was his fiery lecturing self; Buddy slouched in his chair, smiling but dubious, willing to be overwhelmed.

"Liquor ain't a damn thing but imprisoned laughter, Mister Buddy," Mister Satan declared, chuckling. "That's it. I got a volcano inside me, I *know* that much. Okay. The Earth put the mess in there, like it put your beautiful liquor right here in my hand, to be *enjoyed*. God's people will tell you No no no, liquor gonna mess up your behind, you ain't never gonna get to heaven if you take a drink. And then you take a drink, you supposed to feel *bad* about it at the same time the liquor you just drunk is upholding a *good* feeling all through you? Hell no! The worst damn thing you can do is condemn what you do! I feel like smoking me a cigarette, I sure as hell ain't gonna talk some cancer mess and scare myself to death. I'm gonna *smoke.*" He reached through his star necklace into his breast pocket. "Smoke you a Kool and shut up," he laughed, shaking one out for Buddy.

"You know Buddy Guy ain't never gonna do that," Buddy laughed richly, waving him away. "Satan or no Satan."

"I'm waiting on you, sir."

Buddy glanced at his second guitar-player, who had long silky headbanger's hair. "Ain't I warned you about Mississippi? Mother-fuckers are *born* knowing how to preach."

Mister Satan winced as everybody except me chuckled. "Please, Mister Buddy, don't do that."

"What?"

"Profanity ain't no kind of credit to the beautiful music you gonna be projecting."

"Now hold on there, Satan," he complained, smiling. "Hold on, hold on. Shoot. Muddy Waters taught me how to talk like that, dammit."

The two men stared at each other, eyes locked.

Mister Satan suddenly giggled. "Well then Muddy Waters was a no-good mother-effer!"

They grabbed hands, crumpled, almost fell off their chairs. Mister Satan and I pranced onstage a few minutes later, surrounded by an endless blanket of upturned faces. Who were these strange people and what did they want from me? Cognac wrestled with adrenaline; our big moment had arrived and I was buried inside a smeared dizzy fireball, pure shapeless liberated squawk. We found each other after a couple of songs and clung tightly; I was pissed off at myself, suddenly, and blew from that, lifting my eyes to take in our audience. Mister James Gants had hobbled down from Harlem and was standing up front in his gray Borsalino, just below me. He'd been hanging out with us during our June club-plunge—sipping the free drinks we passed him, sharing our late-night burgers and french fries, unkinking his bad leg and creaking onstage to sing "I Feel Good" and "A Change Is Gonna Come" while we backed him up.

"Yes, Mister Adam!" I heard him shout between songs, swallowing his words. "Yes! Lord have mercy!"

Mister Marvin was down there, too, trucker's cap pushed back, punching his fist in the air. Mister Danny flashed his mouthful of broken teeth up at me, jubilant. We'd come a long way from Harlem, hadn't we? I pulled myself together and blew my best for three old friends, the side of us nobody down here knew.

AUGUST'S JUNGLE-STEAMY cicada heat brought with it, at last, our pilgrimage to Mecca: the International BuskerFest in Halifax, Nova Scotia, Take Two. This year I'd played my cards right. The organizers had given us three round-trip tickets on the *Scotia Prince*—a ten-hour ferry leaving out of Portland, Maine—and rental money for a rooftop carrier. All we had to do was arrive in one piece and play our assigned spots, lunchtime and evening, five hours a day for eleven days. Crowds were well trained, I'd been assured, and generous. A Bank of Montreal branch in town would count out our sacks of Canadian change and issue cashier's checks, payable in U.S. dollars.

This time Mister Satan couldn't say no. Outwardly gung-ho, I was quietly panicking. The farthest we'd been from home was Jersey City. Could Mister Satan possibly survive *as* Mister Satan out in the real world? Harlem, Dan Lynch, Chelsea Commons were one thing; Canada was another. Suppose people laughed in his face when he told them who he was? Or took him seriously—God-fearing Christian white people did still exist—and took offense? The downside risk was dizzying. My stomach warped; I'd developed gastritis by now and was chewing Tums.

I needn't have worried. Halifax, international seaport and final stop on the Underground Railroad, had seen stranger than us. Our fellow buskers—twenty-six acts—included Disorderly Conduct, the Bizzaro's, Wyndsong & Cheez, the Checkerboard Guy, and Rebels with Applause. There were jugglers with kerosene batons, ventriloquists with fuzzy-muzzled Snow Dragon puppets. There were breakdancers who shadow-boxed and magicians who rode unicycles, a light-skinned black mime who stripped down to boxer shorts and hurled himself off a dock into Halifax Harbor. Canadian dollars, quarter-sized and brassy, are called loonies. We learned all about loonies, and two-dollar bills, and five-dollar bills. Halifax was a small clean city perched on a hill overlooking a breeze-ruffled bay. Summer twilight lingered late. We sat on the carpeted floor of Mister Satan's hotel room after our first evening's show, Satan and Adam and Macie, and raked our hands through our pile of slippery beautiful change as we clinked beer bottles. They'd given each busker a six-pack of Labatt's Blue on arrival.

"Hey!" I cried, nabbing a familiar coppery shape. "Ten francs. We used to get these all the time over in Paris."

"They *got* to be here!" he barked happily, cigarette jumping. "You got French people, Germans, the whole damn universe carrying on down there in the streets."

Miss Macie, always inscrutable behind huge violet sunglasses, was smiling as she lounged back. She picked up a loonie, rolled it slowly between her fingers. "How you doing over there, Mister Satan?"

"Living my life and enjoying it."

"I'm gonna cook you a pork chop when we get home, 'cause I *know* they ain't got no pork chops up here in Canada."

"I'll bet you I eat it when you cook it."

"Man," I said, swallowing, "you believe the crowd we had?"

He chuckled. "I don't have to *believe* a damn thing. I got eyes."

"Now," Miss Macie continued, as though an imagined meal were a playful accusation, "I might make you cornbread, too. I'm thinking about that."

"Think on, Miss Hat-Passer!"

"Miss Pass-the-Hatter," I volleyed.

"Miss Million-Dollar Tip-Snatcher!" he laughed.

We stayed eleven days in Halifax and had the best busking of our lives. The days were warm but never hot, the evenings pleasantly cool. Our drinking leveled out; my gastritis disappeared. Dozens of kids recognized us from *Rattle & Hum* and requested autographs. I moved three hundred cassettes. We were a blues-playing, money-making organism, one harshly sweet flailing thing doing what it did best. Outdoors, under the open sky. Things couldn't get any better.

*1984.* THE HARDEST THING TO DESCRIBE is how the world looks when you've landed freshly on it, reborn. Guy loses girl in May, takes trip to Europe in June, flies home babbling on the Fourth of July. Wild Bill Rasputin, the savior of Western Civilization! My friends thought I'd lost it. They just didn't know. My soul was a poem now. I was *Leaves of Grass* with plutonium added. Visions had possessed me. I'd discovered a way of opening my heart so that the thousands of Soviet and American nuclear warheads aimed at me *this very minute* would pass harmlessly through, instead of choking me to death with stiff white tentacles. The energy release was extraordinary. I'd filled three hundred journal pages in five weeks, every moment a precious gift. I was waking at dawn these days, shivering with new life. I was going to write a book and explain everything.

The precise sequence of events leading to my rebirth was still unclear. Peter Herman—my Renaissance buddy—and I had flown to Paris with wine and women on our minds. I'd thrown a few harps in my backpack, in case song was required. Our third day in town, as though compelled, I found myself setting out a little box and blowing panicked blues on the Plateau Beaubourg for a crowd of nobody. The Pompidou Center was looming over my shoulder, a red-and-blue pipe-encrusted monolith. Showbiz death. Then a guitar-player—a sweet-tempered Dane named Jakob—came up, asking if he could sit in. Time melted into dream, a flow-state within the groove. An hour later we were sitting on the terrace of a nearby café; counting out a pile of francs and centimes, sipping cold Cokes our sweat had earned. I blinked at my new soulmate in the June afternoon, astonished. I could have been back in New York right now, collapsing. Here I was, blossoming large. Helen had *freed* me, not destroyed me.

How could I explain what had happened next? The bottles of *vin rouge* inhaled, the guitarists jammed with in Avignon and Cannes, the trains careening from Florence to Bologna to Milan, the affair with Gabrielle, an older German woman—thirty-three to my twenty-six—who played blues piano in a Solingen café, sneered at my American accent, and did not want me to leave her bed. Busking Centraal Station in Amsterdam, Leicester Square in London. Punting on the Cam with a pillow-lipped Dutch au pair named Ingrid. Summarized, the plot fell flat. You couldn't do resurrection in a hundred words. Wild Bill Rasputin was real, though. His redeemer's energy was flowing through my veins.

The day after I got home from Paris, I ran up to campus and flew up five flights to Helen's small, stuffy office in Hamilton Hall. Tidings of great joy must be shared.

She seemed surprised to see me, but not displeased. File cards were spread out; she was hard at work on her dissertation, a chapter on Kate Chopin. Books! I thought. What need have ye of *books,* silly woman, when life is pounding at the door! Books are for the scholar's idle times! Cast the poet out of doors! Awake, arise, or be forever fallen!

I jumped around the room, raving. If we'd had a golf course nearby, I would have dragged her out to go skinny dipping. Her face was flushed with feeling. She seemed receptive but residually wary, worried for me. I asked about Jack. She hesitated. They were seeing a lot of each other.

"That's okay!" I cried, dancing forward to kiss her forehead. "All three of us need to keep growing! It'll work out in the end!"

All I wanted to do was shout Yes! She didn't quite believe me. We held hands later, melting a little.

"Don't you see?" I said softly. "You were *right* about Europe. Who would I be if I hadn't gone? You've bequeathed the blues to me, Helen. Thank you!"

She sobbed. I clucked, wiping her tears away. I was larger than her now, infinitely larger. I contained multitudes. I had to sing my song, and save the world.

. . .

MISTER SATAN AND I HAD A STEADY GIG—an experiment—waiting for us when we got home, at a lesbian piano-bar in the Village. Kelly's was owned and operated by Kelly, a tough, sharp-featured peroxide blonde with a compressed sculpted pompadour and a sultry vampirish wife named Barbara. I'd never realized women could marry each other, the measure of my residual innocence. Kelly had seen us one night at Chelsea Commons and felt, for some reason, that we would work well in her room—a mirrored, chandeliered singles bar with a jukebox stuck on Madonna's "Material Girl" and a fevered unhappy clientele used to cabaret pianists crooning "Send in the Clowns." Somebody had played a twisted joke on everybody involved and sent in Satan and Adam.

For two months in the fall of 1990, we held down the five-to-nine slot on Sunday evenings. We'd load in through the back door, past the pool table where trim tough women in jeans with long hair buzzed and gelled on the sides eyed us warily. Men! The waning weekend is tinged with sadness at that hour, if you're loverless. Next Saturday night is a week away, Monday morning is first thing tomorrow. The pool-girls' loneliness seemed to mingle bittersweetly with mine. All of us would have been happier with a girlfriend; at least they had a fighting chance of finding one here. Mister Satan had Miss Macie and was happy for the gig. He'd given up booze entirely these days—would wave it away if you offered—and was his old strong deathless self, a guitar virtuoso with dancing cymbal-feet. I'd sip Johnnie Walker Black and blow the blues from a deep relaxed place, happy to be back in the Big Apple. Autumn was settling in, the air was edged with cool. We'd finally reached equilibrium, it seemed, after an endless spring and summer of boozing and raging, egos swelling and contracting, both of us perpetually on edge. We'd captured our best stuff on tape, become a club act, lifted ourselves off the streets without giving them up. Found our true level.

The story could have ended there. Then one evening, as we were breaking down, Miss Macie handed me a business card she'd been given. Margo Lewis, Talent Consultants International. A Midtown address.

"I don't know," she shrugged, when I asked. "Some white lady."

I called the next morning. Margo had a tough squawk—not unlike Kelly's—and was glad I'd called. Our playing had moved her. Our look, the whole thing.

"I see a lot of acts," she said. "It's rare when I'm touched, you know. You guys touched me. I trust the feeling."

She was currently managing Bo Diddley, Wilson Pickett, the Village People. She knew what it would take. How big did we want to be?

# PART FIVE

# HARLEM BLUES

# CHAPTER NINETEEN

# THE SAME OLD MESS

*First you say you do, and then you don't*
*First you say I will, and then you won't*
*You're undecided now . . . so what are you gonna do?*

—SID ROBIN AND CHARLIE SHAVERS, "UNDECIDED"

MARGO WAS A musician herself, it turned out—former keyboard player with an all-woman rock group named Isis—and her offices were across the street from Carnegie Hall. I subwayed down and took a meeting, demo in hand.

Talent Consultants International was my introduction to the world of professional artistic representation. Margo had a staff of six, walls covered with Bo Diddley and Ron Wood Gunslingers Tour '85 posters lovingly autographed to her by Bo and Ron and Mick, and several framed gold records. I found out about the gold Mercedes later. I never begrudged her. She was a tough shrewd Italian dame—Lewis was a stage name—who'd made it in a man's business and did not flaunt. She calculated, flattered, and cared. Musicians were her love and livelihood. She'd found Bo wasting away in a Florida trailer park and coaxed him back into the big time by making promises and keeping them. She'd rustled up a band and put him back on tour, finagled top dollar from stingy promoters, given him a new life.

"Guys like Bo," she explained as we strolled into the tiny back conference room, "they've been hurt. Stung. Everybody in the business has screwed them at least once. I'm sure Mister Satan's been through the mill. So you're not gonna get anywhere with these guys unless you deal straight up and *prove* what you're able to do. That's all I did with Bo. Eddie Kendricks was the same way."

We were her next big project. She introduced me around the office. Her two prime booking agents, Mitch and Mike, shared a cramped corner room papered with Deicide, Gorefest, and Mucky-pup posters, bumper stickers reading "Deathmetal Lives" and "Lack of Planning on Your Part Does Not Constitute an Emergency on My Part," and a large map of North America shredded with red and blue pushpins. Half-eaten cartons of takeout Chinese perched on desks littered with flung contracts and old copies of *Pollstar*. Plump, balding Mike, who seemed toadishly immobilized in his swivel chair, had an English accent and was on the phone.

"Look, asshole," he said calmly, his voice rising, "that's not my problem. If you—what's that?" He grimaced silently for a moment. "Oh bullshit. Bullshit! Listen to me. If you fuck me over in Newcastle, you're *dead*." The slammed phone rattled.

Mitch was younger, my age, with waist-length black head-banger's hair, glasses, a brutal resentful underbite—like Dana Carvey's Garth in *Wayne's World*—and a sparkless affectless gaze, as though some crucial pleasure center had been burned out. He was Margo's main man; he'd been a musician once, too. She invited him into the conference room. He slumped in a chair and gazed blankly at our Satan and Adam publicity photo—a diptych I'd cobbled together—as "I Want You" crashed and throbbed on the room's compact stereo.

"We're gonna represent these guys," Margo croaked briskly, invitingly. "Festivals, blues clubs. Whaddya think?"

He glanced at me. "This guy Satan, is that his real name?"

"It's kind of a street name, up in Harlem."

He seemed vaguely disappointed. "Is he into gothic?"

"Blues, Mitch," Margo barked. "He's an old blues guy. R and B."

"Like Bo."

"Like Bo. Exactly. The only thing we might want to change," she continued, turning toward me, "is the name. I mean Satan and Adam—I love what you guys do, don't get me wrong. You're beautiful. But the name could confuse people, as far as a blues direction. Promoters, whatever."

"It's who we are," I said.

"I like the name," Mitch grunted.

Margo shrugged. "Fine. Just a thought."

OUR SESSION AT GIANT SOUND back in February had never, in Rachel Faro's eyes, been solely for the purposes of producing a street-salable cassette. She was thinking album deal, producer's fees, peer acknowledgment. She had many powerful friends, including Bruce Kaplan, the president of Flying Fish Records, an independent folk label out of Chicago. The music business, it seemed, was structured around maddeningly extended seductions. Deals didn't just *happen;* that would have been too rational. Deals were floated, fretted over, worked partway through, then forgotten about for months. Somebody lost interest, somebody was in a bad mood, Jupiter was misaligned with the belly chakra. One night the wind blew down out of the mountains, somebody made a call, and the ball was rolling again.

Rachel pursued Bruce relentlessly through the fall of 1990—flattering, cajoling, portraying Satan and Adam as clattering virtuosic avatars of urban contemporary folk-blues. His curiosity piqued, she'd propose a recording budget. He'd balk—this was *Flying Fish,* not Sony—and she'd freak, call me, vent. Men didn't take her seriously! The only thing I didn't take seriously, at first, was her New Age cosmology. Later I came to my senses, or lost them entirely. The fault was clearly in our skewed stars. Her mantra, in any case, became mine.

"When you have a *record,*" she'd exasperate, "you have a *career.* Otherwise you're just playing gigs."

I hungered for all three. Mister Satan remained half-hearted

about the first two. He'd already had a record as Sterling Magee—
several regional hits on Ray Charles's Tangerine label back in the
mid-sixties—and considered himself to have been screwed.

"I had me a Double-Whammo Show-Stopper with 'Oh She Was
Pretty' on WAMO out of Pittsburgh," he complained, "and the label
biggies sat on it until it died. No joke. Brother Ray ain't gonna let no
underplayer on his own label kick his behind. A record will mess you
up, Mister. You might as well forget about royalties; they got a hundred ways of keeping those. Only thing a record is good for, really, is
personal appearances. Get you a hit and you *bound* to get a few
gigs."

He seemed delighted with the attention we were finally getting,
though. "Go ahead on, Mister Business Manager!" he'd cackle at
my periodic reports. Margo, pulling strings, had gotten us on the bill
with Bo at the Marquee in New York; Bruce was days away from
sending Rachel a contract.

One night, late, I got a call from Bobby Robinson. We'd bumped
into each other a few times in the two and a half years since our
abortive session with Plinky and Mitch; he'd talked a good game but
done nothing to advance our career since *Rattle & Hum*. I'd done
that: paid for and sweated our demo, worked up a publicity photo,
hustled gigs.

"Bobby," I cried with strained heartiness, "how you been?"

"Now," he began irritably, "I got Sterling talking to me about all
kind of fish this and that, and talent consultants trying to—from
downtown, he said, somebody trying to horn in on our whole thing
we got going on. What the heck is with all this?"

I did my best to explain, toning down my great expectations.

He cleared his throat. "Well now I gotta set you straight about a
few things. First of all—because we go way back, Sterling and me.
*Way* back. I picked him up off the street after Betty died and got him
an apartment, put a guitar in his hand, the whole thing. Kept him
going when he wasn't nothing but a damn drunk twenty-four hours
a day, drinking himself to death, because I knew what kind of special talent we got going on. So where it stands is, I don't know about
no Flying Fish or Holy Mackerel. I got my own labels—Fire and

Fury, Red Robin, Enjoy—and we gonna move ahead on one of them, as far as another recording session with you and Sterling. I got some things I'm working on, a promoter over in Japan and whatnot. So you can forget about *whatever* downtown things you got going on, as far as another manager." He grunted dismissively. "I been managing Sterling for *years.*"

I PICKED MISS MACIE UP on the corner of 138th and Lenox the following afternoon. She'd just gotten off her shift at Harlem Hospital; we were meeting with Margo downtown. Mister Satan hated business and wanted us to take care of it. I'd barely said three words about Bobby Robinson—venting my frustrations—when she went off.

"Bobby ain't in it," she huffed. "This ain't about Bobby Robinson and what he ain't done for Satan and ain't *gonna* do. Nooooo." She laughed harshly, lighting a cigarette. "You leave Bobby to me."

"I have no problem with *Rattle & Hum*," I admitted. "He did a great job on that. But we've worked too hard for too long to—"

She cracked the window and blew a huge cloud at the bruised fall skies. "Bobby wanna mess all in Mister Satan's business, he's gonna have to deal with me first. 'Cause I won't run away. I'm sitting right here, and I *will* go off, dammit."

We were one cheerful couple, strolling into the offices of Talents Consultants International. Margo, oozing solicitude, ushered us into the conference room and began outlining the bright shining future of Satan and Adam while Miss Macie smoked, nodded, smiled to herself.

"I see you guys as a three-person act," she said. "Everywhere we go—for example, if I send Satan and Adam on tour with Bo Diddley over in England next summer, which is something I'm working on, obviously Mister Satan is gonna need you along as part of the deal. Fine: I tell the promoters I need *three* airplane tickets and a double room for Mister Satan *and* Miss Macie. So you're part of the package right up front. How does that sound?"

Miss Macie showed her teeth, playfully. "I like the way you talk, Miss Margo."

"I can't make any promises this early in the game. This is gonna be more of a building year, as far as introducing the world to Satan and Adam, finishing up the first album—"

"Yes," I interrupted.

"—and playing a few festivals. But looking down the road, I see no reason why *next* year Satan and Adam can't gross . . . oooh . . ." She tapped her lips with the eraser end of a pencil. "Maybe $200,000, which includes merchandizing. Records, t-shirts, whatever. My percentage comes off the gross, so naturally I have an *incentive*"—she brayed as she grinned at Miss Macie—"to work as hard as I can for you guys. You with me?"

Miss Macie tittered, tickled to death.

AS THE FIRST YEAR of the new decade hurled toward its conclusion, we were sitting pretty. Flying Fish had come through with a contract—enough for a second recording session and whatever it took to transform our demo into an album. Margo had drafted a Letter of Agreement, firming up our management relationship. BluesStage, a nationally syndicated radio show, wanted to tape us for broadcast when we opened for Bo Diddley at the Marquee in March. Success was so close I could taste it, inhale it, feel its hot feathery sweetness licking at me.

The day before our big meeting with Margo in early December, Mister Satan called, his voice huge and rough, oracular. He was trashed.

"Mister Adam," he bellowed.

I cringed. "Hello Mister Satan."

"Okay," he began. "I ain't gonna sign no damn contracts with *anybody!* That's out. Not Miss Margo, not Flying Fish. I'm serious, Mister Adam!"

"I'm sure you are, I just—"

"Stop! If you know what's good for you, you'll listen to your black father. A record is a devastation, man! I been through his whole mess before. A record is a *black hole,* and we staring down the barrel of it! The whole damn world and everybody in it, all my little people, we ain't got but a few days left until—I been watching TV,

Mister. I know what's going on. George Bush, Saddam Hussein, everybody preaching death and damnation and kill kill kill. I can't be thinking about no *contracts* with those idiots about to start a war! And in God's name, too! That's what Armageddon is—big old bastard God shouting, 'Ah'm a get 'em!' I already *got* a manager, and that's Mister Bobby Robinson. So you can go on down to TCI and tell Miss Margo thank you but she ain't needed, I ain't signing *nothing* until after the first of the year, and that day ain't gonna come *anyway,* so that's out."

"THIS IS SO *amazing!"* Rachel cried when I called her up. I was devastated; she was exhilarated. "He feels the world's pain. It's almost like a Gandhi, or a . . . a—like a Buddha. His trip is suffering. He's been through so much, it's made him incredibly sensitive to other people's."

"What about *my* feelings, goddammit!" I shouted.

"Hmm," she mused.

"This is insane! You're all *nuts!* I'm trying to make a goddamn *record* happen, all I ever wanted out of this fucking music was a *life,* and you're . . . you're—"

"Calm *down,"* she soothed. "Calm down. When you're dealing with somebody like Mister Satan, you can't take anything they say personally."

Margo was unflappable when I saw her the next day. "He's scared. Success is a scary thing. Bo was the same way." She shrugged. "Nothing moves between now and New Year's anyway."

THINGS REACHED A HEAD at noon on Christmas Eve day. That was the moment, according to Mister Satan, when the world was going to end. He wasn't joking. He'd summoned me, Bobby Robinson, and Miss Harisha, his adopted street-daughter to bear witness. I was intrigued. Most prophets, when push came to shove, wouldn't name the time and place. Mister Satan was adamant: twelve noon on December 24, 1990. He'd worked out the numbers.

We assembled on the sidewalk in front of his Manhattan Avenue apartment, rubbing our hands in the calm, cold, gray morning.

Bobby had showed up, amazingly. He had on a tan camel's hair coat and blue sea captain's hat. We hadn't met face-to-face in months.

"How you feel?" he grunted, his inch-long fingernails brushing my palm as we shook hands.

"Ready for the big day," I said, smiling.

He shook his head, a smile tugging at his small mouth under the remains of his once-dapper mustache. We seemed bound, suddenly, in a fellowship of husbandry for the genius we both loved.

Miss Macie would not be joining us and had stayed indoors. Miss Harisha was there—sad and soft-cheeked, smiling benignly, self-conscious about the curved white ceramic shelf she had instead of right front upper teeth. Mister Satan came striding around the corner, paper-bagged bottle peeking out of his Triple Fat Goose ski parka pocket, euphoric as Scrooge on the morning after his ghostly visitations. He was wearing his red-knit crown hung with costume diamonds and rubies.

"Hello Mister Bobby!" he cried, taking Bobby's gloved hand in both of his own. He beamed wild-eyed at me. "Hello to you, sir! Hello Miss Harisha, ma'am!"

We piled into my car, the four of us, and drove across Harlem to Mount Morris Park, the vantage point he'd selected for the observation of Creation's wrath.

"Go on and take yourself a drink, young man!" he roared, passing me the bottle as I pulled up to the curb. His breath reeked.

I glanced over my shoulder. "I'm gonna defer to Bobby, since he has seniority."

"Mister Bobby!" Mister Satan cried, turning and pressing the bottle into his hand with exaggerated solicitousness. "Please sir, take a drink and put a little of my fire inside you, sir!"

Bobby hesitated, wrestled with his fastidiousness, eyed me, relented. "Man," he spluttered afterward, "I can't see how in *hell* you put that stuff down without no chaser behind the vodka."

"Ain't you feel the fire all up inside your lungs, like?"

"I got more of a heartburn situation."

I took my hit—our germs were one big happy family—and glanced at my watch. "We better get moving."

"Yes!" Mister Satan bellowed, taking the bottle back.

We piled out and flowed into the park, shuffling through snow-dusted weeds onto a path that wound upward toward a rusting water tower at the park's crest. The sky, with five minutes to go, was gray-blue and wisped with unicorn-horn clouds. Bobby paused to brush snow off his scuffed black dress shoes. I inhaled the cold fresh Christmas Eve noon air and suddenly felt wonderful.

"Hell," I joked, "I hope the world *doesn't* end, because we have some gigs coming up in January."

"It ain't my choice," Mister Satan shrugged. "Creation gonna do what it *gotta* do."

"I hear you, Mister Satan," Miss Harisha lisped.

I followed him up the rusting spiral stairway next to the water tower. Bobby was below me, then Miss Harisha.

"You expecting some kind of explosion, Sterling?" Bobby grunted as he came up behind us.

"That ain't for me to know!" he cried, agitated and exhilarated. "You all gonna be very surprised! What time you got, Mister Adam?"

"Two minutes to noon."

We teetered, the four of us, on the gravel-sprinkled crow's nest, shivering. Harlem lay spread out below us—a forest of water towers and tar-papered rooftops—with the rest of Manhattan, Harlem and Hudson rivers, Jersey and the outer boroughs ringed concentrically beyond that. A huge luminous world.

"Great view," I murmured.

"That's the truth, Master," Miss Harisha agreed.

"Just watch!" he cried.

We stood silently, listening to breezes swirl through rusting steel girders, checking our watches occasionally. It was a beautiful day, as Final Days go. Noon came and went. Mister Satan had his elbows against the railing, eyes closed. His smile was beatific. Bobby and I caught each other looking.

"What time you got?" he said.

"Five after."

"I got two or three."

"Well," I finally said.

Miss Harisha coughed. "I guess it ain't happened like you said, Master."

Bobby rubbed his hands, fingernails clicking softly. "How you feel, Sterling?"

"What can I do?" he shrugged, mildly embarrassed but not visibly unhappy. "The numbers must have lied. I can't see *how*, but I sure gotta live with it."

"So we're stuck with it," I said a moment later as we worked our way back down the spiral staircase.

"Ain't a damn thing changed," he chuckled, scratching his head through his red knit crown. "Still the same old mess. I love you all for coming with me, though. You got that much on your behalf."

*1985.* I WAS A FAILED PROPHET in my own land, suffering through slushy February. Lying around the apartment reading *Bright Lights, Big City*—the bestseller of the moment—and wondering where I'd gone wrong.

I'd written a big book, all right. Sat down in mid-July—right after flying home from Europe—and unrolled 555 pages in fourteen weeks, revealed truth hemorrhaging unchecked. The Great American Novel was child's play; I was writing the Great *Russian-*American Novel, with my halfbreed alter ego as protagonist. A loose and baggy road-monster, Kerouac crossed with Dostoyevsky. And it *would* save the world from the Soviet-American nuclear menace. Wild Bill Rasputin could do that. The mad Russian cowboy with blues harps in his hip pockets, the quick-draw street musician who brings healing musical energies to a civilization in need.

Friends, concerned, broke the news gently. I saw what they meant, after the fever had passed. A critic whose critical judgment has been annihilated can't just spew and expect to be published. Dialogue? Pacing? I had no idea how to tell my story. I knew only that it had something to do with rebirth and had happened to me over in Europe.

You go back to the drawing board. Jay McInerney was my age and successful; one blurb on the back of *Bright Lights, Big City* praised his "perfect power-to-weight ratio." He'd gotten that, it seemed, from Hemingway by way of Raymond Carver. I paged through *The Sun Also Rises* and *What We Talk about When We Talk about Love*. Then I started over. I wrote in tight-jawed baby talk about a six-year-old named Adam who recoils in terror during a kindergarten duck-and-cover drill when somebody cries "Atom bomb!" The power-to-weight ratio was skewed. I'd erased every last trace of fun. *Bright Lights, Big City* was fun. McInerney's hero snorted coke, partied with beautiful models, winked at nihilism, and made no attempt to save the world. Why couldn't I write like that?

I'd walk the streets at night, brooding. I'd dropped out of grad school by that point—fed up with theory, disgusted with civilization, humiliated. How could I show my face around the English Department when Helen and Jack were strolling the halls? I'd get drunk in a pub called The Dive Bar on the corner of Amsterdam and 96th, down the block from her new apartment. Equipoise had fled; I missed my baby. One night I floated out of The Dive Bar with a buzz on, reached into my pocket for a harp, and ran smack into the Happy Couple, swinging down the sidewalk arm in arm.

"Hello there!" I blurted out, straining for heartiness.

They glanced up, stricken, swerving away.

I was haunted. Music was my only release. I'd walk the streets with a cupped harp hiding my mouth. Blowing your blues away wasn't just a Tin Pan Alley cliché. Fresh air, obsessively repeated chord-rhythms, and circumnavigated space really could heal, a trance-synergy that wholed your soul. I'd come home refreshed. Sometimes I'd grab a beer out of the fridge, put on "Hoodoo Man Blues," slip on headphones, turn the lights off, and groove along with Buddy Guy and Junior Wells as they worked their smoky little club in Southside Chicago. Junior had the mojo, no question. Enough to make you shiver. How was he getting that sound, with the breathy curled edge? I wanted what he had.

THINGS SUDDENLY BEGAN to fall into place, a delayed Christmas dreamflow as New Year 1991 glided toward late February's brightening salmon dusks. Mister Satan, teetotaling once again, accompanied Miss Macie and me to a downtown meeting with Margo and grinned delightedly as she sketched out our beckoning future. Flying over to England with Bo in June, opening seven dates in big concert halls.

"Hear me well," he pronounced after she'd finished. "Go ahead on, Miss Margo."

I'd finally figured out, dense as I was, that Bobby Robinson required no more from me than the simple courtesy of proper respect. I called him up, sent him a copy of our working Flying Fish contract, paid a visit. Bobby's Happy House Records, just off 125th Street, had a wrenchingly overdriven loudspeaker on the sidewalk out front; the walls inside were hung with dusty shrink-wrapped copies of old Junior Parker and Dinah Washington LPs. The man himself—whom my frustrations had somehow transformed into a malevolent Wizard of Oz—was standing behind an old turntable, relaxed and willing to deal. I took him out for a cup of cafeteria coffee next door.

"The thing of it is," he explained across the table, contract in hand, "you got to make sure you ain't tied up in no *exclusive* agreement with anybody. 'Cause they'll try to lock you in with this and that option clause, say you gotta cut four sides with them and can't work with nobody else, even if you want to."

"You must have gone through some of this stuff with the major labels," I said, "since you had so many artists they wanted, like King Curtis, Wilbert Harrison—"

"It was a *mess*," he interrupted, smiling bitterly. "Give you an ulcer, destroy your sleep."

He'd scrawled notes in the margins. His negotiating points were subtle, and not ones Rachel had made. Sterling Magee and Adam Gussow were still free to record for him, singly and collectively, under any name except "Satan and Adam." We shook hands afterward, warmly. Mister Satan and I signed the faxed revised contract a week later, between sets out on 125th Street. We toasted with Midnight Dragon. The promised land was in sight.

Margo called soon after, breathless. Quint Davis, the largest blues promoter in the world, had just phoned, months after receiving our demo cassette. He'd finally gotten around to listening to it.

"I don't know where you found these guys," he'd raved, "but I'm gonna make them stars!"

He was flying us down to the New Orleans Jazz and Heritage festival in April. He was putting us in the Philadelphia RiverBlues Festival in July, the New York/Benson & Hedges Blues Festival in October. Great money all around, of course.

"Quite a year, huh?" Margo cackled. "This is even bigger than I'd hoped."

A FEW DAYS LATER I CAME HOME to find a message on my answering machine from a harp player named Jack down in Richmond. Nat was in the hospital. He'd just been diagnosed with leukemia.

# CHAPTER TWENTY

# WHAT WE'VE BEEN TRYING FOR, ALL THESE YEARS

*Hey everybody, let's have some fun*
*You only live once and when you dead you done*
*So let the good times roll. . . .*

—LOUIS JORDAN, "LET THE GOOD TIMES ROLL"

MUCH LATER, A couple of years after Nat had died, I was able to cry and get out what I felt for him that way. My eyes still fill, at unexpected moments. When I'm cruising alone down certain stretches of the Jersey Turnpike and remember my last pilgrimage to Richmond. When I walk through Astor Place and remember his finger-in-the-air lectures—backed by Charlie Hilbert on guitar—about how blues was *American* music, the best we had to offer, and Thank you darling for that lovely tip.

When I first heard the news, though, tears wouldn't come. Crying wasn't useful. A death sentence wasn't the same as dead, and miracles were always possible. If anybody had a miracle in him, it was Nat Riddles. One last surprise up his sleeve. I truly believed that. I had to believe that. My throat ached; all the bottled-up feeling collected there, a throbbing cartilage-knot of grief, disbelief, and shit-lousy sadness. I didn't want to lose the guy. I loved him. Passionately, faithfully, in my own way. I hadn't realized how much until the bad news came. The ache in my throat was a pretty good measure.

You could play the blues from a throat like that. He'd taken the trouble to show me how.

ACUTE LYMPHOBLASTIC LEUKOMA was the term he used, when I called. He was in the oncology unit of the Teaching Hospital at the Medical College of Virginia. We had a brief conversation before I drove down. He was sleepy and sounded drugged, but in pretty good spirits. Remember that swollen chipmunk-jaw he'd had last time he was up in New York? It went away, then came back; two weeks ago he'd collapsed on the floor of a friend's apartment.

"I wasn't gonna let *that* go by," he chuckled softly. I've never been one, as you know, to mess around as far as my health is concerned."

I thought about his days with Doreen, the white junkie-prostitute who had died of AIDS the year before. He seemed to read my mind.

"It's not AIDS," he added. "I made them test for that."

"I was worried when I heard."

"No, it's not, ah . . ." He drifted off. I heard a nurse's murmur. He came back on. "Temperature time."

"You have a fever?"

"What's that?" he said hoarsely.

"You running a fever?"

"I'm a little cold right now," he said. "They got some nice cotton blankets down here, some wool blankets. I'm part of an experiment."

A HUNDRED AND THIRTY FLAT STRAIGHT MILES—the length of the Jersey Turnpike—from the George Washington Bridge to the Delaware Memorial Bridge, a clean beautiful lofting arc. Past the Chesapeake House service area, where seagulls stroll the parking lot demanding crab-cake crumbs. You skirt Baltimore, dip through the Fort McHenry Tunnel, fly thirty more southerly miles. The Beltway, a curving roller coaster, drops you off below D.C. There's a blue-grass station at the bottom of the dial—an older D.J. who knows from twang—that lasts you half the ninety minutes to Richmond.

This leg always seems to come in late afternoon; you and the truckers highball it along shadowed twin southbound lanes cut through forested hills that smell cool, leafy, fertile, Virginian. Old backcountry.

I STUCK MY HEAD THROUGH THE DOOR of his hospital room, afraid of what I'd find. He was, amazingly, sitting cross-legged on his bed with an electric bass in his lap, practicing. A notebook was open in front of him. His face was slightly drawn. He looked distinctly undead.

"What took you?" he chuckled, glancing at the plastic I.D. band on his watchless wrist as I came in.

I unzipped my daypack. "I was gonna bring you a Heineken but I figured they had you on a beer-free diet." I pulled out a Ski Mississippi long-sleeved t-shirt I'd picked up in Mount Olive and tossed it in his lap.

"The range of alkaloids they've made available to me, the last thing I need is—hey!" He held it up. "Thank you. Thanks. I will wear this."

My throat throbbed as we hugged and the sides of our skulls met. He smelled baby-clean in the antiseptic, faintly astringent air. His shoulder blade swelled under my hand like an axe-head rippling below flesh.

"You're looking good," I said.

"This period of time is gonna be good for me," he insisted, with incredible aplomb. "I got a space cleared out for some focused study. I got my bass—from Mark, in the Blues Defenders—which I've *always* wanted to learn. I got my—hey, check out my Casio keyboard."

He reached around behind him and picked it up, set it on top of his notebook, tinkled a passable boogie-woogie.

"Damn."

He grinned. "It's *amazing* how much time you get in here, without distractions! Plus three squares a day. The chemo program they got me on—I mean the shit has progressed a *long* way from what we remember leukemia as having been."

Harlem Blues

He chattered amiably while I sat, wondering at his clarity of purpose. He was up but not manic and didn't seem drugged, or afraid. He was Super Nat: curious, absorptive, self-disciplined, fearless, at peace. He'd figured things out. Anything you could figure out couldn't beat you.

He'd certainly charmed his nurses, white and black. The look in their eyes as they bustled around his room, plumped his pillows, handed him the paper cup and stood by while he swallowed his pills, was familiar: this guy was too good—an angel—and didn't deserve the bad luck that had fallen in his lap. Lori, the freckled redhead, came in as I was demonstrating with my B-flat harp how I'd flubbed the instrumental chorus of "Don't Get around Much Anymore" on the second recording session Mister Satan and I had careened through a couple of weeks earlier. Our forthcoming first album, *Harlem Blues,* had just been edited, sequenced, mastered, and sent off to Flying Fish.

"I'm always totally wired when we record," I said, "so I was drinking Johnnie Walker Black, which blunted my edge just enough that when we came out of the double-time section, I caught the seven-hole draw *and* six-hole draw"—I blew the major-second interval—"which is an obvious clam, or at least sounded like one to me."

"I've been there," he chuckled. "I *have* been there."

"So all I can think of—I'm trying for inspired and perfect, right?"

"This would be nice."

"Because a recording is forever. And I've just blown it, a voice inside my head is screaming *You've just fucked up!* So I basically just gave up on the take. My heart folded up shop and went home, and the note I played reflected *exactly* what I was feeling." I demonstrated, a helpless Awwwgghh! on the three-hole draw.

"Awwwgghh!" he echoed.

"I was totally bummed when we finished. Tore my headphones off, started apologizing. Rachel's going No problem, calm down. And of course it turned out that when we edited the song a couple of days later, we were able to cut out the clam. So the Aw-shit-I-just-fucked-up note is still in there—it's the bluesiest note I played—but

371

the fuckup itself is gone. And no one who listens to the album will ever know what the note means, or why I played it."

"*We* know," he laughed, pointing at his chest. "And it's always gonna hurt."

I shook my head. "Always."

"I coulda done better, you know? If only I hadn't had that last . . . that last drop of—whatever!"

Lori was waiting patiently on the far side of his bed, cup in hand.

"This guy," he said, grinning up at her as he thumbed me. "I love it."

"You keeping Nat entertained?" she said.

"Doing my best," I murmured, throat knotting.

THE MYSTERY THAT SHADOWED NAT was why success—on the world's terms—had always just eluded him. I left Richmond convinced that this crisis, if survived, would wake him up. He'd spoken in the past about German blues impresario Horst Lippman's standing offer of a European tour. Maybe he'd finally get off his butt, fly over to Frankfurt, hit Paris and London, become the star he was born to be.

My hope lingered until the next time we spoke. He sounded beaten. The leukemia had stayed in remission only a couple of weeks; cancerous cells had been found in his spinal fluid. The doctors had given him four months, if that.

News travels fast in New York blues circles. Within days, April 11, 1991, had officially been designated Nat Riddles Day at Dan Lynch, an all-star benefit. Once the guy was dying, why hold off until he was dead? He had bills to pay.

The big night arrived; the place was mobbed, a line tailing out the front door. The man himself was being driven up from Richmond and expected momentarily. The bandstand was crowded with his extended family, musicians whose lives he'd touched and changed. We'd all grown, trying to fill the space he'd left. El Cafe Street alumni like Jerry "Slapmeat Johnson" Dugger and Wild Billy Durkin; the Holmes Brothers, a soul-blues trio who'd run the Sunday jam for years and recently vaulted onto the national scene;

singer Lorraine LaRocca, a huge gravel-voiced postal worker whose theme song had always been "I'm So Mean and Evil" but was actually a gentle mama bear, dispensing hugs in the loving Nat style. Altoist Chuck Hancock, an occasional El Cafe Streeter, was ringleading when I arrived, allocating solos with his pistol-cocked thumb-and-forefinger. Chuck had inherited the mantle, if anybody had. Five foot five and frantic, he had Cleanhead Vinson's shaved brown skull, Maceo Parker's shrieking chirp, early Madonna's black leather and bracelets, Charles Manson's demonic glare. He'd leap up on the bar while honking and kick like a Rockette, fall on the floor and baby-flail. He'd thrust the bell of his sax against the crotch of the nearest female and pay his respects: *squawk!* He'd orchestrate collective riffs and repeat them for days, whipping everybody into a frenzy. This was the kind of showmanship Nat had encouraged. Chuck had taken Riddles dynamism to the next level. He reached across the bandstand when he saw me, grabbed my hand and kissed it, hard.

"Hahahahaha!" he cackled fiercely.

Charlie Hilbert, Nat's better half, was slumped at the bar next to his gig-bagged guitar, drinking. His dark hair had thinned; he'd grown a wolfish graying beard.

"Fucking Nat," he growled as I squeezed in. "Do you believe this shit?"

"It's a mess," I agreed.

"I'm extremely depressed."

"You and about two hundred other people."

Charlie I felt for. He'd been around since the beginning, when Nat was taking lessons from Bob Shatkin and Lenny Rabenovets, sitting in with Odetta and Larry Johnson, scoping out Sugar Blue in Washington Square Park. He and Nat had worked the sidewalks in front of Penn Station through the early eighties, honing their groove. I'd caught them late—their last summer, it turned out. Six years ago.

"I *told* him Doreen was trouble," he grimaced over the band's thumping roar.

"It isn't AIDS," I said. "It's leukemia. That's the first thing I asked."

His eyes flashed, despairing. "Is that what he told you?"

"Isn't that what he told you?"

"Fucking Nat." He downed his shot. "You gonna play later?"

"Acute lymphoblastic leukoma," I said. "That's leukemia, right?"

"Maybe he has both," Charlie sighed. "We'll never know jack shit." He signaled for another shot, stroked his beard. "You and Satan need a second guitar player? I can play bass, too."

Chuck and the Irregulars were unison-riffing on "Shake, Rattle and Roll"; one more smoke-clouded, pool table–clattering East Village juke-joint Thursday night was shifting into high gear. Rumors suddenly swirled; the doors swung inward, parting. Nat was standing there—beaming, *radiant,* his face drawn tight against his skull, his arms thrown around the shoulders of a pair of white guys I recognized as his Virginia bandmates. His eyes were watery and huge. The cancer had gotten him. It hurt to look. You couldn't not.

"Hey Nat!" somebody yelled over the thumping roar.

Chuck Hancock bent toward the sax mike. "Ladies and germs, Nat Riddles is in the house!"

He stood just inside the front doors, a scarecrow in a trucker's cap and blue satin Yankees jacket, and accepted everything we had to give—every cheer, every shout, every soul-shake and slapped palm, every hug, every kiss, every arm around his shoulders, every hand gently massaging his upper back, that needy spot between the shoulder blades he'd taught us to notice. A Heineken found its way into his curled bony fingers. One of half a dozen rotating harp blowers, I played the deepest blues I could on "Next Time You See Me" and "Mercy, Mercy, Mercy." Nat's attentions were scattered. His family had showed up: a brother and sister, aunts and uncles, Riddleses and Pendergrasses and Washingtons none of us had ever met. Why hadn't he stayed with *them* after the shooting, instead of fleeing town? He hobbled up to the bandstand later and did his thing, clasping his harp lovingly to the mike I handed him. His wind wasn't good; his tone was weak—a shadow of the True and Beautiful—but not yet gone. He quieted the band down and sang an old Dan Lynch standby, his voice breaking: "Well I've had my fun . . . if I don't get well no more. . . ." People whooped and cheered, toasted him, shook out cigarettes, ordered another round of Jack Daniels, squeezed back past the pool table into the men's room and pissed into cracked urinals loaded with crushed ice. The Soon-to-be Late Nat Riddles. He'd never be more famous than right here, right now. I suddenly wanted more for him and hated the place a little. This was all he was going to get.

MY HEALTH DISINTEGRATED over the next few months as the Satan and Adam juggernaut hurtled skyward. My back went out, cold sores erupted, my gastritis blossomed. Two days before the New Orleans Jazz and Heritage Festival I collapsed on the floor of my doctor's waiting room—feverish, soiled with my own shit. Harmonica playing was the least of my worries: I'd suddenly become our road manager, publicity consultant, sound tech, not to mention Mister Satan's overseer. How should I rein him in when we'd run over our contracted set-length? How should his wooden stomp-board be miked? What sort of backstage hospitality did we want specified on our rider? Margo suggested a deli platter and juices, soda, coffee; I added a bottle of Scotch and a couple of six-packs. Drink exactly the right amount, I'd discovered, and the released tension would settle my stomach. Throw in half a pack of Tums and a few gulps of Maalox and I could get by.

We flew to New Orleans early on festival morning with our new manager, checked into the hotel, chilled briefly. Margo had suggested after the Marquee gig—I'd worn a polo shirt and jeans—that I dress a little more "fly" onstage; I kneeled in front of my ornate French Quarter toilet bowl in my expensive new Italian sport shirt with a finger down my throat, trying to vomit. Better now than later.

The festival was twenty tents and stages scattered across a muddy racetrack infield. Baptist gospel trains rocketing full-bore toward the Promised Land; punkabilly revivalists ravaging electric mandolins; Mardi Gras Indians whirling in blue-feathered splendor. Quint Davis, stroking Margo, had given us our own private minivan behind the Lagniappe Tent.

"Pretty nice, huh?" she brayed as we stepped up out of Big Easy swamp-swelter into air-conditioned comfort.

"I ain't got no complaints," Mister Satan chuckled as Miss Macie attacked the cold cuts platter, wrapping four or five sandwiches in paper napkins and stowing them in her handbag.

I washed down a Tums with Johnnie Walker Black and leapt onstage—flailing wildly for the German video crew that circled us like birds of prey. The kickdrum mike I'd taped to Mister Satan's wooden board came unstuck almost immediately and began chattering, destroying his low-end sound. He glared at me and yelled; I reached down between his pumping legs to fix it, dropping my harp. Misadjusted monitor speakers had shattered our uncanny connection. We were circus fleas under a microscope with floodlights switched on. You thrash and blow, the blurry face-zone out there applauds, you're panting, scrambling to collect your stuff, dodging stagehands as they belly-heave amps, getting offstage as quickly as possible. This was the Big Time? I skipped up into our trailer, wiped out but flying—baptized by fire, grabbing my bottle and swigging down. Mister Satan, teetotaling this week, shook me out a matching Kool. Margo pulled open the trailer door, grinning.

"Hey guys, I brought a fan by to say Hi. You know Harry Shearer?"

I knew he was famous but had no idea for what. I didn't watch *The Simpsons* and had never seen *This Is Spinal Tap!* He had a vulnerable open Jewish face with thick dark eyebrows.

"I really enjoy your music," he said. "Somebody sent me your demo. I have a radio show out in L.A. I've been playing it a lot."

"That's just great," Margo said, encouraging me.

"Man," I raved, "I couldn't hear myself at *all* out there just now. Could you hear the harp?"

He glanced at Margo, vaguely awkward. "Everything sounded fine to me."

"I'm glad you could hear it because *I* sure as hell couldn't."

"Hello to you, sir," Mister Satan said, nodding.

"I love your guitar playing," Shearer said. "I understand you used to play with King Curtis?"

Mister Satan scowled through his gray beard. "That dead bastard used to play with me."

"So you're from L.A.?" I said, cracking open a beer and gulping, sprawled next to the plastic tray covered with carrot sticks, olives, roast beef and cheese slices. I grabbed the last two turkey breast rollups, ravenous.

"I, ah, work out there."

"I'm hoping we can get some gigs out there," I chattered. "Do you know any place out there we can get some gigs?"

IT WAS BURSTING mid-May in New York—perfect busking weather—and Nat was back in the hospital. I'd called to check up; he was telling me about his hemorrhoids. He was on fire, the old Nat—astonished, a crying edge in his voice, ridiculing absurdity with furious laughter.

"You have no *idea*," he said. "They don't tell you about this bullshit. I mean chemo was no picnic, but at least you had a fighting chance of retaining some shred of . . . of—whatever. Mental health, or—"

"Dignity," I murmured.

"*Fuck* dignity, man." He laughed harshly. "This motherfucker ain't gonna give you that."

"No violins and mood lighting."

"Tear it up and burn it. Fuck it up the butt. The first time—" He broke off, coughing. "Forget about Preparation H. I'm talking about *hemorrhoids*. I mean they don't—the doctors *will not* tell you about this shit until you find out on your *own*. And then it's like, Hello? Excuse me. What the hell is this?"

"Mm mm."

"The first time I took a shit after they broke out," he snorted, "the pain was so bad I was beating my head against the bathroom door. They coulda used me for a . . . a . . . whatever. The monster trapped in the closet of some horror movie. *Bang*, motherfucker! You thought we were gonna letcha off easy with this leukemia thing? A little chemo, a little nausea, some hair falls out—you're cool with that? Fuck you. Time for batting practice."

MISTER SATAN, Miss Macie and I were driving down the FDR Drive the next morning, on our way to the Fabulous Fifth Avenue Street Fair in Brooklyn, when my stomach spoke. Three hours from now, it murmured, you will probably vomit. Think about it.

"Ain't no reason to give up these little street fairs," Mister Satan was saying, "just because we gone and got famous. Hell, the best way you got of keeping in touch with the people that *made* you what you are is right out in the street. You got a song that works on those bastards, you damn sure got yourself a hit."

His cymbals clanked somewhere in back. My stomach rolled over.

"I'm feeling a little queasy," I murmured.

Mister Satan chuckled. "I can't *look* at a scrambled egg sometimes when I been partying it up the night before. I gotta drive a few hundred miles and work the mess off, or either take myself another drink and kill it off that way."

"I think I need to pull over," I said, suddenly desperate.

He waved his hand. "Do what you got to."

I pulled off the exit ramp onto Sixtieth Street, stopped next to a loading bay for Lenox Hill Hospital, fell out and leaned against the hood, swaying a little. Mister Satan smoked a cigarette. Miss Macie smoked in the back seat. Huge ventilators whooshed all around me. It was a velvety spring morning, a strained nauseating velvetiness.

"I can't make it," I said after a minute, shivering, wanting only to be home in bed. "I'm sorry."

"We'll live through it," Mister Satan shrugged as he took the wheel and drove us back to his place. "You need you an Alka-Seltzer. A young man *gonna* get himself a bit of a sour stomach in his early thirties, now." He shook out a Kool, pushed in the dashboard lighter. "I had me one so bad around the age of thirty-three, I couldn't even take a drink of water, it near about made me sick."

SATAN AND ADAM were New York's Best New Blues Act, according to *Newsday*'s spring survey of the local scene. The Riverbend Festival in Chattanooga and the Wolftrap Jazz and Blues Festival near D.C. wanted us. A promoter had offered five weeks in Switzerland and Italy later in the summer. *Harlem Blues* was days from release; Flying Fish would be sending 850 copies to radio stations across North America. The old black guy/young white guy thing was an easy sell, Margo said. Mitch was on a roll. This was going to be fun.

WE WERE ON THE BUS with Bo Diddley, an overcast June morning through heavily tinted windows, somewhere between Glasgow and Newcastle. One good show down, six to go. I'd cold-turkeyed coffee and booze; my stomach had stabilized, if barely. Mister Satan was in a beer phase and playing amazingly well, stealing the show. Margo was sitting up front, grinning beakishly behind rimless spectacles; Miss Macie was sharing a friendly cigarette with Marilyn, Bo's lusty, red-faced, Southern-born wife. Bo's band, white New York rock pros in their thirties, were clustered in back around Bo and his programmable rhythm machine.

Bo was dressed as Bo always was, onstage and off: black everything, including the cowboy hat and large squared-off thick-lensed glasses. His hands were massive. He'd been a sheriff out in New Mexico and thrown rednecks in jail. His voice was slow, resonant, bark-roughened, leavened with vulgarity, pitched to cut through the bullshit. "Bo Knows" was the refrain of an ongoing Nike ad campaign. This morning he was giving us a refresher course.

"Now some musicians," he began, "is got the wrong idea. Motherfuckers might try to tell you, 'Bo Diddley ain't done a damn thing new with his beat.' Tell you *they* was doin' the jungle rhumba this and that back with Dizzy Gillespie, and all I did was came along and didn't change a thing about the feel of it, just called it the Bo Diddley Beat." He shook his head sadly. "See, they might throw some bullshit on you, like the Bo Diddley Beat ain't no big thing. Then how come those motherfuckers can't *play* it right? You know? Talk like they some kind of rhythmatic experts, and then get up on the bandstand and throw some shit behind you like—" He flicked on his keyboard, punched buttons until it produced a rinky-dink cha-cha version of the Bo Diddley Beat. He glanced around the circle as his band chuckled. "Ain't that a bitch?" he belly-laughed. "Shit." He flicked the switch off. "Couldn't none of 'em come up with my Bo Diddley Beat 'cause wasn't none of 'em *doin'* what I was *doin'* back then, in the early days. Like I was talking with Satan here—" He lifted his hand. "What say, Satan?"

"How you doin', Mister Diddley?" Mister Satan grinned over his shoulder. He'd been, to my amazement, cheerfully tolerant of Bo's filthy, disrespectful mouth.

"Chasing a dollar, same as you."

"Shut up."

"Satan," he continued, "was telling me about playing on the street, like these guys been doing. Up in Harlem or wherever. Now what most people don't know is, I got *my* start on the streets of Chicago. See, it wasn't about workin' in no clubs at first, 'cause the clubs ain't even gonna look twice at no nappy-headed boy from McComb, Mississippi, 'til you got your thing together."

"Hell no," Mister Satan agreed.

"So we hadda—you'd get a guitar and a little cigar box, get right out there on the street corner, up on Maxwell Street or wherever, Jewtown. Little Walter, Louis Myers, all them jokers did that, when they started out. And we'd play. And I'd do my little dance, too. Sing to myself and hit that dance step, 'cause if you had a good dance step, the people was *gonna* stop and throw money."

"Amen," Mister Satan called out.

"That's all I was doin'," Bo continued. "Just pattin' it out." He patted his feet lightly against the bus carpeting, then doubled the beat with his hands, patting the gray plastic carapace of his silent rhythm machine. *Boomp*-a-*doomp*-a-*doomp* . . . a *Doomp Doomp*. "So when I came into the clubs, and later on into the studio up at Chess Records, you know, there it was. That's your Bo Diddley Beat. Couldn't nobody play it the way I played it, because they ain't had the whole street thing behind it, that little dance move I did."

1985. THE CRAZY HARMONICA player of Morningside Heights, after pacing the streets all winter, was beginning to reconnect himself with reality.

The weakness of my Wild-Bill-Rasputin-saves-the-world-with-spirited-blues-playing scenario was becoming clear: I'd had virtually no exposure to actual blues musicians. I'd learned almost everything I knew about my instrument from records, and a couple of European folkies faking their way through twelve-bar blues changes. How could I celebrate the stuff that had turned me inside out without pushing forward to the vital source?

Recently, drawn by an ad in the *Village Voice*, I'd ventured down to a Sunday afternoon jam session at an East Village blues bar called Dan Lynch. Fourteenth Street and Second Avenue was a rough part of town; the music hit my solar plexus like a thunderclap when I first pushed through. An older white guy with a wolfish beard was center stage, blowing harp in a smoky haze. The band had a plump young black kid on drums, a gaunt black bass player with his brown fedora pulled low. The two guitarists were white, my age, and much better than I'd ever been. People were drinking and shouting in each other's ears. I felt awkward, foolish, hopelessly out of the loop. I'd brought harps with me—a pair in each hip pocket—but didn't dare. It was like being confronted by adult sex after a boyhood shaped by *Playboy*. I sipped a beer as I edged onto a barstool, trembling. Wolfman was blowing the real shit. Half the sounds he made were tricks I didn't know. Tongue stuff? He was *potent*. Bob Shatkin, I found out later. He and another white guy named Bill Dicey ruled.

More recently I'd gone to see Paul Butterfield at a tiny basement club called Tramps. The first white harp player to work his way into Chicago's Southside blues clubs, Butterfield had learned from Muddy and Little Walter. The place was packed with disciples, trading frenzied little licks over beers as they waited for the Man. He walked onstage after a delay—staggering, shading his eyes. Everybody shushed. He had a droopy cowboy mustache, was wearing faded bluejeans and a black leather jacket with the sleeves pushed up. He grabbed the harp-mike, blew a couple of test notes through a pair of cranked-up Fender Twins. Whaaaaugh!

Bluesmen are for nothing but to inspire. I walked out of Tramps two hours later, transported. It was the *spaces* he left. Teasing you with gorgeous burning streams of notes, then pausing, taking a breath. Making you wait as the band chugged on.

My soul felt light, suddenly. Spring was sweeping in. Life after Helen! I had a gig coming up, too. My first as a harp player, with a band.

I'd made friends over the winter with the Special Guests, a quintet of Columbia undergrads who'd been playing a neighborhood hangout called the Blue Rose Lounge. They were happy white kids who wrote bouncy ditties about Vincent van Gogh when they weren't covering Bruce. Three hundred sitters-in had recently occupied Hamilton Hall to protest Columbia University's investments in South Africa; the Guests were one of several campus bands who'd volunteered to play a late-night rally in front of the building. Would I come down and blow?

I'd been steering clear of campus for months—avoiding the scene of humiliation—but this was too enticing, if nerve-wracking. Floodlights? Big stage? They called me up on "Riot in Cell Block Number Nine," a tune we'd kicked butt on more than once. You find a riff that doubles somebody, stay out of the way until your solo. Heart throttling when the nod came, I poured all my anxious hope into a machine-gunned stream of notes that echoed off the building in front of us. Afterward, you slap fives and walk offstage, relieved. I'd warmed people's clapped hands in the cold night air. Helped the cause in a small way, if not exactly saved the world.

I was bopping home down Amsterdam Avenue a few minutes later, harp cupped, lost in the sound of my unleashed notes spiraling up and collecting under the walkway between the Law School and Philosophy Hall. Bird was my model: sweet, angular, endlessly unfolding lines.

A yellow cab heading uptown cruised by me, then slowed. Hung a U-turn and pulled up to the curb. The driver leaned over, rolled down the passenger-side window. He was older than me but not much, and black.

What's this, I thought?

He was smiling as if we knew each other.

ONLY NAT! PEOPLE were still talking when we got back to the city. The Riddles, it seemed, had crawled out of his hospital bed, borrowed a car, driven up to New York, and gone on a weekend bender. Showed up at Manny's Car Wash—a new blues club on the Upper East Side—and sat in with touring pro William Clarke, a white West Coast harp player he'd been singing the praises of for years. Clarke's jaw had dropped, people told me; his dark sunglasses had fallen off, his cool had been shaken. Who was this dying young black guy with the Sound? Later, I'd heard, Nat had made the rounds downtown—buying everybody drinks at Lynch's, boozing it up, desperate and wild, crying in somebody's arms.

He was back in the hospital now, to stay. I got him by phone on the third of July. His voice was hoarse; he sounded weak. Uncontrollable hiccups kept overtaking him. He'd say Excuse me and put the phone down; I'd hear him dry heaving across the room. Then he'd cough and come back on. I told him a few road stories—how we'd played the Bessie Smith Strut in Chattanooga, opened for James Cotton at Wolftrap—but mostly I listened. He sounded happy. William Clarke was the real deal. Forget about the sunglasses, the slick suits and wiseguy look. Clarke could throw down simple shit and make it sound good, inspired shit and make it sound easy. This was what we'd been trying for all these years—both of us, *all* of us. And of course the feeling was there. Any time you found that, you had to celebrate it.

He'd gotten onstage with one of his heroes and shown what he could do. He sounded happy, sick as he was. It was a real triumph. We savored it.

JULY 17, 1991, was the Big Day, a minor miracle: the *Harlem Blues* release party at Dan Lynch. At how many points along the way had disaster and contingency threatened this particular future? Seymour Guenther, our A&R man at Flying Fish, had driven overnight from Chicago bearing a large cardboard box filled with CD jewel cases, several hundred identical shrink-wrapped totems faced with photos of Satan and Adam frozen in mid-beat. On the front cover we're gazing off across 125th Street toward our beckoning destiny, spiritually aligned and serene. On the flip side, a split-second later, Mister Satan is rocking back and cackling as I, who have just blown out a reed, drop my head—juggling a handful of spare harps, searching desperately for a replacement, trying not to lose the groove. My desperation reads as focused intensity. Mister Satan is exuberance writ large; he's got the world in a jug.

I felt a thrill as I gazed at the thing, turned it over, fingered the hard clear plastic. Kill me tomorrow, kill him. This much would stay done—shoulder to shoulder, black-and-white music. The melting flux we'd known.

RACHEL SHOWED UP, Margo and Mitch, a handful of local blues DJs. Two or three hundred others. Nat hadn't made it—in body, at least—despite my last-minute offer of a plane ticket. His spirit lingered on the bandstand, at throat level.

Gail came, another minor miracle. It was only the second time she'd caught Mister Satan and me at work. The first was one afternoon, more than a year after I'd left *Big River*, when she stumbled across us in Times Square on her way to matinee curtain call. She'd moved on, too—shedding her slave gowns to play a chubby astonished blue-black insect with bouncing antennae in a futuristic Broadway musical called *Astro-Zombies*. She invited me to the show, took me out afterward for a drink.

"It ain't exactly Chaka Khan," she said, mouth twisting into a wry smile, "but you don't hear me complaining."

"You're on *Broadway*, Gail!" I cried. "Look at me. Not that I'm complaining either."

She seemed shadowed by residual sadness—still struggling to work things out with her old boyfriend—but the feeling between us was real, a tender friendship between done-the-nasty showbiz survivors. We talked for the first time about true love, which I'd lost and still mourned and she'd never had.

"Seriously?" I said, astonished. "Never?"

She traced a figure eight on the tablecloth with her dawdling finger, eyes lowered. "Not like you were saying, with the whole Fourth-of-July-fireworks thing."

"But the way you sing, you . . . I mean your demo was totally about falling in love. It certainly broke *my* heart."

Her eyebrow arched playfully. "Really?"

"I swear to God. You have an amazing voice."

"Welllll," she sighed, "I wasn't singing about what I've had, I was singing about what I *want*."

She came to the album release party because I'd sent her an invite and we had a mutual support pact: when either of our musical ships finally came in, the other would put in an appearance. She pushed through the swinging doors just before our second set, when Dan Lynch was a smoky whiskied energy-field vibrating to the remembered beat of Mister Satan's feet. She was wearing a sleeveless red dress on the sweltering July night, red heels to match, gold hoop earrings that set off her high cheekbones. Her combed-out natural glistened in the shadowy lights; her eyes chuckled as they caught mine. Whatever self-consciousness about her tall full figure she'd suffered from in the past seemed to have evaporated. More than a few heads turned as she waved and came toward me.

"Gail!" I cried. "This is great."

"You gonna give somebody a kiss?" she joked.

I went for her cheek as we hugged. The smoky-oil scent of her hair conjured up a dozen fleeting memories: how helplessly I'd hungered for her early on, gazing up from the pit with my schoolkid crush; her butt-length t-shirts; endless whirlpooling nights we'd spent in Toledo, Raleigh, Huntsville; the smoothness of her thighs against my lips; the pain my goof with Ron Layton had caused—he'd teased her later about sleeping with me—and the tearful apology I'd made; the awkwardness of our final rendezvous in Pittsburgh after I'd quit the show.

She pulled back and eyed me, pouting playfully. "You gonna kiss me for real, or just do the cheek-thing?"

We had a rollicking second set. Mister Satan was as fierce as he'd ever been—glorying in our official launch as Flying Fish recording artists—and I had a friend in the front row, sipping her Kahlua and cream and grinning. Gazing up at me, for a change, as I sang "Sweet Home Chicago" and warbled through cupped hands, throat humming.

IT WAS THE FIRST SONG I'd written since high school, after the breakup with Sandra: a funky nameless little instrumental, the theme song to "Sanford and Son" turned inside out. "Written" was the wrong word. It had come to me one morning, a few days after the release party. We'd just signed a one-page Letter of Agreement with Talent Consultants International—nine months it had taken for Mister Satan to come around—and I was feeling really *musical* for the first time in ages. My gastritis had vanished. Melodies tugged at me as I took a shit, made coffee. I grabbed a harp and bounced outside, past the salt marsh and the Shorrakapock rock where Peter Minuet—according to a tarnished bronze plaque—had bought Manhattan Island from the natives for sixty guilders in 1626. The Parks Department had recently sponsored a shad-fest-and-pow-wow; upstate Onondagas in bluejeans and t-shirts doing their drum dances, black Shinnecocks from Long Island in moccasins and deer-skin leggings, chain-smoking Vietnam vets who broiled fish on charred planks. My neighborhood.

I skirted Inwood Hill, hiking up along the service road into the shade. Sultry late July is the end of wineberry season; I paused to nibble, then kicked back on an orphaned park bench overhung with sassafras. The salt marsh glistened below, a sprinkle of daylight through the random weave of oak, maple, tulip. I noodled aimlessly. A morning song hovered, pleading to be born.

Like most blues harmonica players, including Nat, I'd based my style around second position, or "cross harp," a way of playing in a key pitched four scale steps below the instrument. This allowed you to bend and wail, mimicking a blues singer's inflections. There was another approach. Third position, which shifted the key signature *up* a scale step, gave you an eerie minor tonality. Unadulterated minor had never been my thing. Blues was about the tension between minor *and* major, tragedy *and* comedy, disaster *and* jubilee.

Minor without major was slack, depressing, Major without minor was Disneyland.

Suddenly, plugging in one of the overblows William had shown me during our *Big River* days, I had it: a minor-major flutter, in third position. I tongued the low octave, threw in a breakaway upward run. Found the groove with my shoulders, a swingy bounce-beat. It wasn't a blues, exactly, but bluesy, funkified, jazzed-up, danceable, new. Whatever our New York mongrel-mix was.

I bounced down out of the hills, plugged into my Mouse, jumped around the apartment, worked it through. Gave the old white lady downstairs a very hard time.

The next day I drove down to Harlem, my five-mile gulp of open road. *Newsday* had done a cover story on us in their Metro section the week before; Mister Danny and the gang were clustered around Mister Satan's shopping cart as he paged through a copy, showing off photos of himself, his mandalas, the spot where he was standing right now.

"I'm so beautiful it *hurts,*" he roared happily, holding up the four-color spread. "I'm brown and beautiful and—hey, Mister Gus, hello to you, sir."

"Y'all gone and got famous on us," Mister Oscar chuckled, palming his polished steel balls as I set down my Mouse and the box of *Harlem Blues* CDs. "I was telling Mister Satan—"

"Get back here you bastard!" Mister Satan called out to Mister Danny.

Mister Danny, ten feet away, spun and spluttered, "I already *got* two dollars! It ain't cost but two!"

Mister Satan held out two more. "Mister Adam damn sure gonna bite the Midnight Dragon along with us, now. Shut up."

Mister Danny snatched them and took off. I noticed the plastic cups scattered across the top of Mister Satan's guitar case, the paper-bagged forty-ounce discreetly shoved behind his shopping cart.

"I was telling Mister Satan," Mister Oscar continued, "y'all gonna get out there in Switzerland, whatever, Italy, and forget the little people back home."

"Hell no," Mister Satan proclaimed. "Harlem *is* home. Switzerland is *money.*" He rocked back on his heels as everybody roared. "We *got* to get on over to Switzerland and make us a little silver, cause my people definitely gone and dried up on me. That's how damn famous I got. Everybody pass by talking some mess about, 'Hello, Mister Satan, we see you in the paper, we see you on Channel 7, we know you don't need our little tip money no more cause you gone and got *biiiig.*"

Mister Larry eased toward me, cool and vaguely irritable as always. "I'm talking about *hot,* Mister Adam," he complained, folding his arms. "Seems like a nice cold Guinness would go down reeeeal smooth right about now."

"I was just thinking the same thing," I said.

"Funny how that works." He smiled as I palmed him two bucks. "We be reading minds out here after a while, getting inside each others *heads,* you know what I'm saying?"

A few minutes later, after I'd Dragoned and propped a couple of *Harlem Blues* CDs against the phone company window behind us, I couldn't hold back.

"Mister Satan," I said, "check it out. I came up with a funky little thing I think we can do."

I played thirty seconds or so, solo. A few people drifted to a stop. I was still something of a curiosity, at least for newcomers just up from the South. Mister Satan's head was bowed, his eyes closed.

"What you call that song?" Mister Oscar asked when I stopped.

"It doesn't have a name."

"It's a funky thing," Mister Satan declared. He chuckled. "A thunky fing. Yeah, I got something we can put behind that." He eased into his hi-chair, strapped on his guitar, tried a couple of fingerings, then glanced up. "Hit it again."

It took him a minute or two to find me, like an elite fighting unit scrambling to triangulate behind a crazed lone grunt leading an impromptu charge. Then he locked in—it was our sound all the way, but fresh—and a crowd collected. The thing had no beginning or end, just a versy part and a couple of chorusy parts. It felt too good. We couldn't stop. Mister Danny flashed his jumble of broken teeth every time I glanced up, Mister Oscar leaned back in his lawn chair, Mister Larry sipped his paper-bagged Guinness and called out, "Go ahead, Master!" The swelling crowd pitched quarters, peashooter-sized scrunched-up dollars. It suddenly occurred to me that I was supposed to feel residual anxiety out here. Bless the Dragon. I'd forgotten all about the Malcolm X guy.

"We got ourselves a sure-enough crowd-stopper," Mister Satan chuckled as we slapped hands after reeling the thing in.

"Thunky Fing," I panted. "I like it."

"Check it out. We gonna lay it on 'em tomorrow at the Philadelphia festival. You watch don't the people down there groove on it just like they be doing up here."

IT WASN'T A CONVERSATION I knew how to have. I'd put it off until the last minute. Mister Satan and I were playing the RiverBlues Festival on Sunday; Monday we'd be flying off to Europe for five weeks. One of Nat's Virginia bandmates had recently called to let me know that Nat, liver failing, had been moved to intensive care.

Goodbye? I love you? I took a deep breath, sick at heart, and dialed the hospital. Nat Riddles was a hard guy to track down. I finally got a hold of a nurse in the ICU, a Southern white woman.

"Nat isn't well enough to come to the phone," she said.

"I know he's very sick. I just need to talk to him for a couple of minutes."

"I'm sorry, sir. I can't do that."

"Look," I said, trembling. "I'm a friend of his, I'm leaving the country for five weeks, and I need to talk with him. This is the last chance I'll have."

"I wish I could help you, sir."

"Please," I begged. "Tell him who it is. We're old friends, I'm sure he'd—"

"Nat is currently under sedation," she said with an edge of twangy impatience. "He needs all the sleep he can get."

The line filled with soft static. So that was how it ended. I'd blown my chance.

"Can I at least leave a message for him?" I pleaded.

"I can give him a message."

"Tell him, ah . . ." I glanced at the harmonica in my hand. My throat suddenly ached. "Tell him that Adam loves him. Tell him my spirit is with him."

"I surely will."

"You're sure he'll get the message?"

"I'll give it to him myself," she said, voice softening.

THE MORNING DAWNED CLEAR AND COOL, July's blanketing mugginess blown away by a passing shower. I made coffee and tuned my harps, bringing five or six worn reeds back up to spec with several flicks of a jeweler's file. I'd blown out several hundred harps in five years with Mister Satan; he was still playing the solid oak Ampeg Superstud he'd been playing the first afternoon I'd stopped by. His callused fingertips had worn teardrop-shaped streaks in the solid oak fretboard.

Ginger showed up at ten in her Dodge van. Ginger was a muscular associate of Margo's who had been assigned the task of transporting us to and from Philadelphia. I heaved my two big amps in the back and we drove down to Harlem, picked up Mister Satan and Miss Macie, and hit the Jersey Turnpike South—windows wide, the midsummer smell of drying mowed hay pouring through. This was our first show since *Harlem Blues* had been released; I'd brought along plenty of product, as Margo called it.

"We've certainly paid our dues," I yelled over my shoulder, happy to be moving.

"You getting what's due you," Mister Satan yelled back. "I'm getting what's *overdue* me."

I'd been to RiverBlues as a spectator several times in recent years and knew the general layout, guiding us across the tautly wired blue span of the Ben Franklin Bridge and around onto Penn's Landing. The Blues Heritage stage was up above; we pulled to the curb and began unloading Mister Satan's dented hi-chair, smelly foam cushions, chipped wooden sounding board, clanking cymbal-bag. We were running late. One of the cymbal-stands closed on my finger as I yanked it out.

"Shit!" I yelped.

"Ain't it pitiful?" Mister Satan chuckled, hand brushing mine as he took it. "They gonna nip at you every damn chance they get."

"There's Satan and Adam!" somebody said excitedly as we walked our equipment through stragglers at the edge of the crowd. It was quite a crowd: standing room only from a hundred and fifty feet out. Several people whooped as we came on stage and began to set up.

"Jesus," I muttered, gazing out across the meadow of upturned faces, "take a look at that."

"They waitin' on us, Mister."

I didn't find out what was up until two minutes before we were introduced, when the stage manager brought me the can of beer I'd begged. I was waiting in the little performer's tent off to the side of the stage.

"They sound pretty lively out there," I joked nervously.

"They ought to. WXPN's been playing your music all week. Jonny Meister is calling you guys 'The Discovery of the Festival.' "

"The *what?*"

He winked. "You ready to hit?"

I finished the beer and veered into a nearby Porta-Potty. Mister Satan strummed a bittersweet chord onstage, thumped his miked stomp-board through the massive P.A. I stood in front of the shadowy, foul-smelling hole, pissing. Suddenly I heard Nat's voice, as though I'd conjured him up.

"*You're* scared?" I could hear him laugh. "How the hell you think *I* feel?"

I zipped up, shivering but ready. Very ready, suddenly. We serve no wine before its time. I shouldered out into the sunny afternoon as the door banged behind me, tucked in my shirt, notched my belt tight. Trotted up the steps as Mister Satan, drawing cheers, roared out my name. This was our day.

# APRIL 1998

I T HAD TAKEN us four and a half years to rise from the sidewalks of Harlem to our first festival stage. We'd refer to those later, fondly, as "the street days." The street days waned during the summer of '91 and ended the following summer when Mister Satan, playing solo, was attacked one afternoon by a couple of kids brandishing the latest Harlem fad, "SuperSoaker" water-rifles. Our uptown tips had already thinned, a function of the success people rightly assumed we'd been enjoying elsewhere; the cops had nailed us the last couple of times we'd ventured down to Times Square. Mister Satan had had enough. He called me that night, fuming.

"I ain't gotta put up with that effed-up bullcrap, man! Not from my own people!"

The next moment he was philosophical. "The streets were there when we needed them. Now we don't and they ain't."

I couldn't argue. Two pay phones had recently been installed on the wall just behind me, to the left of the New York Telephone office's front door. People were tripping over my cables and Mouses;

young B-girls with long painted fingernails answering beeper-calls glared at me as they inserted quarters over the din of my amplified harp. Suddenly, pointedly, I was in the way. We'd already begun to move out into a larger world that seemed primed to embrace us. In the fall of '91 we'd been interviewed by Noah Adams on NPR's "All Things Considered"; we had a well-connected manager, gigs up and down the East Coast. Harlem was still home base but no longer home. We bought a Sears clamshell for the roof of my Honda and hit the road.

We played the Chicago Blues Festival, the Newport Jazz Festival, the Winnipeg Folk Festival, a dozen others over the next seven years. We worked tiny packed clubs and big empty clubs. We drove tens of thousands of miles—sharing cigarettes and stories, farting discreetly, cracking open a window, trading the wheel when exhaustion loomed. We never had an accident or missed a fly-in soundcheck: Dublin, Toronto, Sydney, Kansas City. We recorded two more albums—"Mother Mojo" (1993) and "Living on the River" (1996). Neither sold as well as "Harlem Blues," but we could count on a scattering of fans wherever we showed up. One winter we toured Finland and ended up at a ski resort in Äkäslompolo, two hundred kilometers north of the Arctic Circle. Two drunken Finns staggered toward the stage, tore off their shirts—they were pale, lithe—and dry-humped in front of us as the crowd whooped. What *hadn't* the streets prepared us for?

Minor celebrity beckoned, then faded. We paid our bills, barely. Mister Satan's gray beard slowly whitened; my red hair thinned. We left Talent Consultants International and bounced between smaller booking agencies. Mister Satan bought a car and he and Miss Macie moved down to Virginia, driving up to New York for our occasional weekend gigs. I returned to grad school after nine years away, having finally made peace with Helen's ghost and my own bookishness. The music was a good place to work out our griefs and hopes. "You'll live through it" was Mister Satan's constant refrain, when stomach acid or girlfriend troubles or record company hassles or doctoral qualifying exams wreaked havoc. "You'll damn sure live through it." He was from Mississippi and knew how trivial my gripes were.

Several years ago, after an article about us in *Harper*'s attracted an agent's interest, I began to write this memoir. Mister Satan gave me his blessings, pleased that somebody was finally telling our story. From time to time, curious, he'd ask how it was coming along. We'd reminisce about the street days during our long drives to Pittsburgh, Newport, Saratoga Springs. I'd ask him about people we'd known. Most of them had died. Professor had died, miserable old bastard. Mister Oscar had died. Miss Harisha had died. Mister Danny had stolen some money, run away upstate, and died. Mister Marvin was still around. Nobody had seen Mister James Gants in a couple of years.

One afternoon in the fall of 1997, while he was driving us home from a gig in Portsmouth, New Hampshire, I asked Mister Satan if he'd like me to read him a few pages. The finished manuscript had been accepted for publication; I was anxious about his reaction, particularly to those moments where I'd let his voice speak through me. In the academy this was called "ventriloquizing," a particularly suspect practice when engaged in by white male writers, who had—it was generally agreed—an unconscious need to burlesque, caricature, and otherwise fatally misrepresent the speaking black subject. "Playing in the dark," Toni Morrison had called it. The sin of blackface minstrelsy. I was determined not to fall prey. The only way I could honor my larger-than-life master, however, was to go for broke.

"By all means," Mister Satan said when I asked about reading out loud; he reached for his cigarettes.

I read him the last few pages of chapter 9, in which he and I were busking Times Square on a sweltering August afternoon, defending our territory against a pair of Christian evangelists. It was a strange, dislocating experience. What *were* these words I'd attributed to him? Were they recollected verbatim, fabricated by an apprentice in the master's style, or a combination of the two? Leery of "doing" his vocal inflections to his face, I kept my voice flat and hoped his exuberance would shine through. Which it did, apparently. The diatribe I'd given him—"Love your neighbor? Hell, if you got to *kill* me to *love* me, you might as well go on and hate my ass!"—cracked him up.

"Read that back again!" he said after I'd finished. "Yes sir! That's the life we lived."

# THANKS

To Joan Gussow, who read to her eldest son early and often, taught me to think critically, kept us all going through the lean years, and may yet save the world (beginning with her own organically farmed corner of it).

To my late grandfather, Don Gussow: wanderer, storyteller, supporter.

To Tina Bennett, every writer's dream of an agent, without whose foresight, intellectual passion, smarts, wisdom, and unquenchable energy this book would never have found its way onto the page.

To Charlie Hilbert, Larry Johnson, Lennie Rabenovets, and Ron "Cafe Mojo" Smith, who knew Nat way back when and helped conjure his spirit at crucial moments.

To Karola, Diana, Buddy, Hamp, Jojo, Lester Schultz, Jerry Dugger, Trip Henderson, Chuck Hancock, Johnny Allen, Mason Casey, George "Jersey Slim" Cook, Bob Shatkin, Margie Peters, Bob Bavido, Mark the Harper, Bill Sims, The Holmes Brothers, Bill "Kid Java" Ferns, Frankie Paris, Michael Hill and the Blues Mob, Ron Sunshine, Little Mike, Motor City James, and the rest of my Dan Lynch Blues Bar family, too numerous to name. Keep the faith!

To William Howarth and Anne Matthews, for several shrewd readings of the memoir-in-progress and unfailingly good advice about which roads needed taking.

To Peter Herman, true friend.

To Bobby Robinson, Bobby "Professor Sixmillion" Bennett, Mister Marvin, Mister Pancho, Mister Danny, Mister Larry, Mister Oscar,

Mister James Gants, Miss Harisha, Duke Wellington, Jimmy "Preacher" Robbins, Jackie Soul, Tippy Larkin, Miss Chevela, and Harlem's generous tip-tossers: the best teachers and audience a young blues player could have.

To Danny Clinch, Paul LaRaia, Cynthia Carris, Jack Vartoogian, Cory Pearson, and every other photographer who jammed with us streetside.

To David Sanjek, copyright permissions maven.

To Kate Rothschild, for the gift of healing laughter and support above and beyond the call.

To Rachel Faro and Margo Lewis, fire signs. A better introduction to the music biz I can't imagine.

To Erroll McDonald, editor, who provoked and corrected me when needed, gracing my vision with his steadying hand.

To Mister Satan: gentleman and genius. Thank you for the God Tape!

And to the late Nat Riddles, especially. Your voice still chides, prods, inspires.

rights on behalf of Sony/ATV Songs LLC administered by Sony/ATV Music Publishing, 8 Music Square West, Nashville, TN 37203. Reprinted by permission of Sony/ATV Music Publishing.

*Sterling Lord Literistic, Inc.:* Excerpt from *Dutchman and the Slave* by Amiri Baraka. Copyright © 1964 by Amiri Baraka. Reprinted by permission of Sterling Lord Literistic, Inc.

**Adam Gussow** is a writer and blue professor of English and southern sippi in Oxford.